A JOHN HOPE FRANKLIN CENTER BOOK

UNSETTLING ACCOUNTS

D1367027

The Cultures and Practice of Violence Series

SERIES EDITORS:

Neil L. Whitehead, University of Wisconsin, Madison
Jo Ellen Fair, University of Wisconsin, Madison
Leigh A. Payne, University of Wisconsin, Madison

The study of violence has often focused on the political and economic conditions under which violence is generated, the suffering of victims, and the psychology of its interpersonal dynamics. Less familiar are the role of perpetrators, their motivations, and the social conditions under which they are able to operate. In the context of colonial, national, and postcolonial state building, as well as the collapse and implosion of society itself, community violence, state repression, and the remembrance and inquiry that mark the aftermath of civil conflicts, there is a need to better comprehend the role of those who actually do the work of violence— torturers, assassins, and terrorists—as much as the role of those who suffer its consequences.

When atrocity and murder take place, they feed the world iconic imagination that transcends reality and its rational articulation; but an imagination fed on violence can bring further violent realities into being. This series encourages authors who build on traditional disciplines and break out of their constraints and boundaries, incorporating media and performance studies and literary, cultural, and sexuality studies as much as anthropology, sociology, and history.

Neither Truth
nor Reconciliation
in Confessions of
State Violence

LEIGH A. PAYNE

DUKE UNIVERSITY PRESS

DURHAM AND LONDON 2008

UNSETTLING ACCOUNTS

© 2008 Duke University Press
All rights reserved
Printed in the United States of America
on acid-free paper ∞
Designed by Katy Clove
Typeset in Cycles by Keystone Typesetting, Inc.
Library of Congress Cataloging-in-Publication
information appears on the last printed page of this book.

TO STEVE, ZACK, AND ABBE

FOREVER AND UNCONDITIONALLY

CONTENTS

ACKNOWLEDGMENTS

"Why is a nice girl like you working on a topic like this?" I have received this question more times than I can count in some form or another since I began this project. At first my answer focused on my personal and physical distance from these political matters. I argued that it was precisely because I had not experienced anything remotely like this political violence that I could work on it. That critical distance, however, broke down after spending years working with perpetrators, victims, and survivors, video and photo archives of violence, and confessional and testimonial accounts. While I still had not directly experienced authoritarian state violence, violence and violators formed a large part of my life. Now I have to honestly reply that I did not understand the emotional and physical toll that such a study would have on me. But I have learned a lot along the way. I hope that this project contributes to a comprehension that political violence affects all of us once we begin to acknowledge it. I also hope that it encourages less silence and more combative dialogue to challenge the legitimacy of state-authorized violence.

For the experience and the outcome, I owe many institutions and many individuals a debt of gratitude. This extensive and expensive project, which took place in four countries, was made possible by the generous support of two foundations: the John D. and Catherine T. MacArthur Foundation's Global Security and Sustainability Program, with special thanks to Kennette Benedict; and the Social Science Research Council's Fellowship on Conflict, Peace, and Social Transformation, with special thanks to Craig Calhoun, John Tirman, and Itty Ibrahim. The University of Wisconsin, Madison, also provided research support through the department of political science; the graduate school; the International Institute and its affiliated programs in global studies, African studies, Latin American, Caribbean, and Iberian studies, and the Legacies of Authoritarianism Research Circle; the Hilldale Undergraduate Research Award program; the Letters and Science Honors Internship program; and the Vilas Associate program.

The project and I have benefited greatly from smart and creative colleagues and students in the political-science department at the University of Wisconsin, Madison. Thank you to those colleagues who have talked through parts of this project with me, particularly Richard Avramenko, Richard Boyd, Katherine Cramer-Walsh, Michael Schatzberg, Joe Soss, Aili Tripp, and Crawford Young. Graduate students Yousun Chung, Valerie Hennings, Tricia Olsen, Kerry Ratigan, Marcela Rios Tobar, and Jelena Subotic answered many of the questions that I could not tackle on my own. The participants in the Theory Colloquium generously read and critiqued my work at a critical juncture. Undergraduates now embarking on their own professional careers provided invaluable assistance, particularly Jennifer Cyr, Hillary Hiner, Jessica Menaker, Sheri Wright Linzell, Heidi Smith, and Nicole Wegner.

An interdisciplinary network of scholars at Madison working on violence, memory, narrative, and performance challenged me to explore new areas of research and ideas. In particular, I thank Severino Albuquerque, Ksenija Bilbija, Laurie Beth Clark, Erik Doxtader, Jo Ellen Fair, Susan Friedman, Kenneth George, Richard Goodkin, Heinz Klug, Mary Layoun, Jacques Lezra, Toma Longinovic, Florencia Mallon, Alfred McCoy, Rob Nixon, Michael Peterson, Gay Seidman, Steve Stern, Neil Whitehead, Thongchai Winichakul, and Susanne Wofford.

Scholars and practitioners in various parts of the world have lent support and critical feedback. Among my U.S. colleagues, I am especially grateful to Rebecca Atencio, Michael Barnett, Mark Beissinger, Louis Bickford, Margaret Crahan, Pablo De Grieff, Susan Eckstein, Nancy Gates Madsen, Eduardo González, Frances Hagopian,

Eric Hershberg, Martha Huggins, Brian Loveman, Eric MacGilvray, Kathryn Sikkink, Marion Smiley, and Timothy Wickham-Crowley. Among my colleagues who lived abroad, but not in countries directly related to the nations I studied for this project, I thank in particular David Chandler, Stanley Cohen, and Carlos Iván De Gregori for their invaluable insights.

In Argentina the project benefited from Elizabeth Jelin and Eric Hershberg's Memorias de la Repressión program, which was supported by the Social Science Research Council, housed at the Buenos Aires Instituto de Desarrollo Económico y Social, and possessed of a unique network throughout the Americas. Gloria Bonder of the Facultad Latinoamericana de Ciencias Sociales, Argentina, provided feedback on the project both in Buenos Aires and in Madison. In addition, the Centro de Estudios Legales y Sociales, Valeria Baruto and Patricia Valdéz at Memoria Abierta, and Nora Cortina and Estela Carlotta de Barnes of the Madres and Abuelas de Plaza de Mayo all provided significant research materials and insights that advanced the project.

In Chile Carmen Garretón of the Vicaría de Solidaridad, Teresa Valdéz and Alicia Frohman of Facultad Latinoamericana de Ciencias Sociales, Chile, Elizabeth Lira of the Instituto Latinoamericano de Salud Mental y Derechos Humanos, and Felipe Gonzalez of Diego Portales University's Law School all assisted with this project at different stages. In addition, Rubén González and Pedro Matta helped me work through details of the Chilean case.

It would have been nearly impossible to include the Brazil case if it were not for a few human-rights groups and scholars who struggled against, and made audible, the silence. Of particular note is the Grupo Tortura Nunca Mais, especially Victoria Grabois and Cecília Coimbra. I also thank James Cavallaro, Danilo Carneiro, Glenda Mezarobba, Edson Teles, and Aníbal Castro for their help in the book's final phases.

The South Africa portion of the research depended on my guide, friend, and collaborator, Madeleine Fullard, to whom I am deeply indebted for introducing me to a whole new world of politics and research. The Centre for African Studies at the University of Cape Town housed me during my stay; Alex Boraine allowed me to use his extensive and private archives; and the Centre for the Study of Violence and Reconciliation researchers and staff generously gave me their time, thoughts, and documents. What mistakes I've made in the project will not be easily forgiven by the scholars and practitioners who taught me so much: Janet Cherry, John Daniel, André Du Toit, Nyameka Goniwe, Paul Haupt, Christina Murray, Laurie Nathan, Michelle Parlevliet, Deborah Posel, Fiona Ross, Nicky Rousseau, and Wilfried Scharf.

At Duke University Press I benefited from the uniquely warm and fun guidance of Valerie Millholland and her assistant, Miriam Angress. Three anonymous reviewers deserve my thanks for helping me transform this book substantially from its original manuscript. I extend my gratitude to Pam Morrison and Tricia Mickelberry for their careful and efficient copyediting. I also thank Carol Roberts for her index and Andrew G. Reiter and Kathleen Pertzborn for proofreading.

As in all large projects, intangible forms of support came from individuals who defy easy categorization. It might surprise some of you to be mentioned here, but only because I have failed to effectively communicate how much you have done for me over the years: Peg and Jim Berkvam, Jane Brodie, Catherine Jagoe, Lynn Northrup, Carol and Brad Ricker, Ned Sibert, Minette Vari, Emely Verba, and Sue Williamson. Thank you from the bottom of my heart for being there for me when I needed you. Randy, Janet, Faith, and Grace, I hope you know how much the "escape to Eden" you offered me meant. Thanks again.

To all of you who know me, it won't surprise you that I conclude with the idea of "contentious coexistence." I have to thank my three older brothers Gary, Steve, and Randy, my sister Sara, and my parents for providing ample opportunities to sharpen my dialogic combat weapons while I was growing up. I dedicate this book, however, to my husband Steve and my children Zack and Abbe, who endure contentious coexistence in our home. It has not been easy. We have not always reached consensus or achieved reasonable deliberation. But in case contentious coexistence gets in the way of my expressing myself clearly, please know that I love you forever and unconditionally.

Now that it is time for me to move on and leave this project behind, I find myself missing it. I am not sure I'll miss talking, reading, and writing about torture, killing, and the deep emotional pain of surviving it. I will, however, miss the intensity and the passion that so often gets left out of contemporary academic studies of political life. Fortunately, or unfortunately, many dramatic and irreconcilable conflicts await future study.

AEDD	Asociación de Ex-detenidos Desaparecidos (Association of the Ex-Detained Disappeared, Chile)
AFDD	Agrupación de Familiares de Detenidos Desaparecidos (Association of the Families of the Detained and Disappeared, Argentina and Chile)
AFEP	Agrupación de Familiares de Ejecutados Políticos (Association of Families of Murdered Political Prisoners, Chile)
AI-5	Acto Institucional 5 (Institutional Act Number 5, Brazil)
AMIA	Asociación Mutual Israelita Argentina (Argentine Israelite Mutual Association)
ANC	African National Congress, South Africa
APDH	Asamblea Permanente de Derechos Humanos (Permanent Assembly for Human Rights, Argentina)

Asociación de Madres de Plaza de Mayo (Association of the Mothers of the Plaza de Mayo, Argentina)

CELS	Centro de Estudios Legales y Sociales (Center for Legal and Social Studies, Argentina)
CGT	Confederación General de Trabajo (Confederation of Labor, Argentina)
CIA	Central Intelligence Agency, United States
CIE	Centro do Informacão do Exército (Center for Army Intelligence, Brazil)
CNI	Centro Nacional de Información (National Center for Information, Chile)
CODEPU	Comité de Defensa de los Derechos del Pueblo (Association for the Defense of People's Rights, Chile)
CONADEP	Comisión Nacional Sobre la Desaparición de Personas (National Commission on the Disappeared, Argentina)
DICOMCAR	Dirección de Comunicación Carabinero (Carabinero Intelligence Branch, Chile)
DINA	Dirección de Inteligencia Nacional (National Intelligence Service, Chile)
DOI-CODI	Destacamento de Operações e Informações, Centro de Operações de Defesa Interna (Internal Defense and Operations Unit, Brazil)
ESMA	Escuela Suboficiales de de Mecánica de la Armada (Naval Mechanics School, Argentina)
FAB	Força Aerea Brasileira (Brazilian Air Force)
FACH	Fuerzas Armadas de Chile (Chilean Armed Forces)
GAC	Grupo de Arte Callejera (Street Art Group, Argentina)
GTNM	Grupo Tortura Nunca Mais (Torture Never Again, Brazil)

H.I.J.O.S.	Hijos por la Identidad y la Justicia contra el Olvido y el Silencio (Sons and Daughters for Identity and Justice against Forgetting and Silence, Argentina)
ICTY	International Criminal Tribunal for the former Yugoslavia
IFP	Inkatha Freedom Party, South Africa
IJR	Institute for Justice and Reconciliation, South Africa

Liga Argentina por los Derechos del Hombre (Argentine League for the Rights of Men)

Madres de Plaza de Mayo, Linea Fundadora (Mothers of the Plaza de Mayo, Founding Group, Argentina)

MEDH	Movimiento Ecuménico de Derechos Humanos (Ecumenical Human Rights Movement, Argentina)
MIR	Movimiento de Izquierda Revolucionaria (Revolutionary Left Movement, Chile)
MK	Umkhoto we Sizwe (African National Congress army, South Africa)
NUSAS	National Union of South African Students
OAB	Ordem dos Advogados Brasileiros (Brazilian Bar Assocation)
PAC	Pan African Congress, South Africa
PC do B	Partido Comunista do Brasil (Communist Party of Brazil)
PDS	Partido Democrático Social (Social Democratic Party, Brazil)
PEBCO 3	Three murdered South African Port Elizabeth Black Consciousness activists
PFL	Partido da Frente Liberal (Liberal Front Party, Brazil)
PMDB	Partido do Movimento Democrático Brasileiro (Party of the Brazilian Democratic Movement)

PT	Partido dos Trabalhadores (Workers' Party, Brazil)
PTSD	Post-Traumatic Stress Disorder
SACP	South African Communist Party
SERPAJ	Servicio de Paz y Justicia (Peace and Justice Service, Argentina)
SIDE	Servicio de Inteligencia del Estado (National Intelligence Service, Argentina)
SIFA	Servicio de Inteligencia de la Fuerza Áerea (Air Force Intelligence Service, Chile)
SNI	Servicio National de Inteligencia (National Intelligence Service, Argentina)
SNI	Serviço Nacional de Informações (National Intelligence Service, Brazil)
TRC	Truth and Reconciliation Commission, South Africa
UDF	United Democratic Front, South Africa
UTPBA	Unión de Trabajadores de la Prensa en Buenos Aires (Buenos Aires's Union of Journalism Workers)

THE POLITICAL POWER OF CONFESSION

PAULINA: I want him to confess. I want him to sit in front of that cassette recorder and tell me what he did—not just to me, everything, to everybody . . . with all the information, the names and data, all the details. That's what I want.

GERARDO: He confesses and you let him go.

PAULINA: I let him go.

GERARDO: And you need nothing more from him?

PAULINA: Not a thing.

—Ariel Dorfman, *Death and the Maiden*

PAULINA'S LINES FROM ARIEL DORFMAN'S DRAMATIC PLAY *Death and the Maiden* express a prevailing belief about the political power of confessions made by perpetrators of state violence. She contends that if her torturer confesses to what he did to her, she will need "nothing more" to move on in her life, to settle accounts with the past. What Paulina and Gerardo discover, as the play unfolds, is the complexity that emerges when authoritarian state agents confess. Their confessions do not settle accounts with the past; rather, they unsettle them.

Perpetrators' confessions unsettle listeners, who learn disturbing and lurid details of past authoritarian state violence, sometimes for the first time. They unsettle, or break, the silence imposed over the past by forces within democratic societies that wish to leave the past behind, to close the book on it. These confessions, however, do not necessarily disclose truths about the past. They are merely accounts, explanations and justifications for deviant behavior, or personal versions of a past.[1] As such, they unsettle, or compel, audiences of victims, survivors, and human-rights activists to assert their own, often contending, interpretations of the past. While victims and survivors demand accountability, authoritarian-regime supporters defend the past, denying and silencing negative portrayals of it. Conflict erupts over confessions as social actors dispute interpretations of what happened and compete for power over whose interpretation will shape the political agenda, the terms of public debate, and the outcome of that debate.

The charged political talk generated by confessions of past authoritarian state violence challenges democratic theories. The hope expressed in transitional justice literature—that perpetrators' confessions might lead to reconciliation, defined as resolution of past quarrels or friendly agreement between competing sides—overlooks the often irreconcilable differences between victims and perpetrators. Rather than apologize for their acts, perpetrators tend to rationalize them and minimize their own responsibility, thus heightening, rather than lessening, tension over the past. Key deliberative-democracy texts consider that "decision making by discussion among free and equal citizens" hinges on "rationality and impartiality," a product unlikely to emerge from polarized and emotionally charged discussions about past political violence.[2] Similarly, deliberative-democracy scholars have argued that without "gag rules" democracies will fail to "secure forms of cooperation and fellowship otherwise beyond reach."[3]

Rather than promoting deliberation or reconciliation, dialogue over the authoritarian past appears to threaten democracy. Some groups call for censorship of ideas or vigilante justice. Deep fissures emerge as groups struggle for political power. Governments attempt, often without success, to suppress debate in the interest of peace and democracy. Ideological polarization, antidemocratic attitudes and policies, and dialogic warfare emerge and unsettle democracies.

Even within this unpropitious political climate, democratic debate over past state violence is possible. In *Unsettling Accounts* I explore the nature of that debate by advancing the notion of contentious coexistence, or a conflictual dialogic approach to democracy in deeply divided societies. Contentious coexistence borrows from deliberative-democracy approaches, but emphasizes the reality and importance of competition over ideas and conflict over values and goals. Emotion overpowers reason in these charged environments, but it does not necessarily threaten democracy. Consensus, harmony, and equality are unlikely outcomes. Nevertheless, I argue, contentious debate enhances democratic practices by provoking political participation, contestation, and competition. Through those processes it makes possible public challenges to prevailing antidemocratic attitudes, behavior, and values in society. Contentious coexistence, in short, offers a more realistic understanding of dialogic practices in democracies, as well as a better alternative to reconciliation processes that suppress political talk.

Perpetrators' confessions provide insights into the process of contentious coexistence. Perpetrators speak out despite social sanctions and laws, and sometimes even against their rational self-interest. Their words spark profound political conflict. This conflict, however, is largely discursive. I explore ways that democratic societies can encounter, and even encourage, confessions without threatening democratic speech or political stability. Indeed, it considers perpetrators' confessions a pathway to enrich democracies.

This is not an entirely novel idea. The South African Truth and Reconciliation Commission (TRC) made perpetrators' confessions a central and unique feature of its process toward settling accounts with the past and building a new, democratic South Africa. Apartheid-era perpetrators received amnesty in exchange for confessing to political violence. Valorizing perpetrators' confessions in a public process to reach truth and reconciliation made the TRC a model for other countries emerging from authoritarian state violence. Nevertheless, to date no other country has adopted the confessional model of reconciliation. Truth commissions elsewhere have provided amnesty without requiring confessions; in such cases, confessions have emerged outside the transitional-justice apparatus. South Africa remains a phenomenon often explained by its propitious political climate: the international delegitimation of the apartheid regime, its electoral defeat by its erstwhile enemies (the African National Congress), and Nelson Mandela's conciliatory leadership. Even in the favorable post-apartheid climate, perpetrators' confessions unsettled, rather than settled accounts with the past. South Africa's democracy advanced, in other words, because of contentious dialogue, not because of shared values and goals, reasoned deliberation, or conflict avoidance.

South Africa thus provides valuable insights into contentious coexistence. It demonstrates that new democracies can survive profoundly unsettling and even antidemocratic political discourse. Democracies may even thrive in such climates. Contentious coexistence embraces political contestation as a fundamental pillar of democracy. Moreover, rather than advocating the lofty and elusive goals of consensus or reconciliation, contentious coexistence rests merely on open and democratic debate.

Debate, however, involves more than political speech (the confession). Focusing on speech or confession alone would give undue political power to perpetrators. Contentious coexistence, therefore, includes the interaction of political speech in a wider political context. A political drama unfolds. I examine in chapter 1 the elements of political performance and their relationship to contentious coexistence. Perpetrators and their audiences vie for political power: who tells the story of the past (actor), what they say (script), how they say it (acting), and where (stage) and when (timing) they say it. Sectors of society (audiences), moreover, clash over interpretations of the political meaning behind confessions. Comprising not only victims, survivors, and human-rights activists but also members of the authoritarian regime and its civilian supporters, these audiences use perpetrators' confessions to advance particular political positions. They struggle over the facts, interpretation of them, and their significance for contemporary politics.

Research into the political dynamics of perpetrators' confessions therefore involved several levels of analysis. I chose four countries emerging from authoritarian state violence that had adopted different institutional forms for addressing their past: Brazil's blanket amnesty; conditional amnesty in exchange for confession in South Africa; amnesty without confession in Chile's truth commission; and the full array of truth commission, trials, pardons and amnesty, and retrials in Argentina. Institutional stages and political timing, while significant in shaping the confession and audience reactions to them, did not explain everything; the performance itself also influenced the confession's political impact. Thus, using text, video, and aural recordings of confessions, I analyzed how perpetrators presented their confessions in print, radio, and televised media. I noted which parts of the original performance the media included and excluded, and the political dynamics and consequences of such editing. I further used the media to track reactions to the confessions, finding as many different political interpretations as possible. In follow-up interviews I explored with confessed perpetrators, their victims and survivors, and others who publicly responded to these confessions the political dynamics of the confessional performance as a check on media reports and my own analysis. Since this project is about public politics, I have not often attributed private comments made to me. Anonymity protects individuals whose comments, seemingly innocuous at one juncture, could make them vulnerable in changing political climates. Content and discourse analysis, performance and media analysis, interviews, and comparative historical methods have enabled me to trace the political dynamics of the confessions: the factors that influenced them and the impact they had.

The empirical chapters of this book examine particular confessional forms and their impact on democratic debate. Each chapter begins with an in-depth analysis of a singularly important confessional performance in a particular country. The second half of each chapter compares that confession with similar ones in different contexts. This organizational framework demonstrates not only the profound impact of a single confession on democratic politics in the relevant countries, but also that these confessions are neither isolated events nor determined by culture and institutions alone. The range of confessional forms I analyze emerges regardless of culture or transitional justice institutions. While particular kinds of institutions might produce more of a particular kind of confession—truth commissions engendering remorse, court cases provoking denials—each country experiences a nearly full array of confessional forms. The temptation to consider confession a cultural byproduct of Catholic traditions in particular countries ignores its emergence elsewhere. The rarity of perpetrators' confessions suggests that only a few individuals seek the opportunity to tell their story, make history, and account for the past. Their motivations are simultaneously personal and political. History and political context shape the confessions themselves and responses to them by establishing different political stages and timing in which perpetrators perform their confession and audiences respond to them. Certain processes are more relevant than others. Countries with stronger human-rights organizations contest perpetrators' confessions more effectively than those that do not. Where perpetrators have remained united behind silence they tend to avoid confession and the conflict it might engender. But political capacity and strength change over time and with experience. Indeed, the confessions themselves can often catapult onto the public stage previously silenced and powerless victims and survivors of authoritarian state violence.

The pair of cases on Argentina, which I introduce in chapters 2 and 3, involve the kinds of confessions most commonly associated with reconciliation—remorse—and those least likely to contribute to reconciliation—heroic confessions. The perpetrators confessed to their activities during the so-called Dirty War in Argentina (1976–1983), the period of state terrorism under military junta rule. Security forces kidnapped supposed "subversives" and held them in secret detention centers, torturing, killing, and disappearing an estimated 10,000 citizens and noncitizens. The junta claimed it responded to a call by the democratic government and Argentine citizens to end the threat from left-wing subversion. Widely discredited for its economic mismanagement, its ill-fated war with Great Britain over the Falkland (Malvinas) Islands, and its human-rights abuses, the military issued a self-amnesty and allowed democratic elections. President Raúl Alfonsín (1983–1989) overturned the self-amnesty, ordered an investigation of human-rights violations by the National Commission on the Disappeared (CONADEP), produced an official report (*Nunca más*, or Never again), and tried, convicted, and imprisoned for life members of the military junta and other top military commanders. As civil and military unrest mounted, Alfonsín adopted Full Stop and Due Obedience Laws that ultimately amnestied lower-level officers for human-rights violations. The subsequent democratic government of Carlos Menem (1989–1999) pardoned the military commanders and released them from jail, ending the possibility of prosecutions for human-rights violations. Trials continued for crimes not covered under the amnesty laws, specifically the kidnapping of babies born in the detention centers and their illegal adoption by military or military-friendly families. Lower courts and the legislature, moreover, gradually eroded the legitimacy of the amnesty laws, culminating in the 2005 Supreme Court of Argentina's decision on their unconstitutionality.

Argentine perpetrators spoke out despite the uncertainty of their fates under such fluctuating laws. Neither efforts by the courts, the government, or the security apparatus to silence them, nor their own self-protective interests stopped the perpetrators from confessing. Their statements ranged in character, however, from remorseful to heroic.

In chapter 2 I focus on the dramatic admission by Argentine naval officer Adolfo Scilingo that he had conducted "death flights," or disappeared detainees of the infamous Naval Mechanics School (ESMA) by dropping them alive from an airplane into the ocean. In this first account from inside the military's security apparatus, he expressed remorse for killing thirty people. I explore the factors that contributed to Scilingo's confession, the responses to it, and particularly how the death flights became a symbol of the regime's inhumanity. Far from settling accounts with the past, or reconciling it, remorseful confessions like Scilingo's lead to contentious debate over truth, justice, and impunity.

The confession featured in chapter 3 is the obverse of Scilingo's. Argentine naval officer Alfredo Astiz represents those perpetrators who use confessions to reassert a heroic interpretation of the authoritarian regime's use of violence. Among his notorious acts of violence, Astiz infiltrated the Madres de Plaza de Mayo, a group of mothers who march once a week in the square in front of the government palace demanding the return of their disappeared children. His efforts led to the death and disappearance of some of these mothers and their supporters in the human-rights community. Although heroic confessions like Astiz's include admissions of violent acts, they resurrect the authoritarian regimes' justifications for such acts, specifically their role in saving the country from subversion. Democratic governments and social movements often advocate censoring such confessions to protect democracy and the dignity of victims and survivors. When social movements engage them, however, they expose the acts as un-heroic, leading to an emotional debate over the past and new democratic values.

In chapters 4 and 5 I focus on Chile and highlight two types of confession that would appear to undermine rather than advance democracy: denial and sadism. Such confessions occurred in the aftermath of the dictatorship of Augusto Pinochet (1973–1990). Having overthrown the democratically elected socialist president Salvador Allende and imposed nearly two decades of military rule, Pinochet lost a popular plebiscite over his own constitution, forcing him to hold national elections. Despite significant support for Pinochet's successful economic recovery program, his candidate lost the elections. With Pinochet still holding the reigns of formal and informal power over the democratic process, President Patricio Aylwin (1990–1994) nonetheless established a truth commission, popularly known as the Rettig Commission, to investigate the regime's human-rights violations. The commission documented approximately 3,000 murders and disappearances by the regime. An amnesty law, and Pinochet's continued political power over the democratic transition, protected most of the military from prosecution. Yet even in this context, Chilean courts found ways around the amnesty statutes, specifically by investigating disappearances not covered by the law. After Pinochet was detained in London in 1998, in response to the Spanish judge Baltasar Garzón's extradition request, perpetrators' immunity eroded further. Pinochet himself joined the ranks of the accused for human-rights violations, with the Supreme Court of Chile denying him immunity three times in 2005 and 2006. Pinochet remained under house arrest until his death in December 2006, having evaded two trials on medical grounds.

Given the context, most members of Chile's security apparatus remained silent about the past. In chapter 4 I explore one exception: Osvaldo Romo, a civilian member of Pinochet's National Intelligence Service (DINA). Romo not only admitted to his role in past violence during his televised confession, he exuded a manner of depraved pleasure at the sexual torture of women in clandestine prisons and the disappearance of bodies. The two ideological poles in Chilean society reemerged, each using Romo's confession to stress its interpretation of the military regime's involvement in violence. Unlike with heroic confessions, however, no one applauded Romo's actions. Instead, Pinochet's supporters denied Romo's story. The debate over Romo's confession developed consensus around notions of human-rights violations, while allowing disagreement over the regime's involvement in them.

In chapter 5 I examine the confessional texts of former DINA leader General Manuel Contreras. Contreras seemingly avoids confession by denying his role in the murder of Chilean diplomat Orlando Letelier in Washington, as well as of other opponents of the Pinochet regime within and outside Chile. But evidence of violence compelled Contreras to explain it, to admit to knowing about the violence. His conviction and imprisonment demonstrate that even very powerful perpetrators may fail to successfully argue their innocence.

The confessional forms I analyze in chapters 6 and 7 transpired in the absence of institutional mechanisms for addressing past human-rights violations. Most analyses attribute the slow and weak progress on transitional justice in Brazil to the low level of violations there (estimated at under four hundred deaths). The Brazilian military regime (1964–1985) issued a blanket amnesty in 1979, which continues to protect its members from prosecution. No national truth commission has investigated the violations or held the regime or its members accountable for them. Instead, *Brasil: Nunca mais* (*Torture in Brazil*), an unofficial report of human-rights violations published in 1985, documented military regime violence with data compiled from the regime's own legal records. The report relied on the Archdiocese of São Paulo and the International Council of Churches, not a government commission, for its support. In addition, family members of the regime's victims published in 1995 a *Dossier of Political Deaths and Disappearances after 1964* (*Dossiê dos mortos e desaparecidos políticos a partir de 1964*). The Brazilian human-rights community has made some gains to counteract the prevailing amnesty law: state-level and city-level investigations and acknowledgment of violations; a parliamentary commission to investigate disappearances (1991–94); a 1995 Special Commission on Political Deaths and Disappearances (Comisão Especial de Mortos e Desaparecidos Politicos–CEMDP) that provided reparations; a 2004 constitutional amendment to make human-rights violations a federal offense, shifting jurisdiction away from state courts; and a 2005 decision (still not implemented) to make the archives from the dictatorship available to the public. Whether the recent civil trial of the torturer Carlos Alberto Brilhante Ustra might contribute to the erosion of the amnesty law remains to be seen.

Few perpetrators have confessed in such a protective environment. In chapter 6, however, I observe a—literally—novel confession made by the Brazilian military officer Pedro Corrêa Cabral. Cabral's fictional account, based on his own experiences, describes the military's involvement in a massacre in the Amazon region in the 1970s. His story confirmed victims' and survivors' testimonies, previously ignored or denied by the military. Fiction and even lies can expose truth about the past unrevealed in other kinds of confessional accounts and provoke dialogue over a past otherwise censored.

The Brazilian regime's silence forms the core of chapter 7. This seemingly nondialogic process and nonconfessional form still fits my analysis of perpetrators' confessions, providing an opportunity to explore how words can silence the past and how silence can expose it. Silence may be perceived as the most effective way in which security forces can end discussion about the past. Even entrepreneurial social movements sometimes fail to initiate a dialogue when authoritarian forces or their supporters suppress communication. But audiences sometimes interpret silence as a confession to wrongdoing, a refusal to reveal the truth because it would implicate the narrator.

Looking to South Africa in chapters 8 and 9, I examine confessions made within and outside the TRC. The result of political negotiations that ended the apartheid regime, the TRC encouraged perpetrators to confess in exchange for amnesty. The Amnesty Committee evaluated applications and held hearings to determine each perpetrator's compliance with the criteria of full disclosure of the truth, the political nature of each crime, its occurrence within the mandated period (1960–1994), and the proportionality of the act to political goals. Perpetrators who failed to apply for or receive amnesty were to be subject to criminal prosecution for their acts. The committee received about 7,000 applications, but considered only about 2,000, dismissing the others on administrative grounds. Half of those 2,000 applicants received amnesty. To date, no perpetrators have been brought to trial for their failure to comply with the amnesty process. Some perpetrators have appealed the Amnesty Committee's decision, and others remain in prison for crimes not subject to amnesty, holding out hope for a presidential pardon.

In chapter 8 I explore amnesia by focusing on the apartheid policeman Jeffrey Benzien's confession in exchange for amnesty, which he received despite his failure to provide full disclosure. Benzien offered a sanitized version of his past acts, claiming that he could not remember the names of all of his victims or the details of the torture he committed. The victims present at his TRC hearing challenged his account, transforming Benzien into the poster child for apartheid state brutality. By forgetting the past, perpetrators are not always able to end dialogue about it. They may, in fact, mobilize sectors of society to fill in the "forgotten" details. In those cases, the power behind the confession shifts from perpetrators to survivors who remember and recount the missing facts.

Eugene de Kock's confession, presented in chapter 9, shows what happens when security forces abandon or betray their officers. De Kock, the head of an apartheid police death squad (Vlakplaas), refused to become the scapegoat for apartheid era violence. Instead of quietly accepting his conviction, sentence, and imprisonment, he began to name names of perpetrators and provide the details that brought down the regime's house of cards. Betrayal produces some of the most effective confessions, at least from the perspective of providing the evidence necessary to expose and verify regimes' involvement in past violence. Few who support the regime can ignore the truth behind confessions made by the regime's former golden boys.

The differences in political context among these four countries shape each chapter's discussion of the impact of timing, staging, and audience response to unsettling accounts. South Africa provided the most conducive environment for perpetrators' confessions through the TRC. The electoral victory of Nelson Mandela's African National Congress no doubt made such a full vetting possible by affording victims and survivors of apartheid-era violence political representation in government. Similarly, elections to the presidency of former political prisoners in Argentina (Néstor Kirchner), Brazil (Luiz Inácio "Lula" da Silva), and Chile (Michelle Bachelet) have recently challenged amnesty and silence over the past in those countries. If the background of the president alone determined political outcomes, however, one would see more advances in Brazil. The (long) time that has passed since repression and the (low) level of repression partially explain why Brazil's human-rights groups have proved less successful than others in pressing for investigation and justice. The balance of power between the security forces and the human-rights community also influences outcomes in each country. But even in the inauspicious environment of Brazil, unsettling accounts have strengthened weak human-rights movements to challenge the silence imposed by a united security force. In the empirical chapters, therefore, I look not only at the political context (timing, staging, and audience response), but also at how unsettling accounts alter that context.

In the conclusion to *Unsettling Accounts* I summarize the impact of unsettling accounts and contentious coexistence on democracy. I take the analysis beyond confessional performances in transitional democracies, comparing such performances to the unsettling photographs of abuse from the United States's Abu Ghraib prison in Iraq, a comparison that reveals not only the positive impact of unsettling accounts and contentious coexistence on democracy, but also their limitations. The democratic practices of participation, competition, and contestation do not inexorably lead to democratic outcomes. Indeed, those anticipating reconciliation, consensus, and an end to human-rights violations will find the limited outcomes that emerge from contention over these political issues less than satisfactory. Unsettling accounts and contentious coexistence only make the struggle for democratic ideals possible; they do not ensure its success. The final scene of *Death and the Maiden* captures the real-life indeterminacy of political struggle. Gerardo and Paulina encounter her torturer at a concert. Nothing is resolved; nothing is forgotten. The music "plays and plays." But the actors face the stage. They look forward, not backward.

CHAPTER ONE

CONFESSIONAL PERFORMANCE

If one good deed in all my life I did,
I do repent it from my very soul.
—William Shakespeare, *Titus Andronicus*, 5.3.189–90

THE VILLAINOUS CHARACTER Aaron's confession to committing evil deeds in Shakespeare's *Titus Andronicus* represents a public confession by a perpetrator in a dramatic performance. This is not, however, the kind of performance real-life perpetrators make. Whereas Aaron admits to doing harm and smugly gloats about it, Murray Edelman notes, with an unintended insult to Shakespeare, "Only in bad novels and comic books do characters knowingly do evil and boast of it. In life, people rationalize their actions in moral terms."[1]

Real-life rationalizations, however, are no less dramatic than fictional boasting. Perpetrators' confessions are more than mere political talk: they not only *say* something, they *do* something.[2] They interpret the past. And through that interpretation they advance a political project for democracy. The political meaning behind the confession

Perpetrators' confessions are more than mere political talk.
Photo © iStockphoto.com/Jordan Chesbrough. Reproduced by permission.

generates conflict as others—victims and survivors—challenge perpetrators' interpretations. The ensuing political drama transcends personal stakes in the past and shapes the meaning of the past for contemporary political life.

DYNAMICS OF THE CONFESSIONAL PERFORMANCE

The metaphor of performance is not new to the social sciences. Dramaturgical analyses often emphasize "what performance is taking place or what meaning is being portrayed to an audience and how the elements that make up the performance contribute to that meaning."[3] They focus on "people and groups within the society who have access to resources and who use these resources to invoke and manipulate meaning."[4] The specific characteristics of a performance—scene, act, agent, agency, and purpose—provide a set of categories for organizing observations.[5] Such analyses, however, limit their approach to everyday occurrences by social actors largely unconscious of acting or playing on a political stage.[6] In a confessional performance, by contrast, a social actor deliberately takes a public stage in a political drama that suspends "normal everyday role playing" and "interrupt [s] the flow of social life."[7] Moreover, in addition to the actor and acting, script, and stage, certain theatrical elements—specifically, audiences and timing—produce meaning out of confessional performances.[8]

Perpetrators as Actors; Acting as Perpetrators.   Who are perpetrators and why are so many people fascinated by them? Because they are novel, mystifying, or deviant, they intrigue audiences. Audiences perhaps unconsciously believe that they can protect themselves if they know more about perpetrators. Or perhaps audiences find perpetrators' power alluring. Perpetrators, after all, "do" violence; victims are "done to."[9] Observers of the South African Truth and Reconciliation Commission reflected on the media's emphasis on perpetrators: "The same kind of intensity of reporting is not afforded to victims/survivors, unless they have high-profile images themselves," and even then the media considers newsworthy only the "sensational brutality" that victims have faced.[10] The South African dramaturgist Jane Taylor further notes: "What makes the stories of the perpetrators so compelling is, in part, that they are agents: they act upon others. All of the psychological structures of desire, power, greed, fear, identification are invoked in these accounts. Milton's classic dilemma in *Paradise Lost* was that Satan became the hero of the narrative, because of the inherent interest in his character. A similar effect was evident in the coverage of the stories of [South African perpetrators] de Kock, Coetzee and Mamasela."[11]

Perpetrators themselves rarely find the characterization appealing. They do not, like Shakespeare's Aaron, embrace the role of the evildoer. Even when they boast about their violent past, they do not accept the implied criminality behind the "perpetrator" label, which they resist for its indelible imprint. A former British Loyalist combatant, for example, preferred language that acknowledged the possibility of changing attitudes and behavior: "I used to be a peace-breaker," he stated. "Now I'm a peace-maker."[12] A recent sociological study refers to Brazilian police torturers as "violence workers," which emphasizes the institutionalized creation of perpetrators, rather than innate and immutable individual characteristics.[13] For those who have committed authoritarian state violence, the role of perpetrator is neither neutral nor alluring.[14]

Public attention may result from fictional and news accounts that depict perpetrators as extraordinarily evil, sadistic, and psychopathic. By contrast, most academic studies consider perpetrators of authoritarian violence normal. The psychologist Dan Bar-On, for example, claims that only 5 percent of Nazi perpetrators could be labeled psychopaths. The remaining 95 percent were motivated to commit atrocities as a result of a particular type of training, socialization, ideology, and power structure. The obedience experiments conducted by Stanley Milgram at Yale University in 1961–1962 concluded that most individuals obey authority, even when ordered to inflict harm on individuals without reasonable cause. Philip Zimbardo's 1971 prison experiments and a 2002 study of Brazilian torturers conducted by Martha K. Huggins, Mika Haritos-Fatouros, and Zimbardo claim that environments that authorize and reward individuals for violent acts breed violent perpetrators. John L. Sullivan, James Piereson, and George E. Marcus found that under the right set of circumstances nearly everyone is susceptible to acting violently against individuals who belong to a group they hate. Nonetheless, the media seek explanations that differentiate perpetrators from "the rest of us": abusive or repressive homes or deep psychological afflictions.[15]

Misguided assumptions about perpetrators' psyches run so deep that even those who know better are susceptible to such prejudices. The journalist Tina Rosenberg, for example, wrote, "I did not want to think that many of the violent are 'people like us': so civilized, so educated, so cultured."[16] The journalist Jann Turner fashioned herself a "Jodie Foster staring down the restrained psychotic form of a South African Hannibal Lecter" when she interviewed an apartheid assassin.[17] I recall vividly the way my own heart beat on the way to my first interview with a perpetrator, assuming that some slip up on my part would make me one more victim of his violence.

Perpetrators, therefore, use social fronts to overcome this image when they take the public stage. Erving Goffman defines *personal front* as "expressive equipment, the items that we most intimately identify with the performer himself and that we naturally expect will follow the performer wherever he goes."[18] He includes among its features insignia of office or rank, clothing, sex, age, racial characteristics, size, appearance, posture, speech patterns, facial expressions, manner, and body language. Perpetrators can thus engage in "the whole theatrical array of gestures, demeanors, costumes, props, and stage devices" to "impress or bamboozle an audience."[19] They make and remake their image; their front is "constantly constructed, negotiated, reformed, fashioned, and organized . . . , a pragmatic piecing-together of pre-existing scraps of material recalling . . . 'bricolage.' "[20] These fronts are not cut from whole cloth, but derived from existing and socially acceptable roles. Sometimes perpetrators adopt a front unconsciously and sincerely, believing that it represents their "truer self," the self they would like to be or believe they are.[21] Alternatively, they may deliberately and cynically construct an appropriate front, either alone or in consultation with their colleagues, family members, or lawyers. These cynical fronts provide a pragmatic "means to other ends," but a perpetrator may also derive "a kind of gleeful spiritual aggression from the fact that he can toy at will with something his audience must take seriously."[22]

Perpetrators use other techniques, in addition to social fronts, to diminish negative images associated with their past. Through "doubling," for example, perpetrators present alternative selves and lives.[23] Their social lives appear incompatible with common images of perpetrators, as they portray themselves to be morally upright and religious, good neighbors, and good citizens, doting parents, loving and faithful partners, generous and caring friends. Their work lives appear beyond reproach: they are dedicated, loyal, and efficient employees, willing to go the extra mile, and obedient to authority. In political life, they exhibit patriotism, duty to the nation, and a willingness to make personal sacrifices. Doubling diminishes the negative characteristics associated with perpetrators.

A "born again" narrative device presents a similar opportunity. In these cases, perpetrators admit to past wrongdoing, but consider themselves reformed and, as such, unassailable. Religious rebirth allows individuals to trade their sinful pasts for saintly presents. Recovering alcoholics and drug addicts among perpetrators use a similar trope. They explain their earlier acts as resulting from intoxication and as incompatible with their new, sober selves.

Primo Levi's notion of the "gray zone" points to how perpetrators reverse roles and identify themselves as victims. They recount or demonstrate the physical or psychological effects of their violence on their lives: drug or alcohol addiction, insomnia, anxiety, depression, or other scars of a tormented past. They suggest that they cannot be held responsible for the violent acts they committed when they were also victimized by those acts.

"To agree to perform is to agree to take a chance"; despite elaborate fronts and narrative devices, perpetrators do not always succeed in convincing their audiences of their "normality."[24] They may lack effective acting or narrative skills. Too much contradiction or too many incompatibilities in their performance may render it incoherent to the audience. While they can alter certain personal characteristics (e.g., clothing or hairstyles), other attributes can indelibly mark them as perpetrators (e.g., background, build, movement and carriage, accent and word choice, facial expressions or emotions). Inappropriate performances, as Goffman notes, can derail perpetrators' objectives: "To be awkward or unkempt, to talk or move wrongly, is to be a dangerous giant, a destroyer of worlds. As every psychotic and comic ought to know, any accurately improper move can poke through the thin sleeve of immediate reality."[25]

Contentious coexistence demands performances by political actors, but it understands that such performances shift across time, stages, and in response to audiences. Those shifts indicate political adjustments made through interaction with other elements in democratic society. Subtle changes in the performance may reveal an understanding and sensitivity to political events, institutions, or actors.

Similarly, those parts of the performance replayed or remembered publicly demonstrate how political meaning changes over time and in conjunction with theatrical and political elements.

Confessional Scripts. Adapting Ndebele's elegant formulation, I argue that confessional scripts allow perpetrators to reinvent their past through narrative.[26] Perpetrators do not recount their past as it occurred at the time, nor do they necessarily possess "a claim to truth or accuracy." The stories they tell may be made up, consciously or unconsciously, to fit a particular political moment or personal need.[27] They may even contradict the common understanding of confession as an acknowledgment of guilt or wrongdoing. Perpetrators' accounts, or reinventions, of their past include remorse, heroism, denial, sadism, silence, fiction and lies, amnesia, and betrayal.

Audiences often perceive confessional reinventions as deliberate manipulations that minimize guilt, rather than acknowledge it. And sometimes they are. At other times, however, confessions simply reflect the creative process of trying to piece together the past with partial and selective memory. Memory is imperfect and unreliable, as is well known among psychologists, historians, legal professionals, and law-enforcement agents. Perpetrators and nonperpetrators alike tell "vital lies" about their past, sometimes deliberately and sometimes unconsciously creating stories that add meaning and coherence to their lives.[28] In their confessions, perpetrators describe how they remember their past, or how they want it to be remembered, reconstructing their pasts through narrative.

Creating vital lies involves several processes. Perpetrators employ, for example, "salvage operations," the conscious or unconscious choice to retain certain parts of the remembered past and to jettison others that do not fit "present-day discourses and desires."[29] The present political context acts as a filter, molding and modifying memory "to fit into the understanding and expectations of the society in which it is presented."[30] Salvage operations filter and select facts, seeing only what is convenient to see and transforming memory fragments into a coherent and consistent story.

To fill in memory gaps, perpetrators use contrivance, adding details, sometimes out of sequence, or borrowed from other moments or others' memories, or even imagined, but believed to be true. These details give memory body and life, and accurately represent how perpetrators remember events (or want to remember them), even if they do not match the chronology or factual set of events.

Socialization also frames vital lies. Families, schools, churches, and military institutions shape how people experience events in the past and even teach a specific language for talking about those events, or to avoid talking about them. Over time, social norms or individual attitudes change values and influence the way in which individuals remember their past. Sometimes they may do so according to their new set of values and thus reinvent their past. At other times, they cannot escape the language of memory that they learned originally, and they remain trapped in a particular narrative about the past.

Perpetrators of authoritarian state violence do not speak about their acts of violence at the time those acts are committed. Elizabeth Jelin's ominous statement, "If there are no words . . . there cannot be memories," may explain the absence of confession by perpetrators.[31] Formal and informal gag rules pervade authoritarian periods. It is common for perpetrators to recount official sanctions and self-censorship that prevented them from talking about their violent acts, even to their colleagues, family and friends, and counselors. Gag rules persist into democratic periods, sometimes through violence, threats, and intimidation. Perpetrators may deliberately erase their violent acts more from consciousness, so they can learn to live with themselves without ghosts and haunting memories. Perpetrators' silence and amnesia not only reflect this learning process, but may also be used instrumentally to avoid reprisals.

When perpetrators do speak out, they often evoke the vocabulary they were taught by the authoritarian regime: denial, justification, excuses, and euphemisms that hide their acts from themselves and others. They may do so even when they feel remorse for their past, for they simply have no other language. The language of war, and particularly "unconventional war" (counterinsurgency), pervades their confessions, sanitizing atrocity. The vocabulary of "interrogating" or "eliminating" the enemy in a "war," for example, obscures the reality of kidnapping, torturing, executing, poisoning, raping, and disappearing prisoners held in covert detention centers.[32] Perpetrators characterize the defenseless victims in those camps as ferocious enemies whose defeat requires military virtues of self-sacrifice, patriotism, heroism, and bravery. As soldiers, perpetrators contend, they have a duty to defend the nation from communism, terrorism, or barbarism.

Asserting that the ends (defeating the threat to the nation) justify the (usually unarticulated) means, perpetrators portray themselves as forces of "good" against the forces of "evil."

Perpetrators must justify or excuse these acts only when silence and denial no longer work and evidence of atrocity emerges. In the context of war, as opposed to a human-rights framework, the nature of the violence can be characterized in perpetrators' favor. Perpetrators often blame their enemies, the subversives, for the violence, claiming that the authoritarian regimes in fact prevented more extreme brutality. They point to awards, decorations, promotions, raises, status, and commemorations they received for their bravery against the enemy.[33] And because their accounts "ring true," certain audiences accept them. A Chilean Air Force general's statement is illustrative: "I don't condemn these [military] groups. Probably without them the danger to the country would have been even greater. At first glance into this issue they look like monsters. But the truth is that we owe them a lot for having defeated subversion."[34]

That perpetrators fail to question their "missions" at the time is not surprising. They often live in isolation in security-force communities. Authoritarian regimes control the media and political opposition, eliminating alternative viewpoints from public debate. Social bonds reinforce allegiance to the regime and its acts through family and friendship networks, parties, and festivities. Religious institutions (most notably, the Argentine Catholic Church and the South African Dutch Reformed Church) often support authoritarian regimes and their acts.[35] Only during the transition from authoritarian rule do perpetrators begin to see their acts from a different perspective. Abandoning their vital lies, however, threatens their moral foundations and their beliefs in themselves and in others, so most cling steadfastly to learned, or indoctrinated, versions of the past.

Regime supporters also cling to the heroic version, or salvation myth, of the authoritarian regime. To explain mounting evidence of violence, perpetrators adopt a language of error: human mistakes explain why innocent individuals die in wars; bureaucratic error explains why commanders fail to learn about and stop violence carried out by renegades, rogue forces, and emotionally or mentally unstable elements within the security forces. In pointing to human and institutional fallibility, perpetrators deny moral responsibility for systematic violence. At most, perpetrators may admit to crimes of omission or to failing to halt the violence, but not to crimes of commission or to acting violently. They condemn the violence, without condemning the regime.

Remorseful and betrayal confessions, rare as they are, break out of these narrative patterns and challenge authoritarian justifications and excuses. Audiences rarely embrace these confessions, doubting their sincerity, judging them to be instrumentally driven, or finding within them the authoritarian regime's justifications and excuses. Such scripts therefore rarely satisfy audiences looking for condemnation of the regime. But some audiences nonetheless use them, as well as other confessional forms, to that end.

Confessional scripts often have multiple, intertwining, and even contradictory narrative strands. While one dominant narrative form —remorse, heroism, denial, sadism, silence, lies, amnesia, betrayal— may emerge, other forms intrude. Confessions also change over time as new information surfaces and as political contexts and opportunities change. Even the dynamic dialogic process initiated by confessions alters those confessions. Perpetrators learn new languages for expressing their views only through interaction with victims and survivors who challenge them. Or they adopt new views, refining their positions to make their arguments precise, more or less inflammatory, or to reclaim their confession after editing or excerpting for public consumption has distorted its original intent. Even subtle changes in a script, or what parts of the script are made public, reveal how actors begin to live with each other in contentious coexistence.

Confessional Stages. Vivian Patraka encourages one to extend the notion of the stage beyond its architecture—"land, buildings, and physical props"—and to include its role in the production of meaning.[36] She identifies two types of stage: performance place and performance space. Performance places produce scripted meaning and representation.[37] One would expect perpetrators, therefore, to deny their past, remain silent, or claim amnesia to avoid a guilty verdict in court. Plea bargaining agreements, on the other hand, promote betrayal. Truth commissions and mitigation of sentence hearings encourage remorse. "Made for TV" confessions involve heroic, sadistic, or exaggerated fictions. Performance places heavily influence the kinds of confession perpetrators produce.

Performance space, however, complicates scripted meaning and representation by producing "multiple performances of interpretation."[38] These spaces "not only condition political acts," they become the sites in which meanings of the past are openly contested and reshaped.[39] Performance space opens up access to other political performers. Victims and survivors, for example, may seize the confessional stage, diminishing perpetrators' control over their confessions and even subverting or derailing the political project they hoped to advance.

Audience responses to media coverage of confessions illustrate the concept of performance space. Although perpetrators might prepare their confession for a particular stage, such as a courtroom or truth commission, the media take it over. "Mediatized" versions of confessions, or those "circulated on television, as audio or video recordings, and in other forms based in technologies of reproduction," replace the original, live, and uncut versions unseen by most audiences.[40] Due to official policy, space limitations, location and time accessibility, awareness of the event, or demand, most audiences miss the live version, but catch the mediatized one. Mediatized performances, however, are not faithful copies of the originals. Hours or days of testimony are reduced to minutes on radio and television programs or to a few sentences in a print story. Decisions about what to exclude and include in news stories create meaning that may diverge from the perpetrators' intended message. The media, for example, seek dramatic material and may distort a confession by reproducing only small segments of it: screams and sobs, anger or laughter, sneers or tears. Camerawork can create or diminish emotion: it can zoom in on perpetrators, making them larger than life, or pull back to invite audiences "to see the pain of others but not to feel it."[41] Radio broadcasts eliminate explanatory facial expressions. Print media flattens inflection. The media, in short, possess enormous power over what confession the public views and interprets. Because most audiences witness confessions through mediatized accounts, those accounts actually become the confessional event, not an interpretation of it, reinforcing the adage that "we never 'know' an event but only its media coverage."[42] Mediatized versions thus tend to obliterate the original.[43] Being aware of this potential, perpetrators sometimes demand live, uncut, and unedited air time to present their public confession. Otherwise, they might find themselves in the awkward position of challenging their own confession, or what became of it in the media.

Despite their power, mediatized performances do not "speak for themselves," present one uncontroversial interpretation of perpetrators' confessions, or dictate political meaning to audiences. Sometimes they accurately depict perpetrators in all their complexity: simultaneously brutal and vulnerable, guilty and innocent, powerful and weak, rendering multiple interpretations of their pasts. Sometimes mediatized versions include commentary from other, even contending, social viewpoints. The media, in other words, become the performance space in which audiences debate the political significance of perpetrators' confessions to past violence. Even if the media produces scripted meaning and representation, audiences can use the portrayal to challenge those meanings.

The transitional-justice literature focuses on establishing the right set of institutions, often ignoring the role of the media in generating the political meaning around those institutions. The multiple performances of power that occur on transitional-justice and mediatized stages reveal the dynamics of contentious coexistence and how political actors sort out their differences and learn to speak to each other.

Confessional Timing. We live in an age of confession. Guests expose their deep secrets on widely watched television programs like *Oprah*. On websites like postsecret.com, people send in deeply personal and anonymous confessions in art form. Public leaders admit to personal scandals. Governments, nations, businesses, religious institutions, and political organizations confess to past political or social wrongs. Confession arguably has never played such a large role in political and social life. Despite the prevalence of confession, perpetrators remain reluctant to reveal their deepest secrets about the authoritarian past. For the most part, they remain silent to avoid violent or legal reprisals. Personal, institutional, and political factors only rarely succeed in encouraging perpetrators to overcome their fear of retaliation and speak out about their past.

Proximity to death—terminal disease, aging, tragic accident—or more general psychic and physical healing compels some perpetrators to speak out. Approaching the end of their lives or hoping to begin new ones, they realize they have nothing to lose from revealing their past. Indeed, after reevaluating their actions, some may consider atonement for past wrongs as necessary to their personal salvation.

Facing their own death also appears to inspire empathy among some perpetrators toward their victims and victims' families, motivating them to apologize. Public confession offers some perpetrators a pathway to healing from the physical or psychological trauma induced by past acts of violence—insomnia, anxiety, depression, emotional withdrawal, or addiction. Believing that confession will chase away the demons that haunt them, some perpetrators hope to begin a new and healthier life by atoning for the harm they caused to others.

Perpetrators seeking salvation will most likely choose private, over public, acts of confession. Rational calculation, however, drives some to go public with their story. Perpetrators may speak out against their colleagues, commanders, or the security forces in general, if they perceive the risks of public confession to be lower than the risks of silence. A pattern of mistreatment, betrayal, abandonment, or punishment within the security forces, for example, may convince some perpetrators that they will become scapegoats and that public confession may offer more institutional protections than silent loyalty to the outgoing regime. Most perpetrators, however, fear reprisals from the security forces and wait until other perpetrators test the explicit or implicit threats of disloyalty.

Confessional chains often occur, with one confession unleashing similar ones.[44] These chains sometimes arise only after one perpetrator has tested the safety of speaking out and cleared the way for subsequent confessions. Confessional chains also emerge when perpetrators attempt to "correct" impressions created by earlier admissions, thus clearing perpetrators' besmirched names or reputations. Confessional chaining also occurs when journalists, prosecutors, or other perpetrators "out" perpetrators, encouraging them to go public with their own story. Confessional chains may also result from rumors about financial or legal rewards for incentives. Chaining sometimes affects only particular security branches, since other sectors may prove more effective in ensuring silence.

Political transitions create particular institutional and material incentives that motivate some perpetrators to speak out despite potential reprisals. Perpetrators sometimes consider silence the greater risk, particularly when institutional arrangements offer amnesty in exchange for confession, as in the South African Truth and Reconciliation Commission, the Rwandan gacaca, and state witness programs. Perpetrators' decisions to confess may depend on internal calculations about the likelihood of exposure or trial. Institutional arrangements that reduce prison lengths, such as plea bargaining or mitigation of sentence hearings, also induce some perpetrators to speak out in exchange for their freedom.

Perpetrators may also anticipate material rewards or fame for their confession. Media outlets sometimes pay perpetrators for their stories or make them celebrities. Thus some perpetrators actively peddle their stories, often exaggerating their material value. They write, or plan to write, confessional books, though few achieve significant sales, material benefit, or fame. Only those perpetrators who work with journalists to tell their story gain access to a wider audience. Contentious coexistence emphasizes how unfolding and ever-changing political dramas, and not personal and institutional incentives alone, motivate perpetrators' confessions.

Confessions begin cautiously, reasserting safe euphemisms and coded speech. Over time and in interaction with victims and survivors, perpetrators must learn a new way to speak about their past. Attitudes change when language changes, and perpetrators thus begin to comprehend another point of view. As Jelin notes, "With time, and with historical, political, and cultural processes developing, there will necessarily be new processes of giving meaning to the past, with new interpretations. Thus, revisions, changes in narratives, and new conflicts over interpretations will have to arise."[45] The very act of public confession, in other words, forces perpetrators to understand, sometimes for the first time, what they did and its impact on individual lives and the nation's history. In explaining to those "outside" the repressive apparatus exactly what took place, and particularly in being questioned by victims or their representatives, perpetrators begin to see themselves and their acts without the protective shield of official discourse.[46] The confessional act allows perpetrators to "know" the event: to speak the unspeakable and to inscribe the event for the first time, by breaking with the official version and the silence imposed on them. Sometimes confessions appear long after the end of authoritarian rule. As evidenced by the capture and trial of Nazi war criminals, late confessions can incite political drama and contentious debate long after the atrocities have ceased.

Confessional Audiences. Following Stanley Fish, I argue that confessional texts are devoid of meaning on their own and require "interpretive communities" to create meaning.[47] In the case of perpetrators' confessions, such communities emerge among the audiences who witness them. Although perpetrators try to control interpretations of their performances, audiences hijack them and impose their own meanings. Confessional audiences resemble Augusto Boal's notion of the spectator who "no longer delegates power to the characters either to think or to act in his place. The spectator frees himself; he thinks and acts for himself! Theater is action!"[48]

Alfred Jarry asserts that the process of audiences interpreting performances is inevitable. "In any written work," he writes, "there is a hidden meaning, and anyone who knows how to read sees that aspect of it that makes sense for him."[49] Audiences do not uncover meaning deliberately or unconsciously hidden from them. Instead they use confessional performances to advance their own political projects. Confessions act as catalysts and as tools: as catalysts, they spark debate over issues previously silenced or dormant in society; as tools, they give their audiences a performance they can use for their own ends. Audiences mine confessions for what the perpetrators say and intend, how they say it, who they are, and where and when they perform.

Audiences do not approach confessional performances uniformly or in a political vacuum.[50] They bring to them backgrounds, experiences, political perspectives, and vested interests that shape interpretations. Audiences react to confessions from any of five pre-established positions: cynical, traumatic, healing, retributive, and salvational. Victims and survivors (and those sympathetic to them) approach confessions from cynical, traumatic, healing, and retributive perspectives. Authoritarian-regime supporters approach confessions from traumatic and salvational perspectives. Each position involves a corresponding political project.

Cynical audiences disbelieve that perpetrators will reveal the truth about the past. They consider perpetrators sufficiently powerful to avoid serious penalty. They presuppose that confessions will comprise cover-ups, denials, and blaming-the-victim strategies. They discount remorseful confessions as insincere. They assume that perpetrator confessions are instrumental: to avoid trial and conviction, to reduce a prison sentence, to profit materially, or to heighten power and prestige.[51] In the cynics' view, perpetrators who undergo the transitional-justice process will emerge unscathed and even seem virtuous.

Anticipating a losing power struggle with perpetrators, cynical audiences advocate nonprosecutorial, victim-driven truth commissions that silence perpetrators. El Salvador's truth commission, for example, allowed victims and survivors to name perpetrators, identify their acts of violence, and condemn that violence, while it excluded perpetrators from the political process.

Such a model is inconsistent with contentious coexistence. By endorsing censorship and political exclusion, it encourages antidemocratic processes. Moreover, it tends to isolate perpetrators in an authoritarian enclave, enhancing their potential power and appeal in society. In contrast, subjecting perpetrators' ideas to public scrutiny "narrows the range of permissible lies" and shrinks their political power, preventing them from developing sacred and unimpeachable doctrine.[52] Cynics' rigid position on perpetrators also ignores complex layers of guilt and responsibility for antidemocratic attitudes and behavior within perpetrator and victim communities.[53] Transparency, critical thinking, and practiced debate over the past provides the opportunity to build a stronger democratic culture. In their understandable desire to remove perpetrators from positions of authority, cynics may, paradoxically, enhance their power and weaken democratic practice and outcomes.

Traumatic approaches, like cynical ones, call for silencing perpetrators, but for different reasons: they aim to shield victims and survivors from reliving authoritarian violence, regime bystanders and new generations from witnessing violence by hearing confessions, security forces from institutional breakdown over confessions, and democratic society from political polarization. The traumatic approach is premised on the notion that witnesses, particularly victims and survivors of authoritarian state violence, do not experience confessions at a safe and critical distance, but as part of their present lives. Perpetrators' confessions invade their safe spaces, entering living rooms through the television, kitchens through the radio, daily routines through newspapers and headlines in newsstands, and conversations with friends and colleagues through popular references to the confessional event. Moreover, public confessions catch witnesses unaware, who do not choose and cannot prepare themselves for the encounters. Like smells and words or other mental and physical reminders of a violent past, seeing or hearing torturers in the media traumatizes and retraumatizes individuals, creating states of fear, helplessness, and paralysis.

Perpetrators have a particularly profound impact on victims and survivors. Sadistic and heroic confessions justify violence and exaggerate victims' roles in threatening the nation. Heroic confessions often praise fallen victims and denigrate survivors who "squealed," which erodes survivors' integrity. Denial prevents victims and survivors from confirming the violence they experienced and its traumatic impact on their contemporary lives. Confessions, the traumatic approach contends, assault victims and survivors once again, paralyzing them with fear, forcing them to withdraw into silence and self-blame.

Confessions expose to atrocity, sometimes for the first time, those who did not witness or experience authoritarian state violence; thus they traumatize bystanders and post-authoritarian-era generations, particularly victims of physical or psychological abuse. Bystanders also face the heightened trauma of guilt for disbelieving victims' accounts, for blaming victims, for supporting a regime capable of such atrocity, for failing to act to prevent the violence, and even for benefiting from authoritarian rule.

Democratic society faces trauma when old ideological and political positions reemerge and threaten political stability. Many supporters of the democratic process fear a destabilizing battle of "memory against memory." They imagine that authoritarian forces might remobilize and reverse the transition to democracy. To avoid such an outcome, many support the "pragmatic" solutions of silencing debate over the past or of forming highly proscribed truth commissions, as in Chile, in which neither perpetrators' names nor specific acts appear.[54]

Members of the security force may support the same position if they feel that the military institution is threatened by fragmentation. They may advocate blanket amnesty and silence, as in Brazil, to avoid tensions between softliners and hardliners in the military and between new and old generations of security forces, and to prevent finger-pointing between military branches. Strong and united national defense, this audience contends, protects citizens and the nation from trauma.

Contentious coexistence argues that democracies cannot suppress debate. Efforts to do so will generate conflict between "social forces that demand markers of memory and, on the other [hand], those who seek to erase these markers," and over who is authorized to remember the past and what form of remembering is appropriate and legitimate.[55] Ultimately it may prove more disruptive to democracy to censor political memory than to allow it, no matter how painful the trade-off between psychological harm to individuals and potential benefits for the political system.

Healing audiences consider open dialogue, including participation by perpetrators, essential to the health of individuals and society. The healing process begins with perpetrators' acknowledgment, through confession, that violence occurred. That acknowledgment verifies victims' accounts, allowing them to overcome the taunts of their victimizers that no one will hear or believe their stories. Confessions have the potential to confirm victims' previously unspoken, unheeded, or disbelieved experiences.[56] Psychologists contend that societal silence perpetuates victims' self-blame, confusion, and rage, all of which prevents recovery.[57] To restore their mental health, victims and their families need it to be known that *someone* committed undeserved, unlawful, and immoral violence against them. Even if perpetrators fail to fully disclose details or apologize for their acts, the debates they engender acknowledge and condemn past violence. The South African scholar Hermann Giliomee captures this effect when he states, "A nation . . . is built on great forgettings and great rememberings." Donald Woods adds, "We used to hear so many complaints in the bad old days that the allegations of people like ourselves against the security police were exaggerations, were unpatriotic, . . . and untrue."[58] Confirmation of those "exaggerations," through perpetrators' confessions, restores the credibility of those who witnessed, endured, and condemned past violence.

Confessions further aid the healing process by providing missing details: who did what, to whom, when, where, and how. Sometimes only perpetrators witnessed these acts or survived to tell the story. With this information, families of victims may undertake healing rituals of burial and mourning. Legal death certificates, based on perpetrators' confirmation of facts, also release life-insurance policies or pensions needed by families for their physical survival and well-being, particularly when the victim contributed significantly to the household income.

Therapeutic and religious communities advocate forgiveness as

necessary for individuals building a new life after violent events. Forgiveness releases victims and survivors from harmful, unresolved, and
undifferentiated anger and removes perpetrators' power over them.
While nearly all members of the healing community concur that victims and survivors need to know what they are forgiving for the
process to be effective, they disagree over the significance of perpetrators' remorse to that knowledge and forgiveness.[59]

forgiveness

Perpetrators' confessions, particularly remorseful ones, may contribute to healing societies as well as individual victims. They provide
a route for perpetrators to restore themselves in the community, rebuilding what they destroyed by explaining their past and asking
forgiveness.[60] Confessions also contribute to a clear and official history of violence. When perpetrators admit to what they did, they
render doubt impossible. As South African journalist Donald Woods
states, "Even the supporters of such people in the past have had to
confront the fact. They've heard this coming out of their own mouths,
of these people, now. These unbelievably terrible things for one human being to do to another. And to admit it. And to say 'I hit him on
the head with a steel sjambok,' 'I stabbed him so many times,' 'I
burned the body.' . . . Now at last surely they have to accept [that]
these things happened."[61]

The South African Truth and Reconciliation Commission, with its
institutionalized confessional process in the Amnesty Committee
hearings, its confirmation of victims' testimonies in the Human Rights
Violations Committee, and its array of psychologists, social workers,
and religious figures to encourage healing and forgiveness, embodied
the healing audience's ideal. Advocates of the Rwandan gacaca, or
community courts, also consider perpetrators' acknowledgments of
guilt for violent acts and their atonement through community-service
projects to be crucial components of reconciliation and restoration of
trust in communities torn apart by genocide.

But the healing approach is not without its critics. Forgiveness as a
component of healing and reconciliation, some critics contend, places
undue burden on victims and survivors. Not only must they recover
from their traumatic pasts, but that very recovery hinges on forgiving
those who injured them. Other critics question whether memory-as-
healing may backfire, creating antipathy toward victims and survivors
who resolutely press their demands despite other important concerns
in society. Some observers question whether endless memory heals,

or if health might instead depend on putting the past in the past.[62] Indeed, advocates of retributive justice consider trials, and not restorative justice, healing for individuals and societies because they restore the equality of victims and perpetrators before the law, establish knowledge and acknowledgment of wrongdoing, and set precedents that deter future violators.[63]

Punishment approaches advocate confessions in the context of retributive justice. Such audiences consider trials for crimes committed by authoritarian states to be essential to establishing rule of law, strengthening democracy, and deterring future human-rights violations. Confessions play a crucial role in this process by establishing the facts of the crimes: what happened, when, where, by whom, to whom, and on whose orders. Court trials, moreover, signal the democratic government's break with the authoritarian past and its commitment to legal, procedural, and moral guarantees for citizens—key ingredients for reestablishing the trust between citizens and governments destroyed by authoritarian rule. Blanket amnesties, on the other hand, as Paul van Zyl notes, "undermine the rule of law, provoke anger and cynicism among victims and citizens, and promote impunity."[64]

"Trials," moreover, "are meant to teach a lesson."[65] They demonstrate equality under the law. Illegal activities of all citizens, including elite political forces, will be judged by the laws of the country. When investigation and prosecution indict regime criminals, all citizens recognize that neither silence, nor orders from above, nor political favor provides immunity.[66] Before making or executing illegal orders, potential perpetrators must first judge whether to risk prosecution, whereas past perpetrators, who believed that their crimes would go unpunished, were unconcerned with such considerations.

Most critics of deterrence focus on lack of evidence. Deterrence theories assumed that the Nuremberg Trials established the threat of prosecution for war crimes that would prevent subsequent perpetrators from committing atrocities. They cannot explain why perpetrators of post–World War II genocides and authoritarian state violence ignored that threat. The paucity of other domestic and international trials hardly convinces perpetrators that they will face adjudication for illegal acts; on the contrary, it indicates that most perpetrators literally get away with murder.[67] Until trials become standard procedure, impunity will reign. Moreover, some critics contend that if trials were to effectively prosecute perpetrators of state violence, leaders with criminal records would simply attempt to retain power rather than risk prosecution by stepping down. In sum, existing evidence does not link retributive justice to deterrence.[68]

An additional criticism of the retributive approach is the impact of failed trials. When prosecutors lose cases, perpetrators are fully exonerated. They are not pardoned or amnestied; they are found not guilty. These losses send a strong signal that perpetrators can, if charged, "beat the rap." They also challenge the strength and capacity of the judicial system. The famous acquittals in South Africa of Magnus Malan, the head of the apartheid police force, and Wouter Basson, a chemical-weapons expert working for apartheid intelligence, demonstrate that despite overwhelming (but circumstantial) evidence of guilt, courts do not always convict. Unsuccessful trials may do more harm to building rule of law and deterrence than no trial at all.

A salvational approach emerges among supporters of the authoritarian regime: passive and active, military and civilian, formal members of the dictatorial state, and nonstate actors. Salvation-oriented audiences embrace confessions that defend the regime and glorify its heroic role in saving the nation from subversion. They obliquely accept torture and killing as the only means to end the chaos and violence wrought by the enemy forces. They also point to legal documents that legitimize the regime and its use of force.

Such a view of a regime's duty rejects remorseful confessions and attempts to silence them. Security forces and their supporters employ a variety of tactics to suppress penitent confessions: ad hominem attacks, intimidation, and even violence. Regime supporters raise public questions, for example, about the sincerity and knowledge of remorseful perpetrators, suggesting that they work for the regime's enemies. They produce evidence of financial instability to suggest that such perpetrators have offered up fictitious confessions to the highest bidder. And they drag skeletons out of perpetrators' closets: addiction, mental-health problems, divorce.

At times, these tactics may actually backfire: the existence of financial or personal difficulties may *confirm* the traumatic experiences these perpetrators endured in their secret, violent lives; intimidation and violence against remorseful perpetrators legitimizes their claims by exposing the coercive apparatus that produced their violent acts. Nevertheless, by painting remorseful perpetrators as rogue forces willing to lie for financial rewards, salvational audiences often successfully attribute the violence to immoral individuals, or "bad apples," in the otherwise noble security forces.

Indeed, salvational audiences share, at least publicly, respect for human rights and condemn individual "bad apples" who committed crimes and tarnished the regime. They even appropriate the language of human rights. When they cry "Never again!" however, it is a call for vigilance against the left-wing "subversion" that threatened political stability and required the military to restore order. They accuse the "subversives" of violating human rights and applaud the regime for ending the threat of communism. They sometimes consider transitional-justice mechanisms to be orchestrated efforts by the same leftists who had toppled the nation's security to amass power and undermine their adversaries in the security forces.

Although sometimes dismissed as a lunatic fringe, or as unpopular extremist elements left over from the authoritarian period, salvational audiences are spurred into action by confessions. In addition to denigrating remorseful perpetrators, they endorse heroic ones. The media calls on them to represent regime views. They resonate within some sectors in society precisely because their position does not appear to be a "tissue of lies." They also give voice to a silenced constituency— those who quietly support the past authoritarian regime, despite evidence of wrongdoing and a changing political climate.[69]

Bringing even these extreme views into public dialogue can prove healthy for democracy. Contentious coexistence claims that public debate exposes the weaknesses in the views under discussion. Regime supporters may feel that salvational audiences harm the regime's image more than do victims and survivors. They may continue to support the regime, but distance themselves from the extreme positions taken by salvational audiences. Public debate, therefore, can help erode social polarization by creating a range of different perspectives on the past.

CONTENTIOUS COEXISTENCE AND
THE CONFESSIONAL PERFORMANCE

"Democracy was born in transgressive acts," proclaims Sheldon Wolin, and confessional performances certainly qualify as transgressive.[70] They make profound disagreements over the past audible, visible, physical, and public. They provoke conflict, as audiences clash over interpretations of the past and their meanings for contemporary democratic practice. Deep and irreconcilable schisms emerge in response to perpetrators' confessions, the kind of schisms that had undermined earlier democratic experiments and ushered in repressive authoritarian rule. These schisms divide the armed forces, weakening national security. They retraumatize victims. They reassert authoritarian versions of national values. Multiple, logical, and reasonable motivations therefore exist for stifling perpetrators' transgressive confessions and preventing them from undermining democratic governance and culture.

Because of the conflict they generate, unsettling accounts challenge some aspects of deliberative democracy, the main dialogic approach to democratization. On one hand, unsettling accounts share with deliberative democracy the goal of having "citizens of a liberal state. . . . learn to talk to one another" to "solve their ongoing problem of living together."[71] Yet participants in confessional performances tend to violate some of the prerequisites advocated by scholars of deliberative democracy. They rarely accept, for example, "gag rules" or "conversational constraint." For that reason, some scholars would most likely put contentious issues like past authoritarian state violence "off the conversational agenda of the liberal state."[72]

I argue instead that confessional performances can contribute to democracy through public dialogue and deliberation. I make five central claims about building contentious coexistence in new democracies. First, issues of state violence cannot be kept out of public discussion. Perpetrators confess. And when they do, they generate deep dialogic conflict. Despite efforts by democratic states to legislate and in other ways to prevent such debate, it happens. Explosive emotions overwhelm even those institutional mechanisms designed to steer debate toward constructive and reasoned deliberation. Emotional intensity and irreconcilable differences obliterate such constraints. Issues of state violence remain on the conversational agenda of new democracies because citizens demand it, and the media loves it.

Second, new democracies, and even established ones, would be better served by embracing these issues. By doing so, they would recognize public demand to wrestle with underlying tensions over the past. Confessional performances engage core democratic values: free speech, justice, and protection of human rights. Democracies cannot afford to suppress this debate. Dialogue, as Bruce Ackerman points out, is "the first obligation of citizenship."[73] To repress it is to settle the past through silence and presumed agreement. "We gain nothing of value by falsely asserting that the political community is of one mind on deeply contested matters," Ackerman warns.[74]

Third, dramatic political performances, like confessions, put democracy into practice. They increase democratic participation and debate over important political issues. Audiences pay attention to confessions because of the drama they generate: the rupture of silence; novel, "insider" perspectives; lurid language about violence; engaging acting; emotive speech; exciting media coverage; and loud, visible, intense, and conflictive audience response. These aspects of the confessional performance draw in not only participants among those directly affected by, or involved in, the regime's violence, but include those who were "neutral" bystanders during the authoritarian regime and new generations of citizens. Confessional performances become catalysts for broadening political participation and expanding political debate.

Through participation and debate, citizens exercise democratic rights. Expressing views contrary to those prevailing in society puts free speech into practice. It can also improve the quality of debate. When perpetrators make public confessions, they must carefully consider what content and presentation style is most likely to convince their audience. The ensuing dialogue, moreover, forces confessors to refine their statements, to adopt more effective language, better argumentation, more precision or clarification. Through this process, perpetrators sharpen their own thinking and understanding of the conflict.

Debate is not one-sided. Audiences participate not only in listening but also in speaking. They begin to understand the issues at stake, particularly in highly dramatic political spectacles. Performance makes issues matter to their audiences. Exposed to a range of opinions and responses, listeners begin to formulate their own political views. Confessional performances put democratic contestation and access to information into practice. As Seyla Benhabib succinctly argues, "Deliberation is a procedure for being informed" and for creating an "enlarged mentality" in society.[75]

The process of political speaking and listening teaches a new language and exposes citizens to contending perspectives that are unavailable when debate is silenced. When perpetrators initially speak out, they draw on the terminology and the beliefs they learned through socialization in the security forces; while such indoctrination may not reflect their true nature, it has become their only language and identity. The performance of confession, particularly in its interaction with audiences, teaches perpetrators new words that might more accurately reflect their personal convictions. It also forces them to confront alternative perspectives on the past and to reconsider their own accordingly. Through performance, perpetrators gain confidence in their views, even as those views are altered by the process. When they see and hear the harm they have done to citizens and families, their "insider" ideas of the past may change.

Putting democracy into practice also involves the development of mobilizing skills that allow groups to compete. With regard to participation in confessional performances, Jelin identifies "memory entrepreneurs," or leaders who translate events—such as confessions—into political action projects. "Memory militants" carry out those projects. Both of these political actors play an important role in gaining proximity to the public stage, helping members of the group to overcome opposition and intimidation and to speak out, and establishing the group's moral legitimacy within society. While Jelin cautions that overly successful mobilization may lead to "memory saturation" and "memory backlash," or resistance among even sympathetic audiences to focusing exclusively on past authoritarian state violence, new confessions by perpetrators can energize dormant memory movements.[76]

Fourth, contentious debate shifts power relations in society, which could lead to more democratic outcomes. However, democratic scholars and practitioners fear that contention could cause polarization and a political battle for victory by the more powerful group. Such a victory could then lead to a controlling elite, since the elite possess more political resources in liberal democracies. Jane Mansbridge advocates fostering "enclaves of resistance" that challenge elite power through debate.[77] That model, while attractive in terms of increasing dialogue, could intensify political polarization over contentious issues, since it pits a group of citizens against the state. To prevent the potentially destabilizing effects of polarization, new democracies try to silence competing enclaves (e.g., pro-regime vs. anti-regime) and navigate a middle road toward consensus about the past. The search for neutrality and consensus on highly contentious political issues, however, has proved ineffectual.

Such a search may also be unnecessary. Contentious coexistence claims that dialogue breaks down opposing poles, whereas censorship entrenches them. Mansbridge explores the negative impact of isolated, or censored, enclaves. If the members of a group speak only among themselves, they understand only one language and one set of values. Shielded from public debate and scrutiny and protected from argumentation, loyal members unthinkingly adopt the group's philosophy. Public discussion of these views could expose them as unsupported by available evidence and thus erode their appeal within the group. To avoid such erosion, enclaves may attempt to refine their ideas to better meet rhetorical challenges. In the process, their extremist supporters may split off, accusing the group of capitulating to moderate influences. The dialogic process thus promotes moderation and weakens political polarization.

Iris Young considers dialogic processes themselves as shifting power relations by promoting "a conception of reason over power."[78] Argumentation becomes a political resource accessible to a variety of groups. Opening up the debate to contentious, performative, and emotive forms of speech makes the process more inclusive and shifts power resources toward groups incapable of "dispassionate and disembodied" speech.[79] Young describes this process as understanding "differences of culture, social perspective, or particularist commitment as resources to draw on for reaching understanding in democratic discussion rather than divisions that must be overcome."[80] Contentious debate, in short, not only attracts a wide range of citizens but also increases their access to political resources (talk) so that they can influence political outcomes.

Confessional performances fit Young's analysis by shifting political power away from the authoritarian regime and toward a human-rights and justice agenda. This happens through the public performance that puts into public debate denial, justifications, and excuses for authoritarian state violence. Once such rationalizations become public, victims and survivors and human-rights activists can challenge them. They can mobilize their own constituents in performative acts that produce evidence and argumentation that refute authoritarian versions of the past. They gain access to the media. They expose bystanders and even some pro-regime elements in society to the hypocrisy of such versions. They thereby erode authoritarian notions. Confessions spawn debate around issues of concern to the public, and they also provide the framework to contest interpretations on these matters. Their emotional intensity and significance allow groups to develop effective argumentation for or against them.

Fifth, the bonus of contention is more democratic outcomes. Although deliberative-democracy approaches emphasize process over end results, promotions of such models are certainly motivated by the pay-off of democratic outcomes. And although contention cannot guarantee democratic outcomes, they are nevertheless an expectation inherent in the process: participation in political debate, development of political (dialogic) resources, skillful use of those resources, and the shifting of power balances toward previously silenced or excluded groups.

Public debate can strengthen democratic norms. To participate in public debate, one must develop a new—democratic—language. Thus, perpetrators would not publicly advocate kidnapping, torturing, killing, or disappearing citizens; they would instead use euphemisms acceptable in democracies: detention, interrogation, and defeat in war. They adopt the language of democratic norms, advocating justice (for war crimes committed by the enemy) and human-rights protections (for security-force members and their families). Although a new idiom may merely disguise old attitudes, it can also play a transformative role. In shifting the terms of the debate, perpetrators reflect a shift in norms. By articulating those norms, they diffuse them. In diffusing them, perpetrators not only satisfy the guardians of democratic order but also incorporate the democratic currency of debate into their own segments of society. Everyone, in other words, becomes a democrat, at least linguistically. Authoritarianism, albeit defended as politically expedient in the past, garners little support today.

Democracy as a preferred political system generates little debate, in other words; what is debatable is the quality or extent of democracy and the means by which it is achieved. By using the language of human rights, justice, and free speech, perpetrators' confessions reinforce that language as a measure for assessing democracy. Groups within society may not agree on definitions of human-rights violations, but they agree in condemning them as a whole. How justice is served will evoke deep ideological debates, but consensus around democracy dictates *that* it be served.

Contention over the past does not disappear; it remains unsettling and unsettled. Yet contending groups learn to live together—to coexist

—with their irreconcilable differences in flawed democracies. They learn, through practice, to use the political resources of speech to negotiate the terms of democracy. In the case studies that follow, conflicts generated by perpetrators' confessions exemplify contentious coexistence. In each of these cases, organized groups of human-rights activists, victims, and survivors have found the means to use confessions to advance their particular goals for democracy. They have often overcome great obstacles, including internal conflicts, in the process. They make the case for contentious coexistence as a democratic model.

CHAPTER TWO

REMORSE

What you call the past, for me is my present and my future. To carry in my conscience the death of thirty people is not bearable. . . . I don't think it is possible to speak of the past when the president is surrounded by important people from the military government. . . . The past will only be the past, sad but at least in the past, when those responsible for, participants in, and those who hide the [Argentine detention center] ESMA's genocide speak the truth, leaving positions and honors to those who deserve them because of their clean hands and clear consciences. . . . I belonged to a mafia which is currently entrenched in power. . . . These are the same people who believe that prison walls, threats to my family, death threats to me can silence the inevitable: the definitive knowledge of the truth. . . . [T]hey gave me immoral orders, and I obeyed those immoral orders. I neither lie nor escape my responsibility. . . . The present demands the truth. Until it arrives, we cannot speak of the past, unless we are hypocrites or suffer from senility and amnesia.—Adolfo Scilingo, 17 December 1995

IN 1995 THE RETIRED NAVY CAPTAIN Adolfo Scilingo broke the Argentine military regime's silence and told his story about past violence. He confirmed statements made by victims and survivors about death flights. In 1977, while stationed at the Navy Mechanics School (ESMA), he had received orders to carry out those flights. Twice he had taken approximately fifteen drugged detainees into an airplane, stripped them, and dropped them to their deaths in the ocean. Over the ensuing years, thirty dead men, women, and children preyed on his conscience.

Scilingo's confession shocked the nation. He did not admit to anything new: Argentina's official truth-commission report, *Nunca más*

The infamous Argentine Navy Mechanics School. Captain Adolfo Scilingo confessed to making two "death flights" from there in 1977, dropping an estimated thirty men, women, and children into the ocean. Photo by author.

(Never again), academic studies, numerous human-rights agencies' records, and several survivors' testimonies and testimonial novels had already reported the number and names of the tortured, murdered, and disappeared; the techniques used by the military regime; the secret detention centers where torture and murder occurred; and even the death flights.[1] What surprised the country was that Scilingo, as a member of the regime's repressive apparatus, defied its code of silence and denial, and publicly admitted to committing atrocities ordered by his commanding officers.[2] As Osvaldo Barros, a survivor of the ESMA torture camp and member of the Association of the Ex-Detained Disappeared (AEDD; Asociación de Ex-Detenidos Desaparecidos), stated, "What Scilingo admitted, we already knew . . . but in spite of knowing it, it moved us to hear it from the mouths of those who had carried out that action. The declarations are uniquely important because they come from someone directly involved and we hope that they will awaken the consciousness within our society."[3]

Moreover, Scilingo was not a rebel within the armed forces; he fervently supported the military regime's "war against subversion." He was an avowed anticommunist, proud about fighting a patriotic war and defending his country: "We won a war. I did what I did because I was absolutely and totally in agreement."[4] He even accepted, in the abstract, the need to use "unconventional" methods to eliminate what he and his military colleagues perceived as a threat to the country from the Left. When he applied those methods, however, Scilingo faced an internal dilemma. He could not abide the ESMA's detention techniques, for example. Likening them to Nazi concentration camps, he rhetorically asked, "Have you ever seen photos from Auschwitz?"[5] His horror, compared to the indifference he perceived among his colleagues' drove him to question his suitability for service.

Scilingo reacted similarly to the death flights. In the abstract he accepted them. But when Scilingo himself nearly fell out of the hole in the plane to his own death, he understood for the first time that he was killing people. Tormented by his murderous acts, Scilingo claims that "maybe it would be better if I had fallen out."[6]

Scilingo tried to remain quiet. He anesthetized his internal conflict with drugs and alcohol, which led to addiction. He sought solace from private confessions to military priests, but he found no comfort in their reassurances that he had performed a Christian act, and not a sin, by separating the wheat from the chaff and providing prisoners with a "Christian way of dying." When he recounted his problems to a commanding officer, he received psychiatric treatment, but at the cost of promotion within the navy. With his military career at an impasse, and ravaged by addiction, insomnia, ulcers, and haunting images, Scilingo retired.

Leaving the service, however, did not end Scilingo's nightmares. Unable to live with himself and his acts, he withdrew from his family, nearly abandoning his wife and children. He engaged in questionable financial dealings that impoverished his family. Eventually, Scilingo became a born-again Christian, which he believes helped him pull his life together again.

The Trial of the Generals, broadcast on Argentine television in 1985, provoked Scilingo to confront his military past. The generals, to Scilingo's amazement, refused to accept any responsibility for torture, deaths, and disappearances. They denied the systematic use of repression and claimed that reports of violence were based on lies by ideological enemies and "errors and excesses" committed by lower ranking officers. The generals' denial stripped Scilingo of his only ethical justification for his acts: following orders in a patriotic war. By refuting that they had issued those orders, the generals recast Scilingo and his colleagues as cold-blooded murderers, rather than loyal soldiers. In Scilingo's words, "I entered the Naval School as a sailor and I left as an assassin."[7]

Instead of quietly disagreeing with the generals' interpretation of the Dirty War, Scilingo began a one-man campaign to reveal the truth. He wrote numerous letters, delivering some by hand, and begged military and government officials to publicly admit to the use of unconventional methods in the war against subversion. No one answered his letters or fulfilled his demands.

The immediate catalyst for Scilingo's public confession was the senate's denial of promotion to his former navy colleagues due to their violations of human rights during the military regime. To Scilingo, Captains António Pernías and Juan Carlos Rolón were loyal officers, like himself. They had received rewards and promotions for their bravery and service. That "service" had involved torture, to which they confessed in the senate hearings. None of their commanding officers, however, defended them in the hearings or admitted to the "unconventional methods" required. In Scilingo's view the high command hid behind the generals' "excesses and errors" defense, thereby sabotaging the careers of loyal and effective officers. The cowardly silence that betrayed such officers prompted Scilingo to speak out: "The navy is guilty. What is it trying to hide? Those who criticize me say that what happened during the Dirty War was a patriotic defense to save the country from falling into communist hands. Fine, if they are so proud of this why do they hide the issue of the disappeared? What is the problem? This is inconsistent: I feel proud of my participation in the war against subversion, but at the same time I continue hiding the truth. So, it's clear: we are ashamed . . . they are ashamed to say what we did."[8]

After exhausting military and government channels to express his grievances, Scilingo selected an unlikely confessor for a public act: Horacio Verbitsky. A well-known left-wing journalist and activist committed to human rights, Verbitsky had narrowly escaped detention and possible disappearance on an ESMA death flight. He had built his professional career in the opposition press, *Página/12*, and in books by exposing military atrocities. Scilingo no doubt trusted that Verbitsky would believe and publish his story, confidence he did not have in the right-wing media.

Scilingo initially approached Verbitsky in the Buenos Aires metro, offering him a story about his experiences at the ESMA. Verbitsky mistook Scilingo for another victim of ESMA violence. Nothing about Scilingo tipped Verbitsky off to his role as a perpetrator of that violence; he looked like a kindly neighbor or distant uncle, not a mass murderer. Rather than the erect posture and prideful countenance or the arrogance and self-righteousness Verbitsky might have associated with a military regime officer, Scilingo's stooped and humiliated carriage instead expressed the shame and pain of a torture victim. He had a defeated, rather than proud, attitude about his past. He avoided military trappings. He appeared to be completely normal: neither too educated nor uneducated; neither rich nor poor; neither a religious fanatic nor an atheist; well-groomed and well-dressed, but not ostentatiously so. He neither smiled too much, nor withdrew in anger, exuded neither warmth nor coldness. Little gestures checked his emotion: biting his lower lip, grooming his moustache, or pressing his hands into his face to cover his eyes and mouth. He did not sob or otherwise display horror on his face or body, but subtle gestures expressed his regret and pain. He neither dramatized nor underplayed his actions, only occasionally allowing a discreet tear to roll down his face. He represented, in his appearance, someone who lived by rules of convention, civility, and decency.

Once Scilingo had identified his role in the ESMA, Verbitsky doubted he would see him again. Surprisingly, Scilingo kept their first appointment. And despite Verbitsky's harsh interrogation, Scilingo returned to record his story.

Verbitsky played a key role in shaping the confession, rejecting, for example, Scilingo's use of euphemisms, forcing him to name the atrocities he and others committed. Scilingo grew defensive at times, retreating behind the language he had learned at the ESMA, as in this response to Verbitsky's charges: "No navy officer participated in kidnapping, torture, and clandestine eliminations. The entire navy participated in detentions, interrogations, and the elimination of the subversives, which could have been done by various methods."[9] Scilingo held on to moral justifications for his acts. "Shooting someone is immoral too," he stated on one occasion. "Or is it better? Who suffers more, the one who knows he is going to be shot or the one who dies by our method?"[10] Through antagonism, Verbitsky forced Scilingo to verbalize what he, as an individual, had done. Scilingo argued with him. He changed the subject. He returned to issues he could explain, while avoiding others. When he felt trapped, as if held against his will, he even pleaded, "I don't want to talk about it. Let me go."[11]

By confessing, Scilingo was able to make a clean break with his past and publicly admit to atrocity. Initially, he rejected the notion of remorse: "I am not a repentant, the facts are too out of the ordinary; it's too easy to say 'I'm sorry' and everything is okay."[12] But he began to take responsibility and to feel better about himself in the process: "Though it may be a little egotistical to say so, my public confession has brought me a certain relief. Before, I had a secret I couldn't talk about to anyone. Now I can talk to everyone. But the problem still exists."[13] He added, "It was good for me to speak; I feel better. But I don't feel good. I'm going to feel bad for as long as I live. This is something you don't get over."[14] The protracted pain and guilt he summarized in this way: "I am not a scoundrel. Scoundrels sleep perfectly well, and I, since the first flight I took, cannot sleep without taking Lexotanil or drinking alcohol. . . . I want to tell all of you who are listening: I feel like a murderer. As a human being I cannot get over having pushed from a plane in flight other sleeping human beings."[15] Scilingo recognized, in hindsight, how his public confession had changed his perspective. He remarked, "I always referred to the methods ordered as detention, interrogation, and elimination of the enemy. It was difficult for me to use other words . . . kidnap, torture, and assassination."[16] The process of confession and interaction with the public transformed him.

Before each interview I took a Lexotanil, and I would prepare a hard line. I was afraid that I was going to cry, and I believed that this was not what a soldier should do. For this reason, in Grondona's [television] program, I said that we had won the war and this confused a lot of people. Someone said to me that it seemed contradictory to my position, that they didn't understand if I was repentant about what I had done or not. . . . At that moment I was convinced that what we had done was correct. There are people who would prefer a white lie [novela rosa], that I said what they obliged me to say, that I did things against my will or my opinion . . . but this is not the way it was. We were all committed. Now nearly twenty years have gone by. Of course I am remorseful. More than this, I am destroyed by what I did. But I have begun to break out from under the military's shell. If I have tears in my eyes, it doesn't bother me. Let them come. I am not only feeling like a human being. I am also beginning to think like a regular person. And this has changed my family life. There are things I said to you [Verbitsky] and to Mike Wallace that I had never said to anyone, not even my wife. I almost never spoke with my children, and now we speak every day. So in this moment, it amazes me that we could have done what we did. . . . We were the armed forces and we should have acted differently. We could have acted differently.[17]

Scilingo consistently pursued his goals of restoring dignity to the armed forces. His strategy shifted, however, from respecting the regime to criticizing it and its impact on the honor of the armed forces. He stopped considering violence as a necessary evil and searched for atonement instead. As he put it,

We could offer up a true, permanent mea culpa and pay our debt. And the most important effect of that would be on those who remained in the institution, people who are new or who didn't get their hands dirty. It would help them to reflect, as a reminder of what they must not do. The president should order the chief of staff of the navy to inform the country of everything that happened during those years, to give out the list of the disappeared. It did me good to speak, it would also do the society good, and it would do the navy good. Especially the new generations of the military, so they don't continue to bear the stigma of the ESMA. Otherwise we can't be sure these things won't happen again some time.[18]

Scilingo's confessional performance played out on a number of stages and met with varied responses. Pointing to the importance of the confession, Verbitsky claimed, "There are no longer two histories [about our past], there is only one. We have the truth and this is really important in a country where there is no justice."[19] Scilingo's story became the symbol of military regime atrocities. The decision to build a park for memories on the banks of the Rio de la Plata, for example, reflected the central role of that river in the regime's death flights. In a concert commemorating the foundation of the Grandmothers of the Plaza de Mayo, balloons were released into the air to contrast with bodies thrown from planes during the dark days of the authoritarian regime. When one of the founders of the grandmothers' movement died, her friends gathered at the bank of the river to scatter her ashes and flowers, symbolically uniting her with her disappeared children.

Media attention to Scilingo's confession no doubt heightened its potency in the remembering of military atrocities. The media transformed the unknown Scilingo into an instant celebrity. Verbitsky played parts of the recorded interviews on television and radio programs, and published transcripts in *Página/12* and in the book *El vuelo* (*The Flight*). Scilingo also made appearances on television and radio, and published his own book, *Por siempre nunca más* (Forever, never again). The story hit all of the local media outlets and some of the most important international media sources: *60 Minutes*, *Time*, *Newsweek*, the *New York Times*, and the *Los Angeles Times* in the United States; the *Economist* in Great Britain; and *Veja* in Brazil. Although never confirmed, rumors circulated that he had sold his story to Hollywood.

His high-profile confession generated multiple responses. It set off a chain reaction of confessions, as perpetrators sought financial windfalls, personal atonement, or their fifteen minutes of fame through their Dirty War stories. These confessions corroborated Scilingo's allegations about the systematic use of repression, not just in the navy but in all branches of the armed forces. They confirmed death flights, trafficking in babies and goods stolen from detainees' homes, secret detentions, interrogations under torture, firing squads, disappearances, and rotations of officers into the repressive apparatus to ensure collective guilt and silence.[20]

The media presented Scilingo in a positive light, as an uncomplicated and remorseful figure: "Scilingo took off the mask so that we could see the face of a man transfigured by suffering and who cleared his conscience. The system wants him to continue wearing the mask, like so many other assassins who walk freely and perhaps sleep soundly."[21] But few other audiences to his confession shared that view. Scilingo, for example, received little support from his colleagues. Few publicly shared his remorse, countering instead with heroic confessions and denouncing Scilingo as a "crybaby" and "traitor." They also tried to silence him. One offered him money to remain quiet. An immediate superior expressed concern for Scilingo's family while issuing a thinly veiled threat that he would lose health benefits if he continued to speak out. A friend's wife railed against him for ignoring the impact of his confession on others, to which Scilingo responded, "That's fine, but what do I do with my thirty dead ones?"[22]

The high command also tried to silence Scilingo. Emilio Massera, a former navy chief admiral, simply denied the death flights. His successor at the time of Scilingo's confession, Admiral Enrique Molina Pico, dismissed Scilingo from the navy and avoided any discussion of his confession. When Scilingo confronted Molina Pico's silence in a public letter, demanding that he confirm or deny the death flights, he received no reply.[23]

The army's high-command chief, Lieutenant General Martín Balza, however, did respond to Scilingo's confession and issued an institutional apology. Balza challenged the legitimacy of the military coup and the regime it implanted, and he condemned ordering or implementing "illegitimate methods."[24] As he stated, "No one is obliged to obey an immoral order or to depart from laws and military rules. Those who do incur the sanction that the seriousness of their actions warrant. Without euphemism, I state clearly: those who violate the constitution are criminals, those who obey immoral orders are criminals, those who believe that the ends justify unjust and immoral means are criminals."[25] Some observers interpreted Balza's apology as an effort to halt the confessional barrage by assuming institutional responsibility. In a move that reinforced that view, Balza encouraged soldiers to seek out their commanding officers or priests (and not the media) for confessions. But he failed. Public confessions continued.[26]

The Catholic Church, maligned in Scilingo's confession, responded ambiguously. Monsignor Emilio Bianchi de Carcano, for example, categorically rejected Scilingo's claim that the church knew about or justified the death flights.[27] Cardinal Antonio Quarracino, head of the Permanent Commission of the Bishops Conference, denied personal knowledge of the so-called Dirty War's methods: "Neither the Argentine Bishopric nor its authorities were ever consulted about the legitimacy or viability of the processes to eliminate detained individuals, nor did we provide any support."[28] In the wake of Scilingo's confession, only a few officials admitted guilt and apologized for the church's role.[29] Most notably the bishop of Viedma, Monsignor Miguel Esteban Hesayne, confirmed that the church knew about the regime's use of torture since the minister of the interior had attempted to justify it in a forty-minute lecture before church leaders. Hesayne called on priests to deny communion to members of the high command until they publicly repented, claiming that "the sin of torture and sacrilege was public, which means that repentance should also be public."[30]

The Carlos Menem government, like the military and the church, did not attempt to confirm or reject Scilingo's claims, but instead impugned him. Menem referred to Scilingo as a "scoundrel" and "mythomaniac." To call into question Scilingo's integrity, Menem focused on Scilingo's shady business dealings. And on trumped-up fraud charges, Menem stripped Scilingo of his retired military status and jailed him for nearly two years.[31] Lest anyone miss his message, Menem warned soldiers against media contacts, encouraging them to confess to their priests instead.[32] Minister of Foreign Affairs Guido DiTella focused on the internal inconsistencies in Scilingo's confession that rendered it unreliable.[33] The subsecretary for human rights in the Interior Ministry, Alicia Pierini, accused Scilingo of profiting from his violence: "For those of us who work seriously in human rights, these people who first murder and then want to negotiate with the blood they spilled cause us great indignation."[34]

Menem further accused Scilingo of political motives. Because Scilingo's confession corresponded with national elections, Menem blamed Scilingo for attempting to derail his chances at reelection.[35] Confessions by Scilingo and others challenged Menem's governance, since he had pardoned those junta leaders who had ordered death flights and

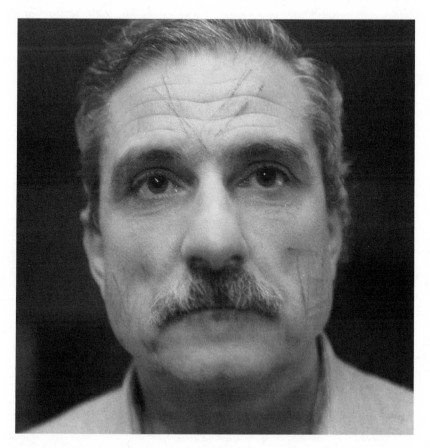

In 1997 a group of unidentified assailants pulled Adolfo Scilingo into a car, drove him to a remote location, carved the initials of three journalists into his face, and warned him that if he continued to speak out against the authoritarian regime, he and the three journalists would die. Reproduced by permission of AP Photos.

other atrocities. Scilingo rebutted that he would probably vote for Menem, not because of his human-rights record, but because he had stabilized the economy.

Scilingo faced physical threats and intimidation that he attributed to government and military forces intent on silencing him. Shortly after his release from prison in September 1997, a group of unidentified individuals pulled Scilingo into a car, drove him to a remote location, carved the initials of three journalists into his face, and warned him that if he continued to speak out he and the three journalists would die.[36] This was not the first threat Scilingo received. In July 1995 one of his children found under her apartment door a letter with the return address "Comando de Liberación" [Liberation Force]; the letter read: "Stop the criminal accusations. Stop the declarations in newspapers, films, and books. Think about your family. Menem cut you off; we'll bury you."[37] Scilingo received another threat, signed "G.T. 3.2.2," referring to the infamous ESMA Grupo de Tarea [Operations Unit] involved in kidnapping, torture, and assassination: "Did you forget what we said about your family? We know about the book. Your days are numbered. Stop soon or we'll take you on a flight. We have people watching your steps. You know how we work."[38] While in prison, Scilingo received a package that included a fake mail bomb and a box with a swastika drawn on it. The handwritten return address indicated the ESMA.

The human-rights community disagreed over how to respond to Scilingo. The Association of the Mothers of the Plaza de Mayo called for Scilingo's conviction and imprisonment. The head of the Grandmothers of the Plaza de Mayo, Estela Carlotto, questioned Scilingo's sincerity and the utility of his confession for the human-rights community: "One does not sit at the same table with an ex-repressor who does not repent and only confesses his crimes, like Scilingo, to advance in the ranks while still saying that the illegal repression was really a war."[39] In contrast, the director of the Center for Legal and Social Studies (CELS) at the time, Emilio Mignone, called on the human-rights community to take advantage of Scilingo's confession.

> I would not demand it [justice for Scilingo]. In the first place, because I do not believe that his confession should be used against him because he is helping us out. His declaration is useful. It shows that those who are responsible are those in the top command. It makes a painful contribution. I believe in remorse in human beings, and I believe that this helps because even if his testimony cannot bring justice, it can bring a moral sanction. In the second place, I wouldn't demand justice because it would be useless. It would end in his exoneration since Scilingo is protected by the Due Obedience Law. But, in addition, there is another factor: we need to encourage others to tell their stories, that ten, twenty officials like Scilingo overwhelm the navy with their declarations and that the institution has to reconsider its position.[40]

Another CELS activist, Martín Abregú, summarized: "Do we love Scilingo? Of course not! But we don't want him or other Scilingos to stop talking."[41]

These different opinions within the human-rights community did not prevent its members from using the confession to advance political goals. Although they hoped Scilingo would help identify the disappeared, his personal recollection failed. Perhaps the lapse in time from the death flights to his confession blocked his memory, or perhaps Scilingo could not match the smiling, healthy individuals in the photographs with the thirty emaciated and tortured bodies he had dropped from the plane.

Scilingo also failed to help the community find the lists of the disappeared to which he and others had referred. At the Trial of the Generals, the ESMA prisoners Carlos Muñoz and Víctor Melchor Basterra had testified that they had seen the lists. Scilingo and other confessed perpetrators further confirmed their existence. One conscript soldier, Luis Muñoz, testified that he had carried lists of kidnapped people every day to military headquarters.[42] Unconfirmed rumors circulated about lists in private archives and Swiss bank vaults. Balza called on soldiers to disclose information about the lists to no avail. In short, Scilingo could not help the human-rights community achieve its most basic commitment to victims and survivors: identifying the dead.

The human-rights community also used Scilingo's confession to pursue restorative justice. In particular, it demanded official and formal acknowledgment, condemnation, and apology for the systematic use of violence under the military regime, to guarantee that it would not be repeated. Balza's apology proved only mildly satisfactory to human-rights groups. The community also demanded the dismissal or retirement of any individuals involved in approving, ordering, or executing violence, but without investigation into crimes, these goals proved unachievable. The human-rights community further demanded an official apology from the Catholic Church for its behavior during the regime. The church finally issued such an apology in September 2000, but it did not disclose the documents that the human-rights community believed would reveal the degree of complicity. A CELS activist emphasized the importance of these restorative projects: "It is only through these actions, since all legal avenues have been cut off, that the country can achieve reconciliation and peace in Argentina."[43]

Despite legal constraints, the human-rights community used Scilingo's confession to end impunity in Argentina. They called on Scilingo to name perpetrators. At first he resisted. He claimed that he could only speak for himself and expressed his hope that others would come forward and assume responsibility. When top leaders not only failed to come forward but also maligned and threatened him, Scilingo began to name names. He did so in a variety of legal venues and contributed to the investigation and prosecution of other perpetrators. He testified in hearings, for example, that indicted General Jorge Videla and Admiral Massera and others involved in kidnapping babies born in captivity, one of the few crimes not covered by the Due Obedience Law. He also participated in the international investigation into the murder of the Swedish-Argentine teenager Dagmar Hagelin and the disappearance of two French nuns.

Scilingo's most noteworthy international testimony involved his 1998 trip to Madrid to testify in Judge Baltasar Garzón's investigation into the disappearance of Spanish nationals in Argentina.[44] Despite rumors to the contrary, Garzón did not offer Scilingo immunity, and within only a few hours of arriving in Madrid and meeting with the judge, Scilingo was imprisoned.

Initially Scilingo tolerated his situation in Madrid, remarking: "I am fine because I knew what was coming when I left Buenos Aires. I hope that all this will serve some good."[45] Garzón used Scilingo effectively to identify and arrest ESMA officers involved in the murder of Spanish citizens and other criminal activity.[46] Scilingo called on these former colleagues to assume their responsibility. In an open letter to Vice Admiral Luis María Mendía, for example, he wrote, "Be a man for once in your life. Show your face in the Spanish courts." He teased, "Ask your colleague, the cowardly Emilio Eduardo Massera, to join you," but concluded that he would await them in vain since neither possessed sufficient "manliness" or "honor" to appear.[47] Referring to the attacks he faced in Argentina, Scilingo said that he "felt safer in a Spanish jail than in Buenos Aires."[48]

As time wore on, however, Scilingo lost his patience with the Spanish process. Without a work permit or job, he began to complain: "I am economically ruined. . . . Garzón cannot ask me to die of hunger."[49] His earlier sense of security, moreover, eroded after several verbal and physical attacks.[50] And his thwarted hope that he might turn state witness for Garzón led him to accuse the judge of having "tricked and betrayed" him.[51] Scilingo lodged numerous legal complaints to win financial support from the Argentine government and armed forces, receive employment or support in Spain, and gain release from his Spanish detention.[52]

Ignored, forgotten, abandoned, and confined, Scilingo reappeared in the public eye in 2005, this time not as a confessed perpetrator, but as a convicted one. Tried, found guilty, and sentenced in Spain, Scilingo faces a 640-year sentence. Judge Garzón's trial succeeded even after Scilingo had retracted his earlier confession and denied being at the ESMA or on a death flight. Indeed, Scilingo refused to remember any details of his past life, responding "I don't know" and "I don't remember" to the specific questions Garzón put to him.[53] Scilingo claimed that he made up his earlier confession to hurt Massera, but Verbitsky defended the truth in Scilingo's earlier confession and brought tapes to Spain to confirm them.

Too many people and groups have grown to depend on Scilingo's earlier remorseful confession to accept his denial and amnesia. To acknowledge that he might have been lying before, moreover, suggests that the Menem government might have accurately identified him as a "scoundrel," which would undermine all of the ways that his confession advanced public acknowledgment of key events in Argentina's political history.

REMORSE IN COMPARATIVE PERSPECTIVE

Scilingo's dramatic revelations catalyzed debate around authoritarian state violence. For victims and survivors he confirmed from within the authoritarian regime's security apparatus the rumors about the death flights. He made it harder for Argentines to ignore or deny the truth about the atrocities committed by the regime and its security forces. His confession, moreover, acknowledged wrongdoing. And Scilingo made clear that the death flights were not accidental, but part of a systematic effort to wipe out the regime's opposition. Knowledge and acknowledgment, apology, and a modicum of justice emerged out of the open debate over the past. But the story proved more complex than that. Comparative analysis of the theatrical elements in the performance—actor and acting, staging and timing, text, and audience—reveals the challenges that remorseful confessions pose for settling accounts with the past.

"The Complex Vicissitudes of Self." Why should anyone have believed Scilingo's story or his apology? There were, of course, those who wanted to believe him because he confirmed rumors they had heard, explanations they could understand, about the disappearances. Similarly, there were those who discounted his words because they did not want to believe them. The perspective of an audience member depends significantly on his or her background, but it also depends on how perpetrators present themselves.

Mark Behr, a South African writer who identified himself as an apartheid regime collaborator (posing as an anti-apartheid student-movement leader), suggests that once perpetrators confess, their identity becomes inextricably entwined with the acts they committed. Confession obliterates all other identities and aspects of their lives. As Behr states, "I was and am a friend, a son, a curmudgeon, a lover, a comrade, a liar, a satirist, a mentor, a disciple, a loudmouth, a reader, a walker, a sulker, a loner and all the many things that make up an identity. Yet I knew, as I know today, that to say that one has been paid for working secretly against the struggle for justice in South Africa would reduce one at once to one thing: an agent of the South African regime. I have always suspected that the only voice people will hear from that moment on—in spite of the complex vicissitudes of self, is the voice of betrayal: a voice that cannot be trusted, that is incapable of truth."[54]

Paradoxically, the act of confession makes perpetrators seem less, not more, trustworthy: that they could commit atrocity casts doubt on the earnestness of their subsequent remorse. Perpetrators only rarely craft the kind of remorseful confessions that convince audiences of their sincerity.

An example of someone who did so was black apartheid policeman Thapelo Mbelo, who confessed to the Truth and Reconciliation Commission (TRC) for his participation in the killing and cover-up of seven anti-apartheid activists in Guguleto Township. His confessional performance continued outside the TRC process, when he met with the mothers of his victims. In front of television cameras, Mbelo apologized to a deeply hostile community that was distrustful of this young black man who had chosen to join the white police and kill his people. Mbelo's confessional performance altered the community's view. He expressed in his words, his face, and his body the grief he felt for his acts. With his back to the camera, sometimes blocking it, he made the conversation an intimate and personal one with the community he had harmed. He cried and he reached out to each individual, asking for their forgiveness. Even skeptical individuals accepted Mbelo's hand and embrace, never forgiving the act, but mostly forgiving him.[55]

Paul van Vuuren, a white apartheid policeman, also offered a televised confession to his victims' family. He had participated in the murder of a black policeman, Richard Motasi, who he believed would expose the police's death-squad activities, and Motasi's wife, Irene, because she had witnessed the murder. After his TRC amnesty hearing, van Vuuren sought out the young son, Tshidiso, who had survived the deadly assault on his parents. In the televised encounter, van Vuuren appeared as the quintessential Boer policeman, hulking, aggressive, and arrogant. He offered the young, handsome, and poised teenage Motasi a meaty palm and the liberation handshake, then immediately got down to business:

VAN VUUREN: All the people always say we must say sorry, we must say sorry. Are you sorry? And to say, just to say I'm sorry is an empty word, do you know what I mean? Can you really be sorry, you know? It's the first time in my life, no, it's the second, no, it's the third time in my life that I meet you, but . . . um . . . sorry. I'm not the type of person that come and say I'm sorry. I don't even know you, you know what I mean? If I look back at the whole [of] what happened and apartheid and now, then I'm sorry about what happened to you, to your parents and to you. Because it was a waste of human life. I'm sorry for that. Um . . . I know that you . . . that you must hate me. I know if somebody killed my parents . . . I would feel . . . maybe I would have been much more hateful than you. And, um, I can't really say how would I feel. I can just imagine how would I feel.

MOTASI: I don't have parents. My granny can die any day, 'cause she's old now. So, if she dies, who's going to take care of me?

VAN VUUREN: [pause] Yes, that's a difficult question. Um, you can come and live with me. I'll look after you. [laughs a bit]

MOTASI: As you told me, it's very hard to say. It's very hard to say you are sorry, but for me it's like you did something very bad, you see, and like I can't forgive you, I can't, because it's very hard for me.[56]

Van Vuuren's remorse backfired. He appeared to be bullying the young orphan into forgiving him, without offering him anything more than an empty apology. Motasi extracted something more from van Vuuren, a televised promise to care for him. But that promise exposed the insincerity behind van Vuuren's visit to Motasi. Van Vuuren's face appeared to reflect a sense that he had been morally ambushed by the teenager. Rumor later supported that view: van Vuuren allegedly left the studio in a rage, drove to his father's game farm, and killed all the impala he could find. Van Vuuren may have felt remorse for his acts, but his performance looked like nothing more than a public-relations stunt.

Mbelo's and van Vuuren's efforts to convince audiences of their remorse demonstrate the difficulties perpetrators face in doing so. How could these men, each of whom had joined the apartheid police force and remained on it even after they learned of its brutality, persuade an audience that they now felt remorse? Neither apartheid supporters nor opponents would easily believe that a person could switch so completely from being a dedicated policeman or violent perpetrator to feeling true remorse. The skepticism remained in the case of van Vuuren, who epitomized the loyal apartheid policeman: white, privileged, and stalwart. While he might feel sorry for the boy he had orphaned, few believed that he had regretted apartheid violence. If he had, he would have left the force and found a less harmful career. Mbelo had lacked those options. As van Vuuren's killing of Motasi had showed, joining the police force did not protect blacks from violence. Had Mbelo refused to follow orders or had he attempted to leave the force, he might have become another victim of apartheid. Because he could have faced death for refusing to commit atrocity, Mbelo's remorse after the fact seemed more believable.

A perpetrator's physical appearance can contribute to the public's interpretations of his identity and sincerity. Very large perpetrators look the part of monsters, as van Vuuren found out, particularly when they confront diminutive victims or survivors. Body language is also important. Scilingo, not a big man to begin with, bowed his head often, as if ashamed of his acts. The tall, thin, and charismatic Mbelo, who did not fill the camera with his frame, crumpled when he embraced his victims' families, giving power to those he had harmed. Clothes and grooming, cleanliness and care, can reinforce, or undermine, perpetrators' motives. For remorseful confessions, perpetrators must appear humble and unassuming, avoiding ostentation on the one hand or an unkempt appearance on the other. Too much style may indicate a cynical performance; too little care may suggest character flaws.

Who one is, however, is often ambiguous, with room for interpretation. Mbelo had to win over those who could not trust a man who had violently betrayed his people and race for his own advancement. Scilingo, explaining why someone with all of the privileges of the middle class could be persuaded to commit atrocity, described his isolation in the military world: having been raised in a military family and surrounded by regime-supporting friends, colleagues, and family; having undergone indoctrination during training; his dedication to the country; his obedience to and faith in commanding officers; his loyalty. He had trusted the military and its values more than he had trusted his own—until it was too late and he had already committed murder.

Perpetrators undergo change as a result of their experiences. Scilingo's religious transformation gave him the tools to admit remorse.[57] Age and maturity may help, as in the case of Virgilio Paz Romero, one of the Cubans involved in the 1976 murder of the Chilean diplomat Orlando Letelier in Washington, D.C. Romero attributed his acts to immaturity: "At the time, I was 23–24 years old. I was a young man full of ideas. I've contemplated that today. . . . In retrospect, it was a grave human error."[58]

Collaborators face more challenges than perpetrators in making a clean break with their past due to their pattern of betrayal. The Chilean collaborators Luz Arce and Marcia Merino, for example, betrayed all of their erstwhile supporters. Both had held powerful positions within the pre-coup Left in Chile: Arce, a member of the Socialist Party, had served on former president Salvador Allende's personal security force and was with him in La Moneda Presidential Palace on the day of the coup; Merino held one of the top positions in the armed guerrilla Revolutionary Left Movement (MIR). Both were picked up by the Chilean secret police, DINA, shortly after the 11 September 1973 coup and collaborated only after they faced torture and the threat of death. They became informers, betraying their comrades, and participated in the imprisonment, torture, and death of those comrades. The security forces rewarded their acts by making them paid DINA agents. At the end of the dictatorship, they confessed to their roles and expressed remorse for the violence they had helped perpetuate. A few empathized with Arce's and Merino's Faustian bargain. Others, on the Left and Right, felt that Arce and Merino confessed primarily in order to reestablish themselves in the new democratic Chile and to sell their testimonies, which only reinforced the pattern of betrayal for personal gain, this time at the expense of their DINA colleagues.[59]

Some collaborators overcome through performance the skepticism that greets their remorse. Kimani Peter Mogoai, for example, admitted to the TRC that he had participated in the apartheid police murder of three Port Elizabeth Black Consciousness Organization leaders, the so-called PEBCO 3. Mogoai worked for the police as an *askari*, that is, as an African National Congress (ANC) activist who the apartheid police had captured, tortured, and threatened to kill unless he betrayed his comrades and worked for the apartheid security apparatus. Askaris, like collaborators elsewhere, were effective weapons used by the authoritarian regime against liberation forces. The security apparatus exploited their background, race, language skills, contacts, and knowledge to infiltrate the opposition movement and eliminate its leaders. Like Arce and Merino, during reconciliation askaris received no support from either their former comrades or their authoritarian masters. Mogoai overcame distrust, however, by expressing visible, audible, palpable, and apparently sincere remorse: "I have taken this opportunity to speak the truth and to express my torturing regrets about the wasted years and my shame about a mean and petty past. . . . I regard myself today as a disgrace to my mother, my family, and my relatives, my friends and the families of the PEBCO 3 and the nation as such. It is with my deepest remorse that I ask for forgiveness. I say it now here today as I could not have done so in the earlier days for obvious reasons. I thank you."[60] During this confessional performance, Mogoai cried, his body seem wracked with sorrow, and he appeared to have suffered physically and psychologically for his criminal acts.

How he acted mattered. Mbelo, too, cried and physically reached out for support from a room full of wounded and angry mothers whose children he had murdered. Scilingo tried to hold back emotions, biting his lip, bowing his head, covering his eyes and mouth in grief, but sometimes allowing a single tear to course his sorrowful face. His slumped posture seemed to bear the weight of insomnia, anxiety, addiction, attacks and threats against him, and the imprisonment he faced for his violent acts and his confession. These physical expressions of pain inscribe on perpetrators the suffering for their past. Arce and Merino, whose confessions were written, could not as successfully communicate their anguish and were thus limited in their capacity to overcome doubt about their sincerity.

Acting can also reinforce insincerity, however. When the stout van Vuuren faced the slight, orphaned, fourteen-year-old Motasi, he seemed to be badgering him into forgiveness, rather than atoning for his past. Van Vuuren even appeared to be using Motasi to promote himself. Many viewed Scilingo similarly, considering him capable of going to extremes for attention, even if it meant lying and facing imprisonment. They believed he had invented the death flights, staged or invented the kidnapping and threats against him, and volunteered to meet with Judge Garzón purely to gain notice. He retracted his confession only when the publicity surrounding his case died out and he faced inglorious imprisonment without media access in a foreign country.

To convince audiences of their sincerity, remorseful perpetrators must act the part. They must construct their role to explain how they could have committed atrocity in the past and feel remorse about it in the present. Those who occupy positions of powerlessness in society or in the authoritarian regime may prove more skillful in this endeavor. Privileged backgrounds usually work against remorseful perpetrators, unless they can persuade their audience that they committed violence under threat of death. Persuasive acting helps. Perpetrators who physically exhibit suffering for their past violence or in some other way perform believable acts of atonement are more likely to sway audiences in their favor. Ambiguity, however, generates intense debate, even within specialized communities, over the sincerity of the act.

"In the Course of a War, Life Is Lost." "I would like them to come and confess so that we can be reconciled," a South African widow-survivor of apartheid violence pleads.[61] But so much gets in the way of producing the kind of confession victims and survivors need to reconcile the violent past, above all the fact that perpetrators tend to excuse and justify acts, rather than sincerely apologize for them.

Scilingo's persistent use of war language in his remorseful confession, for example, was questioned by human-rights leaders, because the terms of war justify killing as necessary and legitimate. Had Scilingo used the language of state terrorism and acknowledged the immorality and illegality of the regime's acts, human-rights groups might have found his remorse more believable.

The confession of Aboobaker Ismail, a commander in the ANC's military wing, further illustrates how war-based justifications can undermine remorseful intent. In his TRC amnesty hearing, Ismail apologized for the Cape Town Church Street bombing, which had killed nineteen people (including eleven air-force officers and two liberation-movement comrades) and injured 217 black and white civilians. In his apology, however, he defended the legitimacy of his acts: "I regret the deaths of innocent civilians killed in the cause of the fight for justice and freedom. In the course of a war, life is lost. The injury to and the loss of life of innocent civilians sometimes becomes inevitable. . . . We fought a just war for a just cause against white supremacy. . . . I am proud of the bravery, discipline and selfless sacrifices of the cadres of the Special Operations Units who operated under my command. Many of them laid down their lives in the pursuit of freedom for all in South Africa." The lawyer for Ismail's victims challenged his assumption that "typists, telephonists, people who worked with books" constituted the "military machine." Ismail insisted, "No military machine will work without all these administrative people as well. They are legitimate targets! . . . When you fight, what do you do? You kill people! The military is the military. They were targets!"[62] By calling his victims "targets," he justifies and excuses their deaths. In this, Ismail's remorse differs little from the apartheid policeman Carl Botha's unapologetic defense: "There is absolutely nothing that I feel ashamed of. . . . I'd very much like to just get on with my life. . . . We were in a war zone. . . . I think by-gones should be by-gones."[63] Victims and survivors await apologies for illegal and illegitimate acts of violence. They usually do not get them.

But sometimes they do. Scilingo's confession came close, but only with the guidance of Verbitsky, who led Scilingo to understand why the military could not, as he desired, defend the atrocities committed. The former Serb nationalist leader Biljana Plavšić accepted blame not only for the methods and consequences of the war but for the war itself, in her confession to the International Criminal Tribunal for the former Yugoslavia:

> I have now come to the belief and accept the fact that many thousands of innocent people were the victims of an organized, systematic effort to remove Muslims and Croats from the territory claimed by Serbs. At the time, I easily convinced myself that this was a matter of survival and self-defense. In fact it was more. Our leadership, of which I was a necessary part, led an effort which victimized countless innocent people. Explanations of self-defense and survival offer no justification. By

the end, it was said, even among our own people, that in this war we had lost our nobility of character. . . . I believe, fear, a blinding fear, . . . led to an obsession, especially for those of us for whom the Second World War was a living memory, that Serbs would never again allow themselves to become victims. In this, we in the leadership violated the most basic duty of every human being, the duty to restrain oneself and to respect the human dignity of others. We were committed to do whatever was necessary to prevail. Although I was repeatedly informed of allegations of cruel and inhuman conduct against non-Serbs, I refused to accept them or even to investigate. In fact, I immersed myself in addressing the suffering of the war's innocent Serb victims.[64]

Plavšić went on to clarify her individual responsibility and remorse for the war: "I have accepted responsibility for my part in this. This responsibility is mine and mine alone. It does not extend to other leaders who have a right to defend themselves. It certainly should not extend to our Serbian people, who have already paid a terrible price for our leadership. The knowledge that I am responsible for such human suffering and for soiling the character of my people will always be with me."[65]

Plavšić's testimony exemplifies a remorseful narrative that avoids the usual justifications for lives lost in war. But it also points to barriers in producing those kinds of remorseful scripts. First, Plavšić erodes her only pillar of support—Serb nationalists—without winning new support from her erstwhile opponents. Her opponents want to see her tried and convicted for those acts. Her former allies want her confession censored. Only rarely will perpetrators abandon all their support in a community to make remorseful confessions.

Second, Plavšić as a woman and a politician may have faced fewer barriers than male soldiers in finding a narrative structure and an emotional timbre with which to express remorse.[66] Soldiers, for example, rarely apologize for their past; they seek praise for it. They generally do not embrace the language of repentance, perhaps fearing that they might sound "phony-ass," as the U.S. baseball legend Pete Rose claimed when referring to the difficulty of expressing remorse about his gambling addiction.[67] Perpetrators often fail to produce convincingly remorseful confessions because they express too little emotion. Apartheid's "superspy," Craig Williamson, for example, shocked audiences with his lack of emotion over killing a six-year-old girl: "When I heard about the child being killed, it was like being hit with a bucket of cold water. . . . There is nothing that has happened to me in my life that I regret more. To carry out an attack on somebody you do not know is one thing, but to do that to somebody you know is very difficult. The fact that the individuals were my enemy and that of my country did not make it easier."[68] Williamson expressed shallow emotion with the "bucket of cold water" analogy. By referring to a six-year-old child as an "enemy," he justified his acts.

Similarly, too much, or inappropriate, emotion can also undermine remorseful confessions. In the TRC's human-rights (rather than amnesty) committee hearings, the South African Yassir Henry expressed remorse for his role in the killing of Anton Fransch, his former commander in the ANC army, Umkhoto we Sizwe. Henry spun a complicated tale in which he admitted to betraying Fransch by revealing his whereabouts to the police. Rather than assume responsibility, however, Henry blamed others. He blamed Fransch himself for having disclosed his location to Henry, who had to give up that information when the police detained and interrogated him and threatened to murder his family. He also blamed the police for setting him up as a stool pigeon, in order to protect their own spy. This testimony, which Henry subsequently presented in various national and international forums, inspired doubts about its sincerity. Why did Henry transform himself into a victim and miss the opportunity to express regret for his role in Fransch's death? How was he able to call up the same depth of emotion in each retelling of the event? His remorse came to seem rehearsed and insincere.

> Where does the culpability rest? I believe I cannot be held solely responsible for the death of Anton Fransch. And the role played by the security police must be exposed. [*cries out*] I wish! To be recognized! For who and what I am! So that the falsification of my history can be rectified. I want to know who the person was who informed on *me*. Only then will I be able to reconcile myself with my experience and with the death of Anton [*voice breaks completely*] that the ANC acknowledges their role in my pain! That they restore my military rank. And that the TRC will grant me the possibility to wake up from this nightmare with which I've been living for so many years, so that I too can share in the process of healing taking place in our country.[69]

Silenced parts of remorseful confessions, like Henry's muteness with regard to his own culpability, often undermine the effect of sincerity. Mark Behr prepared an emotionally deep and remorseful confession, but hid details about which agency he spied for, to whom he directly reported, which member of his family had lured him into his position, how much money he received, and what information he relayed.[70] By guarding this information, he continued to protect himself and those he worked for in the apartheid apparatus. One reporter summarized the impression Behr produced with his confession: "Behr could be forgiven for spying on the anti-apartheid movement, even if it was for thrills and extra ready cash. But, quite simply, he would have to be sorry first. Not sorry for himself. Sorry for what he has done."[71] The combination of deep emotion and vast silence leads audiences to suspect perpetrators of feeling regret for having been caught, not remorse for their acts. Those, like Behr and Henry, with writing and acting talent, artfully craft confessions that look and feel remorseful, but sometimes only convince audiences of perpetrators' desire to find a place in the new democracy, not of their sincere contrition for the role they played in past violence.

Effective remorseful narratives require consistency between script and acting, which was achieved by the apartheid policeman Brian Mitchell.[72] On death row for his involvement in the murder of eleven individuals in Trust Feed (his sentence was later commuted to thirty years), Mitchell returned to the community to apologize: "Brian Mitchell's eyes fill with tears and glaze over as the relatives of those he killed sob. His whole body starts shaking. And he swallows hard frequently."[73] Through sobs, Mitchell explained that he had lost everything: his wife had left him and he had not seen his children. He almost begged his victims to forgive him: "I understand that forgiveness does not come cheaply. It's something that comes deeply from the heart. And I can just ask the people that were involved directly or indirectly and who have been affected by this case to consider forgiving me."[74] Mitchell followed up this effective script and acting with a promise to work with the Trust Feed community to rebuild it. Reconciliation groups in South Africa and business communities in the United States lauded Mitchell's remorse because it extended beyond words and promises into acts of atonement.

Mitchell's off-stage comments and his earlier confessions, however, cast doubts on his sincerity. In previous trial testimony and in private conversations with me, Mitchell had insisted on his innocence, accused the special constables of lying about his involvement, and contended that he had not been present on the night of the attack and that his commanding officer (now deceased) had ordered it. Mitchell also admitted that he would not have applied for amnesty had he not been jailed. Finally, he averred that if he had killed anti-apartheid combatants, rather than "innocent victims," he would have been "overjoyed." Only by overlooking these remarks, and the attitudes behind them, can one trust the sincerity of Mitchell's confession.

Evasion traps remorseful perpetrators. The apartheid police officer Gideon Nieuwoudt walked into such a trap. With a South African film crew, he visited the family of Siphiwe Mtimkulu, whom he had killed, to ask forgiveness. The family received him reluctantly. They knew him from previous visits when, disguised as a bible salesman, he had spied on Mtimkulu. Mtimkulu had told his family to distrust Nieuwoudt. While the cameras captured the high-publicity forgiveness encounter, Mtimkulu's family pressed Nieuwoudt for a confession. They refused to accept his apology without one. But Nieuwoudt, consistent with his TRC hearing, denied responsibility for killing Mtimkulu. Exasperated by Nieuwoudt's evasion of responsibility, Mtimkulu's son took up a vase and cracked it over Nieuwoudt's head.[75] Apology, without admission of guilt, rings hollow.

Perhaps the greatest obstacle to a remorseful script is the perpetrator's unforgivable acts of violence. No words can adequately reconcile victims and perpetrators of atrocity, and perpetrators recognize the impossibility of saying the right thing. As Scilingo said, "It's too easy to say 'I'm sorry' and everything is okay." Luz Arce said, "I believe that I have to pay a price—due to my own actions and those of others. For a long time I have understood that I have to pay a price to live in my country. . . . I ask for pardon, but I don't expect it."[76] Deep remorse requires acceptance that certain acts are *not* forgivable and that speech alone cannot reconcile the past. Dirk Coetzee, head of the police death squad Vlakplaas, reflected this view in his statement about murdering the civil-rights attorney Griffiths Mxenge: "[I feel] extreme mixed emotions of anger, deep-seated anger for allowing me to get involved with this nonsense. Uh . . . humiliation, embarrassment and a helplessness of a pathetic: I'm sorry for what I've done. What . . . what . . . what else can I offer them [the Mxenge family]? A pathetic nothing. So, in all honesty, I don't expect the Mxenge family to forgive me because I don't know how I ever in my life would be able to forgive a man like Dirk Coetzee, if he's done to me what I've done to them."[77]

To convince victims and survivors of their sincerity, remorseful perpetrators must also listen to those they harmed. Rather than over-power them, they need to engage in a dialogue about the past. They must understand what they did on their victims' terms, not on their own. That involves surrendering power to victims in the interest of coexistence.

"Things Went Horribly Wrong." Recent innovations in transitional-justice institutional design—most notably the South African TRC and the Rwandan gacaca—have created incentives for remorseful confes-sions, thereby, paradoxically, increasing doubts about perpetrators' sincerity. Audiences assume that perpetrators express remorse insin-cerely and instrumentally, to benefit from institutional inducements (e.g., amnesty, pardon, reduced sentence).

Brian Mitchell, for example, by his own admission would not have expressed remorse without the inducement of the TRC's amnesty. Mitchell's story was further complicated by his prison experience: after two years on death row, Mitchell was sober and newly religious. Mitchell, moreover, was not alone in taking advantage of the TRC with regard to the Trust Feed incident. Thabane Nyoka, whose mother had died in the Trust Feed attack, had approached Mitchell. Nyoka re-counted that his mother appeared to him in a dream and encouraged him to avoid revenge and seek reconciliation with Mitchell. As Nyoka explained, "I underwent trauma counseling. I have forgiven him and accepted it. I wanted to hear him apologize and ask the community for forgiveness. I understand that he cannot rebuild the community on his own. On the other hand, we cannot wait for Brian to develop the community."[78] Nyoka suggested to Mitchell a reconciliation project which the Institute for Justice and Reconciliation (IJR) helped sup-port. Indeed, Mitchell's work with Trust Feed became a model for IJR's community-reconciliation program. Mitchell devoted his limited time and money to travel to, work with, and raise funds for the de-velopment project in Trust Feed.[79]

For some Trust Feed residents, Mitchell's contribution speaks vol-umes. Others view his efforts more skeptically.[80] Fostus Sibonge, whose store and home were burned during the rampage, represents these doubts in the community: "I never believed Brian from the onset and that is why I told him that I will never forgive him until I see him doing something practical regarding development. . . . For me, he hasn't done enough. I wouldn't stand in the way of the community if they wanted to hear him apologize. That is why I took part in organizing his visit. . . . I think Brian's lawyers advised him to apply for amnesty because they saw the chance to become heroes in the history of this country."[81]

Skepticism also surfaces when perpetrators come forward so late and only after induced by institutional mechanisms, reveal so little, and ignore how long their silence and the uncertainty tortured survivors. Nomonde Calata judged the remorseful confession by the apartheid policeman involved in her husband's murder this way. Nomonde Calata's husband was killed in an incident known as the Cradock Four murders. The four men left Cradock on 27 June 1985 to attend a United Democratic Front meeting in Port Elizabeth. They never returned alive. Their mutilated, charred bodies were found outside the city, but until February 1998, no one admitted to the murder. A leaked document implicated the police in the murder and cover-up. The policeman Eric Taylor admitted to his involvement in the murder in his amnesty hearing in February 1998: "I . . . uh . . . also hit Mr. Fort Calata from the back with this iron object, more or less where the neck joins the head. He fell down and I was under the impression that he was unconscious. The black members [of the security apparatus] then stabbed him with knives [to make it look like a violent robbery]."[82] Shortly before he made this testimony, Taylor had met with Nomonde Calata to offer an apology. As he stated, "The need to meet Mrs. Calata really stemmed from a Christian point of view. I don't think amnesty was more important to me than reconciliation at that stage. I was very emotional. I think it's an experience that will stay with me for a very long time."[83] For Nomonde Calata, however, Taylor's expression of remorse did not erase his murderous act and the prolonged torture of having searched for the truth in vain: "Well, he was expecting me to say I forgive him. But I did not say that. I was terribly hurt when I saw him. I was angry! Uh . . . I felt like somebody who was for the first time hearing the news of my husband. And I thought he was a very hard person. He waited for the right time to come out so that he can get forgiveness. From me? Yet he had let me suffer for so long with these children of mine. I can't forget Mr. Taylor. I can't forget anyone. I can't forgive them."[84]

Timing confessions for personal benefit often undermined the believability of perpetrators' remorse, as Behr, who revealed his past as an apartheid spy only after threats of exposure, discovered. He offered a defensible excuse: that an earlier admission would have hurt the anti-apartheid student movement, which he had infiltrated and learned to respect, by revealing that it had inadvertently contained spies like himself.[85] He further claimed that his experience within the liberation movement had transformed him and convinced him that his infiltration was "morally untenable": "It was not possible for me to see this, hear these people speak, experience their humanity and remain politically and personally unchanged by it."[86] But he also admitted to less admirable reasons: "I lacked the moral fortitude to face the consequences of my treason," and "I still wanted the money."[87] He also worried about his public image: "Having seen the way in which other informers had been publicly exposed and having myself reached a point of comprehending why the act of espionage was shameful and utterly devoid of defense and why informers were publicly humiliated and suspected informers on occasion even killed, I would not speak."[88] Behr's international fame as an anti-apartheid crusader had, after all, won him prestigious grants and fellowships to study and work outside South Africa. His novel, *The Smell of Apples*, became a paean to the struggle against apartheid, described in one (pre-confession) review as "one of the documents the [TRC] commissioners must read as they struggle to understand and come to grips with the soul of apartheid South Africa."[89]

Behr's confession unleashed a torrent of diatribes against him. One journalist described him as a "flamboyant individual interested only in self-promotion" and presumably the promotion of his new novel, *Betrayal*.[90] Others called him a "glamour hunter" who would trade "on his credentials as the contrite perpetrator, as the prodigal son" to differentiate himself from all the other white-liberation activists writing novels and testimonies, to render himself more complex and interesting, his life and his work more intriguing, his perspective unique. His audience judged his confession cynically, characterizing it as a ploy to control his national and international image, and sell more books. His audience, no doubt bruised by his betrayal, exaggerated the personal benefit he would extract from a confession.

Behr's confession was a simple statement without dialogue, preventing those he harmed from directly confronting him or his acts.

· Perpetrators who confess within a deliberative process often find them transformative. Scilingo's remorse, for example, emerged only through Scilingo's confrontation with Verbitsky, who provided a different way of thinking about the past and a corresponding language of remorse. The interaction pushed Scilingo out of the safety of denial or heroism, forcing him to confront the harm he had caused.

The TRC provided a similar environment for some perpetrators. Archbishop Desmond Tutu, at the TRC's helm, tutored perpetrators in the art of remorse. He proved so determined to produce remorseful confessions that TRC leaders from the legal community felt compelled to clarify the purpose of the commission. Judge Hassen E. Mall, who served on the TRC's Amnesty Committee, proclaimed, "We don't take into account, for example, whether a man says 'I'm sorry for what I did.' . . . You know a man may come and say, 'I'm sorry for what I did,' and there may be very little else he might be able to say to justify his offense."[91] Tutu, nonetheless, searched and found opportunities for personal reconciliation between perpetrators and victims. A now famous encounter with the ANC leader Winnie Madikizela-Mandela illustrates his efforts.

> TUTU: There are people out there who want to embrace you. I . . . I still embrace you because I love you and I love you very deeply. There are many out there who would have wanted to do so, if you were able to bring yourself to say: "Something went wrong." And to say: "I'm sorry. I'm sorry for my part in what went wrong." I beg you! I beg you! I beg you! Please! You are a great person and you don't know how your greatness would be enhanced if you had to say: "Sorry. Things went wrong. Forgive me." I beg you!
> MADIKIZELA-MANDELA: I am saying it is true. Things went horribly wrong. For that, I am deeply sorry.[92]

Madikizela-Mandela resisted Tutu's entreaties; her apology evolved after a lengthy period of denial, defensiveness, and evasion. In the end she did not assume personal responsibility for her acts. But she expressed what Tutu desired: the humanity of remorse.

What did Madikizela-Mandela gain from expressing remorse to Tutu or the TRC? Victims and survivors often exaggerate the instrumental gain perpetrators derive from offering remorse. And they ignore the risks remorseful confessions entail. As well-known anti-apartheid activists, Madikizela-Mandela and Behr faced severe damage to their reputations for admitting that wrongdoing had occurred within the liberation movement. Perpetrators within military structures even risk death, as was illustrated by the assassination of the Chilean collaborator Juan René Muñoz Alarcón, who had expressed remorse for collaborating with Chilean intelligence forces in the death of his former socialist comrades. The warning left by his assassins was clear: other perpetrators who told their stories would face a similar fate. Nearly every perpetrator has an example of reprisals that guides his or her decision to remain quiet. Perpetrators express their remorse only after they overcome fear of reprisal. Remorseful confessions, therefore, often occur late, not only in response to institutional inducements but also for self-protection.[93]

Neither timing nor institutional arrangements cause, predict, or explain remorseful confessions. They do, however, generate debate over how to interpret confessional performances. And these debates sometimes lead to the kind of transgressive events that build democracy.

"Remorse Is Irrelevant." Facts alone rarely heal individuals or societies. For healing, individuals want remorse. Dawie Ackerman, for example, confronted his wife's killers at the TRC amnesty hearings. He not only asked for information about their murderous spree at St. Andrews Church, but also for an apology.

DAWIE ACKERMAN: May I ask the applicants to turn around and to face me? This is the first opportunity that we've had to look at each other in the eye. I want to ask Mr. [Khaya] Makoma who actually entered the church. My wife was sitting right at the door where you came in. She was wearing a long blue coat. Can you remember if you shot her?

KHAYA MAKOMA: I do remember that I fired some shots. But I couldn't identify [anyone]. I don't know whom did I shoot or not, but my gun pointed at the people. . . .

DAWIE ACKERMAN: It is important for me to know if it is possible. As much as it is important for your people who suffered to know who killed. I don't know why it is so important for me, it . . . it just is. . . . . . . I would like to hear from each one of you, as you look me in the face, that you are sorry for what you've done. That you regret it and that you want to be personally reconciled.

AMNESTY APPLICANT: We are sorry for what we have done. Although people died during that struggle, we didn't do that out of our own will. It's the situation that we were living under. We are asking from you, please do forgive us.

DAWIE ACKERMAN: I want you to know that I forgive you unconditionally.[94]

Ackerman, like Tutu, seemed unconcerned with the true character of the apology: he emphasized the act of forgiveness over the sincerity of remorse. He needed the apology, however formulaic, for his own healing. As the widower of an apartheid-era assassination stated, "Part of the therapy is to be exposed to, to know and to know, and to hear people say, 'I'm sorry.' "[95] The South African TRC demanded that people heal—through expressions of remorse and forgiveness, even mimicked ones. The mother of one of Thapelo Mbelo's victims summarized her understanding of what it meant to reconcile with the past: "This thing called reconciliation . . . if I am understanding it correctly . . . if it means this perpetrator, this man who has killed Christopher Piet [her son], if it means he becomes human again, this man, so that I, so that all of us, get our humanity back . . . then I agree, then I support it all."[96]

But many victims and survivors did not accept superficial remorse, instead seeking either true repentance and remorse or meaningful expressions of atonement that recognized the financial impact of the deaths of productive members of the family. Many South Africans felt resentment at the shallowness of the TRC process: "Well, if they truly showed remorse, I'm sure the family would accept their apology. But now they are telling lies. They are making us more angry," one South African commented.[97] Another stated, "My first impression was that 'this guy looks really sorry.' But as time went on, after that, 'No, no, no. He's not yet come closer to the truth.' And that now destroyed all the sympathies that I had for him."[98]

"Remorse is irrelevant," said Ana Maria Careaga, a torture survivor and the daughter of one of Argentina's disappeared.[99] Her few words speak for those who cynically interpret perpetrators' remorse. They judge such confessions as opportunities for perpetrators to profit from their past acts of violence legally (through amnesty, pardon, or a reduced sentence), financially (through media appearances and book sales), and morally (by restoring perpetrators' humanity). These confessions, claim Careaga and others, give perpetrators control over and within the transitional process. The human-rights activist Martín

Abregú, referring to Scilingo's confession, stated, "Once again, essential questions of public life are being settled by an army chief and that, in a country like Argentina, is serious."[100]

Victims and survivors are burdened with offering an appropriate response to perpetrators' remorseful confessions. They are expected to be grateful. They are expected to regard the confessions as unexpected and generous gifts. But to accept them, victims and survivors must overcome trauma, fear, and anger. They must forgive the unforgivable. Victims and survivors, in other words, are held to a standard of mental health and magnanimous spirit not expected of perpetrators. Merely by admitting to the violence they committed, on the other hand, perpetrators meet, and even surpass, societal expectations for their role in the reconciliation process. Reacting against the double standards for victims and perpetrators in the reconciliation process, the South African poet, writer, and radio broadcaster Sandile Dikeni writes, "The Europeans love it [white confessional literature]. It pushes the moral high-ground back to white people, forces me to accept that they're not entirely bad. They feel sorry, man! We'll kill you if you don't forgive. They'll hug you to death, and you don't have an option. And I hate it!"[101]

Dikeni's comments epitomize the reluctance with which audiences encounter remorseful confessions. Where the authoritarian regime retains power, audiences in society and in the government censor remorseful confessions to protect the image of security forces. In the case of Scilingo, audiences publicly denigrated his version of the story, physically attacked him, intimidated him, and sent a clear message of intolerance for disloyal "crybabies." Where remorseful confessions threaten to disrupt peace and reopen old political wounds, democratic governments will censor them, sometimes, as in Scilingo's case, with fines and imprisonment.

What these audiences try to censor—the truth—is what so many desire. Remorse is irrelevant, in Careaga's words, not because it lacks a profound impact on audiences' responses, but because it is intended to end, not begin, dialogue.

CONCLUSION

Remorse offers the possibility of closure, or of settling accounts with the past. If perpetrators would only admit to their wrongdoing, the theory holds, society could move on. Remorseful confessions thus have great political stock.

Such views exist only in the abstract. In reality, few audiences believe remorseful confessions, instead considering them to be instrumental and insincere, manipulative, a way to avoid painful political and personal discussions. Remorseful confessions are felt to place undue burden on those who have already suffered—victims and survivors—in the name of individual and national healing.

Contentious coexistence acknowledges that few societies accept the remorse bait. They do not allow such confessions to settle accounts with the past. Instead, they interrogate them, digging for sincerity, deeper meaning, or concrete forms of atonement. Most societies, in other words, do not let remorseful perpetrators off the hook so easily. Remorseful confessions generate conflict.

Through that conflict, however, perpetrators begin to understand a different perspective. They hear and begin to comprehend the harm they committed, the personal, financial, and emotional losses they inflicted on individuals and communities. They learn this not by mimicking apologies, but by learning a new language and form of interaction in communities.

Moreover, because not all victims and survivors or regime supporters share the same response to remorseful confessions, political polarization fails to surface. Instead, a diversity of views emerges, generating debate and forcing perpetrators and their audiences to sharpen their expressive and interpretive skills.

The process of fragmenting memory, avoiding memory poles, and engendering debate over the past is not a byproduct exclusively of perpetrators' remorseful confessions. Indeed, most confessions, if used effectively by memory entrepreneurs, can have the same effect. Remorseful confessions may be "irrelevant" to political memory, but only because other kinds of confessions may be equally effective in producing conflicting versions and public debate over the past and its significance for the present.

CHAPTER THREE

HEROIC CONFESSIONS

HEROIC CONFESSIONS

I never tortured. It wasn't my job. Would I have tortured if I had been ordered to do so? Yes, of course I would. I say that the navy taught me how to destroy. They didn't teach me how to build, they taught me how to destroy. I know how to plant mines and bombs. I know how to infiltrate and disarm an organization. I know how to kill. I know how to do all of this really well. I always say: I'm thick [*bruto*] but I've had one moment of clarity in my life, that was joining the navy. . . . I never debated [my orders] first of all because I am a military man from my soul and the first thing they taught me is that one must obey orders from superiors. But besides that I agreed [with the orders]. They were the enemy. I had a lot of hate inside of me. They had killed two thousand of our men. Do you know why a military man kills? For a lot of reasons: for love of his country, for machismo, for pride, for duty. . . . I am the best man in this country, technically speaking, to kill a politician or a journalist.—Alfredo Astiz, interviewed by Gabriela Cerruti

Astiz –
Unreported?

THE FORMER NAVAL CAPTAIN ALFREDO ASTIZ shocked the nation of Argentina with his confession to the journalist Gabriela Cerruti, which she published in the news magazine *Trespuntos*. Astiz was already known in many circles as the man who had infiltrated the Mothers of the Plaza de Mayo. In 1977, posing as a young man looking for his "disappeared" brother, Astiz quickly won the affection of the Mothers of the Plaza de Mayo. They called him the Blond Angel because of his good

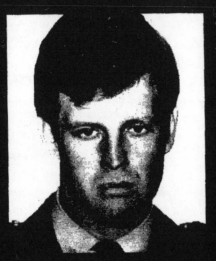

"On behalf of our comrades, spit on him." Posters of former navy captain and perpetrator of authoritarian state violence Alfredo Astiz appeared throughout Buenos Aires in January 1998.

looks and sweetness. After discovering that he had organized the raid on the Santa Cruz church and several homes that led to the kidnapping and disappearance of twelve people (including two French nuns) associated with the Mothers of the Plaza de Mayo and other opposition groups, they referred to him as the Angel of Death.[1] His identity as a naval officer was revealed only after he left Argentina and attempted to infiltrate the Argentine Solidarity movement in Paris. A former prisoner of one of Argentina's notorious torture centers recognized him and alerted the movement. Tipped off by a fellow infiltrator, Astiz escaped to Spain. But news filtered back to the Argentine human-rights community that the navy captain Alfredo Astiz had posed as Gustavo Niño, a young man looking for his disappeared brother, and as Alberto Escudero, the young Argentine exiled to Paris. When his face appeared on the front pages of Argentine newspapers in 1982, surrendering to the British during the Malvinas-Falklands War, the opposition community had proof of the connections.

After the dictatorship, survivors from torture centers filled in more details of Astiz's involvement in other political murders, most notably that of Dagmar Hagelin, a Swedish-Argentine teenager whom he shot after mistaking her for a leader in the Montonero guerrilla movement. The human-rights community began to build legal cases against Astiz. Although the Supreme Council of the Armed Forces found him innocent of murder in 1987, civilian courts later convicted him. Astiz claims that he spent nine months during the Raúl Alfonsín presidency awaiting trial and serving part of his sentence before the Due Obedience Law freed him. French courts found him guilty in absentia for the murder of the two nuns, and other countries demanded his extradition to stand trial for murdering citizens.[2] The military appeared to sanction Astiz with forced retirement, but later secretly rehired him into the National Intelligence Service (SNI).

Astiz faced the courts again in response to his *Trespuntos* confession.[3] Charged and convicted on a range of crimes, including justifying a crime (*apología del delito*) and threatening democracy, Astiz received a three-month suspended jail sentence and a fine. The armed forces also sanctioned him for conducting an unauthorized interview and showing disrespect for military hierarchy. He was discharged and stripped of the privileges of his rank, including pension and insurance benefits. International courts continued to press for extradition. Judge Baltasar Garzón used Astiz's statements in *Trespuntos* to advance cases against him in the Spanish courts and called for his immediate arrest by Interpol should he leave Argentine soil.[4] Charges against Astiz resurfaced again with the abrogation of the immunity laws under President Néstor Kirchner (2003 to present).[5]

Astiz's background and physical appearance attracted public attention. As the son of a well-known navy vice-admiral, Astiz seemed positioned to climb to the commanding heights of the most respected branch of the armed forces in Argentina. And he looked and dressed the part. One North American journalist described him as "a young blond man with the face of an angelic five-year-old and a Kennedy smile."[6] His blond hair and blue eyes, rare in his country, signified for many beauty, wealth, and power. His sartorial style reflected good breeding, manners, education, and taste. Like a Ken doll, Astiz had an outfit for every occasion and photo opportunity: navy whites, navy blues, casual-but-elegant jeans and sweater, polo shirts, and swimming trunks. He "accessorized" with beautiful Argentine women. News cameras captured the tan and fit couple in the company of the nation's elite at exclusive beach resorts, yacht clubs, and discotheques. His passion for Calder and Van Gogh completed the image of a cultured man. But these images of beauty, civility, and refinement clashed with the one that emerged within the human-rights community during the dictatorship and became public with the *Trespuntos* confession and its aftermath.

Astiz's physical deterioration matched his social demise. Although still accompanied by Argentine beauties and spied in exclusive clubs, Astiz no longer possessed the physique of his youth. He looked like an average middle-aged man who might spend weekends and weeknights sprawled on a couch, watching soccer matches on television and drinking beer, and not like the buff navy hero of yore. Cerruti described buttons on Astiz's still perfectly pressed shirt that seem ready to pop from his extra girth. She noted that his eyes, no longer brilliant blue, were rimmed in red, as if fighting back tears or a psychotic rage.[7] Nervousness replaced verve and swagger. Journalists depicted Astiz alternatively as a frozen form in the courtroom who only occasionally blinked his eyes or as twitching constantly and involuntarily throughout the hearing. His slumped posture hid his once adored face and expression from view. He spoke almost inaudibly, forcing the judge and the spectators to strain to hear him.

His "Kennedy smile" lost its allure and turned sinister. Cerruti recounted that smile as having been constant throughout her two-hour interview, "whether he was talking about a murder or telling what he considered to be a joke. It was as if he was trying to seduce me, and was pathetic, or scare me, and was pathetic."[8] When they next met, the smile had disappeared. Astiz had perhaps lost his capacity or desire to seduce, impress, or scare. Cerruti described his face as red and swollen as he pounded his hands and yelled at her to retract her article. She wrote that she could not tell if he wanted to kill her or run away and cry.[9] Journalists alternatively used the terms "cold" and "hostile" to describe his appearance in court, never mentioning his smile.

Astiz also lost his self-confidence and sense of humor. In *Children of Cain* the journalist Tina Rosenberg described the younger Astiz by his laughter: "Astiz laughed, with his head tilted back and his teeth flashing as he strode away, just as in the newspaper photos. His laugh was mocking, victorious, the laughter of a man who knew he would walk in liberty for the rest of his days."[10] Astiz himself recalls his mocking humor; referring to infiltrating the Mothers of the Plaza de Mayo, he stated, "What I did was infiltrate and this is why they will never forgive me. Because I infiltrated them two times. When they accuse me of other things, I get mad, but about this [infiltration] I laugh."[11] But now, Cerruti noted, when he laughed, one could see that he had lost some of those flawless teeth. A metaphor, perhaps, for the holes time and truth had bored into his perfect facade.

Astiz compensated for his loss of status and looks with stories. In the *Trespuntos* interview he glorified his role in the military regime: "We did everything," he claimed. "They would say to me, 'Go and look for so-and-so.' I'd go and bring him in. Dead or alive, I left him in the ESMA. And then I'd go out on the next action."[12] When asked specifically about how many people he had killed, Astiz conspiratorially warned, "Never ask a military man that question." "Why not?" Cerruti persisted. "Because we prefer not to know." Yet Astiz offered up information about specific acts, such as his involvement in the murder of Juan Roqué, the third in command of the Montoneros. In a shootout in which Astiz claimed he nearly died and that left him shaking for days, the navy eventually killed Roqué by blowing up his house.[13] Astiz also claimed credit for heroic work in the ESMA detention center. "What do you want me to say [about the ESMA]? That it was for Barefoot Carmelites [monks or nuns] run by Mother Teresa?

No, no it wasn't. It was a place for jailing the enemy." He went on to talk about the danger he had encountered in his work.

> If one doesn't keep perspective [on the goals], you can't go on doing your work. It's not like an accounting firm. It is risking the only thing you have: your body. It is about protecting your mind. Do you know what shit you go through? Every day, at every moment, I know that someone could kill me. My legs shook in every shootout, your whole body hurts, I go through so much fear, I went through a lot of fear. I died of this shit. And the next day you have to go out again. Do you believe that you can do this if you're challenging orders every day? And this is how you learn not to question orders when you're in the lower ranks. And you learn to watch out for your people when you're on top. That is the first thing they teach you: you are responsible for your people. The worst thing you can go through in life is that they kill one of yours. And I'm not even talking about when it is responding to one of your orders. So what I'm going through now isn't anything compared to what I've been through.[14]

Astiz's confession revealed the secrets behind the military's silence and denial. He did not attribute the violence to "left-wing propaganda" or to "mistakes" and "excesses by rogue officers," but to his own actions and orders. This led one journalist to probe whether Astiz "spoke without realizing [that he was exposing] what the navy had been trying to hide."[15] Astiz confirmed, for example, the systematic process of rounding up and exterminating the opposition:

> In '82 I said to a friend who asked me about the disappearances, I'm sure there are 6,500. I suspect that there may be more, but I don't know exactly how many more. There aren't more than 10,000, I'm certain. Just like I think the people who claim there are 30,000 [disappeared] are crazy, those who say that they are living in Mexico are also delirious. We cleaned them all out. There was no other way. They killed them. What else could they do? There was the experience in '73 when they had put them all in jail and then they were amnestied and they got out. It was too risky. There was no other way.[16]

He also implicated the navy in the disappearances of individuals who only mildly threatened the regime, including the journalists Mario Bonino, Rodolfo Walsh, and Edgardo Sajón, who had never taken up arms, but used only the weapon of opinion.[17] Astiz turned his infiltration and the disappearance of the Mothers of the Plaza de Mayo members into a soldier's heroic act, by branding them subversives. "I did my job," he explained. "They were Montoneras. They received orders from the Montoneros. I respect them for looking for their disappeared children, but they are exploiting them for money and politics."[18] In Astiz's world, any opposition to the regime, regardless of how mild, constituted subversion.[19]

Astiz considered his confession a heroic act that his commanders lacked the bravery to carry out. "The juntas were cowardly," he asserted. "The truth is that they were cowards. They didn't come out and say that they had to shoot them all."[20] He also considered the army general Martín Balza a "cretin" for suggesting that soldiers should disobey unethical or illegal orders: "How are you going to claim that some orders should not be obeyed? There wouldn't be an armed forces if this were the case."[21] And Astiz criticized the commander-in-chief, President Carlos Menem, as "the worst of them all. A lot of 'my brother, my brother,' and then he kills you. My brother, my brother, and then he forced me to retire. Alfonsín would not have done that."[22]

Although Scilingo and Astiz shared the opinion that their commanders were cowardly, they took diverging views on their own violence. Astiz considered his acts noble: "I don't regret anything. I am not perfect. I might have made a minor mistake. But in the big picture I do not repent anything. Scilingo is a traitor. And there is one thing that I learned from my mother and it is the only advice I can give: watch out for traitors. He who betrays once will always betray."[23]

Astiz had not expected the notoriety he received for his heroic confession to *Trespuntos*. He responded by retreating into silence and shunning the press, which relentlessly hunted him. He turned down even the most prestigious media opportunities, including a chance to be interviewed by the popular and sensationalist television journalist Mauro Viale.[24] Astiz limited his public appearances to trials and hearings and spoke as little as possible in them. But journalists from every news outlet in the country covered each trial and hearing, reported every word he uttered, regardless of its triviality, and improvised stories out of each tic and twitch he made, every article of clothing he donned, and every public response to him. Astiz's confession and postconfessional performances dominated the news media.[25]

Multiple images of Astiz emerged from this coverage. Most obviously, Astiz appeared as a ruthless killer and a symbol of the danger of granting perpetrators immunity from prosecution. Astiz's confession and postconfessional confrontations contributed to this image. To Cerruti, Astiz referred to himself as the best-trained assassin, who could be convinced to act against journalists, politicians, and others who threatened the country.

> Journalists now believe that there wasn't any subversion. They need to watch out, they're going to end up in a bad way. . . . Don't continue cornering us, because I'm not sure how we are going to respond. [You're] playing with fire. It's as if Cassius Clay comes into your house and hits you, one day, two days, three days . . . by the end you get tired and even though you are smaller, you hit him over the head with a chair. Only we're not smaller. The armed forces have 500,000 men technically prepared to kill. I am the best of them all. They always come to see me. And I give them the same message. Calm down. You've got to wait. This happens in all countries. But I don't know for how long [I can hold them off].[26]

Several subsequent acts and statements bolstered Astiz's threats. *Trespuntos*, for example, received a call from someone asking for Cerruti. Evoking the language of the dictatorship, the voice issued a warning: "Tell her that we are from the Cave Commando. She should watch herself or else she's fried."[27] And it was hard to miss the threat implicit in Astiz's response to his prosecuting attorney: "Killing an ant and an elephant is the same thing, you use different methods but they both die in the end. If you shoot someone in the head, they will die regardless of whether they are a lawyer, doctor, or whatever."[28]

Astiz's image thus came to represent not only his past acts but also what those acts augured for contemporary Argentine democracy. Identifying the danger his immunity posed to democracy, Nora Cortinas of the Mothers of the Plaza de Mayo, Linea Fundadora, stated that Astiz "exalt[ed] the crimes that he and his band committed, but he also threaten[ed] to commit them again." The Union of Workers in Journalism in Buenos Aires demanded that Astiz stand trial and disclose the information he claimed to possess regarding the navy's involvement in journalists' deaths. The union wanted justice not only for past murders, but also for the continued violence against journalists after the end of the dictatorship.

The democratic government focused on Astiz's contemporary threats, not his past.[29] It censored and condemned Astiz's *statements* about violence, not his *acts* of violence. The former spokesman for President Alfonsín, Federico Polak, defended this censorship: "That a figure like Astiz has the possibility of putting on the pages of the dailies how they killed people but do not repent, does not contribute to reconciliation. These people do not have the right to free expression. This issue is more important than freedom of the press, and these types of articles should not appear."[30]

Menem treated Astiz like a "scoundrel," throwing him in jail to censor him and warn other would-be confessors about the danger of speaking out.[31] Astiz's comments reflected badly on Menem's pardon. As one of Menem's colleagues in the Peronist Party noted, "These people should not be free, they should not be on the street. . . . Those who benefited from the pardon today are exalting the violence, as if the barbarities committed had been virtuous acts, and this provokes outrage."[32]

Taking a slightly different tack, some audiences countered Astiz's heroic image with evidence of his cowardice. The president of the Abuelas de Plaza de Mayo, Estela Carlotto, referred to Astiz as a "cowardly assassin" who did not confront an enemy in battle, but shot an innocent teenager running from him on the street. He had not tested his military mettle, but sequestered and disappeared unarmed mothers searching for their children and others defending human rights. One journalist ironically captured Astiz's bravery: "Like it or not, there is a man in this world who is called Alfredo Astiz. He is forty-seven years old, blond, considers himself handsome, and brags about knowing how to kill people. His specialty is young women and defenseless nuns. But regarding the English, we can't say a word."[33] The last line refers to Astiz's role in the Falklands-Malvinas War, which deepened his image as a coward. The journalist Miguel Bonasso reminded the public that Astiz surrendered only forty-five minutes after the war began—some say without firing a single shot—and spent the rest of the war as a political prisoner in Great Britain.[34]

Journalists also challenged with numbers Astiz's notion of fighting an evil enemy. Contesting the legitimacy of the war against subversion, Bonasso claimed that only 200 members of the security forces died between 1974 and 1976, while the security forces killed 1,500 "subversives" during that same period before the dictatorship.[35] Uki Goñi also questioned Astiz's claims of 2,000 security force deaths. He found that during the dictatorship (1976–1983), the ESMA alone killed

4,000 subversives. During the entire decade of the 1970s, in contrast, only 21 navy personnel died, seven of them prior to the 1976 coup.[36]

These responses to Astiz's heroic confession challenged power relations in Argentine society. They revealed that Astiz was no longer feared and that his threats of violence proved idle. To further demonstrate his loss of power, citizens confronted him directly. Protesters greeted Astiz at each of his court appearances, demanding justice and loudly assailing him as "assassin," "torturer," "genocidist," and "son of a bitch." Protesters sometimes pelted Astiz with eggs and bottles. When a man walked through one rally shouting "Viva Astiz!" the crowd seized and pummeled him, bloodying his face. Authorities heightened security and crowd control inside and outside the courthouse to prevent violent eruptions. Even so, members of Sons and Daughters of the Disappeared (H.I.J.O.S.), posing as law students, occupied the front row of spectator seats in the courtroom and took off their jackets to expose T-shirts emblazoned with the messages "Jail for those who Torture" and "Jail for Assassins," as they sang their trademark song: "Just like the Nazis, it's going to happen to you." Posters of Astiz appeared around Buenos Aires with the caption "On behalf of our comrades, spit on him." The Mothers of the Plaza de Mayo plastered posters of Astiz near his favorite boîtes, urging young women to avoid consorting with a known assassin. Astiz could not travel within Argentina without being confronted by protests. When he arrived to visit an uncle in Luján, protesters turned him away. In Rosario 150 people took to the streets to condemn him. A number of towns deemed him persona non grata.[37] His escape hatches disappeared: fewer towns offered refuge; international indictments prevented exile; and his enemies spotted him even when he used back entrances and undisclosed exits. Protests even confronted Astiz in his own social circles. Two prominent individuals from the military and legal communities, for example, left a wedding reception in Bahia Blanca when Astiz arrived.[38] His natural allies in military and civil society began to distance themselves. Aldo Rico, responsible for a military uprising that prompted the Due Obedience Law, simply referred to Astiz's comments as "lamentable." The former general Antonio Domingo Bussi, found guilty for a massacre in Tucumán in the 1970s, pardoned as a result of Due Obedience Law, and subsequently elected governor of Tucumán, publicly repudiated Astiz's declarations: "It is time to definitively heal the scars. Returning to the past never helps."[39] Few of Astiz's former political and military allies remained loyal to him.

Astiz endured verbal and physical assaults in the restaurants, bars, dance halls, and other social venues he frequented. A former ESMA prisoner, for example, spotted Astiz in the famous Bariloche ski resort. Yelling "son of a bitch" and "murderer of teenagers," he punched Astiz in the face twice and kicked him in the genitals. Explaining his response, the former prisoner stated, "What happened at that moment is that I could not bear the reality of seeing him walking the street. . . . I felt I had to do something. . . . It was a punch of indignation, of impotence."[40] But it was also a punch that symbolized a power shift in Argentine society. On the street in Buenos Aires, two university students without any direct connection to the disappeared or torture centers recognized Astiz in his car. They spat at him, smashed his car, and punched him in the face, knocking out a dental prosthesis. Passengers on a city bus applauded and shouted their approval. One woman yelled, "Good boys! Kill the son of a bitch!"[41] Astiz initially pressed charges against these physical assaults, but they became too frequent and costly to pursue. He thus changed his attitude, referring to his tolerance as an "act of service for the country and the [military] institution."[42]

The human-rights community viewed these vigilante forms of justice against Astiz as a natural, but unfortunate, result of his legal immunity from prosecution. Nora Cortinas remarked that she found it "healthy when people see a pardoned murderer on the street that they react the way they feel at that moment." But she added, "We don't want revenge; we continue insisting on justice, that all of the genocidaires are put in jail." She and the former CELS director Emilio Mignone blamed impunity for the increase in vigilante acts against former perpetrators.[43]

Astiz's confession mobilized those demanding legal prosecution for past authoritarian state crimes. With local legal remedies cut off, groups petitioned Judge María Servini de Cubria to arrest and extradite Astiz to stand trial abroad.[44] Human-rights activists together with the political coalition Frente Grande marched through Buenos Aires streets holding a huge banner and shouting, "Astiz assassin! Extradition now!" They also prepared a letter to the minister of external affairs criticizing President Fernando de la Rúa's stance against extradition.

For former political prisoners, Astiz's prosecution seemed largely symbolic. They considered Astiz no worse, and maybe even less evil, than other military-regime officials. Astiz's visibility and symbolic power, however, allowed them to advance justice claims. As one survivor stated, "Unfortunately we needed symbols. I'm sorry it was Astiz. . . . I wish it had been Acosta."[45] Jorge "El Tigre" Acosta had been Astiz's superior in the ESMA and Naval Task Force 3.3.2, and was described by most of the surviving prisoners as a psychopath who enjoyed the pain he caused others. By staying behind the scenes, he avoided public notoriety.[46] A navy insider described Astiz as an "emblematic figure," who along with Massera received all the blame for the dictatorship's excesses, as if no one else had been involved.[47]

Astiz, and not Acosta, became the face of the regime because he sought attention through high-risk behavior.[48] During the dictatorship an ESMA survivor claimed, "He had to have an audience. . . . We had to be at his disposition."[49] He dated Montonera women, dressing them up and taking them outside the torture center. When he infiltrated the Mothers of the Plaza de Mayo, he publicly confronted the police, posed as a spokesman for the families of disappeared on the BBC, and appeared in weekly marches in the Plaza de Mayo.[50] He engaged prisoners in debates on Marxism. He defended Fidel Castro to his superiors. He asked to go undercover as a Jewish man named Abramovich.[51] The *Trespuntos* interview seemed consistent with the thrill Astiz derived from risky behavior.

Many, however, consider the interview an ambush, claiming that Astiz's lack of intelligence prevented him from accurately calculating public response to his confession. One navy officer stated, "He isn't as brilliant as they would like you to believe. He has the mentality of a twenty-four-year-old. He hasn't matured at all."[52] Arrogance, not skill, characterized for some the Task Force 3.3.2 that had trained Astiz: "There are naval officers, ex-montoneros, and researchers on the ESMA theme who maintain that the GT 3.3.2 functioned like perfect clockwork, with a rigorous logic behind precise objectives. But some police who tried to teach the navy how to repress more efficiently and certain surviving non-Montoneros from the ESMA assert that the GT acted in a chaotic frenzy, resulting from their own ineptitude for the tasks they had to fulfill. This book inclines toward the theory of disorder and error."[53] Puzzled by Astiz's behavior, a judge ordered a psychological evaluation to determine whether Astiz could understand the consequences of his actions and if his "unusual pride" resulted from pleasure derived by causing others' pain. The results determined Astiz to be "normal."[54]

Others explain the "ambush theory" according to Astiz's characteristic submission to others. Alfredo Bravo, a deputy from the Frepaso Party, described Astiz's subordination in this way: "Cerruti describes the Astiz automaton. . . . He arrived in the morning, they told him who he should go kidnap, he did it, and he brought them dead or alive. There didn't seem to be any superior intelligence that he needed, nor any ideological project."[55] This view suggested that someone encouraged Astiz to confess. Captain Aurelio "Za Za" Martínez, according to Cerruti, told Astiz to accept the interview to burnish his image. Others suggested that Massera masterminded the confession, with Martínez's help, to discredit the Menem government and the navy leadership under Admiral Carlos Marrón and thus restore Massera's prestige.[56] Massera himself provided no insights in this regard, refusing to become "meat for the tigers."[57] He did, however, refer to Astiz as "crazy" and his confession as "foolish."[58]

Astiz claimed in court that Cerruti had ambushed him. He charged her with violating professional ethics by publishing an off-the-record conversation. Some journalists believed Astiz's assertions, pointing to his typical reluctance to speak on the record; they claimed that Astiz had frequently agreed to speak, but only after assurances that his comments would be attributed to "an informant," "a source," or "a friend."[59] Books about Astiz included no personal interviews, relying instead on second-hand accounts. Tina Rosenberg wrote, "I knew he had never talked to reporters."[60] Even in Cerruti's interview he confirmed his reluctance to speak publicly, claiming that he had not given an interview in seventeen years.[61] Cerruti quoted from him thus: "I don't want to talk. For this reason I don't give interviews. I won't allow my picture to be taken. Because it's over; there is no reason to talk anymore."[62] Indeed, Astiz described his effort to stay silent as a "war": "I was in four wars and more than thirty battles: I was in the war against subversion, I had infiltrated the Chilean enemy lines when we decided that we wouldn't go to war, I was in the Malvinas, and I was an observer in Algiers. This is my fifth war: staying quiet. I have had to endure a lot of time without saying anything, that's my last war."[63] Cerruti denied that she had won that war, asserting instead that Astiz, as in the Malvinas, had surrendered without a fight and later lied about the circumstances.

Cerruti described the interview not as an ambush but as a convergence of interests. She had sought a story on the hotly debated issues of razing the ESMA and transforming it into a memorial site and of eroding the immunity laws. Martínez had desired a place in the limelight again. Astiz she viewed as an unwise military officer who had felt cornered by society, abandoned by his colleagues, and anxious to look again like the good guy in a cowboy western movie. Cerruti accepted that Astiz might have misinterpreted her background. He might have mistaken her for a "navy brat," since he knew that she had grown up near the naval base of Bahía Blanca. He might also have misread her friendship with Acosta's daughter as signifying sympathy toward the military regime. A cursory glance at her book *Herederos del silencio* (Generation of silence) would have dispelled such illusions. In any event, Cerutti denied that she had agreed to an off-the-record interview with Astiz, claiming to never hold "informal conversations" with murderers. Astiz, she asserted, understood her plans to publish the results and even called her after the interview to clarify a statement, presumably before the article went to press.

Astiz publicly challenged Cerruti. He denied outright the particular comments about Balza and Menem. He also claimed that as a military man he would have referred to "combat," not "killing." He denied any knowledge about the deaths of journalists or leftist leaders. Astiz confirmed his most incendiary comment about his preparedness as an assassin, but characterized it as a joke.[64] Astiz concluded, "I didn't say what the journalist said I said, and I emphatically insist that I don't think or feel about the past or the present in the way she has made it appear that I think and feel."[65] To set the record straight he stated, "I was a navy official by trade, and I dedicated my life to an institution that I respect and love. Because of my position in the navy, I was required to participate in a harmful conflict in which I believe I performed correctly and on the right side."[66]

Judge Claudio Bonadío ruled in favor of Cerruti, rejecting Astiz's charges against her. He questioned why Astiz would submit to an "informal conversation" with an unknown journalist during such a "charged political climate" without demanding a formal agreement that the interview remain off the record. The judge concluded, "There was never an explicit agreement that the interview would not be published. Astiz knew what he was doing, its importance, and the effect his words would have on the public."[67]

In response to the judge's findings, Astiz's allies presented an alternative image: a man of Astiz's integrity could not have made the comments Cerruti attributed to him. The lawyer Juan Aberg Cobo—Astiz's friend and later his publicity agent—referred to Astiz as "loyal," "loved," and misunderstood by the media.[68] Even before Astiz's *Trespuntos* interview, Aberg hinted to the press corps that they had failed to discredit Astiz despite their efforts to do so: "I'll tell you something so that you understand. We were walking along the street together one day not long ago when an older couple stopped us. 'Are you Astiz?' the man asked. 'Yes,' Astiz answered, a little worried about what his reaction might be. But the man put out his hand. 'I want to thank you for everything you have done for our country.' . . . And you know, he didn't say anything. But as we continued walking I saw from the corner of my eye how the tears streamed down his cheeks."[69]

Astiz's supporters turned out for this trial. Fifteen character witnesses, including four former heads of the navy, described Astiz in superlative terms, as a "gentleman," "exuding a positive, civilized, not at all violent, attitude in the navy," a "role model" for young people, and a "democrat."[70] This delegation condemned his sentence as "the clearest example of the illegality, persecution, and discrimination to which those of us who wear the uniform of the victorious fighters against terrorism are subjected." They further used the trial to show how Astiz's confession had diverted the country from peace: "It will not be possible to achieve the formula of conciliation that we have been demanding, and to definitively bury the hatred and revenge that continue devastating the project of coexistence in our country."[71]

Astiz had attempted to project this image of personal and military integrity in the *Trespuntos* interview. He claimed, for example, to have objected to the regime's kidnapping of babies: "No, I never [kidnapped babies], and I strongly opposed this. This was one of my big challenges; I returned babies."[72] A former political prisoner confirmed Astiz's story, recounting how he had posed as her husband (whom the navy had disappeared) so that she could baptize her child born in prison, how he had allowed the child to visit her family, and how he had helped her leave the country with her child.[73] He continued visiting her parents after her exile, mistaking as affection their reliance on him to guarantee their family's safety. Astiz also believed political prisoners learned to like and respect him for his integrity: "What they don't want to tell, and for that reason most of the survivors don't talk about the ESMA, is that the majority of them collaborated and even liked us. Because people begin to like those with whom they have to live over time."[74]

Astiz viewed his loyalty to colleagues and superiors as central to his military integrity. He refused to "rat on" guilty colleagues, even if his testimony would clear his name. He explained that the eyewitness to Hagelin's murder identified a blond, *brown*-eyed man, not the *blue*-eyed Astiz. Astiz intimated that he could, but would not, name the murderer: "I'm not going to tell. I speak for myself. I'm not like Scilingo. This is why they respect me so much in the navy. I'm never going to speak against a colleague."[75]

The activities that might have damaged his reputation as a gentle-man soldier, he denied. Job specialization, he claimed, prevented him from knowing about deaths and disappearances: "I don't know [how subversives were killed], I wasn't part of that."[76] "I never tortured," he claimed, "It wasn't my job." He also could not identify any specific victims or events. "I don't remember. I remember only a very few names," he claimed, because the raids became "routine, everyday jobs." Or, he stated, his memory failed him because "I did a lot [of operations]. It was a daily task. I arrived in the morning, they gave me my orders and I went out to do them."[77]

By the time of his trial, Astiz claimed to have forgotten even the details he had discussed in the *Trespuntos* article. When Nora Cortinas asked him about his infiltration of the Mothers of the Plaza de Mayo, he pretended not to remember. "You understand," he explained, "that a lot of time has passed." In denying memory of the ESMA's location and Massera's position during the dictatorship, he exposed his am-nesia as a strategy to derail the legal process against him.[78]

Goñi considers Astiz's shift from heroism to amnesia and denial detrimental to democracy. Astiz's confession broke the pact of silence implicit in the security apparatus. Open discussion, public contesta-tion, and political engagement over the past and its impact on the present democratic system flourished in that environment. That ended with the "law of silence" imposed after Astiz's confession, dis-charge from the military, trial, and sentence. The law of silence termi-nated the possibility of debate. The military, democratic government, and elements of the human-rights community reinforced the silence. Perpetrators remained quiet to avoid public and private reprisals— including violent assaults, shunning, and the loss of privacy, salary, pension, insurance, and status—or prosecution.[79] As problematic as heroic confessions may be for exposing the truth about the past, Goñi considers them preferable to the absence of political engagement of the past and its influence over the present.

Argument

But Goñi overstates the imposition of a law of silence in Argentina. Even after Astiz stopped talking, his case generated discussion. For example, debate erupted over the conditions of his detention. Mercedes Meroño, of the Mothers of the Plaza de Mayo, reflected on Astiz's "holding cell" at the Azul military base, which included a chalet reserved for high-ranking military officers, a golf course, and a swimming pool: "I believe that this sentence is almost a prize for Astiz. It ridicules the people and seems like a perverse game in which we judge him but we don't judge him; the [military] is guilty but they are not guilty."[80] The charges themselves bred cynicism among victims and survivors, but as Cerruti stated, "We all know that Astiz should be condemned for what he did and not his declarations to the press. But the only thing we can celebrate is that in this country it is prohibited to defend state terrorism."[81] Some viewed his fine and suspended sentence as insignificant in light of his acts. Yet no form of justice could have adequately compensated for his crimes, as the son of one of Astiz's victims recounts: "I wouldn't want to kill him. Perhaps it is utopian, but I'd like it if he had to live with [what he did] for the rest of his life. Or put him in jail so that he pays for what he did, so that the whole world knows he's guilty, so that he doesn't feel invincible, and so that he doesn't feel that he was right. If he's killed, he is going to die thinking that he was right. No. Somehow he needs to know that he is not right."[82]

Indeed, Astiz faced the most severe punishment he could imagine: a loss of identity. He had described his fierce attachment to the military to Cerruti: "No, I never married," he said. "The navy is my life, my family, my home."[83] By stripping his military rank, the military high command robbed Astiz of his identity and pride. Journalists reported with unsuppressed glee when Astiz answered "unemployed" to a judge's question about his profession.

Hebe de Bonafini, of the Mothers of the Plaza de Mayo Association, worried that Astiz would become a celebrity: "What seems wrong to me is that now the media will begin to look for him and pay him so that he can tell how he kidnapped and tortured, like they did with Scilingo."[84] Astiz did become a celebrity, but more infamous than famous. With his image so tainted and out of his control, he withdrew into silence, denial, and amnesia. His supporters could not overcome the public stigma. Instead of promoting the regime, or his own heroism, Astiz's confession isolated and discredited him and his ideas. Even those who might have otherwise shared his views distanced themselves from him.

COMPARING HEROIC CONFESSIONS

Astiz's confession reveals how heroic confessions can do as much, and maybe even more, to catalyze democratic debate over the past than remorseful ones. While resurrecting the regime's language of military valor, they provide an opportunity to contest that vision of the regime and its past acts. As the journalist Horacio Verbitsky contends, even the "efforts by Alfonsín and Menem to impose forgetting and impunity produced the paradoxical effect of deepening social conscience around the facts" of the country's recent history.[85] To have one of the regime's "gentleman sailors" admit to the systematic use of atrocities—even if boasting about them—made it impossible for the regime's supporters to pretend otherwise. For bystanders to hear that groups within the active duty military still consider coups and killing an acceptable form of political engagement makes palpable the danger of impunity and the false reassurance that the past remains in the past. Astiz's confession and its aftermath show how different audiences can use heroic confessions to advance particular political goals, stimulate debate, and even equalize some of the terms of that debate.

"Superspy." Who perpetrators are, what they have done, and how they present themselves are key components of heroic confessions. Astiz enjoyed notoriety even before his confession appeared in *Trespuntos*; indeed, Cerruti interviewed him because of his reputation. Who he was, and what he had done, primed his audience to confront or defend him.

Craig Williamson had a similar reputation in South Africa. His background and accomplishments as apartheid's top spy attracted public attention. From a well-off English upbringing, Williamson had attended exclusive and liberal schools that turned out white progressive supporters of the liberation movement. But Williamson, defying his past, or perhaps exploiting it, joined the apartheid police, infiltrating and killing those elites who shared his social background. First, he infiltrated the anti-apartheid student movement National Union of South African Students (NUSAS). Later, falsely claiming threats to his life, he left South Africa and infiltrated the Geneva-based International University Exchange Fund (IUEF), which maintained extensive ANC contacts throughout the world. As a member of the South African police, Williamson orchestrated the bombing of anti-apartheid activists and centers outside South Africa's borders. He described his work in heroic terms: "The enemy was blowing us up and killing us, and we were blowing them up and killing them. We were not policemen, we were soldiers used to fighting a secret war."[86]

Williamson seemed to fashion himself as an apartheid-era James Bond, and some of his exploits—most notably the bombing of the London ANC headquarters in 1982—may have fit that image. But he undermined the image by sending parcel bombs that killed Ruth First in Mozambique in 1982 and Jeanette Schoon and her six-year-old daughter, Katryn, in Angola in 1984. Williamson apologized at the TRC for Katryn's murder: "I want to say I am sorry. What I did was wrong. . . . I believed at the time that it was justified, but I never deliberately targeted the innocent."[87] Williamson had tried out other responses earlier. At the time of the murder, for example, he blamed the Schoons for using their children as "bomb detectors" by allowing them to play with suspicious parcels in their yard. By the time of the TRC he could state unequivocally, "The killing of a child can never, in any form, be justified."[88]

By defending his killing of First and Jeanette Schoon as honorable, Williamson provoked debate. He described both women as "our revolutionary enemies," but the media countered by portraying him as a "vindictive" man whose targets posed no real threat to the apartheid state.[89] Neither First nor Schoon had ever been involved in the armed wing of the ANC. Both were teachers in exile, posing only a distant ideological threat to the apartheid regime. Perhaps recognizing that his justification of the murders stood on very thin ice, Williamson suggested that the bomb that killed First had been intended for her husband, Joe Slovo. As the head of the South African Communist Party and the ANC army in exile, Slovo could have constituted a legiti-

Craig Williamson was known as a superspy for his infiltration of anti-apartheid movements while serving in the apartheid-police intelligence branch.
Photo by Jillian Edelstein. Reproduced by permission.

mate political target for the apartheid state. But Williamson could not explain why he would have sent a parcel bomb intended for Slovo to First's office in the Centre for African Studies at Maputo's Eduardo Mandlane University.[90] Moreover, Williamson's killing of Schoon and her daughter enabled the media to portray Williamson's modus operandi as inept or vindictive, neither characteristic flattering to a "superspy." Reproducing photographs of the young and smiling Jeanette Schoon and her daughter, and of the fashionable and stately Ruth First, the media further undermined Williamson's defense that he had successfully combatted the external communist threat to South Africa. Instead, by killing these three individuals, the media suggested, Williamson had blundered horribly or, at worst, had deliberately targeted them in a terrorist act.[91] As one reporter wrote: "Killing Slovo, the chief of staff of Umkhonto we Sizwe and head of ANC special operations, would arguably have been an act of war. Killing his wife was an act of naked terror, no matter how radical her anti-apartheid politics. The death of the Schoons was no less barbaric in its callousness. Rather than providing a justification, the pages of evidence on the density of Cuban anti-aircraft sites around Lubango, where they were murdered, and the suggestion that the young girl and her mother were somehow assisting the Cuban military against the South African defense force, only underline the terrorist nature of the act."[92]

Williamson lacked Astiz's panache, which led to far less flattering media portrayals. Rather than likening him to a Kennedy, one journalist poked fun at Williamson's "role of anticommunist gladiator, up there with Ronald Reagan and Margaret Thatcher, the winners of the Cold War."[93] Many commented on his size: "There is Craig Williamson, whose gargantuan girth gives him more the appearance of a trencherman than a policeman and whose taste for personal betrayal won him the tag of South Africa's 'superspy.'"[94] Others connected his size and background to psychological disorders: "His bulk is his protection. . . . Beneath that fat is a thin man in pain. . . . His size, his deep allegiance to a system that despised his Anglo-Saxon background even while it worked to recruit English-speaking supporters, his videos of ANC attacks to justify his own bombings, and his hours of lectures to the committee on communism suggest that something is hiding in there. . . . Certainly, if Williamson were to tell the whole truth he would have to delve deep into his own psyche."[95]

That psyche is what obsessed the press, particularly the white liberal press, and its readers. Williamson posed a conundrum. As a man with every opportunity and all the capacity and connections to choose a different path, he decided to work for the apartheid state and kill its unarmed opponents.

> He is the product of the finest schools English-speaking Johannesburg had to offer. He is articulate. He is intelligent. He possesses business acumen as his venture supplying a range of commodities to the Angolan government shows. . . . And yet he found it necessary to make a home for himself at the heart of a system declared a crime against humanity by the member countries of the United Nations; a home at the heart of a culture that was not his, a language that was not his. . . . Is this why so many middle-class white South Africans have taken a disproportionately close interest in his application [for amnesty]? Their abhorrence signals something beyond the fact that many of them knew and valued one or more of his victims, knew him when he masqueraded as an opponent of the system. Many of them have attended the hearings, many more need to talk about him.[96]

Williamson, perhaps recognizing his limited success in achieving heroic status from his unheroic deeds, shifted toward the less intrepid image of the unsung hero, the loyal and hardworking patriot. Williamson's lawyer stated, "Advocate George Bizos [the lawyer for the First and Schoon families] painted Williamson as duplicitous but everything points to how well he did his very difficult job."[97] Williamson challenged his "superspy" image: "Quite frankly, I wish I had never heard that term. I am sick and tired of this war I have been fighting for 26 years. I want to get away from the urban legends and half-truths which surrounds [sic] my life as a spy."[98]

The confessional performances by Astiz and Williamson illustrate how audiences exploit contradictions in perpetrators' self-presentations to challenge their heroism. By emphasizing physical characteristics, grooming, or posture, audiences can replace heroic with cowardly imagery. They can also exploit particular acts, flaws, or blemishes in a perpetrator's background to challenge heroic labels like "superspy" or "gentleman sailor." Rumors circulated about Williamson's illegal financial gains, for example. Just as the once untouchable heroes Alberto Fujimori, Augusto Pinochet, and Ferdinand Marcos discovered, corruption accusations can dramatically curtail support.

Their adversaries' acts and theater of operations also affect perpetrators' heroic status. Few will hail perpetrators for their use of violence against unarmed children and women. Killing detainees in a clandestine torture center lacks the heroic cachet of the battlefield. Because certain acts lack heroism, particularly summary execution, rape, or the killing of nonmilitary targets, perpetrators usually avoid confessing to them.

Torture, however, is a special category. At least in the abstract, military and government officials defend it. The former Brazilian dictator Ernesto Geisel, for example, stated: "I believe that torture in certain situations becomes necessary, to obtain confessions."[99] The typical "ticking bomb" defense for torture, however, involves extracting from a known terrorist enough information to safely defuse a bomb that is about to kill innocent victims, usually children. Torture in this case is perceived as heroic because it effectively saves lives. The Brazilian journalist Elio Gaspari states, "What makes torture attractive is the fact that it works."[100] Another Brazilian torturer admitted, "Things got complicated when I discovered that the method produced rapid results. All you had to do was take them to the torture chamber, and you had it [the information]."[101]

Justifications for torture in the abstract, however, rarely coincide with its everyday manifestations. Torturers never know for certain if children or other innocent victims are in danger. They also do not know if the detained individual has the knowledge they need to save innocent victims. Torture victims, moreover, often die holding on to their secrets or lacking the information the torturer seeks. The information torture victims provide to end torture and save their own lives may be fabricated or misleading, sidetracking investigations that might save lives.

During the early months of the U.S. war in Iraq, the ticking-bomb justification prevailed. U.S. citizens tolerated torture, at least in the abstract, as a way to find Osama Bin Laden, protect U.S. citizens from terrorism, and win the war. Public opinion began to shift, however, once photographs of torture from the U.S. prison Abu Ghraib were broadcast. Those images made clear that torture was not abstract, but involved the debasing of individuals for unspecific purposes. Soldiers and officers faced trials for conducting methods previously accepted as legitimate. No confession could transform their acts into heroism. The visual imagery undermined heroic defenses of torture.

The more elevated the perpetrator's status, the less likely it is that

specific acts of violence will undermine their heroic status. Such perpetrators possess the trappings of power that allow them to retain
their authority long after they have left office. High-level perpetrators
look like, and even represent, power. Their status, moreover, dis-
tances them from unheroic acts that soil the image of lower-level
officials. They use "plausible deniability" arguments to claim that
they did not know the specifics of day-to-day operations by rogue
officers or soldiers. They often succeed at hiding their complicity in
state terrorism behind the vague and noble language of war, patriotism, duty, and leadership.

Heroic confessions might succeed in obliterating debate if they
could remain abstracted from actual and unheroic events and contradictory images of perpetrators and their acts. Heroic confessions,
however, offer audiences an opportunity to present counter-images of
barbarism, depravity, and incompetence that subverts the glamour
once associated with "war."

"Get Lost!" Perpetrators, even discredited ones, may resurrect their
heroic status by seizing control of the stage and the confessional process. The apartheid leader P. W. Botha tried this strategy. He refused
on principle to appear before the "blatantly biased" TRC or to apologize for "the struggle against the revolutionary communist onslaught
against our country." Botha literally and figuratively held court outside the TRC, forcing the press to come to him, replying with his
signature political banter, complete with the wagging finger. He told
the TRC to "get lost," and he succeeded. Using a technical legal maneu-
ver, he outwitted the commission's lawyers, avoided a subpoena to
appear at the TRC, distanced himself from apartheid atrocities, and
retained his heroic status among his supporters. The journalist Rian
Malan described his performance: "It was vintage Botha, and entirely
predictable. Afrikaners stood up behind him, as if cheering a rugby
try. '[South Africa] is on a most dangerous path and heading for an
abyss,' he said last week, glaring into the cameras like a cantankerous
old buffalo. 'They are attempting to destroy my image and, through
me, to humiliate my people.' It was brave and pathetic."[102]

Botha's reenactment of power worked, but only because of his
political skill. He avoided the TRC with legal mechanisms. But he also
condemned it for fueling "racism and division" in the country. Botha,
in other words, trotted out his old nostalgic power, but packaged in

democratic wrapping: "The answer is that we Boers are terminally fed up. Even those of us who were initially sympathetic to the truth commission have been alienated by the princely salaries of the commissioners, the flashy cars they drive courtesy of the taxpayer, and, above all, by the insufferable self-righteousness with which they go about their business."[103]

Botha could successfully control the staging of his confession by controlling the stage itself. He refused to appear on a stage where he would appear guilty. His heroic confession occurred offstage, in the media, where he reasserted his power and withstood threats to it.

The former Yugoslav president Slobodan Milosevic pursued a similar strategy, but despite his best attempts, he failed to create his own stage. His refusal to participate in court ended with his capture, arrest, and trial at the International Criminal Tribunal for Yugoslavia (ICTY) in the Hague. So he controlled that stage with his oratory skill. He condemned the ICTY as "illegal," because it "does not exist in legal framework but exclusively in the media framework, because it in itself represents a means of war and part of the crime that is being perpetuated against the Serbian people."[104] He presented his heroic mission as combating lies propagated around the world by those who hated Serbia and the Serbs and of correcting the errors created by the tribunal: "Contrary to the intentions of the creators of this unlawful Tribunal, [you] have enabled the world to get a glimpse of the truth and to start to understand the truth as it stands. And in the proceedings to come, this will be made even more evident and the truth will be victorious."[105]

When perpetrators seize control of the stage—either physically or through oratory prowess—they reinforce their heroic image and power. The Argentine Navy admiral and junta leader Emilio Massera appeared in court with all the trappings of power: erect posture and clenched jaw, navy-commander uniform with brass buttons and medals of honor, starched collar, polished shoes, and manicured fingernails. He asserted his oratory strength, commanding, "No one should have to defend himself for winning a just war." He took charge, "I accept responsibility but not guilt, because I am simply not guilty."[106] He pretended that the democratic government had no control over him. But, of course, it did. The sight of Massera in the court's dock of the accused receiving a guilty verdict and a life sentence shifted power away from military rulers and toward victims and survivors of past violence.

Massera tried to reassert his power offstage. After his presidential pardon he appeared on *Hora Clave*, an Argentine political talk show. He controlled the production. The cameras came to him. He set himself up in an office filled with books and trophies. He read uninterrupted from a prepared text with his reading glasses on, until his time ran out. And then he was gone, without any comments or questions from the talk-show host, panel of experts, or television audience. He said what he wanted, where he wanted, and without response. Despite his manipulation of the medium, the program had little effect. Massera repeated the old (war) defense for violence; he excused "excesses and errors," and confidently trusted history, not the newspapers, to absolve him. Massera controlled his stage, but failed to resurrect his power.

A perpetrator's capacity to control the stage depends on the nature of the media coverage. Unwilling to risk negative coverage, Massera received little attention at all. Cerruti gave Astiz full coverage, but turned his heroic confession against him, reviling rather than flattering him. The art of staging lies in asserting power not only over the venue but also over the debate that takes place within it. Few confessing perpetrators have enjoyed power over both.

"Twisted Rationalizations." "Torture is rarely recognized and never openly defended," states Gaspari. "All of the architecture surrounding its defense comes from twisted rationalizations."[107] Such rationalizations, whether about torture or other methods of authoritarian state violence, are at the core of heroic confessions. The audience is burdened with the project of untangling the rationalizations from the unheroic acts they disguise.

Heroic texts involve pithy language and few details, leaving much to audience interpretation about the past and its meaning for the present democratic era. Ten years after the end of Brazil's dictatorship, for example, the military president Emilio Garrastazú Médici (1969–1974) summarized his heroic role: "It was a war, after which it was possible to return peace to Brazil. I ended terrorism in this country. If we had not accepted the war, if we had not taken drastic measures, we would still have terrorism today."[108] Similarly, just when the TRC had begun to expose atrocities, P. W. Botha glorified the heroic struggle of his apartheid regime.

Can you all hear me? Those who can't hear me put up your hand and salute me! I'm a believer and I'm blessed by my creator. I stand by everyone who carried out legal instructions in our struggle against revolutionary and communist attacks on our fatherland. This total onslaught went hand in hand with some of the most gruesome acts of violence against the civilian population. But the truth commission and some politicians conveniently forget this. It's incredible how short their memories are. No struggle is fought by only one side and no cause is so noble as to justify violent murders and destruction. I'm talking about the liberation camps outside our borders where people were intimidated and tortured. The necklace murders. The incitement of people. I'm not prepared to apologize for the views I voiced on removing racial discrimination. Likewise, I'm not prepared to apologize for my government's legal actions in resisting attacks on our political system. I reject the vilification of brave soldiers and policemen. They're not that bad. They are the ones who maintained order in this country day and night. I honor them. I salute them. Read my parliamentary speeches and you will see that this is a hollow cry—this parrot-cry of apartheid. While I expressly stated in the open that apartheid is an Afrikaans word and can be easily replaced by a proper positive term: good neighborliness. Good neighborliness. . . . Who's laughing? Who's laughing?[109]

Regime supporters survive political transitions and attempt to influence public opinion. If they were only relics of the past, they might even appear laughable and quaint. Botha comes close to that image. But the memory is too fresh and his powerlessness untested. Because heroic confessions implicitly or explicitly promise the regime's return to restore "order" if the democratic system goes "too far," audiences contest them whenever and wherever they appear.

Skillful heroic confessions update their language, rather than rely on archaic war metaphors and euphemisms. They also expropriate language used by their opponents. Botha, therefore, refers to the TRC as "justifying violent murders" and congratulates himself for fighting racial discrimination. In a similar move, the Argentine police perpetrator Miguel Etchecolatz calls for "nunca más," or never again, echoing the words of the human-rights community, but with the intent to end "subversion," not state terrorism.

At times, the heroic confession is a perpetrator's only defense. The case of the Chilean collaborator Miguel Estay (El Fanta) is illustrative. A relatively unknown Communist Party militant before his capture and detention in 1974, Estay agreed to collaborate as a security agent in Dicomcar, an intelligence division of the armed forces. He participated in slitting the throats of three Communist Party leaders in 1985.[110] In an inquiry that year, Estay initially denied his involvement. But after material proof connected him to the murder in 1993, he retracted his earlier statement and confessed. Remorse would have conflicted with Estay's earlier denial.[111] A heroic confession, on the other hand, could weave together his complex history. It made sense. Estay revisited his past and his conversion to the authoritarian regime's vision of the world: "My involvement with the PC [Communist Party] had been so great that I had no alternative. I felt that it was my obligation to work against what I myself had helped to create."[112] The heroic confession transformed Estay from a coward who had betrayed his comrades into a brave cold warrior. Estay expressed regret about the murders, but only because he had failed to interrogate his victims and avert future Communist Party atrocities before he killed them.[113]

Replete with ambiguities, contradictions, imprecision, and uncertainty, heroic confessions are open to challenge. Audiences can dispute confessions with evidence. Or they can reinterpret events to show the unheroic nature of those events. They can present additional information that impugns the claims made by perpetrators. Heroic confessions almost seem to be set up for audiences to strike down.

"Over the Sights of an AK-47." When Craig Williamson's lawyer asked Marius Schoon, the husband and father of two of his victims, to meet with him "in the spirit of reconciliation," Schoon refused. He considered the request manipulative, an attempt to secure Williamson's amnesty on false pretenses: "For a legal representative to place me in the position where I publicly have to state that I do not want to be reconciled is both embarrassing and unfair. I felt I was being badgered."[114] Schoon, instead, took the opportunity to repeat a comment he had made earlier about Williamson: "I haven't come away feeling cleansed by the truth. I have no intention of speaking to Williamson ever in my life. . . . The only time I want to see Williamson is over the sights of an AK-47." Schoon died of cancer before the TRC granted Williamson amnesty.[115]

Schoon's response represents the pain and anger engendered

among victims and survivors by heroic confessions. The act of violence and the loss to victims and survivors alone would incense them, but by subsequently boasting about their exploits, perpetrators add insult to injury. It is no wonder that perpetrators who have issued heroic confessions travel with bodyguards, seek hidden entrances and exits, and isolate themselves. They must stay alert to avoid violent reprisals in courtrooms, on ski slopes, or on city streets. Potential avengers include not only the direct victims or survivors of "heroic" violence, but also members of society who wonder what it takes—beyond truth commissions, trials, testimonials, and memory projects—to change attitudes about the past. Heroic confessions do not simply endorse an authoritarian regime's progress on economic or social fronts; they embrace the state's violence as necessary and valorous. Heroic confessions, in other words, give voice and renewed power to a view that victims and survivors had hoped would erode with the transition from authoritarian rule.

Mobilizing and finding common ground in a shared abhorrence for state terrorism—not only among victims and survivors, but also among regime bystanders, new generations, former regime supporters, current security forces, and the democratic government—prevents despair. Political projects aimed at acknowledgment and knowledge of past violence become a collective healing mechanism to overcome the injury and insult of heroic confessions.

Paradoxically, heroic confessions offer a unique set of opportunities to audiences intent on condemning the violent past and its influence over contemporary democratic politics. Furthermore, the negative response among forces previously allied with perpetrators unites diverse audiences to heroic confessions around the repudiation of human rights—an unanticipated outcome. Heroic confessions also keep the memory of the violent past alive, reminding citizens of the atrocities committed by the authoritarian regime and the importance of remaining vigilant against future human-rights violations. Heroic confessions, finally, highlight the danger of immunity from prosecution. Outrage over the amnesty laws that allowed Astiz to promote his heroic vision of the regime's violence contributed to the pressure on the Argentine courts to try past human-rights cases, a process still under way. Schoon's and First's surviving children have challenged Williamson's amnesty on the grounds that their mothers were not legitimate political targets. They hope to have him tried and pros-

ecuted for his violation of human rights. The attention generated by
Williamson's heroic confession may help them in their endeavor.[116]

CONCLUSION

As if reflecting on heroic confessions, a scholar of memory writes,
"Memory is never shaped in a vacuum; the motives of memory are
never pure."[117] In the case of heroic confessions, the motive is not
simply to restore the dignity of the old regime and its security forces.
In many cases that motivation shrouds a more personal goal: to clear
one's name of wrongdoing by claiming a different version of the past.
It might also mask the desire to reclaim power, not necessarily over
the government, but over history. Underlying that history is the possibility of remobilization: the regime may need to reemerge if threats
to the country recur in the future. Heroic confessions, in other words,
constitute what the scholar James Scott calls "enactments of power,"
which employ "affirmation, concealment, euphemization and stigma-
tization, and finally, the appearance of unanimity" to sustain the official and dominant version of the past.[118] This is especially true since
the audiences for these confessions are not only victims but also colleagues and supporters who may need to be reminded of the official
line. Scott states, "Elites are also consumers of their own performance."[119] Heroic confessions provide the means to reinforce, maintain, and adjust the official story to sustain its dominance.[120]

Heroic confessions might seem to undermine the possibility of contentious coexistence, to debate, to understand, to accept (without
agreement) different versions of the past and of democracy. Heroic
confessions might seem to impose a hegemonic interpretation of the
past, to overpower competing views. But that has not proved to be the
case. Instead, conflict erupts over heroic confessions as different
groups mobilize in favor of or against them, to silence them or to use
them to advance particular political objectives. Some audiences perceive this conflict and instability as threatening to the democratic
order, but paradoxically offer only the undemocratic alternative of
censorship to end such threats. Contentious coexistence thrives on
the process of forming political positions, contesting viewpoints, and
actively mobilizing to bring about political change.

In addition, heroic confessions involve accountability. Perpetrators
boast about their past acts. In the process they disclose some—albeit

sketchy—details of those events. They provide investigators and the public with clues about events previously shrouded behind silence and denial. Their acceptance of responsibility for past political violence, moreover, makes them accountable, even if courts fail to prosecute. Atrocity becomes connected to specific perpetrators. Knowledge cannot replace personal losses, but the justification for the atrocity can be challenged.

Accountability also disrupts memory poles. Those who previously supported the regime, interpreting the silence as innocence and believing the denials, must confront whether they can continue to support the regime and its ideals once they know the truth about the violence. Some decide they cannot. They join those condemning past practices and share, even if only passively, in the respect for human rights and justice.

✳ Evidence but new consensus was found? Or progress bowr's on?

CHAPTER FOUR

SADISM

You apply the current like this: to the breasts, the nipples, you put two electrodes up here, see, and two in the vagina. And then you turn up the machine and they get an electric shock. . . . If you give them shocks to the head, or the face, or any part of the body, it leaves marks. If you beat the person, if you flog any part of them with a rubber hose filled with steel, you're going to leave marks. But if you give them a bath first, get them nice and wet, and you use the hose with other things that are more important which means you stick a wet cloth on them and zap them two or three times, nothing will show up. People will just laugh at you [if you say you were tortured].—Osvaldo Romo Mena, televised interview, 11 April 1995

IN 1995 OSVALDO ROMO MENA scandalized television audiences with his confession on Miami-based Univision's international cable program *Primer Impacto*. Shown three times in one day in the United States and transmitted throughout Latin America and parts of Europe, Romo's confession offered a rare and disturbing glimpse into the depraved, sadistic pleasure some perpetrators derive from harming their victims. Within the human-rights community, Romo already had something of a reputation before he appeared on television. The Chilean Truth Commission considered no fewer than eighty accusations of rape and other forms of torture by Romo during his two years (1973–1975) as a civilian member of the dictatorship's secret military-police unit, DINA.[1]

Because of Romo's particular role in DINA and his personal style, victims and survivors were able to identify him after the end of the dictatorship. They referred to him as "the personification of terror in 1974 and 1975 and the best known man in . . . DINA," "perhaps one of the cruelest and bloodthirsty torturers," and "proud of his cruelty."[2] They claimed that he was the agent who had picked them up off the

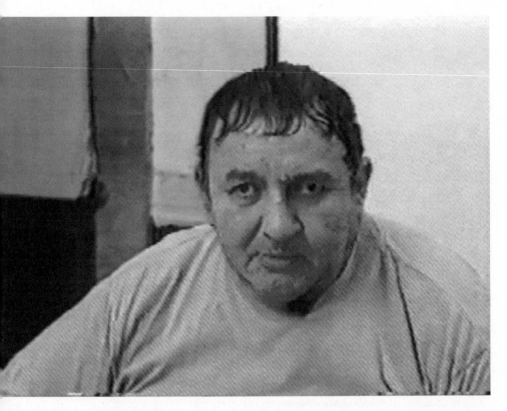

Osvaldo Romo Mena appeared on Univision's *Primer Impacto* on 18 May 1998, recounting atrocities he had committed while working for the Chilean dictatorship's secret military-police unit, DINA.

street, in their homes, or at meeting points secretly arranged with comrades who, under torture by DINA agents, had revealed the plan. They recounted that Romo had sometimes tortured them without blindfolds and sometimes called himself by name. Their family members contended that his penchant for "war booty" led him to enter and steal goods from their homes and in full sight. At other times, he extracted additional goods or money from the families, falsely promising to release the detainees, even when he knew that those relatives had already died.

His nickname Guatón (Big Fat) Romo seems like a term of endearment compared to his menacing presence. During his confession, his looks were hard to ignore: he had a small round head sitting on an almost imperceptible neck, both of which seemed too small for his big, but slumped, shoulders. Ballooning arms connected to huge, clubbish hands with long swollen fingers. One foot dragged behind him when he walked. One of his eyes wandered. His face was covered with gouges, deep pockmarks. His skin was greasy. To cover baldness, the least of his physical deficits, he combed his oily hair forward, like an ancient Roman despot. An extremely large, dirty T-shirt clung to the lumps of flesh on his shoulders and chest. An odor seemed to emanate from his image on the screen, a stench his victims and survivors still remember two decades later.[3] He was, in a word, repulsive.

He transformed his body into an instrument of torture on-screen. His arms and hands acted out the different methods he used: applying imaginary electrodes to nipples, wetting down women's bodies, cranking up the power, and giving jolts of electricity. His face alternated between bliss and delight over his acts, boastful pride in his acumen, and taunting indignation at false accusations. He massaged his hands in apparent pleasure and arousal, interrupting the motion only to simulate how he might use a bolt cutter to snap off fingers or cut through internal organs, which were efforts to hide the identity and evidence of detainees' dead bodies.

His speech patterns intensified the sense of horror. A speech impediment, poor schooling, and eighteen years speaking Portuguese in Brazil produced a garbled Spanish with barely discernible words. Despite the insider terminology he used to describe torture, nonspecialists still understood their debased meaning.[4] Romo appeared coarse, crude, and provocative. And he seemed deliberately so, fixing a stare and cocking his head to one side in an implicit dare to the listener to defy him.

Romo is unlike most perpetrators. He does not have the guy-next-door look that might dissimulate his past as a torturer. And *Primer Impacto* exaggerated his affect to bring out the horror of his acts. Other portrayals presented a less-daunting image of Romo. For example, an earlier interview with Carmen Castillo—a former Chilean political activist who went into exile and became a filmmaker in France —for French television situated Romo at a safe distance from the camera. He is almost invisible, almost inaudible. By keeping Romo in the shadows, avoiding close-ups, and lowering the volume, Castillo robbed Romo of his capacity to threaten. Romo looked and acted more or less respectable, holding his head up straight, keeping his hands still, and wearing a freshly cleaned and pressed white button-down shirt. He did not mention torture himself, but the film's protagonist, his former victim-turned-collaborator Marcia Merino, labeled him a "natural born torturer . . . perverse."[5] Castillo gave center stage to the victims and survivors, not to the torturer.

Romo also appears less revolting in portrayals subsequent to the *Primer Impacto* program. In the many trials in which he appeared, he sported clean clothes, an ordinary haircut, and a stylish goatee. Rather than drag his leg behind him like a figure in a horror movie, he rode in a wheelchair. In fact, his healthy image belied rumors that he had nearly died due to complications resulting from diabetes and high blood pressure, that he was practically blind, and that his leg might require amputation.[6]

Romo's political past, like his image, changed over time and depended on who presented it. Prior to the 1973 coup, Romo had left the Socialist Party to join a splinter party, Unión Socialista Popular, to pressure President Allende for a more radical distribution of rights and income. He had run as a Socialist Party candidate in local elections, participated in slum-dwellers' movements, and even stood next to Allende at a funeral for one of the fallen militants of the Lo Hermida land invasion.[7] Soon after the coup, Romo resurfaced as a civilian member of DINA's Halcón (Falcon) unit, which specialized in infiltrating and destroying the Revolutionary Left Movement (MIR) by kidnapping, interrogating (with torture), and eliminating its leaders and members. Romo's political past ideally situated him for the job, since he could make contact with and identify leaders without raising suspicion.

His rapid incorporation into DINA suggests that he might have worked for the right wing as an agent provocateur or infiltrator prior to the coup. Circumstantial evidence fuels those impressions. Some observers emphasize Romo's flirtation with right-wing politics prior to his "conversion" to socialism. Others mention frequent run-ins with the police and the possibility that he had agreed to infiltrate leftist movements in exchange for his freedom, as he himself maintained after the coup.[8] Romo's own stories contradicted themselves. During the dictatorship, he goaded political prisoners with tales of having infiltrated their movements, but he later insisted that his collaboration with DINA occurred only after the coup, when he began to understand Chile's political history. One of Romo's intrinsic characteristics was his search for recognition and power at any cost.

That Romo confessed, for example, makes little sense except with regard to the visibility it guaranteed. He did not know Nancy Guzmán, the Chilean journalist who interviewed him in his holding cell in the Santiago Penitentiary and who set up Univision's *Primer Impacto* program. As a civilian, Romo did not have immunity from prosecution for human-rights abuses during the dictatorship. Chile's democratic government had successfully extradited Romo from Brazil, where he had been hiding since a 1974 investigation into DINA's activities. Recognizing that he might take the fall for the military dictatorship's human-rights abuses, Romo may have viewed his public confession as leverage over his former superiors. Or he may have anticipated gaining money and fame for it.

Romo met with Guzmán over a six-month period ending on 11 April 1995, when she brought a television crew from Univision and filmed a ninety-minute interview conducted by Mercedes Soler at the prison. A seven-minute version of that interview debuted on *Primer Impacto* on 18 May 1995, and an even shorter version appeared on Chilean television. Guzmán subsequently published a book on Romo that included additional material culled from her earlier meetings with him.[9]

Romo's *Primer Impacto* performance contributes to the uniqueness of his confession. *Primer Impacto* tends to focus on human deformities and disfiguration, bizarre illnesses or disease, freak accidents, and heinous crimes. Romo's story fit the heinous-crime category. The slow-motion filming, dim lighting, slanted image, eerie music, and sexualized imagery situated the interview unmistakably as infotainment. Romo obliged with a sadistic performance and script.[10] He joked about disappearances: "When you don't have [bodies in] cemeteries, you don't have anything [incriminating], you just have to throw them into the sea. You gotta feed the fish." He engaged in banter about the best method for disappearing bodies. "If it's in the water, when the bladder bursts, the body will rise, of course it will rise because it's going to float. And so that it will stay under water you have to use some sort of chemical so it won't rise anymore." Romo also suggested disguising the identity of corpses by snapping off fingers and toes with a bolt cutter. Ultimately, he rejected the ocean as an appropriate site for disappearances: "The Chilean sea isn't a good one for throwing corpses into. The sea off Chile is full of currents; it's a violent sea." As an alternative, he proposed volcanoes: "You know, you just fly along in a helicopter, open the door, and out they all go. Who's going to look for them at the bottom of a volcano? No one!"[11]

Despite his insolence, Romo expressed pride in his work. He believed he had fought a noble cause, defeated a fierce enemy, and restored order. After the coup, he stated, "Those who worked, ate. There was plenty of everything. Disorder by the unions ended."[12] Violence, he contended, was a necessary weapon to end the evils of communism and civil war. Referring to Allende, Romo claimed that "the political parties and the unions run by 'the rich brat' [el pije] from La Moneda [government palace] drove the country to ruin."[13] He elaborated for Guzmán.

> No, look, I understand that you do not know what happened here in Chile because you were very young, but there was anarchy here. Perhaps those MIR guys had good ideas but they were impossible. You know that the army here is really strong. Here a Prussian discipline exists and nobody is going to allow a revolution, except Pinochet did by changing the country. Here only the military can have a revolution. But in any event a civil war would have been worse, there would have been even more deaths.
>
> Here "el Chicho," this is what we called Salvador Allende, began to trick half the country and the people believed in him, but he was telling pure lies. . . . he was a rich brat, we called him this because he enjoyed the best [food] and had the people eating pure rubbish and standing in lines for everything.
>
> I saw all this before the military pronouncement. But the military didn't take power, they only did so when the people screamed for them to step in. This is why I decided in the end to cooperate with [Pinochet's] national reconstruction.[14]

Romo presented evidence of Chileans' demands for military intervention: "People arrived wanting to give us information about what they had seen here or there by John Doe. That their neighbor was strange, and that they had seen him dig a hole in the yard to bury books or arms. There were a lot of people who wanted us to kill all the Marxists, but DINA's task wasn't to kill them. . . . It was intelligence, to check all the information and then go look for the bandits. Yes, they were bandits. Just because they went to university doesn't make them saints."[15] Some of these "bandits," however, gained Romo's admiration: "After they are detained, information has to be gotten out of them. They don't give it up easily or right away. They are indoctrinated to not give up anything. So at times those who had that job went too far because the MIR militants were really stubborn. You'd say to them, 'You might as well talk because they're going to get the information out of you anyway.' You've got to recognize that these guys were brave and they bore it until the very end."[16] Romo referred to the MIR leader Miguel Enríquez as dying "like a man, on the front line. He didn't hide behind anyone's skirts. He was really intelligent, that guy. He was a doctor."[17] Romo implied that to defeat such fierce opponents, the Chilean Army had to be even better. His pride led Romo to exaggerate, rather than minimize, his responsibility for the violence. He even took personal credit for defeating the MIR: "I'm going to say one thing. I have a conviction, a very clear conviction: what I did in life, as a man, on earth, I did it well. If some people didn't like it . . . they are the ones upset that Big Fat Romo, Slum Romo, caused MIR's complete fall. This is clear. They don't accept having lost a battle when they had everything to win: money, arms, networks, people, everything."[18]

Romo's pride in his work and inside track conflicted with his desire to avoid prosecution. This led to numerous contradictions in his confession. In one sentence Romo would admit to and deny violent acts: "If you say that I disappeared prisoners, no, then I'm innocent. But I also did bad things . . . I destroyed whole families."[19] Despite his glib discussion about DINA's involvement in disappearances, Romo later attributed rumors of disappearances to "international Marxism."[20] He denies that he bragged about killing the enemy with the simple comment: "I didn't kill anyone." He seeks to defend himself against accusations of torture and stealing: "I didn't torture. Those who say this are upset because they were defeated, defeated in the war. I am innocent, I never did any harm to anyone. I didn't steal from any-one."[21] But then he plays semantic games: "I don't believe that apply-ing [electrical] current is torture,"[22] or "A slap isn't torture, and at times one has to slap people because they get so furious and they have a hysterical fit. I, for example, hit some prisoners when they were coming with the electricity, but this was to save their lives."[23]

He cast himself in various roles at DINA to diminish responsibility for his acts. As "an analyst," for example, he would not have partici-pated in interrogation or torture.[24] Because he was in an intelligence unit, and not counterinsurgency, he would not have conducted inter-rogations. His rank was too high, he claimed, to have been involved in the torture of low-level members of the MIR: "I didn't hunt down students . . . our concern were the big guys. My role only involved the Central Committee and the Political Commission."[25] He also asserted, "No. I never applied it [torture], I only trained people to apply it. It fell to me to make sure they did their job well."[26] At other times, he claimed to have ranked too low in DINA to perform torture. Against Erika Hennings's charges that he tortured her, for example, he stated, "The lady is lying, because at that time I was only in charge of locating the homes of MIR leaders."[27]

Romo's characteristic ambiguity disappeared in his ardent and steadfast denial of rape. Perhaps Romo understood that rape, unlike other forms of torture, lacked justification. Defeating MIR might ex-cuse torture or killing, but not rape. Luz Arce, Romo's former victim-turned-collaborator, recounting a comment Romo had made in the torture center, believed he understood his vulnerability around rape charges: "We're going to have to kill these women because we've all slept with them."[28] Yet he vehemently denied rape in his confessional performance, "Rape never happened. . . . I invite . . . I defy the women who were DINA prisoners to come forward: who was raped by me? . . . Not one!"[29] Romo invented stories to defend himself. He alleged, for example, that Luz Arce apologized to him for having accused him of rape, but Arce claimed he apologized to her.[30] He maintained that former women prisoners had sought him out to gain information on their relatives and had never accused him of rape. Conflating rape with extramarital affairs, he also denied that he had any reason to rape prisoners: "These are false [charges], I did not take advantage of any woman. Why would I when I have my own [woman] and I am a family man and I have my principles. Look, I am a father of three women and

I'm not going to get involved with prisoners."[31] Continuing to confuse rape with sexual attraction, he stated, "Who would rape these women who were disgusting, dirty, urine-covered, with blood running down their legs, and covered in grime? You don't know what you're asking because these women were living in a room that didn't have a bathroom, where they couldn't wash, where they did everything, everything, that is they urinated and shat in pots, yes like paint cans. In other places they took care of their needs on the floor where they slept, so you can imagine the smell that they had. Yes, you see there was no toilet paper for them to clean themselves. Do you think that someone would get close enough to them to get infected by some disease?"[32] Romo further suggests that women prisoners mislabeled, or misunderstood, his acts as "rape": because he had to "grab them where he could," while they were kicking and fighting back, they may have interpreted this as a sexual assault.

While denying rape, Romo admitted to violence against women. He justified that violence in terms of their ferocity: "If they got really wild—they were more obstinate, tougher, and resisted more than the men. If you gave the men a combo, they'd quiet down, right? But the women, you had to grab them anywhere you could, because they would resist and bite you or kick you, and all those things. Our work wasn't an everyday thing, it wasn't easy at all. You had to use a lot of psychology to deal with [female] extremists, yes, and you forget that they were extremists who went around armed and if they got you they'd put a bullet in you. They were hardly little saints."[33] He also tried to downplay the harm he had caused to women by suggesting that they had a biological capacity to withstand violence: "Look at what women put up with to have a kid . . . a man's never had a kid. . . . So that says it all. If a woman is capable of having a 30-centimeter baby . . . without a Caesarean, a woman can take anything, because women don't give up or give in, they just won't give up. They're not that weak. Women are stronger."[34] Ultimately, Romo insinuated that women prisoners deserved violence because they neglected their traditional roles: "They are more evil than men, they get involved in politics without thinking about their family. Later they cry for their daddy, their kids, but they don't understand the situation they got themselves into."[35] He described Carmen Castillo as "irresponsible because she was pregnant and ran around making trouble."[36]

Romo suggested that the military treated women "subversives" more generously than it treated their male comrades. Regarding Castillo, for example, Romo stated, "If we had been really terrible we could have killed her, and she deserved it. But we respected her because she was pregnant, big and fat. Do you realize how irresponsible the MIR guys were to put their pregnant women in combat?"[37] He claimed to have saved Erika Hennings's life by removing her name from a death list because she had a young child and had become involved in MIR only because of her husband, Alfonso Chanfreau, who was a disappeared MIR leader.

Romo's traditional attitudes about gender extended to men as well, and he challenged the masculinity of MIR males, commenting on their failure as husbands and fathers for putting their families at risk, as well as on their unmanly behavior in prison and in exile. Even though Romo claimed that "everyone talks under torture," he condemned those who did. Speaking about Chico Videla, he stated, "His woman could bear it all without saying a word. She didn't speak, she tricked us, she screwed us around, and nothing. But when we got Chico . . . he shat it all out and sang like a canary. Can't you see that they are all a bunch of faggots?"[38] He referred to exiled leaders in a similar vein: "They're faggots; they pulled out when things got ugly. They went to cry over there in exile and they left the poor people who believed in them to fight when they were defeated from the start. . . . [N]o one beats the Chilean Army."[39] Romo also scorned those who remained quiet or worked underground during the dictatorship: "Do you know what bothers me? It's that they are all faggots in this country. One day they are with you, but when things get ugly, they throw you aside. My General Contreras and the rest of us in DINA fulfilled the duty that had been ordered. DINA had to end Marxism and we did it. Some remained. We should have silenced them at the time, but they escaped us . . . If we'd gotten them then, they'd be quiet now. Do you get it?"[40]

Romo blamed the survivors, not his own acts, for his imprisonment. As he stated, they "are now free and I'm here behind bars. For saving the country from chaos and from the scoundrels [sinverguenzas] and petit bourgeoisie who thought a proletarian revolution would be fun."[41] Romo condemned centrists and socialists alike: "Aylwin, Correa, and all of them, have put me in prison. I am the only political prisoner in Chile, I am the only political prisoner. Those who put me in prison are the ones who drove this country to ruin and now they are back."[42] He continued, "What is happening is that they want to fuck me and they want to fuck me because Aylwin hasn't been able to get any of the others and they have me in prison, but I'm going to get out and then they'll see."[43]

Lest his audience overlook his threat, Romo repeated it often. He indicated his willingness to repeat his past role: "I know I would do what I did all over again. . . . Yes, I'd do it much bigger now. . . . I wouldn't leave jack [a single one of them] alive. . . . I say lock 'em all up. That was DINA's mistake. I argued with my general 'til the very end: 'Don't let these people live. Don't let them go.' Just look at the consequences."[44] When asked, for example, how he would feel about a tombstone inscription "Here lies the executioner, the torturer, the murderer," Romo expressed pride and promise: "That could be, that could be, I accept it, the torturer, yes. For me that is a good thing. . . . What can be said is that I fulfilled a role and I did it well. I have a clear conscience and clear beliefs. I believe in what I did and I would do it again."[45]

Romo's hubris reflected his belief that he had achieved social status in Chile. He invented a past that he never lived: a student at the School of the Americas in Panama and the University of Chile, a consultant in South Africa, an instructor at a large business in Brazil, and even a political-science professor.[46] Those who call him "Romo from the Slums" or "Romo the torturer," he warned, forget that he will always be "Romo-who-knows-Chilean-history-like-the-back-of-his-hand."[47]

His desperate need for status explains his quest for celebrity fame on foreign television. Romo told Guzmán that he had rejected interviews with Chilean journalists because they lacked "seriousness."[48] While *Primer Impacto* could not offer Romo seriousness, it had advantages over national venues. Romo claimed that the interviewers offered him money and an opportunity to make an "effective and high impact" statement that might help him resolve his "personally conflictive situation." Guzmán denied having offered financial compensation.[49] Romo clearly expected favorable coverage from the U.S. broadcast: "Look, I'm going to give you the best interview and even if the shit hits the fan, I don't care, because you say that they are going to show it in the United States and there the people are going to understand. It's not like here where one says something and everyone starts screaming."[50] Univision's link to the anticommunist Cuban-American community may have reassured Romo. The composition of the television crew may also have influenced his decision. The father of the cameraman Raúl Hernández had been an army official during Fulgencio Batista's Cuban dictatorship and had fled Cuba just days after the end of the dictatorship—and only after he had murdered one of the leaders of the new popular army. Hernández, Guzmán contended, considered himself an "admirer" of Pinochet who, like his father, had fought against revolution and for freedom. "He did not understand who we were going to interview, but neither did he want to know," wrote Guzmán.[51] The Cuban-American interviewer for Univision, Mercedes Soler, also came from a staunchly anti-Castro background and viewed "the disappeared" as sympathizers of the Cuban Revolution and Fidel Castro. That they produced such an unsympathetic portrayal of Romo suggests that profit and fame meant more to them than the political message, or that their support for antirevolutionary forces had limits.

When Romo hinted at "the shit hitting the fan," he appeared to be only slightly concerned by the potential repercussions he might endure. At least during the early days of his imprisonment, he flaunted his belief that the military would protect him. Joking with the judge in the Alfonso Chanfreau disappearance case, for example, Romo commented, "Madame Judge, why so much work when they're going to get me out of this thing anyway?"[52] Romo's worries centered on the possibility that the television program would be competition for the autobiography he planned to write, but Guzmán assured him that the global broadcast would serve as a marketing event to boost his sales. Convinced and enthusiastic about the opportunity, Romo promised to meet with the Univision journalists when they arrived in Santiago.

If Romo emerged at all as a hero during the ninety-minute interview, those segments remained on the cutting-room floor. The program presented Romo as a psychopath, an unrepentant murderer, torturer, and rapist, who deserved to be incarcerated for life. Guzmán described the impact of Romo's confession: "This would be the first and last time that a torturer would speak in front of cameras to explain, without a trace of shame, a small part of what women, men, and children had suffered in the dictatorship's torture centers in Chile."[53] Unlike the "Scilingo effect" in Argentina, Chilean perpetrators avoided the public spotlight before and after Romo's confession.

The controversy the program generated, however, centered less on the authoritarian past than Guzmán had hoped. Instead, the broadcast's sensationalistic portrayal of Romo's sadism led some audiences to call for censorship. This group included authoritarian-regime supporters, the democratic government, opponents of the authoritarian regime, and the victims and their psychologists. Each group interpreted the program's political meaning and impact differently, but converged in the desire to silence Romo.

Guzmán knew the military hoped to suppress the interview. Romo told her that "as a military man [which, incidentally, he was not], I have express orders from the high command not to speak or give interviews."[54] Romo also referred obliquely to a "visitor" who had tried to persuade him to deny the interview lest he jeopardize coverage for his legal and medical expenses and financial support for himself and his family. Since Romo derived his income and benefits from the military, Guzmán concluded that the visitor must have represented the armed forces. Romo hinted at his reliance on military benefits when he added that his doctor had also warned against the interview because of its negative effect on his blood pressure. Guzmán ultimately convinced him to submit to the interview by appealing to his honor. He responded to her pressure: "Okay. When I give my word, I come through. And I gave it to you. So come what may, I'll do the interview. . . . My interview is going to make you famous. Do you think the gringos will like what I have to say? Either way, you tell me if it is good or not."[55]

Guzmán further assumed that the threatening phone calls she received subsequent to the televised confession came from the military.[56] Romo, moreover, allegedly received help from Col. Enrique Ibarra when he tried to legally retract his confession due to its "distortions."[57] The military had obvious reasons to avoid any association with a psychopathic torturer like Romo, but Romo, consciously or not, exploited those links as his only protection. As late as 2000, when Pinochet and other top leaders faced criminal prosecution, Romo still asserted, "I am a Pinochet-man and I will die a Pinochet-man."[58] But his loyalty was not reciprocated. Pinochet's former minister of the interior, Sergio Onofre Jarpa, dismissed Romo and his declarations as lunatic: "He is crazy. If you go to an insane asylum, many will tell you the same thing."[59] Manuel Contreras, the infamous director of DINA, denied that Romo had any official role in that organization and identified him as a mere civilian informant.

Guzmán attributed the military's reaction to the Romo confession as motivated not only by public relations but also by legal strategy. Romo's case complicated the 1978 amnesty law. The military had understood the law to cover all human-rights violations prior to 1978, regardless of who perpetrated them, but the courts, by charging Romo, interpreted the law to provide amnesty only to individual and military perpetrators, not for acts that occurred in military installations. Romo, as a civilian, did not have legal protection. Similarly, certain acts, like disappearances, still required investigation to determine criminality. The courts had interpreted the amnesty as protection against prosecution only after the finding of the victim's body or the determination that the victim's death had taken place prior to 1978. Romo's trial thus threatened the military's amnesty by opening investigation into matters they considered closed.

Convicting Romo, and creating the possibility of trying other perpetrators, did not seem to be a high priority for Chile's democratic government, despite military accusations to the contrary. The government in fact shared the military's desire to keep the "dark and obscene side" of the dictatorship hidden from the Chilean public, "to avoid tarnishing the image of the democratic transition."[60] Consistent with this attitude, the secretary-general, José Joaquín Brunner, remarked about Romo's interview, "His declarations do not merit further commentary. They are the utterances of a sick and deranged person without moral values."[61]

Romo's trial seemed to advance almost despite, not because of, the democratic government. Lower courts charged, tried, and sentenced Romo for the detention and disappearance of Ester Lagos Nilson, the MIR press secretary under President Allende. But before Romo had served his sentence, the Supreme Court of Chile, stacked with military-regime supporters, annulled the sentence and sent it to military courts, which absolved him of committing a crime. His release from jail in October 2000 outraged many Chileans, prompting rallies and protest letters from around the world and threatening democratic peace and stability. Vigilante-style justice seemed imminent, as evident in the words of an adult child of one of Romo's victims: "The fact that he [Romo] is free clearly justifies justice by our own hands. They're going to do him a favor by detaining him and giving him a life sentence. If he is free, he is condemned."[62] Prison, however, did not protect Romo from reprisals. In March 2000 Romo asked to be moved from the hospital within the Colina II prison because he had received death threats from four former MIR militants serving time in the same cell block.

Some members of the human-rights community also hoped to silence Romo's confession because of its psychological impact. The Latin American Institute of Mental Health and Human Rights criticized Guzmán for reproducing violence against those "directly affected" by torture. By "advising, stimulating, and calmly provoking the feared person [Romo]," the report contended, Guzmán had encouraged his use of sadistic language, ignoring the profound impact on his audience.[63] "These people have already suffered a lot and should not continue being assaulted by the harmful words of this former agent."[64] The report also claimed that the confession would affect nonvictims: "At times a strange phenomenon occurs: the reader is taken over by a mystifying force that emanates from the interview, as if we were his victims."[65] This effect, the review continued, occurred both because of Romo's power over the interview and because of the public's lack of critical distance from Chile's authoritarian past: "We are still too affected, too diseased."[66] At least one victim tried to express his trauma at seeing Romo again, writing a letter to the editor of a Chilean newspaper in which he described Romo as a "loyal, bloodthirsty dog, sadistic to prisoners." After listing Romo's abuses in the clandestine torture center, the victim stated, "I was detained by him, and I am only alive today to tell all of this because of an inexplicable miracle." He finishes by condemning the culture of impunity in Chile.[67] Another former victim, Alejandra Holzapfel Picarte, recounted how long it had taken her to recover from her torture and how hearing perpetrators like Romo could derail that process: "I spent eight very bitter years [in exile] in which I tried to forget. But each day, Big Fat Romo and the rest of the torturers came into my head. I created a process by myself: each day I repeated, 'I have to be capable of having a sexual relationship again. I have to be able to get pregnant.' . . . I gave myself goals. We all had to find a way to move on."[68]

Some observers viewed Romo's confession as a deliberate strategy by regime supporters who hoped to instill fear by reminding Chileans that individuals like Romo might surface if the democratic government went "too far." Minister of Interior Carlos Figueroa hinted that "certain groups interested in creating an insecure climate" had backed Romo's interview to influence the Supreme Court of Chile's decision on the assassination of the former Chilean diplomat Orlando Letelier.

Others suggested that Romo's confession reinforced the regime's notion that a few renegade individuals, and not the armed forces as a whole, had committed the violence attributed to the regime. Romo embodied the exception, the aberration, to the regime's otherwise noble mission, thereby exculpating the regime.[69] Most directly, Romo's confession offered an opportunity to effect personnel changes in the prison. Director of Gendarmerie Claudio Martínez was forced to resign after he allowed foreign journalists access to the Santiago Penitentiary. With the socialist Martínez gone, regime supporters hoped to influence prison management, given the fact that two top DINA commanders (Manuel Contreras and Pedro Espinoza) were likely to face imprisonment for the Letelier murder.[70]

Romo's confession also offered an opportunity to advance human-rights objectives. Guzmán described her book as "a document directed at the nation's memory, a memory of humanity that opposed the dictatorship of Augusto Pinochet and has remained loyal to the demand for justice."[71] By exposing Romo, she envisioned making it more difficult for "torturers to walk the streets with their heads held high." She hoped to "out" the perpetrators:

> They are the owners of farms, executives in security firms and transnational corporations, the less fortunate work as security guards, telephone-company contractors, public employees in right-wing municipalities, owners of liquor stores or subsidized schools. They are in private offices and public services. They are our neighbors. They sit beside us in restaurants.
>
> In addition, the majority of those torturers have their retirement protected with armed-forces pensions.[72]

The confession certainly brought visibility to perpetrators and the "enormous brutality that had gone without punishment" in Chile.[73] The program's ratings afforded Mercedes Soler an award from Univision.[74] Chile's Channel 11 received a flood of telephone calls from its audience, including one from a woman, self-identified as the wife of an army general, who stated, "It embarrasses me to find out that the army used these types of criminals to commit perversions."[75] This woman admitted that she had not believed victims' accounts until she heard Romo's confession.

Romo's confession also catalyzed action against Chile's immunity laws. An open letter to the Chilean government, signed by nongovernmental organizations throughout Europe, referred to *Primer Impacto*'s portrayal of "one of the most sadistic torturers" and called for Romo's trial and imprisonment.[76] Chilean human-rights groups, like the Association of the Families of the Detained and Disappeared (AFDD) and the Association of Families of Murdered Political Prisoners (AFEP), called for Romo's imprisonment. Mireya García, secretary-general of AFDD, described Romo as "a total perversity of a human being. His declarations about what prisoners had suffered and what he had done to disappear the remains of the disappeared prisoners remain engraved in [the minds of] anyone with a minimal sense of humanity."[77]

The human-rights community tried to link punishment for Romo to a broader framework of justice for past authoritarian state crimes. Luz Arce, despite her own collaboration with DINA, expressed this link: "First I must confess that it is difficult for me to kick someone when they're down. This doesn't mean that Romo Mena should be absolved, which will certainly happen since everything seems to indicate that all of the cases of disappeared prisoners will be amnestied. When I think of Romo Mena today, I remember that in 1974 he would take to hell and back those his boss, Miguel Krassnoff Marchenko, ordered him to [torture]. And today he is the only one in the hands of justice. It is difficult for me to understand how Romo is responsible and the rest of them are not."[78] Guzmán further developed the notion that DINA depended on individuals, like Romo, with certain pathologies. She described Romo as "a bully, but nothing more," who pleased his superiors with extraordinary acts of violence against adversaries.[79] When Romo simply admitted that he had fulfilled his obligations, and done them well, he captured DINA's environment, which rewarded brutality.

Although two of the DINA leaders Romo identified—Miguel Krassnoff and Marcelo Morén Brito—faced trial, conviction, and imprisonment, few would attribute such justice directly to Romo's confession.[80] The debate his confession engendered, however, encouraged contentious coexistence in Chile. By challenging Romo, his victims and survivors were able to find their political voice and power. Several of his victims and survivors remarked that they remembered him being bigger; when they faced him after the dictatorship, he no longer towered over them physically or metaphorically.[81] Holzapfel compared Romo's physical deterioration and isolation to the regime's atrophy: "I'm happy to have been able to say: 'How good it is to see you alone and sick. All of the damage you did to us has returned to you, and I hope that you live and suffer for many years.' "[82] The capacity to debate restored political citizenship to others as well. Erika Hennings viewed Romo's confession as a chance to engage in political life again: "Romo . . . denies the torture and sexual abuse, but he wants to talk. Perhaps the other victims won't forgive me for saying it, but despite everything, I feel he has a human side. He's bearing a great weight of guilt."[83]

COMPARATIVE REFLECTIONS ON SADISTIC CONFESSIONS

Hennings captures the most troubling aspect of sadistic confessions: human beings commit atrocity and enjoy it, even if they are guilty pleasures. Very few real-life confessions express that pleasure in words or actions. Such appearances permeate fictional accounts, however. The character Roberto Miranda, Paulina's torturer in Ariel Dorfman's *Death and the Maiden,* for example, describes his transformation from professional doctor attempting to save prisoners' lives to sadistic torturer: "Bit by bit, the virtue I was feeling turned into excitement—the mask of virtue fell off it and it, the excitement, it hid, it hid, it hid from me what I was doing, the swamp of what—By the time Paulina Salas was brought in it was already too late. Too late . . . too late. A kind of—brutalization took over my life, I began to really truly like what I was doing. . . . She is entirely in your power, you can carry out all your fantasies, you can do what you want with her."[84]

Authors of fiction release their perpetrators from the taboo of admitting pleasure at inflicting pain. Romo resembles literary characterizations of perpetrators by ignoring the taboo. Only fragments of other confessions around the world come close to breaking that taboo and unsettling their audiences.

"I Was Really Good at the Paddle." Sadistic texts are extremely rare. That is not surprising since text allows perpetrators to disguise their sadistic pleasure. What distinguishes Romo's text is his failure to find the language of denial to hide his pleasure. Even when he tries to deny rape, for example, he mistakes it for a sexual, pleasurable act, not physical and psychological torture. Thus, he claims he could not have raped (enjoyed sex) with filthy and diseased detainees.

Romo is called on to express that view due to the eighty accusations of rape against him. Where evidence of sadism exists, perpetrators often fail to find an appropriate text to excuse their acts. The U.S. prison guards caught in photographs smiling while inflicting sexual torture in the Abu Ghraib prison in Iraq, for example, needed a text to explain away the appearance of sadistic pleasure. They failed to find one. How could Private Lindy England place strategic value in holding a naked prisoner on a dog leash or pointing at prisoners' exposed genitals? How could strategy explain the uninhibited delight her photographed image revealed?

Narrative techniques fail to disguise sadism when they do not make sense. Investigation into the abuses at Abu Ghraib revealed that some guards believed the photographs would aid in interrogation and assist in the success of the war.[85] Were they saying that the photographs were supposed to look like the prisoners were having fun with the guards? Do they not reveal instead that the guards were having fun at the prisoners' expense? For whom were these photographs more humiliating? Where photographs, performance, or other evidence hints at the pleasure derived, text can rarely disguise it.

Text attempts to minimize atrocity behind the act. Torturers may claim, for example, that they did not kill anyone, leave physical marks or scars, or even really hurt their victims. They may imply that the acts look or sound worse than they actually were. Thus Romo's claim that women endure torture better than men suggested that his methods did not produce much harm (at least to women).

Text attempts to dissimulate sadism with technical language, but often produces the opposite effect. Romo detailed methods of disappearing bodies that improved on the techniques of his less-intelligent superiors. The Argentine torturer Juan Del Cerro, known as "Colores" due to his red hair and freckles, claimed to have invented a particular kind of electric prod (*picana electrica*) that effectively, and without leaving marks, extracted confessions from victims. He expressed outrage at his superiors' lack of appreciation for his total devotion to his work, especially his fourteen-hour workdays in his patriotic "service to the nation." The army lieutenant Marcelo Paixão Araújo—who topped the list of torturers presented in *Brasil: Nunca mais*, an unofficial report of human-rights violations—gave news magazine *Veja* a dispassionate and clinical version of his three-part torture technique. First, he would throw the detainees down on the floor in the middle of the room, strip them, and shout at them until they gave up information. If that did not work, he began the second—more violent—phase, transforming the detainees into human punching bags by "smacking them in the face, punching them in the stomach, slugging them in the kidney." If they still refused to speak, the third stage commenced: "I really like the paddle. It is really painful, but it makes the person talk. I was really good with the paddle." He described the paddle as "making the detainee show you his palm and then hitting it really, really hard ten or fifteen times" with the paddle. Araújo described other forms of torture he used as well, taking particular pride in the "telephone" as a 100-percent-Brazilian invention. That method involved sending through the body a low-level electrical current "that wouldn't risk serious injury." "I really liked to run it between two fingers, but you could also run it between the hand and the ears." Araújo made it clear that he had followed orders, but not blindly. Instead he proudly defended his contribution to saving Brazil from communism: "I did it [torture] because I thought it was necessary. It is obvious that I followed orders. But I accepted the orders. I don't want to give the impression that I was a patsy. I received orders, directives, but I was ready to accept them and fulfill them. Don't think that I was forced . . . no way. If we let [left-wing groups like] VPR, Polop, or whoever take power or hand [power] over to them, the communists would take advantage. We didn't want Brazil to become the Chile of Salvador Allende."[86]

Sadistic perpetrators often emphasize the socially acceptable aspects of technical skill: intelligence, creativity, innovation, drive, and dedication. What they seem to miss, however, is that when they apply those characteristics to torture, they reveal themselves as sadistic. Although they may not express pleasure specifically in harming individuals, that is nevertheless what the work they enjoy entails. Moreover, not one of these torturers justifies their acts as saving lives. They view their technical skills as essential to the success of the war or to the defeat of communism. But such perpetrators usually fail to produce texts that justify their specific acts as heroic, or even rational.

"You Filthy Pig, You're Still as Nauseating as Before." Perpetrators try to avoid looking like sadists. Perhaps they know that admitting to past violence will conjure up the image of criminal psychopaths in their audiences' minds. To counter such images, they try to appear above reproach.

As Romo's changing image demonstrated, different media outlets will enhance or diminish perpetrators' sadistic characteristics. The infamous Argentine torturer Julio Simón (El Turco Julián) also experienced how the media could create or disguise sadistic images. Accused of disappearing 200 people and found guilty of fifty-eight crimes, Simón enjoyed the freedom of the Due Obedience Law to peddle his story. For his first media appearance, on the sober news program *Telenoche*, he looked and acted the part of a sadistic assassin: wearing a grubby beige turtleneck sweater and with long, messy hair, an unkempt beard, and a boorish attitude. When he later appeared on Mauro Viale's popular infotainment show, he had transformed: beardless, with a neat haircut and stylish clothes, shown mainly from behind, and largely silent. He looked respectable.

The media tells perpetrator stories not only with the assistance of camerawork and wardrobe and make-up consultants, but also through editing. As if Romo's revolting Univision image had not been enough, the media reported a subsequent encounter between Romo and a former victim that clinched his despicable image. Romo had accidentally urinated on a courtroom chair, and one of his former victims, Alejandra Holzapfel, reacted: "At that moment I unleashed all of my hatred [toward him]. 'You filthy pig, you're still as nauseating as before. You've gone and pissed on the judge's chair! . . . Get out of here, you swine!' "[87] The media report portrayed Romo, who had dominated Holzapfel and countless others in the dictatorship's torture chambers, as pathetic and powerless in democracy's courtroom.

Presenting a respectable facade to the democratic public was particularly difficult for individuals, like Romo, who had climbed to a position of status through their violent jobs during the authoritarian regime. The security apparatus had brought them out of obscurity and turned them into Somebody. They gained power, salaries, bonuses, access to social elites, and reputations. And they enjoyed their positions, even if it meant causing harm, as one apartheid policeman recounted: "I was really like a young lion, you know. For me, to participate in this kind of—to serve my country at such a level was a great honor. And when I was in the security police it was one of the elite squads in the police and we worked day and night. And, yes, it did; it gave me a kick."[88]

To have declined their roles would have involved giving up the "kick" of working "day and night" in "elite squads." Thus some perpe-

Julio Simón, also known as El Turco Julián, appeared on *Telenoche* (channel 13) on 1 May 1995.

Julio Simón appeared on the television program *Mediodía con Mauro* (Argentina Televisora Color, channel 7) five times: 15 and 25 August 1997, 15 September 1997, and 13 and 21 November 1997.

trators wanted recognition for their part in the struggle. They viewed themselves as the intrepid defenders of the regime, just as they viewed themselves during the authoritarian period as the ones who got things done. Sadistic confessions helped the foot soldiers claim power over the desk generals by exposing the truth. Araújo, for example, scoffed at former military-regime president General Ernesto Geisel's denial of torture: "Whoever says there wasn't torture is an idiot."[89] He elaborated: "According to Geisel's testimony, he didn't know anything. He was innocent. This is really funny. Everyone in the [military] government who writes about the era of the military regime were really comedians. Clowns even. They didn't know anything, they were saints. . . . But who signed the AI-5 [Institutional Act no. 5]? I didn't. When they suspended constitutional guarantees, they let anything go in the torture centers."[90]

But for perpetrators, letting "anything go" still involved some rules of civility. All perpetrators believed that they had upheld those rules. They also pointed the finger at those who did not. For example, when asked about perpetrators who became monsters, Araújo replied, "Monsters? No . . . the only monsters I found were the sadists. I had to get rid of two sergeants myself. I didn't want sadists working for me."[91]

Similarly, sadistic performances involve recasting past interactions with victims in a less-aberrant light. Romo recounted having close contact with his former victims. Araújo claimed that his victims believed he had treated them "fairly." And some perpetrators, like the apartheid police torturer Jeffrey Benzien, believed that they had developed a bond with their victims. Benzien's victim Ashley Forbes reminded Benzien of the various techniques he had used to torture him: suffocation with a wet bag and in a rug, beatings that burst his eardrums, and anal rape with a metal rod. Benzien did not deny these accusations, but essentially ignored them and focused on the "special relationship" they had forged in prison. Benzien recounted taking Forbes out for steak and Kentucky Fried Chicken. He seemed almost nostalgic when he described how Forbes had seen snow for the first time with him. He had taken Forbes fresh fruit to eat and westerns to read when Forbes was hospitalized for a suicide attempt. Benzien's portrayal of their relationship juxtaposed against Forbes's testimony made his acts look like homoerotic psychological and physical torture.[92]

Perpetrators who make sadistic confessions often have less to lose and more to gain from them. Judging those who make sadistic confessions as uniquely perverse or evil, therefore, ignores the strategic calculations behind them. It also ignores how the acts they reveal link the regime, and not just a few bad apples, to the atrocities committed.

"Torture Is Eternal." Staging dramatically enhances the sadism of confessional performances. The transcript of Romo's confession is disturbing, but it invokes nothing like the sensation of horror one feels when witnessing it on television. The camera's political message about how to interpret perpetrators and their words is often more influential on audience response than the confessional text itself.

Creating a sadistic image does not always involve exaggerating the perpetrator's features, as in Romo's case; sometimes it involves diminishing them. When the diminutive, redheaded, and freckled Colores appeared on a Barcelona television program, he spoke from the shadows. Because the program revealed his full name and alias, his obscured appearance did not conceal his identity. What it masked was his normality. Colores became an indistinct torturer lurking and only semi-visible in the shadows of history. He certainly would have appeared less mysterious and frightening under full view of the camera.

Telenoche similarly calculated its presentation of the well-known torturer Simón. Simón himself attempted to minimize the importance of torture, and therefore, on his own, he did not deliver much of a program. He flatly stated that he had played a role in three different Argentine clandestine torture centers where the regime's goals included killing all of the detainees. He admitted to using torture, albeit only in a "very few" instances. He confessed that torture proved counterproductive to revealing information because it left the victim "too destroyed." His job was to get the "subversives," and not to "waste time" engaging in political discussions with them. When he had only limited time to extract information, he would use torture. He delivered this confession in a matter-of-fact, almost bored, manner, trotting out the usual heroic justifications: "What I did, I did for my Fatherland, my faith, and my religion. Of course I would do it again."[93] And he contrasted his own attitude with those of Scilingo and Ibañez: "I am not repentant. I'm no crybaby like that sorry Scilingo. That drunkard Ibáñez. This was a war to save the Nation from the terrorist hordes. Look, torture is eternal. It has always existed and always will. It is an essential part of the human being."[94] In contrast to his alternating bored and heroic language, however, Simón's body shook nervously throughout the entire segment. He tried to recover his pluck at the end of each sentence by delivering a punctuating thrust of his chin into the air or a cold glare at the interviewer.

Neither Simón's words nor his performance resembled a sadistic confession, but the program transformed it into one. The program spliced in commentary by Simón's victims. Mario Villani, a survivor of five Argentine detention centers, recounted an incident in which Simón, a notorious anti-Semite, tortured a Jewish prisoner to death. Unsatisfied with electric shocks alone, Simón rammed a broken stick up the torture victim's anus. The stick tore open his internal organs each time he twisted in pain from the electric current. Although Villani's testimony enhanced Simón's sadistic image, Villani does not consider him unique among the regime's torturers.

Subsequent to his *Telenoche* debut, Simón pursued a more lucrative option on Mauro Viale's program, *Mediodía con Mauro*.[95] In an isolated booth above the studio and with his back to the camera, Simón listened and occasionally commented on the political battle under way on the studio stage between supporters and opponents of the military regime. Mediators frequently intervened to prevent violence from erupting onstage between older upper-class Argentines, who considered Simón a war hero, and the young students and children of the disappeared, who considered him a Nazi, torturer, assassin, and son of a bitch.[96] At one moment in the program, a young woman who had lost family members during the dictatorship climbed the stairs to Simón's perch, entered, and hit him from behind with her purse. When he turned to defend himself, his face was revealed to the camera. Once exposed, he left his refuge and joined the fray on the main studio stage.

As on *Telenoche*, Simón limited his comments to vacuous defenses of the military regime and kept them devoid of sadism. But also like *Telenoche*, the studio transformed Simón's account into a sadistic one. It simulated Simón's torture of Mónica Brull. Presented in sepia tones and with a voiceover of recorded oral testimony, the reenactment portrayed a young, beautiful, blind, and pregnant Brull being taken to a torture chamber, stripped, shocked with electric prods, and raped, while one of the perpetrators, resembling Simón, smoked and laughed in perverse pleasure at her pain. Although it certainly depicted Simón's sadism, the dramatization itself bordered on pornographic, a voyeuristic male fantasy about sadomasochistic sex, rather than a reflection on past violence from the perspective of its victims. Viale's show hardly made Simón a hero, but it did make him a celebrity: the star villain in his own miniseries, trading on his credentials as a former torturer.

The print media has the same power, but uses different techniques. Interviewing style, for example, encouraged the sadistic confession of Borislav Herak, a young Bosnian Serb condemned to death in 1993 by a Sarajevo military court for the rape and murder of Muslim women. During an interview with the journalist George Rodrigue (G) of the *Dallas Morning News*, Herak (B) tried to limit his comments to details of the case. He initially told the interviewer that he considered rape "stupid," but that his commanding officer considered it essential for troop morale. The reprisal for failing to follow orders—specifically being sent to one's death on the front lines—forced him to comply. The journalist encouraged a reluctant Herak to admit that some part of him enjoyed the rape and murder.

G: Was there anything good about fighting with the Serbs? A feeling of togetherness or being part of a team? A feeling of being important?

B: The only good time was when we found schnapps and we could drink together. Or when we had barbecues. And then we could be together and drink and eat.

G: But I think that in the same way your bosses gave you the drink and food, they gave you the women. As a way to show you were important. Is that right?

B: Yes. For me and for all the soldiers. They wanted to keep us together.

G: Because the way the women are here, you would never be able to have so many women as a normal person, would you? In fact, you had not had any women before, had you?

B: Yes, that is right.

G: Now was it important, not to you personally but to your friends, that they had this chance? Did they enjoy it?

B: Yes, they did.

G: How would you know that? What did they say or do that let you know they were enjoying themselves?

B: Those guys, they tried to make themselves important. When we had meals together they would talk about what they had done there.

G: Specifically what would they say?

B: That they were there [in the restaurant Sonja's] and had a good time . . .

G: Okay. So there was a part of you that felt like your friends did? A part that really enjoyed this chance to rape and kill these women?

B: As for me, it was just a little part . . .

G: What did you feel? There must have been something, or you would not have known that this part was inside you.

B: I know that it was good because when I got back I would drink and celebrate.[97]

Rodrigue secured from Herak a confession that he enjoyed raping and killing. And yet he hardly appeared sadistic in the interview. Was that because Herak held back his views or because he was not a sadist?

In stark contrast, *Veja* resisted the temptation to portray Marcelo Paixão Araújo as a sadist. The article emphasized his elite family background. His father was president of Banco Mercantil, a thriving company that Araújo joined after leaving the armed forces and later inherited. *Veja* described Araújo's large apartment in the most fashionable section of Belo Horizonte, his country house, and his boat. It focused on the 2,500 books in his personal library and his commitment to reading an hour each day before starting work. The article reported on his law degree and extensive psychotherapy, which Araújo insisted he had undergone for reasons that had nothing to do with his past violence. By presenting him as a normal man with a wife, two kids, and economic ambitions, and one who also committed more torture than any other Brazilian perpetrator, *Veja* suggests that anyone, in a particular situation, might be motivated to commit sadistic acts.

To the question, "Why are you coming forward with your testimony now?" Araújo replied, "Because no one has asked me about this before."[98] Araújo's simple words signify the role the media plays in staging, planning, and producing sadistic confessions. *Veja* sought him. They had failed to find the other top offenders listed in *Brasil: Nunca mais* only because those offenders had disappeared from sight, perhaps gone underground to avoid public recriminations. The Barcelona television station found Colores. Univision found Romo. The media looks for sadism because it sells. Audiences, however, do not necessarily accept the media's portrayal. Instead, they use the material presented in the media for their own political ends.

"Wow, What a Bizarre Individual!" The media seeks out and creates sadistic perpetrators. But perpetrators also play a key role in constructing a sadistic image. No one ambushed or otherwise forced Romo, Araújo, Colores, or Herak to broadcast their stories. They willingly complied with the interviews, even if they lost control over the content of the final report.

Financial need might explain perpetrators' compliance; with the exception of Araújo, all of the perpetrators who produced sadistic confessions that I found survived at the margins of society. A media interview offers perpetrators an opportunity to escape their precarious financial lives. Simón, for example, had been peddling his story for years. He had allegedly asked the Permanent Assembly for Human Rights to pay him $30,000 for his "archives." Rejected, he then offered to sell them to the former Montonero leader Roberto Perdía. He also tried to sell them to the North American writer Marguerite Feitlowitz, who suspected, based on his disheveled state, that the rumors she had heard were true: having no income, he was living in a hotel and supported financially by a Brazilian prostitute. Simón even hit up his former victim Mario Villani, asking for cash and help in finding a job. He had originally asked *Telenoche* to pay him $1,000 for his story, but later reduced his demand to transportation costs. When *Telenoche* refused to pay even that amount, he defected to Argentina Televisora Color. His financial arrangements with the latter remain a mystery, but his haircut, shave, and respectable wardrobe indicate some material benefits.

Perpetrators, in other words, may intentionally accommodate the media's desire for a sadistic confession. In promising "I'm going to give you the best interview," Romo suggested a willingness to generate exciting copy. In this regard, perpetrators may resemble other celebrity wannabes. The boxer Mike Tyson once remarked, "I want your grandkids and great-grandkids to remember me and say, 'Wow, what a bizarre individual.' "[99] By biting off a chunk of his opponent's ear and engaging in other "bizarre" acts, Tyson provided the theatricality that heightened his public reputation. His celebrity status depended on his dramatic performances, perhaps even more than on his boxing prowess in later years. Tyson and the perpetrators who give sadistic confessions may believe that bad press is better than no press at all.

This desire for media attention of any sort may explain why, among those perpetrators who gave sadistic confessions, only Romo protested the media's "distorted" portrayal of his performance. Even his remonstration seemed staged, albeit this time by the military. It may be that the military was attempting to protect Romo from the unanticipated consequences of his media interview, but a more plausible explanation is that the military stepped in to protect its own image. Romo and the other "sadistic" perpetrators accept, and maybe even desire, their negative public images.

Sadistic confessions made before other perpetrators tell their stories may provide perpetrators with political leverage. Later ones, in contrast, may offer little more than entertainment. Mauro Viale's program with Simón hardly constituted serious journalism. Parallel story segments, like one on a hermaphrodite's struggle with abusive "corrective" surgery, interrupted the political narrative on the television screen. The banter at the end of the program also seemed incongruous with a political message. Viale and the pretty blond host of the subsequent program giggled and rolled their eyes at the intense fight between regime supporters and opponents that continued on-stage behind Viale. They treated the political conflict as if it were nothing more than a lovers' brawl on Jerry Springer. Sadistic confessions presented long after the violence occurred may only find media venues that treat them as examples of the weird and wacky modern world, and not as serious reflections of the struggle over political history.

"Feel Sorry? That Goes a Bit Too Far." "The crazy torturer," the Brazilian public intellectual Elio Gaspari states, "victim of perversion, is in general a product of political fantasy. For the dictatorship, it functioned as an alibi. If one day the opposition managed to prove the allegations and identified the torturers, they would have this insanity-of-the-agent defense at hand to save the honor of the regime."[100] Gaspari thus identifies a brand of "holocaust denial" in which authoritarian regimes or their supporters plant (or manipulate) sadistic confessions to pin the rumors of violence on rogue forces or "sick-os" and thus deny a systematic policy of torture or extermination.

Gaspari goes too far. Empirical evidence supports his claim that regime supporters do label as "crazy" perpetrators, like Romo, who make sadistic confessions. It is also true that authoritarian regimes and their supporters create a distance between the security apparatus and the individual "sadistic" perpetrator. Yet no evidence supports Gaspari's claim (shared by conspiracy theorists in Chile) that regime supporters pin violence on particular sadists to exculpate the regime and confirm the "rogue forces, mistakes, and excesses" explanation for that violence. Such a strategy may prove too risky. It draws attention to the torture centers and what occurred in them. It opens up investigation into the failure of commanding officers to stop such violence. Although regime supporters may indeed hope that sadistic individuals warn the democratic government and social groups against moving too far and too fast against the authoritarian regime, no evidence suggests that they manipulate them for that purpose.

Democratic governments, nonetheless, often attempt to silence sadistic confessions. For example, the Argentine prosecutor Julio Strassera, reacting to Colores's televised confession, stated, "The media should not give space to those who defend the electric prod as a method for interrogation. These types present themselves as the nation's saviors and in our country there are still people who believe that there was a war here, who speak about bombs, kidnapping, and view the state in the same way that they view the victims. . . . There is no reason to interview these perpetrators. On the contrary, democrats have a responsibility to isolate them." Strassera recognizes that he may be threatening freedom of the press with such a position, but he perceives a greater threat in allowing perpetrators to boast and to flaunt their immunity from prosecution: "Having to see and listen to perpetrators who defend [what they did] is too much." He distinguishes, moreover, confession from justification: "It is one thing to have a dialogue between a journalist and a repentant person who considers what he did during the dictatorship as negative or aberrant. It is another thing to give space to an assassin who glorifies his use of torture." Strassera believes that the harm to society caused by sadistic confessions justifies some infringement on speech rights.[101]

Strassera focuses only on the harm to victims and survivors traumatized by these confessions and to society by allowing public justification of human-rights abuses. He ignores, however, that his remedy —silencing sadistic confessions—may perpetuate a positive image of the past regime and its violence. He also disregards how audiences can use sadistic confessions to expose past violence and build a human-rights culture.

Regime supporters tend to support Strassera's call for silencing sadistic confessions, but for different reasons. These supporters fear that sadistic confessions damage the regime's image, associating it with sadism and systematic violations of human rights, a charge the regime consistently denies. Thus a well-known supporter of Brazil's authoritarian regime and former head of the National Intelligence Agency, General Newton Cruz, reacted negatively to Araújo's confession to *Veja*: "A testimony like this can only engender hatred for the military and for Brazil. . . . With the amnesty law, all of this should be left behind. There were slip-ups on each side and errors on each side."[102]

Within the human-rights community, some groups endorse Strassera's vision of suspending speech rights to protect victims and survivors from the harm of sadistic confessions. But others recognize the potential power of these confessions in exposing the regime's acts. Toward that end, these groups must link the sadistic confession to systematic policy, a process that may be facilitated by identifying with the sadistic torturer as a fellow victim of the regime, as Mario Villani shows. In a conversation with me, Villani recalled a chance encounter with Julio Simón in Buenos Aires after the end of the dictatorship. Simón had neither work nor money and complained about how he had been "sold out" by his commanders, whom he referred to as "sons of bitches." Villani reminded Simón of a conversation that they had had in the torture center during which Villani had likened Simón's role in the security apparatus to a condom: his commanders would use him to satisfy their pleasure, protect themselves, and then throw him away. Breeding disloyalty could encourage perpetrators to reveal the identity of those who gave the orders for sadistic acts, as in Romo's case.

How victims deal politically, as opposed to personally, with their former torturers has received little attention. The psychological phenomenon known as the Stockholm syndrome, in which a hostage sympathizes with the hostage-taker, perpetuates the notion of continued dependence on the perpetrator. But much more complex relationships have evolved. Forbes, for example, went so far as to reach out to his torturer, Benzien, at his TRC hearing: "People were critical when I shook his hand at the hearing. Those who were not part of the process—who are looking at it from outside—are more emotional," he said. Forbes claimed that he did not really think about it: "It was just what I did when I saw him." Contemplating it later, Forbes found that he identified with Benzien: "It [the past] is traumatic for me, but for him it is much worse. . . . In my case, I can speak with pride about what I did [as a member of the ANC's army]. He can't even speak about it. Because what he did was wrong." He went on to describe how Benzien's life had been destroyed by the political transition: "He got divorced. It seems that his family didn't know much about what he was doing. There was a lot of exposure." But while this may have sounded like sympathy for Benzien and his situation, Forbes clarified in a conversation with me: "Feel sorry? That goes a bit too far. But I can relate to him and what he has gone through."

That humanity between perpetrators and victims is what many, particularly the anti-apartheid activist Bishop Desmond Tutu, call "reconciliation." While it may seem surprising that this could emerge from sadistic confessions, victims and survivors sometimes have insights into low-level perpetrators that outsiders do not share. They know that perpetrators are brutal. They also know that perpetrators have little choice about their acts if they plan to remain within the authoritarian security forces. They recognize, in other words, that those who make sadistic confessions are not the only, or even the worst, sadists in the security apparatus. What victims and survivors with militant backgrounds also know, but may not publicly admit, is that they might have acted similarly if the tables had been reversed. One of Benzien's torture victims commented to me: "I was trained to kill. It was my job. I had to really think through whether this was something I could do or should do. I decided that I needed to do it and so it became my job. He [Benzien] also had a job. Torture is something that the government generally accepted and all of us knew that we would be tortured if we were caught. So he was doing his job. And I survived it. He did his best to do what he had to do. And I did what I had to do."[103]

Comparative evidence suggests that such humanity (or reconciliation) depends on accountability. Where victims viewed perpetrators as equals, they did so only after perpetrators faced official hearings or trials. This was the case for Romo and Benzien, for example. Without official forms of accountability, victims and perpetrators tended to lock into a struggle over memory, as evidenced by Simón, Colores, and Araújo. In a passionate encounter on Mauro Viale's program with Simón, an observer challenged a regime supporter for her treatment of a child of the disappeared: "Why are you blaming ideology when she is telling you she lost her whole family? . . . Use some common sense! What does Marxist theory have to do with this person who has lost her whole family?"[104]

CONCLUSION

Sadistic confessions have the potential to shut down debate over the past, reinstilling fear in the population, retraumatizing victims and survivors, and restoring power to regime supporters. Perhaps because of this risk to political debate, mobilizing around sadistic confessions becomes singularly important.

Moreover, the very dramatic nature of such confessions tends to elicit intense response. Sadistic confessions expose previously undisclosed details, including specific acts of shocking violence and the individuals involved in them. Sadistic confessions reveal the horror behind the regime's acts, otherwise obscured in perpetrator accounts that deny, glorify, or disguise violence behind generalities and euphemisms. Sadistic confessions make audiences understand, feel, smell, and witness that violence, sometimes for the first time, making it nearly impossible for anyone to deny the violence and its impact on victims and survivors.

Audiences interpret sadistic confessions differently. Some consider them to be evidence of crimes of omission. Others see them as admission of guilt for crimes of commission. Some desire to silence them, while others demand investigation and prosecution. Comparative cases show that the multiplicity of responses engenders democratic debate and contributes to contentious coexistence. Sadistic confessions force audiences to agree, for example, on protection of human rights and prevention of atrocities. While the various audiences may not agree on who committed those atrocities in the past, or for what reasons, a language that repudiates the violations themselves emerges. Less polarization, and even the possibility of unity on some democratic principles, can be achieved through discussion about sadistic confessions, and perhaps only sadistic confessions.

With regard to justice, sadistic confessions also play an important role, by showing that certain acts, regardless of immunity laws, fall outside any legal protections from prosecution. Neither regime supporters nor opponents would defend the kinds of acts these confessions expose. They defy justification. The discussion, therefore, challenges the notion of impunity for *all* authoritarian-state crimes. Those who make sadistic confessions, moreover, seem to have little to lose, and something to gain, from revealing truths about the past regime. They therefore participate in investigative and truth processes more readily than other perpetrators, thereby dramatically breaking the code of silence that protects authoritarian regimes from negative publicity.

By fomenting debate, sadistic confessions create possibilities for equalizing or even inverting power relationships between victims and perpetrators. Such confessions graphically demonstrate that victims and survivors did not imagine or deserve the brutality they received in torture centers. The capacity to stand up to those who debased and intimidated them contributes to the process of creating political citizenship.

Despite sadistic confessions' potential contributions to contentious coexistence, they also pose three potential threats to democracy. First, the appeal of taking justice into private hands increases in response to sadistic confessions and without formal processes of accountability and prosecution. Such retributive acts of violence both silence debate and threaten perpetrators' rights. Second, a stark trade-off exists within the human-rights community between freedom of expression and censorship designed to protect individual victims and survivors. There is no doubt that these unsettling accounts harm individuals more deeply than other kinds of confessions, that they offend their audiences and traumatize vulnerable groups. But endeavors to censor them have failed. In addition, human-rights groups have shown that sadistic confessions can be used to promote accountability. Finally, making scapegoats out of sadistic perpetrators can limit awareness of the past and justice. Although the heinous acts revealed certainly invite condemnation, the victims have sometimes shown the greatest capacity to recognize the acts as political, and not personal. The victims have thus played a key role in using sadistic confessions to reveal torture as emblematic of a greater political issue and not only as a common crime perpetrated by an individual psychopath. They have kept open debate despite the widespread desire to silence and shun those who admit to sadistic acts.

CHAPTER FIVE

DENIAL

Here there were no personal or individual excesses as they try to claim, because there are no individual excesses in urban combat in a clandestine guerrilla war. . . . It is precisely that: a war, a subversive war provoked and initiated by Marxist, socialist, and MIR communism. The military government had no choice but had to declare an internal war to confront it.

Here there was a Marxist comedy that produced only good electoral dividends. The Chilean soldiers were never trained to assassinate, abduct, torture, or make people disappear. They were trained to defend their country, with their lives if it were necessary. . . . We mourn our losses with men's tears; we didn't leave and undermine our country abroad.

Here there was no demonstrated proof that human rights were violated. There are only presumptions from Marxists who yesterday destroyed their Fatherland. And these presumptions do not consist of charges that can merit parading in front of the courts hundreds of men who yesterday only carried out their duty.—Manuel Contreras Sepúlveda, *La verdad histórica*

THUS SPOKE THE RETIRED GENERAL MANUEL CONTRERAS SEPÚLVEDA, the infamous head of the Chilean military regime's notorious secret police organization, DINA. The Chilean truth commission documented that in its three short years of official operation (1974–1977), DINA was responsible for 2,500 forced disappearances, executions, and deaths under torture. Evidence of DINA's involvement in criminal violence prompted the dictatorship to investigate and close DINA in 1977, replacing it with the National Center for Information (CNI). Contreras slipped into quiet retirement, reemerging on the political scene only in 1991 to stand trial for his activities as DINA's head. He denied wrongdoing and confessed, instead, to his sacrifice to the nation in the

Police officers guard General Manuel Contreras on his way to court on 28 January 2005.
Martin Bernetti/AFP/Getty Images. Reproduced by permission.

antisubversive war. Despite the comprehensive amnesty law, and to surprise throughout the world, Chilean courts found Contreras guilty and sent him to prison.

Few could have predicted such an outcome given Contreras's special relationship with Pinochet. Contreras had a distinguished military profile, having come from a long lineage of military officials and placed at the top of his military-academy class. Pinochet overlooked other deserving and more senior officers when he promoted Contreras, the youngest officer in his rank, to general and appointed him to lead DINA. He thus made him the second most important leader in the country—Pinochet's right-hand man. Contreras enjoyed more access to Pinochet, including daily private breakfasts, than any other military leader.

Contreras's involvement in international crimes undoubtedly factored into his conviction. Belgium, France, Italy, Spain, Switzerland, and the United States had all pressured the government to extradite Contreras so he could stand trial. Claiming sovereignty and jurisdiction over these cases, Chile refused extradition, but began its own prosecution. In 1995 Chilean courts found Contreras guilty of the 1976 murder of Orlando Letelier, Chile's former foreign minister and defense secretary. Contreras was sentenced to seven years in prison. Contreras and DINA's second in command, Brigadier Pedro Espinoza, became the first high-ranking Chilean officials convicted for human-rights violations; they inaugurated the Punta Peuco cell block designed for offenders from the regime.

More trials and convictions followed for Contreras. He was sentenced for the abduction and forced disappearance of the Socialist Party leader Victor Olea Alegría, the disappearance of the MIR member Miguel Ángel Sandoval, the Colonia Dignidad clandestine torture center case, and complicity in the 1974 murder of the former army chief of staff Carlos Prats and his wife, Sofia Cuthbert, in Buenos Aires. Due to his advanced age and his illness, Contreras served some of these sentences and awaited trial for new cases in a home attached to a military installation. He still faces trial within Chile and abroad for an increasing number of cases, including the attempted murder of the former vice-president Bernardo Leighton and his wife, Anita Fresno, in Rome; the organization and operation of a regional, violent, repressive network throughout South America (Operation Condor); the murder of the Spanish diplomat Carmen Soria; and the disappearances of Alphonse Chanfreau and Jean-Yves Claudet-Fernández. With additional documents, testimony, other forms of evidence, and decisions by some courts to bypass the amnesty law, trials against Contreras continue. But so, too, do his appeals.[1]

What remains unclear is whether the military could not or would not protect Contreras from prosecution. Evidence suggests deep distrust among his colleagues and superiors within the military. Several had reported his abuses to Pinochet before the end of the dictatorship, including an incident in which he shot several longshoremen in the chest when they appeared to ignore his orders to unload bags of food supplies at a faster rate.[2] Colonel Edgardo Ceballo Jones, head of the Air Force Intelligence Unit (SIFA), reported that he had begun to hide his released prisoners from Contreras after he discovered that Contreras had been picking them up and disappearing them. General Sergio Arellano Stark, who enjoyed his own reputation as the "Butcher of the North," referred to Contreras as a "Gestapo leader." General Odlanier Mena accused Contreras of trying to poison him and to murder two other officials (Lieutenant Carevic and Colonel Vergara). Contreras's commanding officer, General Orozco, attempted to fire him for violent excesses.

Contreras also had a reputation of disloyalty within the armed forces. His colleagues accused him of "build[ing] his own power base at the expense of the older branches of government." He allegedly recruited members of other branches of the armed forces into DINA to prepare "reports, gossip, and blackmail material from their former organizations."[3] Contreras then used this material to gain power over his colleagues. Pinochet's biographer, Gonzalo Vial, claims that Contreras made himself invaluable to Pinochet by fabricating "frequently and with great detail, plots to assassinate him [Pinochet], or members of his family, and how DINA had crushed them."[4] Within and outside the armed forces, and within and outside Chile, Contreras had a reputation as "one of the most shadowy, ruthless men in the world."[5]

His final vestige of support within the armed forces may have eroded with the declassification in 2000 of the U.S. Central Intelligence Agency (CIA) documents concerning Chile, which revealed that the CIA had Contreras on its payroll. This news scandalized U.S. audiences, since the CIA had previously identified Contreras as "the principal obstacle" to improving human-rights abuses in Chile and knew that DINA was involved in tracking down and eliminating opponents outside Chilean borders.[6] Contreras attempted to dismiss the charges as a CIA conspiracy against him, responding, "This is the most untrue, absurd and ridiculous thing I have read recently. The CIA is not declassifying documents; they are making them up as they go along."[7] Few of his colleagues could forgive him for serving another government and betraying his country, the armed forces, and the regime.

Despite his reputation within the armed forces, it remains surprising that his former colleagues contributed to his prosecution. One journalist directly attributed Contreras's indictment to one DINA agent's testimony before the Chilean truth commission, popularly known as the Rettig Commission.[8] That agent, Luz Arce, revealed DINA's role in kidnapping, torture, murder, and disappearing "subversives" within and outside Chile. Arce personified one of DINA's signature tactics: DINA had detained her as a left-wing militant, tortured her, forced her to collaborate in the detention, torture, and disappearance of her former comrades, and subsequently hired her as a paid agent. In February 2001 Radio Cooperativa transmitted a broadcast by an anonymous former DINA agent who testified in court that Contreras had participated in throwing detainees' bodies into the sea.[9] When the retired general Sergio Arellano Stark faced charges for the Caravan of Death, a campaign of political assassinations following the coup, he blamed DINA and Contreras. The human-rights community seized on this acknowledgment of Contreras's guilt from within the armed forces: "General Pinochet says that he believes him [Contreras], but not that Contreras is innocent. Moreover, personnel who figured prominently in the Letelier case, such as the then subsecretary of the interior, Enrique Montero Marx, have declared your [Contreras's] guilt."[10]

However, Chilean civilian courts, and not the military, tried, convicted, and imprisoned Contreras, a success that depended on institutional and societal transformations. The human-rights community pressured for convictions in cases beyond the amnesty law's reach, including crimes committed outside the time period covered by the law. But disappearances, crucial for Contreras's conviction, also fell outside the amnesty provision. Amnesty, the courts determined, required a crime. Without a death certificate, a body, or any other evidence of a crime, the courts could not grant amnesty. Thus, in addition to his involvement in international crimes, Contreras faced investigation and prosecution for disappearances, most notably of the detainees at the Tejas Verdes and Villa Grimaldi torture centers and the 1976 disappearance of five Communist Party leaders (Calle Conferencia). The Supreme Court of Chile, no longer stacked with Pinochet appointees, further reduced Contreras's guarantee of winning amnesty on appeal.

Contreras therefore appealed to the Chilean public. Between 1991, when he condemned the Rettig Commission's findings, and his 2003 conviction for the Prats murder, Contreras made at least five major television appearances.[11] The frequency of his appearances led one journalist to refer to Channel 13 as "General Contreras's permanent [public] platform."[12] Newspapers and radio programs covered his television appearances and produced independent stories and interviews with him, heightening his media profile. Despite this extensive coverage, Contreras maintained control over his image. The reporting proved surprisingly uncritical: Contreras spoke unchallenged in interviews; journalists failed to analyze or report on courtroom drama, including his testimony or responses to it; and the media reproduced Contreras's response to the attacks on him as "ridiculous," "absurd," "infantile," and "Marxist falsehoods." Describing his own relationship to the media, he said, "I have been mentioned in vulgar, undignified, slanderous, and absolutely false terms, which is why I feel obligated to respond, and to ask you to include this response in your newspaper."[13]

Contreras also found independent outlets to make his public appeal. He organized his own website (now defunct) to document his version of the past. He subsequently published that material in two volumes titled *La verdad histórica* (The historic truth). Each book contains nearly 600 pages, consisting primarily of documents of questionable validity. One of the few journalists who reviewed the books referred to the materials they contained as "assumptions, unknown or unidentified sources . . . and documents of dubious legitimacy or written by Contreras himself [or] . . . anonymous sources, difficult to check or corroborate."[14] Neither the books nor the website attracted much attention, which allowed Contreras's supporters to refer to them as "undenied" truths.[15]

Contreras's confessional denial, repeated in the courtroom, the media, and his independent communication, contends that (1) he was engaged in a heroic war against subversion, not in human-rights violations; (2) subversives, not the military, committed past human-rights violations; (3) those subversives had reemerged and allied with the democratic government to seek revenge against him; and (4) he did not act alone and cannot be held personally responsible. As he left the Punta Peuco jail, Contreras denied wrongdoing in a few simple words: "I have nothing to repent. I did what I was told to do, and I did it well."[16]

Heroism and accusations against "subversives" with regard to human-rights violations merged in Contreras's recounting of history. According to him, the armed forces responded to Chilean society's demand to save the country from communism and to end the bloodbath. The military ended the Allende government's human-rights violations, restored order, reestablished democracy, and promoted economic success. As Contreras stated, "The citizens of our country suffered between 1970 and 1973 at the hands of the Chilean and foreign Marxist guerrillas."[17] He further asserted, "The Chilean people must not forget their soldiers, sailors, pilots, and police who yesterday saved their lives and recovered this land of ours from the ashes where [it] was thrown by the atheist, criminal Marxists. Sarcastically today the same Marxist perpetrators who ruled the people during the thousand black days of the Popular Unity [government] have charged them in court."[18]

Contreras admitted that the military used "unconventional methods," but only to protect the population from guerrilla tactics: "We fought with these people covertly because these individuals used the same tactic as in Vietnam. During the day they were workers, college students, doctors, or any other profession. At night they were guerrillas. This is who fought. Until 1990 there were more than 300 confrontations between the army and [the guerrillas]. It is very easy to attack as a civilian because the military doesn't see you. So they ordered us to dress as civilians like [the guerrillas] and we entered the underground fight as well."[19] These methods, he claimed, did not violate human rights: "I have never acknowledged that there were human-rights violations during the military government, not in my case, nor by my people. We acted under the law."[20] He stated that rather than the "human-rights violators" label attributed to them, the correct terminology would be "military combatants against terrorism in the Subversive War of 1973."[21]

Contreras used military terminology to explain away the "disappeared." War, he claimed, produces disappearances, or bodies that cannot be found. Contreras further contended that only 300—rather than 1,197, as cited by the Rettig Commission—disappeared in Chile and that the number included losses incurred by the military as well as by the guerrillas. He accused "Marxists" of cynically manipulating the numbers, including those of individuals "hurt in combat," who were subsequently "evacuated by the same group of guerilla fighters," but listed as disappeared after they had died. He described the process.

> The Marxist system was to flee secretly from the country, assuming false identities or using other identities conferred on them by the head of the party and taken from guerrillas who had died in combat. They continued to operate abroad under the orders of the Southern Revolutionary Coordinating Junta located in Buenos Aires, which united under its command all of the revolutionary movements in South America. . . . Then they returned secretly to the country to continue to work in operations for the guerrilla war, reintegrating themselves in the unit.
>
> The family, conscious or not of the truth, reported the individual as "detained and disappeared," on the date that proved most convenient and in agreement with the party, who coerced them to do it.[22]

Contreras continued, "It's more advantageous to their cause to make the enemy responsible for having made them disappear, that is, to allow public opinion to consider them 'the detained and disappeared,' even though they were buried in secret places by the same guerrillas."[23] He further contended that "Marxist doctrine" would not acknowledge that the military government took prisoners, housed them in special units, and released them. Instead, those prisoners had been coerced into claiming that they were "tortured terribly" and told what kind of torture they must reveal to heighten the image of military cruelty. As "proof," Contreras reproduced documents that purported to show that individuals who appeared on the list of disappeared had instead left the country. Although a DINA agent had revealed that Operation Condor agents had used the national identification documents of the detained and disappeared to enter neighboring countries, Contreras still boldly asserted that his documents proved that the disappeared were "dead and buried by the MIR, by the Communist Party, and by the Socialist Party."[24]

Contreras's denial involved a dizzying game in which he denied some data produced by the human-rights community while using other data they put forward, employed the language of war but denied the use of conventional wartime methods, and presented numbers without verifying their source. He used a "just war" defense that spoke of "battlefields," for example, even when his own discussion of "unconventional methods" defied such a notion. He denied disappearances, but then used Rettig Commission numbers to claim that the Chilean military caused fewer deaths and disappearances than its neighbors in Latin America's Southern Cone.[25] He denied the military's involvement in human-rights violations, yet claimed that "both sides" were guilty of committing them. As he stated, "If reconciliation is desired in reality, it must be accepted that if excesses and violations of human rights occurred, they occurred on both sides, and this is natural because it occurs in all wars and it is not fair at all to try to judge only the military side without considering that the true 'cause' of the country's destruction and the violation of human rights was initiated by the Marxists. The war against the guerrillas that developed after 11 September 1973, although they don't . . . want to call it this, was in reality the "effect" of the provocation of three years of human-rights violations by the Marxist left in our country."[26]

Contreras's logic included a willingness to admit to violations of human rights *only* if the "subversives" also admitted to an equal level of violations. Because they would not, he denied the regime's violations and characterized the legal processes as revenge taken by the "Marxists" allied with the democratic government for losing the war.

> Today, when the country was saved from the ashes by the armed forces and public order, responding to the desperate pleas of the people oppressed by Marxist tyranny, when the military government succeeded in reconstructing our institutions, when we became recognized as one of the emerging economies in the world, [the Marxist leaders] have appeared again, those who yesterday fled the country, abandoning "the poor young idealists" who fought alone, abandoned by their bosses who were enjoying their excellent lives in far-off American and European lands. They returned "transformed," sincerely in some cases, and improbably in others. The hatred, resentment, and desire for revenge is even greater. It couldn't be otherwise; Marxists don't accept defeat and even less at the hands of the Forces for National Defense, who were their natural enemies.[27]

Contreras further accused the left-democratic government alliance of sowing disorder and chaos again, this time under the banner of human rights.

They poison our youth every day, a youth that didn't know about and had nothing to do with the past events, events that should remain in the memory trunk, but are presented as if they happened yesterday. Certain groups, who have already been brainwashed, have created a sad spectacle of screaming in the streets against the military government, demanding solutions for events that don't concern them and without knowing anything about the reality of the situation, the truth. Their impulsive and negative attitude against everything related to the military government, remind us of the past difficult times that we all wish we could forget, but that the extremists of yesteryear, cowardly runaways to new, more prosperous, lives abroad, and who return to the country converted into white doves, won't let the youth forget and instead try to convert them into furious crowds full of hate, resentment, and revenge.[28]

Contreras believed that the Left had achieved the highest positions of power in the democratic government due to "the poor memory of a healthy people who forget the past and believe again in the hot air of those who destroyed the Fatherland. They have no shame about asking the courts to investigate the 'human-rights violations' of the military government. For them, Chile was born on September 11, 1973."[29] He continued: "What appeared to be an unbelievable story, perhaps from an imaginary country, became a tangible reality: the victors considered heroes yesterday have become, thanks to the psychological action carried out by Marxist elements that have infiltrated the government, today's villains to be judged and condemned to sentences in Hell. But the Marxists, violators of human rights yesterday, are not touched, are not investigated, are not condemned, but, on the contrary, are rewarded, praised, honored in monuments, and, in the end, pardoned."[30]

The Marxist skill at deception, in Contreras's estimation, produced the distortions in the Rettig Commission's report on human-rights abuses (known as the Rettig Report).[31] The commission received its information from the Catholic Church's Vicaría de la Solidaridad (Vicariate of Solidarity), an organization he considered to have been infiltrated by Marxists.[32] He referred to the Rettig Report as the "Marxists' bible," which he felt exaggerated the number of losses that the Left incurred and minimized losses caused by the Left.

The Rettig Report . . . considered only those Marxists who fell between 1973 and 1991, which it established at 1,132 dead and 957 disappeared.

But it didn't take into consideration at all those fallen between 1970 and 1973 as a result of guerrilla actions carried out by the Marxist guerrilla army against the Chilean civilian population.

Between 1970 and 1973 there were . . . 953 fallen among the civilian population and 111 fallen among the armed forces and public order [units] and 134 fallen among the Marxist guerrillas, producing a total of 1,198 dead. . . .

Between 1970 and 1989, there were 760 fallen in the armed forces and public order [units] that are not considered in the Rettig Report which only accepts 132 fallen. This demonstrates a blatant effort to hide the truth from public opinion and to lower the value of the subversive war. There would be no reason for anyone to die if this were a peaceful country. The Chilean military, obligated by the guerrilla war that provoked them, fell in urban combat with the guerrillas throughout those years.[33]

In what appeared to be a retraction from his steadfast denial, Contreras occasionally acknowledged human-rights violations by the military. He denied his own responsibility for those violations, however, by blaming others or asserting that he was following orders. He declared, for example, that he would defend himself and DINA, but not violations that other branches of the armed forces had committed. He blamed the FBI agent Robert Scherrer for inventing Operation Condor while he was stationed in Argentina in the 1970s, even though Contreras had earlier denied the existence of the operation, deeming it "leftist fiction." He attributed the murders of Chilean leaders outside the country to the CIA.[34]

Contreras began his second book with the epigraph "If you repeat a lie enough times, even those who know it is not true will begin to believe it."[35] But instead of generating "lies," the human-rights community used Contreras's confession to demand his prosecution and the disclosure of documents. As Viviana Díaz, the president of the Association of the Families of the Detained and Disappeared, stated, "The [Contreras] book reaffirms what we have always said, that the information concerning the whereabouts of those who were detained and disappeared exists and that the military refuses to release it."[36] The community also questioned Contreras's "just war" defense, as in this excerpt from an open letter to Contreras published in the left-wing news magazine *Punto Final*: "In what war did you participate, general? Or do you mean to call 'war' the secret prisons, the torture chambers, the battles—supposed and real—against handfuls of combatants, and the disappearance of detainees? You might be able to convince your comrades in arms that ['war' means] the Lonquén massacre, or the killing of peasants in Chihuío in which even children died . . . or the executions of prisoners by General Arellano Stark in October 1973."[37]

But not everyone in Contreras's audience of human-rights activists, leftists, and democratic government leaders wanted to engage him. Some wanted to silence him, refusing to dignify his words with a response. President Allende's widow, Hortensia Bussi, refused to contest his statements, stating only, "He is such a despicable person that I cannot place any value in his words."[38] President Eduardo Frei called for silence, or at least moderation, to avoid destabilizing political polarization over Contreras's conviction: "Let us not be dragged down by the divisions of the past."[39]

Frei had little to fear. Multiple interpretations rather than ideological poles emerged from Contreras's confessional performance. The human-rights community fragmented into groups ranging from those who considered his imprisonment a major victory for ending the culture of impunity in the region to those who saw it perpetuating that culture.

Those buoyed by his imprisonment pointed to Contreras's failure to resist incarceration. Contreras had nearly provoked a showdown over it. He accused the supreme court judges of bowing to pressure from the "Marxists" and condemned the court because his "constitutional rights were not respected." Threatening military insurrection, he stated, "When they come for me, I will decide what is necessary at that moment. As a general I am not going to run away because I am going to face the battle. I am a winner and do not want to lose."[40] When the Catalan Brigade, a group identifying itself as "reactivated" members of DINA and CNI, took over Chile's state-run television signals to protest Contreras's imprisonment, it looked like he was calling the court's bluff.[41] But Contreras ended the brinkmanship by succumbing to authorities. He also gave up his 700-hectare country house, Viejo Roble (Old Oak), in 1998 because he owed an estimated 234 million pesos that he could not pay, which further diminished his power. For some within the human-rights community, his precipitous fall meant not only justice within Chile, but in Latin America more generally: "It could be said that this cornered man, 65, pudgy with neatly combed, gray-streaked hair, represents the decline of a once feared species: the authoritarian Latin American general. Once coddled by despots who often came from the same ranks, immune to public scorn and beyond the reach of the law, Latin America's old generals are not having an easy time."[42]

Others interpreted Contreras's imprisonment as merely symbolic, not retributive, justice. They protested his short—six year—sentence for murdering Orlando Letelier. Gladys Marín, secretary-general of the Chilean Communist Party, whose husband's disappearance constituted one of the many cases against Contreras, vehemently condemned his release from prison after he had served his term: "Contreras is one of the principal actors in the events after the coup d'état and his freedom represents torture for the society."[43]

His cell in Punta Peuco reinforced the view of symbolic justice. He had a suite of rooms that included a library full of books, primarily relating to military history. Visitors, admitted around the clock, could meet with him in his "living room," containing two armchairs with accompanying side tables. He displayed a photograph of his wife on one table and an open Bible and rosary on the other. "Everything about the ambiance is French," noted one journalist: "French Provincial chairs, the small French obelisk on the enormous oak desk, a French artist's sculpture of a woman's head in the corner, French lace curtains."[44] In this prison Contreras could avoid looking or acting like an inmate, and he did. A journalist described him as "rather short and slightly paunchy, but in dress and comportment he is the essence of refinement. His suit . . . is an expensively tailored pinstripe cut in the European style. He speaks formal Spanish, never uttering a word of slang."[45] The only detraction from Contreras's image of European refinement, the journalist noted, involved the "standard American Muzak" softly emanating from speakers on the bookshelves. Contreras "worked" on a modern computer system and enjoyed unlimited access to the Internet, fax, and telephone. To help him care for his deteriorating health (colon cancer, hypertension, diabetes, and thrombosis), Contreras had a personal chef and an exercise room equipped with a treadmill and stationary bicycle. Such lavish conditions led one journalist to remark that the security system at Punta Peuco seemed better designed to keep certain people from entering than to keep Contreras from leaving.[46] As if to confirm that perspective, Contreras rhetorically asked an interviewer: "Is this a prison?" and answered, "No, this isn't a prison, it is a military installation—mil-i-tary. . . . And I'm going to tell you something. I didn't have to come to Punta Peuco if I didn't want to. I could have gotten out of it."[47]

Contreras attempted to turn his imprisonment into a badge of honor. "Espinoza and I are in Punta Peuco," he stated, "precisely because we told the truth, although it is not recognized as such. We have accepted our destiny like men, without harming anyone, or being disloyal to anyone."[48] He referred to himself as a "political prisoner" and expressed pride in his political leadership: "I feel proud of having been the peacemaker in Chile and I am proud that none of my people are in prison. It's not important that I am."[49]

Observers wondered how much it would take before Contreras might begin to resent his scapegoating and bring down Pinochet's house of cards.[50] Protesters took to the streets bearing placards that read "Contreras today, Pinochet tomorrow." The journalist and literary critic Christopher Hitchens stated that Contreras "remain[ed] in prison, doubtless wondering why he trusted his superiors."[51] Rumors circulated that Contreras had provided the information Judge Garzón needed to detain Pinochet in London.[52] But Contreras denied those accusations, stating, "I haven't sent anything but straw [*maitre*] to Garzón." Yet his loyalty to Pinochet appeared on shaky ground when he admitted, "DINA is a military organism that depends first, directly on the president of the honorable government junta, and then on the president of the republic."[53] He went on to say, "It is not an autonomous organism that could make decisions on its own, particularly a decision so serious and with so much responsibility as the assassination of Orlando Letelier."[54] Contreras made these statements in documents "leaked" to the Spanish newspaper *El País* and later reproduced in the Chilean news media.[55] Pinochet responded harshly: "It sounds as if he were accusing me," which would be a "horrific betrayal." But Pinochet moderated his remarks by adding that Contreras was "an excellent official," whom he "love[d] like a son." Distancing himself from Contreras's legal disputes, Pinochet confirmed, "I created the doctrine on intelligence, but he had to develop how to carry it out."[56] Contreras covered his gaffe: "My explanation intended to demonstrate a truth established in law: my direct subordination to the president. And to this day I remain totally loyal to Captain General Mr. Augusto Pinochet Ugarte."[57]

Contreras enjoyed some support within Chile, although it was more symbolic than real. Gonzalo Townsend Pinochet, Pinochet's nephew, linked his uncle's detention in London to Contreras's detention in Chile: "Those who yesterday saved the nation, today are prisoners; those who tried to destroy it, today are celebrated."[58] *Despierta Chile*, a newspaper organized in the 1990s to defend the regime, took up Contreras's defense as one of its central causes, stating, "The blame for what happened in our country, and the excesses that have been exposed, especially in the courts of justice, should belong to those who wanted to burn up the country. But it turns out that today the guilty are the firefighters."[59] *Despierta Chile* accused the democratic government of hunting down and prosecuting war heroes, and it warned, "Watch out for corrupt governments where trickery hangs its nets, where justice is hated, where truth hides, and lies and revenge are the authority."[60] The retired general and senator Santiago Sinclair agreed: "There is a clear intention to sully the honor of the army, but I warn those who have such intentions that they will not be able to do so."[61]

Contreras's supporters also included those who believed he had taken the fall for the regime. They judged his efforts to establish Pinochet's responsibility for DINA's orders as "the actions of a wounded man who [felt] that he [had] been abandoned after having carried out his job during the most difficult period of the dictatorship."[62] The retired major Carlos Herrera Jiménez, serving a ten-year prison sentence at Punta Peuco for a murder committed as part of the military regime's repression of the Left, stated that Contreras's violations "could not have been committed without the express orders of a general. . . . It must not be overlooked that when the death of Mr. Letelier occurred, Contreras was a lieutenant colonel and the other [Pedro Espinoza], a major. Anyone who knows even a little bit about the military world will understand how difficult it would be for a lieutenant colonel and a major, without anyone knowing, to organize the murder of a diplomat by placing a bomb in the heart of the civilian zone of the most important country in the world."[63] Herrera Jiménez continued: "Although it is painful to admit it, this is the only army in the world that, when the time comes, the generals have failed to take their responsibility for the orders they gave."[64]

Pedro Espinoza concurred. He confessed that a letter leaked to the press in 2000 had been written by him and notarized in 1978. The letter attested to the chain of command: that Contreras had taken his orders directly from General Pinochet. It further indicted Hector Orozco, the military's investigating officer in the Letelier matter, for pressuring Espinoza to state that only Contreras, and not Pinochet, had given him orders. The pressure included threats to harm Espinoza's wife and children if he said anything that would make Pinochet responsible for the crime. Espinoza had stated, "The order to eliminate Letelier was given to me by Colonel Contreras," and had wanted to add that the order was "authorized by the president of the republic."[65] "Contreras," as one journalist noted, "is not just another prisoner. He is an emblem of the dark side of the military regime's repression, a symbol of the efforts by the Concertación for clarifying crimes of the pasts, and, not unimportantly, a permanent headache due to his episodic allegations against Pinochet and the others who gave him orders."[66]

Contreras's son, Manuel Contreras Valdebenito, added to this perspective on his father's guilt. In what some consider to be a plot by the elder Contreras, his son called on his father to admit everything about his past and stop protecting the military and Pinochet. The younger Contreras portrayed his father as devoted to the regime's political strategy and personally loyal to Pinochet, driving him to commit atrocities, including throwing bodies into the sea. He begged his father to accept responsibility for his past acts, but also called on the rest of the military command to assume their own, rather than scapegoat his father. The younger Contreras explained his personal plea, stating, "It is I who gets insulted on the streets and called a son of a murderer."[67]

Other regime supporters distanced themselves from Contreras to deemphasize the regime's association with violence and embrace its role in economic modernization. The right-wing National Renovation Party president Andrés Allamand, for example, criticized Contreras for his flagrant defiance of the law: "In a nation of rights, no one can avoid the law, and Contreras is no exception."[68] He questioned Contreras's justification of violence, stating that it "leads to two unacceptable aberrations: first, that the end justifies the means; secondly, that to deal with terrorists one must use their same criminal methods. From my point of view, both are ethically, morally, politically and legally wrong."[69] When Contreras hinted at Pinochet's orders, the director of the party's Youth League retorted, "The Left applauds General Contreras's lawyer and they beg him to continue with this attitude that favors the case of the Communist Party against Pinochet. . . . I am Pinochetista, not Contrerista."[70] Pinochet's biographer rebuked Contreras's allegations with "No one watched Contreras."[71] When Contreras claimed that the deceased general Otto Carlos Paladino, former head of the Army Intelligence Service (SIDE), would have cleared his name of allegations, Paladino's lawyer remarked, "It is curious that after so many years he [Contreras] uses words from someone who has died and who cannot ratify or deny what he attributes to him."[72]

Church leaders also distanced themselves from Contreras. When Luz Arce accused a priest of having made frequent visits to DINA headquarters to meet with Contreras, he attacked her for lying. Expressing the degree to which an association with Contreras would damage his reputation, the priest stormed: "I never went to a DINA barracks, I never met with Manuel Contreras. I will not tolerate this continuous stain on my name and my honor. You cannot play around with my honor."[73]

Contreras grew increasingly isolated in prison and abandoned by his colleagues in the armed forces and other regime supporters. But he steadfastly clung to his version of events. In May 2005 Contreras prepared a document allegedly disclosing the location of nearly 600 disappeared detainees. The human-rights community decried the document for failing to provide any new information, for contradicting existing information, for covering up evidence, and for misleading the Chilean public.[74] But something had changed. In the document Contreras attributed responsibility for all actions carried out by DINA to Pinochet—and he did so not once, but seven times. He insinuated that Pinochet's "ominous silence" and failure to defend DINA, an agency totally dependent on his direct authority, had led to the "unjust and intolerable" treatment of DINA's staff. He criticized Pinochet for lacking the "courage," "honor," and "manliness" to assume responsibility for his orders and protect those who carried out his orders from humiliation, trial, and imprisonment.[75]

Pinochet responded with his own denial, reiterating that he had had no direct influence over DINA. But Contreras's mounting accusations provoked Pinochet to retaliate with his own. He incriminated Contreras in a plot to overthrow the government and disclosed that Contreras had created so many problems in DINA that Pinochet had had to fire him.[76] Contreras's betrayal not only drew Pinochet out of the shadows, according to Peter Kornbluh of the National Security

"One more for the Punta Peuco jail." A poster mounted in 1999 in the headquarters of the Association of the Families of the Detained and Disappeared in Santiago, Chile; it called for the imprisonment of the former dictator General Augusto Pinochet.

Archive, but it also made a "small step forward" in the criminal investigations against Pinochet.

Contreras never recanted his denial of wrongdoing. Neither imprisonment nor isolation changed his view. This is hardly surprising not only because Contreras believed in his own innocence, but also because no other narrative would have saved him from prison. He was simply too important to let go in a plea-bargaining agreement.

COMPARATIVE PERSPECTIVES ON PERPETRATORS' DENIAL

Denial and silence constitute the most common forms of perpetrator accounts for past violence. In confessional denials, perpetrators admit to their roles in the past, but deny wrongdoing or knowledge of wrongdoing. Denial has its logic. It protects individuals from legal and social reprisals. But even without the threat of such reprisals, most perpetrators must actually believe in their innocence, as well as the legal justifications and excuses for their acts, to continue committing them. How they defend themselves, and who they offend in the process, makes for dynamic political drama conducive to contentious coexistence.

"The Guardian of Divine Principles." The sociologist Stanley Cohen refers to a "spiral of denial" in which timing influences text. The spiral begins with simple refutation, a perpetrator's claim that torture, murder, and disappearance never occurred. Sooner or later, however, evidence makes it impossible for perpetrators to simply deny violence, so they then try to explain it. Contreras thus constructs his "war" explanation for death and disappearance, an explanation that allows him to continue denying criminal acts. The third part of the spiral transforms the violent act into a virtuous one. Perpetrators, like Contreras, refer to their past in terms of duty, patriotism, or heroism. Contreras even challenges the patriotism of those who accuse him of criminal acts.

The spiral of denial plays out in many confessional texts. Héctor Pedro Vergez, a former army captain and director of the La Perla torture center in Argentina, at first simply denied his own involvement in the murder of Luz Mujica de Rearte: "I know that they have attributed the death to me. But the truth is that when I found out about it I put my head in my hands. It was a barbarity and I didn't have anything to do with it."[77] Despite his denial, Vergez was convicted and spent nearly two years in jail before he was released under the Due Obedience Law. Other information about Vergez's criminal acts surfaced at the end of the dictatorship, including the establishment of a store in Córdoba that sold goods stolen from the homes of detainees, the extortion of money from their families, the sexual torture of women detainees, and his involvement in the murder and disappearance of detainees. Vergez was also assumed to have been the leader of the right-wing Peronist organization Comando Libertadores de América, the Córdoba version of the Argentine Anticommunist Alliance, which had carried out much of the repression prior to the 1976 coup.

Vergez later abandoned his simple denial in favor of a more elaborate one that he peddled in various forms. He tried to sell his story, for example, for $30,000, but found no buyers. He then wrote and published his own book, *Yo fui Vargas: El antiterrorismo por dentro*, and accepted media appearances. In these subsequent confessions, Vergez adopted the "war" explanation, and his heroism in that war, to deny his involvement in state terrorism or repression. Vergez claimed that the Argentine war constituted a difference in degrees, but not in kind, of casualties. Having taken place on Argentine soil and among Argentines, its physical and emotional toll proved particularly high. As Vergez stated, "I know the horror of war because that is war; simply a horror. . . . We worked [hard] so that it would never occur again. We must make clear, really clear, that this painful and terrible war between brothers developed in the same way and with the same methods, and was not unique to the military period, but also to the period that occurred at the end of the government of General Lanusse and throughout the Peronist government."

Vergez elevated himself to the honorable role of heroic, self-sacrificing soldier. In war, he said, "you kill or you die." And while he said, "I love my army," he regretted that he "had the bad luck of serving during that time." Having responded to the call of the Argentine people and democratic government, and performed his duty to his country, Vergez had participated in defeating the "murderous Left" and ending the international conspiracy in Argentina at the time.

Vergez insinuated that torture might be included among his heroic acts. To direct questions posed to him by journalists, Vergez characterized torture as "harsh interrogations, very harsh." But he further discussed its use: "Let's not fuck around about torture. Every army and police [force] in the world tortures to get information and we've always known this. If you grab someone who bombed AMIA [the Argentine Jewish cultural center], aren't you going to give him the stick so that he sings?"[78] He even hinted that he himself used torture: "Listen to how strange this is: the other day an Israeli military leader said that the only thing that you can't do in an interrogation of a terrorist is kill him. I did some courses with people in the Israeli services in 1972."[79] Vergez, in other words, admitted to the regime's, and his own, acts of violence, but characterized those acts as heroic and widespread, thereby absolving himself of wrongdoing.

The notorious former Buenos Aires police commissioner Miguel Osvaldo Etchecolatz taunted the human-rights community with his own version of a simple denial: "Many times I have asked forgiveness from my God and I will continue doing so. I am guilty of many things, but, notably, none of them are included in the [crimes] for which I have been charged."[80] The prosecution did not share his view. He was convicted on ninety-five counts of torture and sentenced to twenty-three years in prison, although he was released under the Due Obedience Law.

Etchecolatz subsequently launched a cynical and aggressive version of the spiral of denial through his book, *La otra campana del nunca más*, and media appearances. "The only thing I did was combat the Marxist subversion, the demonic enemy," he claimed.[81] Justifying his acts as "combat," he boasted, "When I was ordered to take on the responsibility of fighting terrorist organizations, I confess that I was honored to be selected. Fate proved what I could give to my country, to millions of Argentines who did not want to live with those assassins."[82] He went on to deny guilt for his operations: "I state that I never had, nor thought I should have, a guilty conscience. For having killed? I executed a law written by men. I was the guardian of divine principles. For both reasons I would do it again, giving all I had, which for this [important] mission is very little."[83]

Etchecolatz's confession did not involve a defensive denial, but an aggressive offensive. On the television program *Hora Clave*, Etchecolatz grilled his former torture victim, Deputy Alfredo Bravo, demanding that he publicly recount his torture experience and suggesting that Bravo had invented it. He then contradicted his own denial by claiming that the actions taken against Bravo might have been beneficial: "From his youth he [Bravo] had flat feet and plantar warts. . . . The treatment we gave him could have cured him." He denied having raped Lidia Papaleo Graiver, but regretted having forfeited the opportunity since, in his words, "it would have been a privilege." Similarly, Etchecolatz denied using torture but advocated it to "save lives": "This sacrifice of lives would have been diminished in numbers if the military government, recognizing the necessity of rapidly restoring internal peace, had adopted the wise policy adopted by the government of Israel, 'the use of torture for interrogations in those cases in which there is a risk of loss of life, and when there is strong suspicion that the detainee is holding back information that could prevent those deaths.' "[84]

References by Vergez and Etchecolatz to Israel and the AMIA bombing might seem surprising given the notorious anti-Semitism of the

Argentine military regime. They used these references deliberately, however, to show the hypocrisy of supporting torture in some cases and not in others. They also used it to legitimize the use of torture to save innocent lives. They thus linked the Left to threats to the innocent to justify the regime's use of torture. Etchecolatz, for example, accused Bravo and Graciela Fernández Meijide, a human-rights activist and mother of a disappeared detainee, of "sending kids to their death." He attacked "subversives" for using their children to shield themselves from security forces. He described the "ferocity with which pregnant guerrillas, soon to become mothers, fought to the very last bullet."[85]

Even in the face of mounting evidence against them, perpetrators hold on to denial. Pinochet's forces clung to denial, for example, despite the publication in November 2004 of the National Commission on Political Imprisonment and Torture Report (known as the Valech Report), which documented the systematic illegal detention and torture of detainees by the Chilean military, eighteen types of torture, and 800 clandestine torture centers. Pinochet did not react to the findings, but his former spokesman, General Guillermo Garín, simply stated, "The investigation has failed to prove people were really tortured."[86] Vergez's book jacket portrayed him on horseback leaping over burning walls with the words "nunca más" and the names of "left-wing villains" written on them. He claimed that the accusations against him made him laugh.[87] Similarly, Etchecolatz refers to the CONADEP report *Nunca más* as a "novel," intended "not to cleanly inform, but to create a state of repulsion and revenge . . . a plan to discredit the armed forces that defended the nation in its difficult moments . . . and condemning those of us who were protagonists on the battlefields."[88] Denial does not disappear or erode over time; it escalates and spirals.

"Whispered in the Corridors." "Plausible deniability" allows perpetrators to claim that who they were—their rank or position—exculpates them from committing or even knowing about violent acts. Perpetrators at the very top of the security apparatus, for example, claim that their distance from day-to-day operations proves their innocence and lack of knowledge.

Yet these very individuals, as heads of state or commanding officers, bear ultimate responsibility for those crimes. Or so their audience contends. And to make this point, audiences often point to the absurdity of the plausible-deniability defense. In perhaps one of the most famous contradictions, Pinochet had claimed throughout his dictatorship, "Not a leaf rustles in Chile without my knowing." Yet he expected audiences to believe that he had had no knowledge of the abuses that occurred while he was in power.

Middle-level officers, who issued orders, could not invoke this "distance" form of denial. Instead, they claimed that those who had committed crimes had done so on their own (rogue forces) or had misunderstood orders. At the South African TRC, for example, commanders argued that they had given orders to "eliminate" or "take out" the enemy, not to kill. An incredulous Glen Gossen, a TRC legal representative, countered, "No reasonable person can possibly not foresee that a reasonable man would interpret such statements to mean you can kill, you can assassinate, you can bomb, you can annihilate."[89] F. W. de Klerk, the former president of South Africa, defended the innocent nature of the orders: "Those quotes about 'eliminate' simply mean to 'neutralize politically.'" Similarly, the former minister of law and order Adriaan Vlok acknowledged only that his orders had been misunderstood, not that he had ordered illegal acts: "I didn't know that they were torturing people. I never approved it. . . . I'm sorry it happened and I can't turn a blind eye. . . . From my discussions, meetings, speeches and orders, there can be no doubt that I possibly used words and expressions which could have been interpreted to mean 'act illegally.'"[90]

A cagier version of plausible deniability also emerged in South Africa: apartheid leaders suggested that they had investigated, albeit not forcefully enough, the allegations and rumors of violence that had come to their attention. As Leon Wessels, former deputy minister of law and order, stated, "I . . . do not believe that the political defense of 'I did not know' is available to me because in many respects I believe I did not want to know. . . . I had my suspicions of things that had caused discomfort in official circles, but because I did not have the facts to substantiate my suspicions or I had lacked the courage to shout from the . . . rooftops, I have to confess that I only whispered in the corridors."[91] Although they denied either issuing orders or committing violence, top commanders could admit some knowledge of the violence and even express remorse for it. They assumed responsibility only for failing to act (crime of omission) and not for ordering, approving of, or committing violence (crime of commission). As the former minister of foreign affairs Pik Botha stated, "The decisive question is not whether we as a Cabinet approved the killing of a specific political opponent. We did not do so. The question is whether we should have done more to ensure that it did not happen. I deeply regret this omission. May God forgive me."[92]

Lower-level officers also used a form of plausible deniability, claiming to have trusted their commanders to issue legal orders. When they carried out such orders, they could plausibly deny that they understood the criminality behind those acts. In addition, some low-level officers pointed to their rank as evidence that they could not have committed violence; they simply did not have the power or position to do so. Directors at the Villa Grimaldi torture camps used such claims. The DINA officer Marcelo Morén Brito, for example, claimed, "I only passed through Villa Grimaldi." Miguel Krassnoff Marchenko, also of DINA, called himself an "analyst," thus denying his commission, or knowledge, of human-rights violations. The well-known torturer Basclay Zapata claimed to be nothing more than a "driver" during the dictatorship.

Masculine pride often creates inconsistencies in and thus weakens perpetrators' confessional denials. Etchecolatz, for example, claimed, "Cowardice does not find any place on my list of defects," which leads one to wonder what kind of "brave acts" he committed inside the clandestine torture center.[93] Vergez described how growing up in the pampas taught him the harsh lesson of dominating others before they dominated him.[94] Vergez attempted to follow the path forged by the Tucumán governor Antonio Domingo Bussi, who committed a famous massacre during the dictatorship and parlayed it into political office. Bussi, however, had confronted a mobilized insurgency in Tucumán, which made his claim to heroism more plausible among regime supporters than Vergez's violations of detainees and their families in his clandestine torture center. When Vergez ran for office in 1999, he had to close his headquarters and end his bid due to lack of support.[95]

"There Is Only One Terrorism." Court cases tend to produce denials, since perpetrators rarely self-incriminate when facing prosecution. Perpetrators employ a set of stock phrases to deny having committed, witnessed, or known about institutional violence. Milorad Krnojelac,

the Bosnian Serb commander at the Foca Kazneno-Popravni Dom (KP Dom) prison, responded with stock phrases in his ICTY testimony, during which he denied charges of torture, beating, killing, forced labor, and forced removal of detained Muslims at the prison in 1992–93.

> I never saw anything like that in the prison yard, because I usually went to the furniture factory at the time when there were no detained persons in the yard.
>
> . . .
>
> I never saw anything like that.
>
> . . .
>
> I can swear on the lives of all the members of my family . . . that I never heard any moans, any screams, any cries of pain, during my stay in the KP Dom.
>
> . . .
>
> I affirm that I never heard about any beatings, any batteries, any killing, except suicide. . . . I mean—I mean that I heard, I did not see, I did not see it.
>
> . . .
>
> I was not responsible for detained persons. . . . In other words, nobody ever told me, nor was I ever aware, of anything like that, of somebody there being punished. . . . I do not know of any such thing.
>
> . . .
>
> I never heard from anyone that the Muslims were used for any such thing, nor am I aware of any such thing.
>
> . . .
>
> I'm not aware of any such thing either.[96]

While frequent, denials do not necessarily serve perpetrators' goals. Contreras, Vergez, Etchecolatz, and Krnojelac discovered that courts do not always believe perpetrators' denials. Perpetrator denials may not surprise audiences, but guilty verdicts that reject denials often do.

Denials that occur in media spots vary in coverage and audience response. Some audiences object to the fact that perpetrators have access to such outlets to deny past violence. "Is it fair," one journalist asks rhetorically, "that proven and sentenced (although not jailed for their full term) assassins simply appear in public spaces and raise their flags to defend the death and vandalism that they carried out during the last bloody military dictatorship?"[97] Most objections surface when media programs present perpetrators on their own terms and without any possibility of contesting their versions of the past. Vergez, appearing on television in his conservative suit and tie, did not look the part of a torturer, killer, and thief. Lacking any debate, the program *Hora Clave* may have appeared to endorse Vergez's denial of past violence.

But several aspects of Vergez's confessional performance undermined it. He may have dressed the part of a business professional to avoid association with his past as a torture-camp director, but his rigid and expressionless face, mechanical speaking style, and the sinister dark bags under his eyes made him look shifty and untrustworthy. In addition, Vergez's television appearance prompted news outlets to rebroadcast Sara Solarz de Osatinsky's testimony at the Trial of the Generals about her detention by Vergez at La Perla. She recounted that Vergez had threatened to kill her "with the goal of wiping the name Osatinsky off the face of the earth"; that he had told her that he had personally killed her eighteen-year-old son and kidnapped and dynamited her husband; and that he had expressed joy at the disappearance of her fifteen-year-old son.[98] The media also reported on Vergez's involvement in kidnapping and torturing Patricia Astelarra, his effort to extract a ransom of $80,000 from her family, and his continued threats after the end of the dictatorship. The media also drew attention to ongoing international cases against Vergez, specifically the United Nation's charge for his role in killing Luz Mujica de Rearte by beating and electrical current and for his sexual torture of the Swiss citizen Teresa Meschiatti. One journalist directly challenged Vergez's concept "war is horror" by raising the specter of these past cases: "No war policy can justify the criminal sadism that he used as head of the concentration and extermination camp, La Perla, in Córdoba."[99]

Etchecolatz's confessional performance included such an aggressive attitude toward his former victim Bravo that it seemed to demonstrate his capacity for torture, even if his words denied it. The politician Elsa Carrió felt she had witnessed Bravo's torture onscreen, though she did not consider it negative for national dialogue. On the contrary, she believed that the confrontation opened up a dialogue about the past and made at least one thing clear: "There is only one terrorism and that is the [authoritarian] state's. [Etchecolatz] demonstrated that there are not two demons [so-called subversives and the military], because what we saw on television was a torturer harassing a teacher."[100]

Efforts to overcome Etchecolatz's confessional performance and present a positive view of the regime failed. Etchecolatz and his supporters had planned to launch his book at the 1998 Buenos Aires book fair. The program for the fair listed the book launch, but Etchecolatz's supporters cancelled the event, claiming that Etchecolatz had received death threats since his confessional performance on *Hora Clave*. The book-fair organizers also feared that his appearance would provoke violence and the destruction of property as audiences acted out their rage at his treatment of Bravo and the country's past.

"Make the Country His Jail." In South Africa F. W. de Klerk, who along with Nelson Mandela won the Nobel Peace Prize for ending the apartheid regime, nonetheless clung to denials about it. Although he did not deny that violence had occurred, he insisted that he had not known about it.

> I should like to express my deepest sympathy with all those on all sides who suffered during the conflict. I and many other leading figures in our party have already publicly apologised for the pain and suffering caused by former policies of the National Party. I reiterate these apologies today. . . .
>
> . . . If I, Mr. Chairman, or the previous government had known what had happened and who had committed this crime, the perpetrator or the perpetrators would have been arrested, tried, and, if found guilty, sentenced. . . . No stone was left unturned in efforts to ascertain the truth. . . .
>
> . . . I want to make it clear from the outset that within my knowledge and experience, they [the orders] never included the authorisation of assassination, murder, torture, rape, assault, or the like. I have never been part of any decision taken by [the] Cabinet, the State Security Council, or any committee authorising or instructing the commission of such gross violations of human rights. Nor did I individually, directly or indirectly, ever suggest, order, or authorise any such action. . . .
>
> . . . It has now become clear that certain elements misused state funds and were involved in unauthorised operations leading to abuses and violation of human rights. . . .
>
> . . . I think it would have pleased everybody if I said it was our official policy. But I can't speak an untruth to satisfy the call for blood, which there is. I can only speak the truth as I know it and the truth is I never participated in such a policy and I was never aware of such a policy. . . .[101]

De Klerk's supporters joined the chorus, reminding audiences that as a civilian, he was shielded from violent events: "If there ever was a civilian in our ranks, that was Mr. F. W. de Klerk. Always, always warning and saying, 'Don't allow yourself to be militarized.' That was F. W. de Klerk."[102]

The human-rights community would not let such absurd claims stand, however. The broadcast journalist Darren Taylor described Desmond Tutu's response to de Klerk's denial: "The image of Archbishop Desmond Tutu sunken in his shoulders with a dazed look on his face won't go away. Tutu portrays the shock, sadness, anger, and frustration of the audience at the National Party hearing. 'How can F. W. de Klerk make such an impassioned and handsome apology that apartheid was wrong,' asks Tutu, 'and then negate that apology by going into a state of denial?' "[103] Taylor quoted Tutu saying "I feel sorry for him that . . . I mean, maybe he didn't know. He didn't know? I told him!" The journalist Antjie Krog concluded, "Tutu finds it difficult to accept that de Klerk didn't know, when he [Tutu] and so many others gave the government an avalanche of information on widespread abuses. How can de Klerk describe the actions of former security police as only 'aberrations' when they were so uniform?"[104]

Because these denials seemed so unbelievable, fellow perpetrators raised questions about their self-serving nature. The South African police perpetrator Eugene de Kock considered de Klerk's denial preposterous. He listed all of the evidence available to any thinking person—especially de Klerk—during the apartheid era: Steve Biko, the forty-sixth person to die in detention, had been kept naked and manacled for twenty days, according to the evidence; Neil Aggett committed suicide in detention, and evidence showed that he had been deprived of sleep for sixty-two hours and given electric shocks; the physician Wendy Orr in 1985 made an appeal to the Supreme Court of South Africa to bar the police from torturing hundreds of detainees under her care in the Port Elizabeth prisons, an appeal that was confirmed by affidavits from 150 detainees; in 1987 the University of Cape Town psychology professor Don Foster published a study showing that 83 percent of detainees had suffered some form of torture, including beatings (75 percent), electrical shocks (25 percent), and strangulation (18 percent); the anti-apartheid activists Ric Turner, Ruth First, Katryn and Jeanette Schoon, Zweli Nyanda, and David Webster were murdered; and Albie Sachs and Michael Lapsley survived murder attempts. Reminding the public of the lies promoted by the apartheid regime to explain these deaths, de Kock stated, "Did a shrewd and legally trained man like him [de Klerk] really believe detainees were prone to slipping on bars of soap and diving out of windows?"[105]

De Klerk could not overcome public skepticism of his denial. He had no answers to give. Etchecolatz had to answer in court for slandering Bravo. Etchecolatz countered that Bravo had also slandered him by referring to him as a sinister figure in history, an assassin, and a thief. But Bravo won the case. The Permanent Assembly of Human Rights also took Etchecolatz to court. It accused Etchecolatz of committing the "apologists' crime" (*apología del delito*) in his *Hora Clave* appearance and in his book because his actions "harmed public peace by trying to provoke fear" through the "public eulogy and praise of the . . . most serious genocide in the country." Etchecolatz lost the case, with the judge ruling, "To say 'no more to never again' implies that these men of the armed forces should never be criticized, judged, or punished for their excesses. That is, they arrogantly believe that their work was justified and that constitutes a [violation of law] since they excuse, defend, approve, and exalt criminal acts."[106] As part of his three-year suspended sentence, Etchecolatz was ordered to take a course on human rights and encouraged to avoid alcohol and seek psychiatric treatment.

Vergez and Etchecolatz have also confronted reprisals in the streets where they live in response to their denials. Vergez admits that he has "won a broad public," but not a united one. Defenders of human rights have mobilized to declare Vergez persona non grata and bar him from particular cities. He claims that the public recriminations he received in Patagonia forced him to move to the relative anonymity of Buenos Aires.[107] Etchecolatz, too, has endured public recriminations. One of these encounters sent Etchecolatz back to court: he had drawn a gun and threatened to kill four university students who had called him an assassin while he was out walking his dog in a public park. H.I.J.O.S. organized an *escrache*, an Argentine method of publicly "outing" perpetrators, against him in 1998. Although his neighbors came to his defense by pouring flour and confetti on the escrache participants, and although the police used tear gas to disperse them, one organizer considered the response a victory: "The escrache bothers them because from now on Etchecolatz is not going to be able to [freely] walk in his neighborhood. . . . We'll make the country his jail.

We can and we should fight until all of the assassins and their accomplices are given the sentences they deserve for the abuses they committed: life sentences."[108]

CONCLUSION

Through denial confessions, perpetrators disclaim responsibility for past violence. Though they rarely deny that violence occurred, they deny that they themselves committed criminal acts. Perpetrators do so through two broad types of denial. The first resembles heroic confessions. Perpetrators admit to violence, but not to wrongdoing. They justify the violence as necessary and patriotic acts of national defense against a fierce enemy. Audiences respond to these kinds of denials in much the same way that they respond to heroic confessions, that is, by arguing that the atrocities committed failed to meet standards of legal and legitimate warfare or heroism. Some audiences want to believe perpetrators' stories because they are consistent with their own experiences and ideologies. Others make it a mission to silence or refute denials. In short, "heroic" denials provoke audience response.

In the second kind of denial perpetrators admit to wrongdoing, but deny personal responsibility for criminal acts, instead laying the blame on others, on mistakes and misunderstandings, or on oversights. By admitting that wrongdoing occurred, however, perpetrators make it almost impossible for anyone to deny the regime's involvement in criminal activity. Through their very denials, therefore, perpetrators acknowledge the stories of victims and survivors and challenge the regime's justifications.

Once perpetrators and other supporters of the authoritarian regime admit to wrongdoing, some of the polarized attitudes about the past begin to change. Former regime supporters begin to understand what victims and survivors experienced. They also feel betrayed by the regime's lies and cover-ups. Some former regime supporters may even find themselves enraged by the denial confessions and wondering why once-respected political leaders did nothing to prevent the criminal activity they knew about, or suspected. Such former regime supporters distance themselves from the regime. They grasp, at least in the abstract, the importance of human-rights norms.

The second kind of denial, moreover, provides opportunities for human-rights audiences to write a different version of the past, a version that acknowledges victims' and survivors' trauma. But it also acknowledges the importance of remaining vigilant so that well-intentioned leaders are not hoodwinked by individuals and groups who hide illegal acts behind justifications. Perpetrators' acknowledgment that omission, or the failure to act, prevented individuals with power to stop the violence from carrying out that responsibility also speaks to the importance of democracy, laws, and courts to protect human security.

Denial, at least in this second form, may begin to bring individuals together across different social strata. Individuals with varying life experiences and ideologies may find common ground around democratic principles of dissemination of information, contestation, and justice.

CHAPTER SIX

SILENCE

We are in a moment of definitively turning the page of history, but not in a negative way. . . . Society is definitively reconciled.—General Alberto Cardoso, Minister-Chief, Brazilian Casa Militar, 1995

Brazil

IN THE NAME OF RECONCILIATION, the Brazilian military silenced debate on the authoritarian regime (1964–85) and particularly on the most repressive era (1969–74), which took place under Institutional Act no. 5 (AI-5). The military made clear that it would not publicly account for violence, and it effectively imposed a code of silence on its members. One source cited the military as commenting, "We no longer talk about it. Let us blot this page from history as if nothing has happened."[1]

Silence does not always mean the absence of words. Instead, the military crafted statements that avoided either denial or admission, as in this statement by the former military president General Ernesto Geisel: "Many accuse the [military] government of torture. I don't know if there was, but it's probable that it happened, principally in São Paulo. It is really difficult for someone like me, who didn't participate in, nor live directly with, these events to judge what happened. On the other hand, it seems to me that when you are directly involved in the problem of subversion, in the middle of the struggle, you cannot, in general, limit your action."[2] The Brazilian military used silence effectively as a performance of power. It stayed above the fray, with its dignified image intact, by simply refusing to speak about or become associated in any way with past violence. Its success resulted in part from the specifics of the regime's violence, which neither marked the initiation of the regime, as in other dictatorships installed by military coups, nor lasted throughout the authoritarian period. The concerted and systematic use of repres-

Last change of guard under the military dictatorship, Brasília, Brazil.
Photo by Julio Etchart. Reproduced by permission.

sion began with AI-5, four years into the regime and lasting about six years. Violence did occur before and after the AI-5 period, but not as deliberate regime policy. And because the armed forces guided the political transition, over a decade passed between the repressive era and democratic elections. Brazil experienced much less of the domestic and international outcry over human-rights violations than its neighboring countries. With under four hundred deaths and disappearances, it experienced a lower level of violence than neighboring countries. The repression, moreover, could be attributed to a specific sector within the military—intelligence—that lost power over time and was checked by moderate members of the regime before the transition to democratic rule.[3] Authoritarian state violence in Brazil thus looked more like an aberration, a dark and misguided period, rather than its raison d'être. The Brazilian military's violence became its dirty little secret, which it kept well under wraps.

To protect this secret, the military "silenced" and purged its members who spoke out. Soldiers who remained loyal to ousted president João Goulart faced an inquest into their "subversive" activities. The military reported that one of the accused soldiers, Third Sergeant Ivan Pereira Cardoso, killed himself after his interrogation. A human-rights report, however, questioned that Cardoso's death was due to suicide, referring to it as the beginning of "a pattern that would become commonplace in political investigations."[4] Because the "military acted swiftly and decisively to eliminate all sources of opposition within its own ranks," few voices of conscience remained in the military to tell the story of repression from the inside.[5] Those who did remain understood the dangers of disloyalty.

An unofficial investigation and report, Brasil: Nunca mais, dared to reveal the details of the regime's violence. The International Council of Churches, the Archdiocese of São Paulo, and members of the Brazilian legal community supported and disseminated this instant bestseller.[6] Drawing its information from official court records, the report identified the high percentage of military personnel among the regime's victims and the names of perpetrators. Ten years later, human-rights organizations produced a report documenting the dead and disappeared.[7]

Identifying perpetrators did not provoke them to speak out. Many of them simply dropped out of sight. Carlos Alberto Brilhante Ustra, alias "Dr. Tibiriça," who had commanded São Paulo's military intelligence unit (DOI-CODI) during the peak of repression and was repeatedly identified in *Brasil: Nunca mais*, refused to speak to journalists or create any written record of his acts. He reportedly would not allow his name to appear anywhere, including in the telephone book. As his brother described it, "He has suffered so much from the torturer stigma, that today he won't keep anything in his own name."[8] *Brasil: Nunca mais* may have done more to reinforce the code of silence than to break it.

Silence has protected the military from prosecution. The 1979 amnesty law has remained intact, thwarting the investigation, trial, prosecution, and sentencing of past acts of violence. In 1995 President Fernando Henrique Cardoso (1995–2002) officially acknowledged the regime's responsibility for past violence and established an indemnity program for victims' families and survivors of military-regime repression. By holding the regime accountable for violence, his position has provoked some grumbling within the military. But no further accountability exists within Brazil. Trials for past violations have rendered no judgments, either locally or in the Inter-American Court of Justice. Brazil faces no pressure from countries demanding extradition for individual perpetrators. Indeed, even the decrees from the Inter-American Commission of Human Rights and Brazil's Amnesty Commission have failed to produce those documents.[9]

Silence, nonetheless, has cast a pall over traditional celebrations of military power. During the dictatorship, the military used the anniversary of the coup (31 March) each year to advance particular national goals.[10] During the Castello Branco years (1964–68), the anniversary celebrations emphasized order and ending political corruption. The AI-5 and the "economic miracle" years (1968–74) highlighted economic progress and combating terrorism. Restoring democracy on a stable foundation dominated the anniversaries of the transition years (1975–85). Even after the end of the dictatorship, the military continued to commemorate the coup. As late as 1994, the three military ministers issued a statement to the troops on 31 March, blaming the Goulart government for driving the country to a "difficult situation of crisis in four areas of authority—political, economic, social, and military" and justifying military intervention as necessary to respond to citizens' demands to protect the nation's values and institutions. This decree referred to the 1964 military coup as "democratic" because the Brazilian "people" had willed it. Just one year later, after the inauguration of President Cardoso, the military ceased public commemorations of 31 March. Referring to Cardoso's imprisonment and exile by the regime, Admiral Mauro César Pereira, minister of the navy, commented, "It would be embarrassing for President Fernando Henrique Cardoso to participate in a commemorative act for a regime that politically harassed him."[11] Cardoso's government treated 31 March like any other work day.

The military as a whole did not protest the end of these annual celebrations. Some officials even embraced the change as necessary to building a stronger democracy. Pereira, for example, stated, "In a democratic regime it only makes sense to celebrate dates that are truly national, such as the Proclamation of Independence or the formation of the republic. Days like the 31st of March have both advocates and detractors. Why should we continue this debate within our society?"[12] Brigadier Mauro Gandra, minister of the air force, commented that the 1964 events might be treated like other military-sector occasions (e.g., the Paraguayan War and the 1930 Revolution). He added, "We need to end confrontation" over the past.[13] By 1997 the military's official calendar of activities included no commemorative activities on 31 March. Thirty years after the coup, the celebrations became "dispersed, isolated events, without a central core, organizational strands, or guardians of memory."[14] Public support for the coup's anniversary moved into the shadows. In 1995 the Military Club organized a mass on 31 March that included General João Figueiredo, the former military-regime president, and ninety military officials. Minimizing the official importance of the event, General Newton Cruz referred to it as "an opportunity to get together with old friends."[15] The armed forces found private, publicly silent, venues for celebrating their past.

While disbanding public commemorations on the anniversary of the coup, the military nonetheless continued to issue official statements. On 31 March 2000 a military publication commemorated the 1964 "revolution," resurrecting the regime's view of its "heroic" historical role. Peppered with quotes from President Cardoso, the declaration promoted the myth of a shared vision of the regime as national savior.[16] But it provoked little response, either in favor of or against its position. In 2007, the Folha de São Paulo announced that the army general Enzo Martins Peri decided to break tradition and neither make a proclamation nor publish a message on the forty-third anniversary of the coup. The article reported that this has occurred only one other time, in 2003, when President Luiz Inácio "Lula" da Silva took office for the first time.[17]

Silence ensured the Brazilian armed forces' unity. Insisting on 31 March celebrations reawakened old animosities and political polarization within the armed forces. The dictatorship had consolidated two firm ideological and strategic positions within the military. The hardliners, represented by former military president General Emilio Garrastazú Médici, had promoted AI-5 and repression as a means of combating subversion. Ten years after his rule, Médici declared his "war" strategy as effective: "It was a war, after which it was possible to return peace to Brazil. I ended terrorism in this country. If we had not accepted the war, if we had not taken drastic measures, we would still have terrorism today."[18]

Softliners within the military had also supported the 1964 coup and the early years of the military regime under General Castello Branco. They condemned the regime's eventual hardline and repressive direction, particularly the domination by the intelligence division and the suspension of civil, human, and economic rights. These officials did not remain completely silent after the dictatorship. They issued statements for a book titled *Military Confessions*.[19] They did not deliver on their evocative title, instead offering a paean to Brazilian military's history as "the people in uniform," committed to social and economic progress of the country, and characterizing the military regime's "fascistic" control and bond with big business and international interests as an unfortunate lapse in an otherwise brilliant past. The confessions made in this volume contrasted sharply with the military's typical silence and its occasional defense of the regime's violence, most notably represented by the group "Terrorism Never Again" and in the books *The Years of Lead* and *Visions of the Coup*.[20]

If the softliners could have controlled the military, or could have attributed all of the violence to a tiny extremist element within the armed forces and still protected themselves from blame, they might have done so. They recognized, however, that their failure to stop this group reflected its strength and implicated them in the violence. One colonel admitted, "[Torture] was carried out by a small group of officers, working within the security agencies. [Their work] allowed the rest to relax and take classes on 'tactics.' "[21] Silence, therefore, not only protected the hardliners from prosecution and a paralyzing rift with softliners; it protected softliners from revealing their complicity.

Quietly, without disrupting the internal peace, some softliners expressed their disagreement with the regime's tactics: "Not all of the military heads were disposed to live indefinitely with the official lie and even less with the sad reality of what it hid. Several of them—in the three branches [of the armed forces]—became uncomfortable with the increasing isolation of the regime with the proliferation and sprawl of parallel military organs who were carrying out the 'dirty war' and later specialized operations of state terrorism."[22]

A fragile truce exists around silence. To maintain unity requires the silent tolerance of different viewpoints. When one officer publicly balked at President Cardoso's pronouncement of the military regime's responsibility for state violence, another met privately with officers to assure them that Cardoso would not weaken the amnesty law. The armed forces as a whole adopted neither the position promoted by the softliners in the *Military Confessions* book nor that of the hardliners' 31 March coup commemorations, but silently tolerated both. Silence created space for contending viewpoints on the military regime—condemnation and praise—to coexist. A commitment to silence united an otherwise deeply divided military behind a shared goal of institutional protection.

Silence also enforced a truce with the democratic government. The military implicitly agreed to remain outside political discussions over the past as long as the democratic government protected it from retribution for that past. Occasional hardliner outbursts, however, may reinforce the leverage a silent military has over the democratic government. Without them, the military offers no resistance to erosion of the amnesty law. With them, the military can hint that threats to its amnesty will create either destabilizing tensions within the armed forces or potential threats to democracy from an uncompromising sector within the armed forces intent on restoring authoritarian rule.

Silence also succeeds in dampening debate within democratic society over the past. Without a response from the military, social groups —either in favor of or against the regime—find few catalysts to mobilization. Causal factors are difficult to identify, however. Does the military's silence prevent groups from mobilizing? Or does the absence of successful mobilization in Brazil allow the military to remain silent? Both scenarios apply to the Brazilian situation. Efforts to mobilize around the authoritarian past have tended to be weak and fragmented. But mobilizing around military silence has also proved challenging.

Human-rights groups have nevertheless attempted such mobilization. Cecília Coimbra of Torture Never Again (GTNM), for example, asserts that military silence implies guilt for past violence. Referring to a military action in Araguaia in the 1970s, she remarks: "It was recently published that two priests were decapitated in Araguaia. These publications denigrate the reputation of the army, and the military appears as truly monstrous, capable of killing people and leaving their cadavers in the open, they begin to rot, and then someone goes by and pulls off a finger, and another passes and pulls off an ear, and another pulls off a lock of hair. . . . I mean, these are truly monsters. And from the other side, the military one, all we get is silence. So silence conspires against the image of [military] combatants who defeated the guerrillas."[23] Coimbra suggests that silence undermines the military's heroic image, but the problem is that it also conspires against remorse for, or acknowledgment of, the past. Silence denies human-rights groups a particular public image or position on the past to combat or defend.

Thus, human-rights groups work on their own, without catalysts. They have lobbied to find details silenced by the military, by documenting past events on websites and in publications and by lobbying government officials and state human-rights commissions to disclose information. Activists have sought justice in local and regional courts. They have struggled to open up important archives, like the DOPS files, in various parts of the country to discover the facts about the deaths and disappearances carried out by the regime. But despite these strategies, the community cannot point to successful outcomes for retributive justice.

A recent civil suit against a police torturer, Carlos Alberto Brilhante Ustra, illustrates the assistance that perpetrators' confessions can make. The case depends at least in part on Ustra's own admissions made in his testimonial book titled *Breaking the Silence*. In that book he states:

> It is important to refer to the case of a married couple . . . who were imprisoned because they were both militants in a [subversive] organization. . . . Their very small children did not have any place to go. So that we wouldn't have to send them to Juvenile Court, a female sergeant of the Women's Police Force of the State of São Paulo offered to watch after the minors in her house until relatives of the couple arrived, so we took responsibility for their care. Every day, on my re-

quest, the children were taken to DOI to visit their parents. Now, I'm upset to see this couple in the book *Brasil: Nunca mais* accusing us of having taken the children to them to "see their parents harmed by the process and to pressure them, by saying that the children would be tortured if they did not confess to what we wanted to know."[24]

The lawyers representing the Teles family—the married couple to whom Ustra refers, their two children, and their aunt—used this paragraph as evidence of Ustra's torture of the parents and the children. "There is no other reason," one of the lawyers contends, "that he would have brought the children to such a place and to show their parents in such conditions."[25]

Restorative-justice projects have experienced greater success. Media and film projects have exposed the past. Brazil's main television network, TV-Globo, for example, produced a popular telenovela (soap opera or miniseries), *Anos rebeldes*, that represented the repressive era. The songs produced for the program recalled student struggles, and when young people took to the streets in the 1990s to protest President Collor's corruption, they sang those songs. The news media has also promoted other dates of commemoration—like the imposition of Institutional Act no. 5 in 1968—as points of reference and reflection.[26] The internationally acclaimed film *Four Days of September*, based on a testimonial by the left-wing leader Fernando Gabeira, portrayed the armed revolutionary movements and their adversaries, including torturers. Surprisingly, the film's director chose to depict perpetrators in a sympathetic light, rather than as psychopaths. At least one of the torturers in the film suffered internal conflicts over his duty as a police officer and his moral opposition to the methods used.

Because they have remained silent, perpetrators have limited exposure outside of a few fictional accounts. Moreover, the media has tended to avoid sensationalizing the past. An event organized by the newspaper *Folha de São Paulo* to discuss the military regime, for example, emphasized its "balanced" reporting by including a former exiled political dissident, a former guerrilla fighter, a former minister from the dictatorship, and a "progressive" military figure.[27] The media have also trivialized the anniversary of the coup. *Veja*, for example, profiled individuals born on 31 March 1964, but not one of the individuals expressed a political thought about the significance of their birth date. Yet *Veja* ignored the significance of their political silence.

These obstacles have challenged human-rights activists to devise creative methods of overcoming security-force and societal silence. Innovative among these is seizing the coup anniversary for counter-commemorations. Since 1987 GTNM has held protest events near the anniversary of the coup. One study suggests that GTNM picked "April Fool's Day," or "Liar's Day" as it is called in Brazil, for its commemorations, claiming that the coup had occurred on 1 April, and not on 31 March. Because the military had conferred its Peacemaker Medal to the most serious offenders of human-rights violations on that anniversary, GTNM subverted the idea of an award ceremony.[28] It now confers the Chico Mendes Medal on or about 1 April to individuals working to end violations of human rights. By selecting the name of Chico Mendes, who was killed in 1987 because of his active mobilization of rubber tappers in the Amazon region to resist the destruction of the forests by ranchers, the group acknowledges that human-rights abuses did not end with the dictatorship and that the struggle for justice continues. GTNM expresses both pride and frustration in its unique role in remembering and mobilizing around the anniversary of the coup: "Of all of the entities and groups of people who work with human rights and the question of memory of the dictatorship, we are the only one that remembers the day of the coup. In Rio no one does anything, neither commemorations nor events. We are the only ones who remember this day and want to organize other activities that recall this date long forgotten."[29]

Silence and lack of interest may also reflect Brazil's acceptance of the military's past and a desire to move forward. Some evidence supports that view. Brazil has advanced further than its neighbors in writing an authoritative history about the dictatorship that "corrects" interpretations of it. A study of classroom textbooks finds that most of them refer to the 1964 uprising and regime as a "coup" and "dictatorship," instead of using the military's "revolution" terminology. These texts list the regime's involvement in repression, fear, torture, and censorship, seeming to reinforce the notion of "never again."[30] And despite such threats to its image, the Brazilian military has remained silent. The regime's "never reveal" strategy seems to hide not only past violence but also an uneasy consensus around "never repeat."

The Brazilian case suggests that perpetrator silence is an effective way to avoid prosecution and suppress debate over the past. Recognizing its effectiveness, nearly all authoritarian regimes attempt to impose silence over the past. And while few perpetrators confess, those who do often risk legal and social reprisals, and demonstrate the difficulty in imposing and maintaining silence. Thus, silence is usually partial, never total. In that partial silence—somewhere between what remains hidden and what is revealed, between who speaks out and who does not—rests the possibility of debate over the past.

"Silence Is Health." "Silence Is Health" could be a slogan for authoritarian regimes. During the early years of the military dictatorship, a banner bearing those words was draped from Buenos Aires's landmark obelisk. While the sign was probably an admonition against noise pollution, it is remembered by many Argentines as a warning about the life-threatening consequences of speaking out against the dictatorship.[31] It could also have been the slogan for the military in postdictatorship Brazil, because without silence the military would have become plagued by in-fighting between hardliners and softliners.

Silence is healthier for the military than denial or remorse. If the Brazilian military had denied the past, it would have made that past visible. It would have prompted debate within the military and between the military and social groups. Silence is also safer for the armed forces than a mea culpa, which can prompt heroic declarations from hardliners to reject shame in favor of dignity. Silence, in other words, does not offer a safe or neutral path between erupting landmines of memory. Instead, it provides the military with a "healthy" alternative to both sides: obliterating the past through deliberate disengagement.

Ironically, silence and silencing involves text. To silence Scilingo, President Menem pointedly avoided addressing the existence of death flights. He sought to silence discussion of that topic by challenging the integrity of those who evoked the past: "To go out and make these types of statements publicly, to resurrect that past, and what's more some media outlet or some journalist gets involved again in this theme, to again dig the knife into a wound that we are trying to close up, seems aberrant and repugnant." Menem's message was intended, therefore, to censor not only Scilingo but anyone else who might delve into Argentina's past. Menem called for a healing silence: "The repentant must face God. When someone repents something that they have done, they must look for their priests and confess."[32]

Private confession makes the matter personal, putting it off the democratic agenda for public discussion. Perpetrators often view their past acts as personal, and therefore not subject to public interrogation. Thus, when he was "outed" as a torturer, the former Brazilian police officer Miguel Lamano refused to make a public statement: "I've already recounted my version to my family. The rest doesn't matter."[33]

The military puts its past beyond public debate sometimes by characterizing it as a specialized—that is, military—issue that involves protocol that only certain leaders can address. Thus, one Brazilian perpetrator commented, "There is no way I am going to open my mouth about this event. Only the army minister will do that."[34] The military institution can assert a particular position on an issue, and that position is assumed to reflect the views of all its members, as one Brazilian official suggested: "You're not going to get one [an interview]. It is not our mission to give out information. No version of events interests us except our own. We know the truth. What is published out there doesn't affect us or interest us. The general is not going to become involved in one of these [media] events."[35] But some militaries may choose to deflect discussion away from the armed forces, claiming that while the matter may involve military personnel, it remains essentially a political issue, a position reflected in a comment from Menem's minister of defense regarding Scilingo's confession: "I don't have any commentary. I don't think it is a military theme, but rather a political one. Therefore, I repeat, . . . I don't have any comment."[36] Or perpetrators might argue that the matter belongs in the justice department and not in the public realm, as one Brazilian torturer asserted: "I don't have to defend myself against allegations and accusations. If there were a problem, the justice system would resolve it."[37]

An expert in the art of silent texts, General Augusto Pinochet employed a number of devices, including the justice claim, to prevent public discussion of Chile's military regime. One journalist described the Chilean military's silence as "a strategy led by Pinochet himself, whose goal is to avoid making trials and accusations a theme for general discussion" that would be turned "completely and unjustly" against him.[38] Pinochet referred to charges against him for human-rights abuses as "the most unfair accusation that [had] ever been made against a man" and claimed that if the charges had merit, the Chilean Justice Department would have stepped in. He used both humor and dismissal to deflect attention from and trivialize past violence: "I don't have any problem with my conscience. If I did I would say so and I would confess about this problem. . . . [I do have, however,] a problem with my back, a hernia that bothers me when I walk, but nothing more. . . . Why should I be involved in this when I don't have anything to do with human rights? . . . How am I supposed to help? I have asked people I know, but no one knows anything. Do you think I've just stayed silent? I've asked around, but no one knows anything."[39]

The key to silent texts, as Pinochet and others demonstrate, is not necessarily avoiding words and public stages. Effective silence involves ambiguity: neither denial nor admission. It requires the right words to make the past disappear.

"Everything to Lose." Indeed, the failure to say anything at all, the absence of a performance, may undermine the effectiveness of silence. Perpetrators may try to stay off the public stage to avoid discussions of the past. But their absence and silence leaves much to the interpretation of audiences.

The head of the Argentine Navy, Admiral Enrique Emilio Molina Pico, for example, probably hoped that avoiding public comment and stages would end, or at least limit, discussion about Scilingo's "death flight" disclosures. If Molina Pico made no comment, in other words, the press and the public would have nothing to dissect. Instead, his absence generated more discussion than his appearance might have. To avoid commenting on Scilingo's revelations, Molina Pico even missed one of the navy's most solemn occasions, the annual homage to the navy's founding father, Admiral Brown. Never before had the navy's top commander failed to appear and deliver the keynote address. His absence left a void that the press and the public filled with their own interpretations. The news media reported his absence as an obvious attempt to avoid confirming Scilingo's accusations.[40] In the public eye, he confessed to the death flights by failing to present any opinion.

Due to illness, General Videla, of Argentina, sent his lawyer to represent him and deliver his statement at the Trial of the Generals. Perhaps Videla and his lawyer hoped the sudden onset of gastrointestinal problems would demonstrate the unfairness of a legal process that accused a national leader of wrongdoing. Many in the public and the news media, however, interpreted his illness and absence as a silent confession of guilt. In their failure to appear at key moments and deliver carefully worded texts, such military figures surrendered the stage to their audiences. Rather than silencing the ongoing debate, therefore, they stimulated it. Audiences actively engaged in discussion about the political meaning of their silence and absence.

If all perpetrators conform to the silence, it may prove effective. A comparison between South Africa's apartheid regime's police force and military illustrates this effect. Only a small percentage of South African perpetrators, for example, confessed to the TRC, and most of them came from the police; almost no military personnel confessed. Some attribute the decision to go public or not to the top leadership of those security institutions. The head of the apartheid police, Johan van der Merwe, assumed institutional responsibility for the atrocities committed.[41] Some analysts viewed his decision as consistent with national goals of reconciliation, while others considered it strategic.[42] Early confessions by policemen in prison, specifically Almond Nofemela and Eugene de Kock, had exposed police death-squad activities. By naming particular individuals in their confessions, they forced those individuals to confess for amnesty or risk prosecution. Van der Merwe could not stop the hemorrhaging of personal testimonies made by individuals in jail or fearing prosecution. His own confession, in fact, gave these individuals the language they needed to show that they had followed orders from above and had acted politically rather than for personal or racist motives. One of the chief lawyers representing the police at the TRC told me he had encouraged his clients to confess only if they had already been exposed, faced probable prosecution, and had a good chance of winning immunity because their activities fit the criteria for amnesty.[43]

Despite possible inducement to confess within the police force, the legal community, and the TRC itself, most apartheid police remained silent. They believed that silence protected them more than confession. As the apartheid policeman Joe Coetzer stated, he had "everything to lose" from a public confession to his involvement in a massacre in Lesotho that killed eight ANC members.[44] Members of the apartheid police viewed van der Merwe and all the other perpetrators who confessed as traitors to the institution. By speaking out, the confessors had made the institution the scapegoat for apartheid-era violence and undermined the institution's integrity. Other perpetrators preferred gambling their personal freedom with silence to submitting to a process over which they had little control. In hindsight, they seem to have played their cards right, since the prosecutorial team has not yet charged any of those perpetrators who refused to confess.

General Constand Viljoen, the head of the South African armed forces, pursued the silence strategy. He attempted to derail the "truth" part of the TRC by demanding a blanket amnesty without confession. He struggled to block the TRC and sent a clear message to his rank and file against cooperating.[45] Almost without exception, members of the South African military remained silent. Perhaps the military calculated its risk differently than the police. Because the military acted outside South Africa's borders, their confessions could unleash a set of trials in foreign courts and international tribunals that would not respect South Africa's amnesty process.[46] The TRC investigative team exposed cross-border raids by the police and military, but the military, following Viljoen's lead, did not take the bait and expose individuals or the institution as a whole. Neither did the intelligence apparatus face extensive probing into its activities, aside from individual police-intelligence agents like Craig Williamson. Viljoen and Neil Barnard, head of intelligence, successfully protected their institutions and their rank and file from political "witch hunts," as Viljoen called them. Those institutions presented a silent, but united, front in opposition to the TRC and in praise of heroic acts of self-sacrifice for the nation and its borders. They remained vulnerable only to images and information generated by their enemies, not from fellow perpetrators' confessions.

When perpetrators seize control of the stage, they can erect a wall of silence that shields individuals and security institutions. Consensus provides the foundation for that wall. Once consensus breaks down, neither leaders nor rank and file enjoy the protection it once provided. Audiences interpret silences that follow the ensuing public confessions as guilt.

"Talking Too Much." Perpetrators remain silent for self-protection. Audiences often discount the threats posed by perpetrators' colleagues

and superiors for speaking out, but most perpetrators acknowledge and respect it. An Argentine conscript, Luis Muñoz, explained that he had not come forward sooner with the information he possessed about the lists of disappeared, "for fear that they would make me disappear. That's what we thought because of the way they talked and the things they did."[47]

Some perpetrators understood the reality of such threats, since they had personally participated in violent reprisals. Andrés Antonio Valenzuela Morales, a member of Chile's Air Force Intelligence Service (SIFA), confessed to his role in silencing fellow officer Guillermo Bratti Cornejo, who was shot by SIFA agents for having spoken out about the intelligence division's activities. Valenzuela had helped hide his body by tying heavy rocks to the corpse so that it would sink after they threw it into the river.

> After that we returned to the vehicle and went back to "the firm" [headquarters] where we had another bottle of pisco and later they dropped me off at home. Logically they told me not to make any comments to anyone about what had happened. But within the service, everyone knew what had occurred. . . . . Up until that moment I believed that he had betrayed us. Because they told us that he had passed information to MIR and the Communist Party. I felt sad, but underneath it all I was angry because they told us that he had handed over lists with our addresses, the places we went, etc., so that they could kill us.[48]

Valenzuela later discovered that Cornejo was killed not for exposing military intelligence to MIR, but for feeding information about SIFA to DINA, another military-intelligence branch. Valenzuela worried that having participated in Cornejo's murder made him vulnerable to reprisals. When the journalist Mónica González took down his story for *El diario de Caracas*, she expressed concern about his safety: "I don't want them to kill you when you leave." Valenzuela replied, "It is bound to happen, but at least I spoke." Valenzuela had already risked reprisals when he had privately confessed to the Vicaría de la Solidaridad, a legal, educational, and ecumenical human-rights task force. But he publicly confessed only after leaving Chile.[49]

Samuel Enrique Fuenzalida Devia, a Chilean military conscript posted as a prison guard in a clandestine torture camp, spoke out despite knowing the risks of reprisal. He recounted how in 1975 a parachutist, while drunk, had told some civilians about killing prisoners by cutting open their stomachs and throwing them into the sea, and how he was later detained for "talking too much." Fuenzalida confirmed others' accounts about formal declarations that perpetrators had signed, swearing to remain silent and understanding that the military would deny responsibility even for those acts they had committed while on active-duty. As Fuenzalida stated, "I have a document that I signed in the FACH [Chilean armed forces] that says that I agree not to tell about anything I did. If they fire me tomorrow I can live a normal life, but I cannot let anyone know [about my past]. It also says that if I fall prisoner, I fall alone, all of the operations I carried out I did alone and I never had any support from the institution."[50]

The Chilean collaborator Juan René Muñoz Alarcón did not survive his confession. He confessed to the Vicaría de la Solidaridad and was murdered just days later. He had left the Socialist Party in 1973, following an internal dispute, and had sought revenge on his former colleagues by collaborating with the military regime shortly after the coup. He became the infamous "Hooded Man" in the National Stadium who identified people on the Left, subjecting them to torture and death by the military security apparatus. When he refused to identify one comrade, his new military colleagues decided they could not trust him, so they imprisoned and tortured him. Muñoz later decided to confess to the Vicaría de la Solidaridad, even though he knew it sealed his fate. As he put it, "When one doesn't perform a service, it is better to render the witnesses silent than leave them talking. It's safer. . . . I know I am going to die sooner or later and I'm not going to die by a bullet because they are not that stupid. I'm going to have a heart attack or I'm going to slip while I'm waiting for a bus, or I'm going to fall somewhere else. People don't die by bullets, for security reasons."[51] *Últimas Noticias* reported his death as a common crime on 25 October 1977. His body was covered with multiple stab wounds, but they did not completely disguise the signs of security-force torture: blows to his skull, cigarette burns on his forehead, and marks from handcuffs.

The fear of reprisals and the reprisals themselves last long after the end of authoritarian rule. Eugenio Berrios, a Chilean biochemist and DINA agent, disappeared in 1993 after the Supreme Court of Chile ordered his arrest. Because Berrios had possessed evidence that linked Pinochet and Contreras to the murder of diplomats outside Chile's borders in the 1970s, Pinochet subsequently faced investigation for the murder of and intent to silence Berrios.

Silence also follows confession as a way for perpetrators to retreat from public recrimination. The South African novelist and former apartheid spy Mark Behr took refuge in Norway after his confession, refusing to hold interviews with the South African press. The apartheid-police torturer Jeffrey Benzien completely dropped out of public view after his confession turned him into the poster boy of apartheid-police torture. To this day, he refuses interviews, telephone conversations, and any other contact with researchers and journalists. Through a colleague he simply states that he is "too raw" to speak about the past. He has lost contact with the psychologist and lawyer who handled his case in the TRC. His former friends and colleagues say that he moves his home frequently to avoid recognition and that he no longer socializes with his former friends. His wife and children have left him. Perhaps isolation offers him anonymity and the only possibility of an identity other than his public one as a torturer.

Silence after confession also minimizes the risk of prosecution. Scilingo and Astiz retracted their confessions to avoid guilty verdicts. Benzien may fear that the family of Ashley Kriel, whom he murdered, will successfully reverse his amnesty decision. The South African police perpetrators Eugene de Kock, Craig Williamson, and Almond Nofemela, once anxious for public attention, have sought refuge in silence. Since their legal remedies have not been exhausted, their lawyers worry that speaking out will jeopardize their cases. Survivors of Williamson's murders have challenged his amnesty decision. De Kock and Nofemela hope that President Thabo Mbeki's decision to pardon nineteen incarcerated liberation-movement activists will make their own pardon more likely. Their silence is unlikely to convince a skeptical government that their controversial release from prison will occur without fanfare. Silence in these cases becomes a form of damage and minimizing loss, not maximizing gain.

"'Scorpion' Who Stung with the Electric Prod."   In 1985 Argentine television broadcast the Trial of the Generals live to a riveted nation. The image of the once omnipotent leaders on trial was powerful. But image was all the television audience received; the broadcasts excluded sound. Argentines could watch the trial, but they could not

hear the testimony. They could read full transcripts the following day, but with neither sound nor image. The final sentencing occurred in December 1985 on radio—sound, but not image.[52]

Apparently the democratic government hoped to defuse public outrage over the trial by eliminating either sound or image from its coverage. The strategy did not work. The image of the criminally accused generals, even without sound, had the power to mobilize advocates of human rights and regime defenders. The sentencing, even without visuals, catalyzed their supporters and their opponents to spar over the meaning of the past and democratic justice. Audiences, in other words, subverted the silence, turning the trial into dramatic political debate. The absence of media coverage, or sound, therefore, does not mean the absence of confession or debate over it.

Prior to traveling to Chile in 1998, I spoke to a number of researchers, all of whom assumed I would find no public confessions there. However, the Vicaría de la Solidaridad director Carmen Garretón contradicted those views and offered me a set of files containing information on confessed torturers. With follow-up research, I managed to find some media coverage of these cases. But only the most politically aware Chileans remembered any confessions besides those that were politically dramatic (Contreras) or sadistic (Romo). Romo's confession had to create an international outcry before it appeared in the Chilean media. Valenzuela's confession appeared in a Venezuelan, not Chilean, newspaper. Muñoz appeared in the news, but without any hint of the suspicious details surrounding his murder.

The media's failure to cover confessions does not always mean complicity with the regime. Sometimes journalists use silence to protect themselves or their news outlets. At times, they hope to shield perpetrators who have risked their lives to tell their stories. Journalists do not always succeed, however, in securing their own safety or the safety of perpetrators. Nor can they prevent the political drama that can accompany perpetrators' silence.

When silence prevails, human-rights communities often use innovative strategies to force confessions and public debate. French television, for example, followed a group of Chilean survivors as they confronted their perpetrators. The survivors first approached the perpetrators as neighbors, making small talk while they gardened, then wheedled an invitation to sit down and talk. With cameras rolling, the survivors forced the perpetrators out of hiding, confronting them with their past lives as torturers in clandestine centers. These survivors turned silence into a confessional event.[53]

The Argentine escrache outs perpetrators through popular public performance. In August 2002 I participated in an escrache in Buenos Aires against the former federal-police commissioner Ricardo Scifo Modica, alias Alacrán (Scorpion). About two weeks before the scheduled event, small flyers began to circulate in the streets of Buenos Aires, providing details about the event and the perpetrator to be outed. The flyer included a picture of Scifo with "perpetrator of genocide" stamped on his forehead and a caption reading " 'Scorpion' who stung with the electric prod" (*picadura de picana*), which identified his particular brand of torture. Scifo's address and telephone number appeared on the flyer, with the warning that participants should call him from a public telephone to avoid detection. According to the flyer, Scifo had held posts at the clandestine torture centers with the highest rates of abuse: Atlético, Olimpo, and Banco. Despite his record of human-rights abuses, and due to the amnesty laws, Scifo had become the director of the sexual-crimes unit of the federal police after the dictatorship. The flyer proclaimed, "If there is no justice, there will be an escrache!"

At the designated time and day, the lead sponsor, Sons and Daughters of the Disappeared (H.I.J.O.S.), along with co-sponsors from other human-rights, public-art, student, union, and neighborhood-association groups, led us on a carnivalesque march down several blocks to Scifo's house. Marchers, puppets, and people on stilts, bicycles, unicycles, and motorcycles all chanted and sang along the way. The Street Art Group (GAC) painted messages on the pavement, put signs up along the route, and replaced the typical words on traffic signs with those that warned of their proximity to a perpetrator of genocide. A riot squad met the demonstrators at Scifo's house, complete with armed guards on rooftops throughout the neighborhood and a tank parked a block away. Scifo's house was draped in canvas, and the squad stood fully armed and protected behind barricades and his house. At the house, survivors gave testimonials about Scifo's acts and read the litany of his crimes. The group called for justice and threw red paint at the draped house, sometimes splattering a policeman.

Neighbors reacted in various ways to the escrache. Some welcomed

About two weeks before the August 2002 escrache against the former federal-police commissioner Ricardo Scifo Modica, alias Alacrán (Scorpion), flyers circulated throughout the streets of Buenos Aires calling on citizens to publicly out him as a torturer.

the outing, having lived silently with the knowledge of his actions and feeling powerless to do anything about it. One neighbor showed me her private archive of newspaper clippings about Scifo, stating that she had secretly followed stories about him since she had recognized him as her neighbor when he was publicly exposed during the Trial of the Generals. Those worried about violence blamed its possibility on the lack of justice, rather than on the presence of protesters in their neighborhood. Another neighbor, however, argued with his neighbors about the escrache, complaining about its invasion of private property. He did not defend the dictatorship, but claimed, "The police are here to protect us." His neighbors retorted, "No, the police are here to protect Scifo from justice."

Neither escraches nor other practices of outing perpetrators force them to confess. They can and do remain silent about their past. But the outings allow audiences to engage an otherwise silent or silenced confession. In the process they create dialogue. And for some audiences the knowledge that perpetrators must live isolated with their pasts can bring some sense of justice or healing: "Torture work, regardless of when and where it occurs, is almost always unconfessable. In the end, torture is . . . an inhuman act. Those who torture do not speak about their acts with friends or family, nor do they brag about it directly in interviews with academics or journalists. In their solitude, torturers only speak with their ghosts, their eternal companions in darkness. We can only hope that they will never rest in peace in their shadowy underworld."[54]

CONCLUSION

Perpetrators use silence to control collective memory. They try to erase the past from memory by failing to evoke it. Or they prevent any one interpretation of the past from dominating public opinion by imposing a conspiracy of silence. Silence can protect individual perpetrators and even some victims and survivors from additional harm and trauma. Silence can also end debate over the past and allow individuals and societies to move forward, to escape from the trap the authoritarian past has set. Silence attempts to turn the past into a non-event.

But silence rarely succeeds in fulfilling those objectives. A fellow researcher on silence has drawn a parallel with a crime scene cordoned off by police.[55] The presence of law enforcement acknowledges that something has happened, and yet the officers, trying to get their work done and to manage the crowds, attempt to hide that event with barricades and words like "Nothing to see here, folks, move along." This invariably excites curiosity; spectators want to see the "nothing" that is so obviously present behind the concealing text. Trying to silence the past, especially when it has already been partially revealed, often backfires, attracting more attention and debate.

And silence is always partial. Someone will speak out and reveal the past. They may not place the same value on silence or understand the danger of disclosure. They may have personal reasons—dignity, security, legal protection—for abandoning the institutional norm of silence. Consensus usually breaks down. And once shattered, silence becomes nearly impossible to restore. The Argentine military withstood the Trial of the Generals and maintained its silence until Scilingo spoke out. The Chilean military maintained its silence through Contreras's indictment and until Pinochet's arrest in London. The South African military sustained its silence, but the police did not.

The breaking of silence is a public act. Perpetrators do so on their

own. But audiences, particularly victims and survivors, can also sup-
ply the missing dialogue. Their ability to do so depends on creativity
and organizational strength. Their success in drawing perpetrators
into the debate depends not only on the actions of audiences but
also on the consensus and leadership within the armed forces and
impunity.

Silence

CHAPTER SEVEN

FICTION AND LIES

FICTION AND LIES

"Let's get out of here, Rafael. This is too much to stomach. These guys
have lost their minds. They're crazy, irrational, complete animals," says
João Pedro, with his mask off his face and his disgusted expression visible. The two returned to Sapão, completely transformed.—Pedro Corrêa Cabral, *Xambioá*

THIS IS AN EXCERPT from an autobiographical, or confessional, novel
written by Brazilian Air Force officer Pedro Corrêa Cabral. The novel,
Xambioá: Guerrilha no Araguaia (Xambioá: Guerrilla War in Araguaia),
recounts Cabral's experience in the infamous Araguaia massacre. An
estimated sixty young militants disappeared in the military's attack,
nearly half of the estimated total (125) of Brazil's disappeared political
prisoners.[1] Despite the significance of Araguaia in the regime's history
of violence, and despite countless testimonies and demands by victims and survivors to reveal the truth, it was two decades before
Cabral's confessional novel offered the first evidence and apology
from within the military regime. Some confessions, loosely based on
fact or as pure fabrication, resemble fiction disguised as truth. Cabral
employed the reverse technique: writing fact as fiction.

The massacre occurred after a group comprised primarily of university students organized by the Maoist-oriented Communist Party of
Brazil (PC do B) arrived in a remote region of the Amazon in the
late 1960s. Araguaia offered these militants not only an escape from

Michéas ("Zezinho") Gomes de Almeida, a survivor of the Araguaia massacre carried
out during the military regime, searches for his former comrades in clandestine graves at
the former military base in Xambioá, Tocantins. Vanderlei Almeida/AFP/Getty Images.
Reproduced by permission.

the regime's urban repression, but also a possibility of building a revolutionary *foco*, or armed cell, to resist or combat the regime. The militants established strong links within their new community, offering medical supplies and services in exchange for food and community support. Villagers still remember fondly the early years of collaboration with the group they called the "Paulistas" (residents of São Paulo).

> She [Lucia Correa, or "Sonia," one of the PC do B militants killed in 1973] was a good doctor. I don't know why they killed them. Weren't they Brazilian like us? And they treated them badly. They were terrorists. But they gave us assistance. They provided medicine. They extracted teeth. And they delivered babies.[2]

> Everyone liked them because these were refined people, different kinds of people. They helped others out. They were well-mannered, more or less everyone knew they were good people, they weren't like anybody else. Everyone liked them.[3]

Discovering the existence of the cell, the Brazilian military sent troops to the region to eliminate it.[4] After two unsuccessful military expeditions, the intelligence branch assumed control and changed tactics. Abandoning their uniforms, donning shorts and tennis shoes, letting their hair and beards grow out, and posing as employees in fictitious mining and agricultural operations, the combined military, police, and intelligence forces infiltrated the region and convinced villagers to betray the militants. Members of the security apparatus claim it did not take much, that they could persuade villagers to kill a militant for a mere pack of cigarettes. Villagers, in contrast, recount exorbitant bounties, as high as $1,000. They also remember coercion—torture and threats against their families—to join the military's side.[5]

Cabral's role involved flying tortured prisoners from the detention center back into Araguaia, where they revealed to their captors the location of weapons, food, and medical-supply caches. After destroying the supplies, the captors executed their prisoners and buried their corpses in clandestine graves. Cabral knew about these methods because he had not only flown the prisoners to their execution but also participated in "Operation Clean-up": digging up the cadavers, flying them to a remote location in the jungle, and dumping them on a pyre of tires and wood, set afire to burn beyond recognition.

To guarantee the operation's secrecy, the military unleashed a reign of terror in the region. Villagers recount horrific tales of the military's violence and intimidation: torture, decapitation, severed body parts as war trophies, and the exhibition of mutilated bodies in central plazas to scare the population into silence.[6] Scorched-earth tactics, including napalm, eliminated the guerrillas, their base of support, and any possibility of revealing the truth.[7] Seventeen militants survived the massacre and subsequent imprisonment, and twelve are known to be alive today.[8]

Certainly no one within the regime spoke out during the massacre. The military president at the time, General Médici, never once mentioned Araguaia in his public statements. General Geisel, his successor, made only passing reference to the event in a message to congress in March 1975. He confirmed that guerrillas had attempted to build bases of operations in unprotected regions in the country, including Xambioá-Marabá, but that they were "completely curtailed."[9] Commanders of the Araguaian operation made only a few vague statements about it. General Hugo Abreu referred to the guerrillas as "the most important armed movement in rural Brazil."[10] Echoing this view, General Olavo Viana Moog referred to Araguaia in 1978 as "the most important rural armed movement that had ever existed in Brazil, principally as a result of its organizational strength," and noted that to defeat it would require "the largest movement of army troops, similar to the FEB [Brazilian Expeditionary Force] that combated European fascism in the Second World War."[11] Despite its alleged size and threat, Araguaia evoked barely a whisper from the press. Only the *Estado de São Paulo* published an article, without follow up, in September 1972 about the troops' arrival in Araguaia. The regime maintained an incomparable silence about the military actions in Araguaia, which some attribute to its desire to thwart copycat focos elsewhere, but others attribute to the military's desire to hide the atrocities it committed there.[12]

Decades after the massacre, despite the protection of the amnesty law and persistent demands from families of the disappeared to reveal the truth, the military maintained its silence. As information about Araguaia began to reach the public, General Viana Moog refused to "confirm or deny" it. "Only the army high command can deal with this event. Don't bother trying; I won't say anything about it."[13] The army minister insisted on the secrecy: "The documents about episodes of armed struggle, whether it is the guerrilla war in Araguaia or urban events, should only be revealed 50 or 100 years from now."[14] Silence surrounding the event led one journalist to observe: "Even the officers decorated for their bravery in repressing the guerrillas avoid speaking about the event. In contrast to those military who fought in World War II, who show with pride the medals they earned in the fight against Nazism, the heroes of Araguaia in the armed forces are discreet. After all, how does one justify decorations in a war that officially did not occur?"[15]

Cabral might have remained quiet like the rest of the Brazilian military. He had more than adequate legal protection. In addition to the 1979 amnesty law, Cabral enjoyed the immunity of anonymity. No one could single him out as a perpetrator. He had not tortured anyone. The prisoners who had seen him had not lived to tell their stories. His fellow perpetrators would not identify him since they shared complicity. The high command's resolute silence on Araguaia, moreover, reassured those involved that the military would protect their secrets. In addition, Cabral had no responsibility for military policy or orders. He described his relationship to the Araguaia incident: "I never agreed to this; I was just a mere pilot."[16]

To speak out, moreover, was to face personal security risk. Rumors circulated about violent retribution for revealing information. Villagers attributed the mysterious death of a Xambioá gravedigger to the military, explaining that he had threatened to disclose the location of the militants' bodies.[17] Cabral's novel depicted the military's capacity to silence dissent among soldiers through fear and loyalty. Two characters in the novel—the autobiographical character João Pedro (Joãozinho) and his friend (of Japanese descent) Tiago—privately condemn the military's methods, but recognize the danger and futility of disclosing or disobeying them.

> "Hey, Japanese, what's going on with the prisoners?"
>
> "Shit, they probably disappeared them. After they showed them where the two depositories were, they 'took a trip.'"
>
> "Man, I don't know what you think, but I don't agree with this. They are carrying out cold blooded murders, man!"
>
> "Joãozinho, I'm as upset as you are. What these guys are doing is the dirtiest trick in the book. They say it's an order from Brasília. But how could that be? To leave no one alive? Man, this is not right."

"What's worse is that we can't do anything about it. We have to be part of all of these crimes and keep our mouths shut."

"I'm not part of any of this shit! They can go to hell. If I get called to testify, I'll turn them all in."

"A lot of good that will do after all of these guys are dead and buried."[18]

Despite ample reasons to remain quiet, Cabral did testify and "turn them all in." He did it through fiction. But he followed up with media interviews, testimonies to parliamentary commissions of inquiry, and expeditions into Araguaia to find evidence of the massacre.[19] Cabral's novel became the first public account of the atrocity from inside the security apparatus.

Cabral wanted Brazilians to know what happened. "My objective," he stated, "was not and is not to take anyone to trial, but rather, as the saying goes, to sweep the dirt out from under the rug and to reveal this dark page of Brazilian history that must be understood so that new generations understand what happened."[20] Through his confession, Cabral hoped to protect, not destroy, the integrity of the armed forces, to live up to his responsibility to reveal the truth to fellow Brazilians whose children died in the massacre, and to heal spiritually. As his novel's preamble states,

A complicated set of circumstances put me at the center of those sad events. Because of my unfortunate luck, I was not simply a witness of those events, but also, and principally, someone who lived them, knotted up with disgust and shame. Even today my insides are twisted and bitter. Disgust for having experienced events over which I had no power to change. Shame for having participated, completely powerless, in the torture and assassination of Brazilians, by other Brazilians, in a nauseating massacre of brothers against brothers.

As the years have passed, I think that the time has come to bring to light that black page of our history. This is not about finding the villains and laying blame, or to look for scapegoats and demand punishment. No! Time itself has taken over the responsibility for those crimes . . . through the so-called Amnesty Law.[21]

As ironic as his effort to restore the integrity of the armed forces may seem, Cabral's logic involved exculpating the armed forces by blaming the extremist—intelligence—faction within it. General Médici's "take no prisoners" order in 1973 strengthened the Center for Army Intelligence (CIE) in its goal of defeating "subversion." The CIE, in Cabral's view, perverted the military's mission. "There was no war," Cabral contended. "This was extermination of guerrillas without any scruples commanded by the then Major Curió [Colonel Sebastião Rodrigues de Moura] . . . and by other officials of the Center for Army Intelligence. . . . Cold-blooded murder is never laudable."[22] Army intelligence, Cabral asserted, abandoned the military's mission and its historic commitment to national values and ideals, giving way to ruthless power by a few individuals. Cabral believed that the armed forces, similar to the idealistic guerrillas, succumbed to demagogues who led them astray, harming the institution and the nation. A character in his novel lamented the military tactic: "I don't like communism, but I can't abide the injustices that are being committed here. Can it be true that to preserve democracy you have to kill, in cold blood, young and politically misguided Brazilians!"[23]

The novel further explored how the lawless violence unleashed in Araguaia by army intelligence encouraged sadistic behavior. It depicted a major of the army infantry as "having a mission to accomplish, and he would accomplish it at any price."[24] Such an environment, Cabral suggested, legitimized and rewarded sadism.

> "Shit, man, I have really learned to hate these guys [guerrillas]," Blond Devil said to João Pedro, Tiago, and Fabio. . . . The Capivara One patrol had just unloaded. . . . A nauseous smell exuded from their bodies. It was sweat, filth, brush, earth, all mixed together. "When I shot him, I saw the bastard rise into the air and fall down dead. The bullet from my gun had gone through him. I had an orgasm; I swear to God!"
>
> "This guy is out of control; he's turning into an animal, man. He needs to be pulled out of this place right away. He needs psychiatric treatment. What's going on?" thought João Pedro.[25]

Cabral denounced the intelligence division's responsibility for the Araguaian atrocity, but characterized the event as a mistake, an aberration, a stain on an otherwise unblemished military past. He called on the armed forces to overcome that blemish by investigating wrongdoing, assigning responsibility to the culprits, and locating the bodies of the disappeared. Cabral carefully followed military protocol in making his public disclosure. He waited until he had resigned from active-duty service to write his novel, which liberated him from contractual obligations prohibiting soldiers from making unauthorized public statements. He also avoided identifying specific perpetrators. In the preface, he wrote that individuals might recognize themselves in the book, but he did not intend to create heroes and villains, to cast blame, or to seek punishment. Some of the characters, however, were only thinly disguised. "Osvaldão," for example, corresponded to Osvaldo Orlando da Costa, a well-known PC do B guerrilla leader. Cabral named his own autobiographical character "João Pedro," his personal code name, and he used his Araguaian lover's real name, "Joaninha." He more carefully disguised those he denounced. Cabral, for example, transformed Colonel Curió's code name, "Luquini," to name his fictional likeness "José *Lu*cas *Qui*ntino *Ni*coline."[26]

Cabral considered his views on the massacre to be consistent with military values: "I am a military man who was trained to use violence in an orderly way and within a dignified framework. But there in the Araguaian guerrilla war, I witnessed facts that fall completely outside of this [military structure], like the killing of prisoners."[27] He described as unnerving the moment in which he discovered the CIE's policy of executing prisoners: "I remember that I lay down on my bunk and I became completely distraught over it. I didn't want to believe it. Thinking about it today, some twenty-odd years later, I still get emotional. Tears come to my eyes." Cabral further stated, "It was the most difficult mission in my life. It completely disgusted and transfigured me. I felt powerless."[28]

The trauma deepened when he became involved in the clean-up operation. He recounted the horror of that event to the parliamentary commission: "The odor was terrible. Initially we used gas masks, but it was impossible to keep them on because we had to be in communication with the helicopter the whole time, and the gas mask impeded normal contact via microphone with the crew. Then we tried to wear handkerchiefs steeped in cologne or deodorant and tied on our face like bandits, to be able to bear in some way the terrible smell of that macabre cargo that we had to transport to the Andorinha Mountains."[29] The trauma of the operation did permanent damage to his psyche, which he described through his fictional character, João Pedro: "Ever since this fucking 'Operation Clean-up' began, I can't manage to eat anything. Meat, forget about it. I take a thousand baths, but the smell stays in my nose."[30] Flying out of Araguaia did not end his nightmare, which he also recounts through his fictional character.

In response to his co-pilot's offer to take over the flight while he recovered from an affliction, João Pedro answered, "No, no that is not necessary. It'll pass. It's just a pain . . . deep in my soul."[31] Moving out of his fictional role, Cabral closed the book with these words.

> That pain, very deep in my soul, has lasted for almost twenty years. I told my friend Parise that it would pass, but it didn't!
>
> Who knows? Maybe now that I have finished writing this book I will recover, at least a little bit, from that suffering trapped in my punished heart for so long.[32]

Hence Cabral considered his confessional novel therapeutic. But it had its limitations. Cabral could not recover certain memories, a condition he attributed to trauma-induced amnesia, or an incapacity to remember that which will harm him. He became aware of this protective forgetting when he attempted to find vestiges of Operation Clean-up in 1993. As he described it, "I left Rio de Janeiro and I had total awareness about where to go in the Andorinha Mountains. But, believe it or not, when I arrived in Xambioá, I drew a mental blank. I believe it was a psychological defense. I don't know how to explain what it was. I could not remember the place at all. I did everything. We went around the top of the Andorinhas by helicopter for several hours, and I could not get myself to remember. I had a mental block. I imagine that profound trauma explains it, because that mission was so terrible. I wouldn't wish upon my worst enemy the responsibility of carrying out a mission like Operation Clean-up."[33]

His personal recovery also hinged on a moral duty to the massacre's victims. Cabral expresses human, not political, sympathy with the militants and their families: "When I refer to the youths, I am not assuming they were all angels. I know that many went there already well-trained with courses in Cuba and China, etc. But others were very naïve. The majority wanted the best for Brazil, although in a different way than ours."[34] Their guilt or innocence was irrelevant to Cabral. At issue for him was the military's violation of its own code of conduct and international law. The military, he asserted, had a duty to the families and all Brazilians to expose the truth about the atrocity, including the location of the remains of the disappeared guerrillas.[35]

Religious conversion may have also played a role in Cabral's decision to risk reprisal and speak out. In his parliamentary testimony in 2001 Cabral admitted that he had become an evangelical Christian:

"Today, as an older, more mature man I understand that people did these things because they didn't have, or still do not have, something that I have: God in my heart. Because to coldly kill a human being, someone near you, goes against any law, but, above all, God's law. I am not referring to killing that occurs in combat—I understand, military man that I am, that this is normal."[36] He ended his parliamentary testimony with these words: "Happy is the nation whose god is Our Lord. If the god of our nation were really the Lord, omniscient, omnipotent, and omnipresent, none of these events would have occurred."[37] To concerns about his own security, Cabral responded, "My protection is Jesus Christ."[38] But he concluded that he did not fear reprisals, "I want to say to everyone that I sincerely do not fear harm because I am doing work to benefit my country."[39]

Cabral did not write the novel to protect himself, he contended, but rather to fill in the gaps in his memory. He had not kept notes or a diary to accurately document events. With the novel he told the story the way he remembered it, replacing forgotten or fuzzy details with invented ones, merging memory fragments of several individuals into one character, and fully fabricating other scenes. The story was essentially true, Cabral claimed, even if some of the passages were not. Fiction, moreover, allowed Cabral to express the emotional truth behind the story: "If I wrote a journalistic account I would run the risk of it being cold, sterile. And if I decided to write an autobiography, it would turn out to be a silly book."

The novel had the intended effect. It was taken seriously in Brazil as a testimonial account of the Araguaia massacre. One journalist attributed its power to who and what Cabral represented: "The one who is telling this sinister story isn't a communist, predisposed to attack the armed forces. He is Air Force Colonel Pedro Corrêa Cabral. And he is not telling stories he heard from others. Cabral was in Araguaia as a helicopter pilot. He himself transported the cadavers and watched them burn; he smelled the bitter odor of incinerating human flesh."[40]

The Brazilian parliament considered the new evidence provided in Cabral's confessional novel serious enough to open an inquiry on Araguaia. Military regime opponents on the commission praised Cabral for exposing the truth about the past. Haroldo Lima (PC do B-BA), for example, stated, "The military owes explanations to the party [PC do B] and to the relatives of the dead. Perhaps it is time to come clean on the Araguaian story. . . . The death of our comrades in battle is one thing. What we cannot forgive is the fact that comrades were taken alive to prison and then annihilated."[41] Deputy Orlando Fantazzini (PT-SP) stated, "It is no longer acceptable to live with the official version of the Araguaia guerrilla war that accuses the Left of distorting the facts. Salvaging the truth is fundamental and extremely important. We must try to make this truth part of our country's recent history so that future generations become aware and never allow what happened in the past to occur again."[42]

But not all of the commission's members shared Cabral's interpretation of events. Some felt that Cabral too easily let the regime and the armed forces off the hook by scapegoating the CIE. Deputy Aldo Arantes (PC do B-GO) on one hand praised Cabral's "courage" to speak out and "clarify the facts so that Brazilian society can become aware of and overcome Brazil's negative and grave political history"; on the other hand, he questioned whether responsibility for the atrocity rested only with one leader and unit: "In this case we are not discussing an individual. We are discussing the responsibility of the Brazilian government. This is not the responsibility of people, of individuals."[43] Cabral concurred that silence and cover-up about Araguaia constituted an institutional policy, not an individual decision: "Operation Clean-up had as its goal to clean up, as its name indicates, the area of whatever remains, of whatever proof that guerrilla warfare had occurred. Disguising the airplanes and disguising the people who fought had this goal: never to admit nationally or internationally that there had been a guerilla situation in our country."[44] Cabral nonetheless insisted that the intelligence division held full responsibility for the extermination policy. He thus grew defensive when Deputy Socorro Gomes (PC do B-PA) commented, "I could not hear these things and not say, once again, that it is an embarrassment that the armed forces systematically used torture techniques and failed to protect those under its guard." Cabral responded,

One cannot, with a clear conscience, impute these crimes to the Brazilian Army or the Brazilian Armed Forces, the navy and air force. These crimes, as I said, were committed by this notorious intelligence community that also involved the civilian federal police. The intelligence community was composed of people in the National Information Service (SNI), the CIE—Army Information Center—and by other organisms. These individuals, at one specific moment, gained so much power that they remained separate, unconnected to the armed forces. Various colleagues in the navy, the army, and the air force fought the guerillas, but they fulfilled their mission as soldiers and did not engage in this other type of thing. The soldier who entered the jungle on patrol was in combat, the lieutenant who was in charge of that troop also. The pilot, in the case of myself and my colleagues who were flying helicopters, were completing a military mission, which is very different from the role that this intelligence community took on: to take justice into their own hands, torture, kill. We must object to this. It is common to hear the expression: "The armed forces did this and made that happen." No! The majority of the armed forces during the military dictatorship was in their barracks completing normal missions like they do today.[45]

Some commission members defended the intelligence unit from Cabral's accusations. Deputy Nice Lobão (PFL-MA), for example, presented an alternative view of Colonel Curió, who she referred to as "very eloquent" and "very intelligent," and someone who "appealed to people because of his conversational manner." She had met people who had worked with him who deeply respected him. She admitted that she "admired this man for the good things that were said about him and the way he acted. . . . I learned to like this man for his courage, for the seriousness of his words, and for his actions . . . he was an idol for me. . . . I don't want to be an admirer of someone who doesn't deserve it." Cabral defended his position: "I am not here to accuse anyone. I came to tell the facts. . . . I am not here to accuse Col. Sebastião [Curió] of anything. But was he in the situation I described? Yes, he was. I cannot deny this. It is the truth. I am evangelical; I don't lie. And Curió commanded those operations. He went out on those patrols and he exterminated those youths."[46]

The parliamentary hearings received mixed reactions among other government officials. Deputy Roberto Valadão (PMDB-ES), vice president of the Human Rights Commission of the Brazilian Bar Association, referred to Cabral as a "credible source." Senator Jarbas Passarinho (PDS-PA), a strong supporter of the military regime, concurred with some of Cabral's claims. He agreed that an "extra-institutional extermination squad," "a semi-parallel force without separate units or command structures," had operated within the military. "These groups grew a lot," Passarinho stated. "I'm not saying as a parallel government, but as parallel action . . . [i]ndependent action." And he concurred that the group lacked support within the military as a whole. General Antônio Bandeira, he claimed, represented a conventional military position that refused to participate in the counterinsurgency operation "precisely because it had been determined that none of the guerrillas would leave the region alive."[47] But Passarinho fell short of condemning the operation. He posed the possibility that the rules of warfare might not hold up in "antisubversive campaigns": "Guerrilla warfare, subversive wars, these are dirty wars. And I think they end up being dirty on both sides. Because they are wars of terrorism. They are dirty wars, filthy wars. So the Geneva Convention goes to the devil, it disappears."[48] Passarinho seemed to suggest that noble ends—defeating subversion—justify illegitimate means.

Passarinho's words resonated somewhat with the military response to Cabral's confessional revelations. The office of the army minister General Zenildo de Lucena, for example, called Araguaia "an irregular war and it was fought like that. Fought efficiently."[49] General Hugo Abreu asserted that Araguaia constituted "a true war of extermination," but denied any use of torture. He firmly stated that he had never agreed with the practice of torture and that it never occurred under his command and in any of the units that he led.[50] Abreu thus contradicted a statement attributed to him by the newspaper *Jornal do Brasil*: "Torture is always possible in a war like this." Violence occurs when combating subversives, he claimed, "but never torture."[51] The army general Adalberto Bueno da Cruz, who had been involved in the Araguaia massacre from 1972–1974, said that the army did the right thing. By defeating communism in the guerrilla war, he asserted, the army had shown that it was twenty years ahead of its time, anticipating the collapse of communism around the world.[52] General Tasso Vilar de Aquino of the reserve claimed, "We acted to maintain public order and peace for families. We aren't ashamed of the past. The guerrillas committed crimes and they should assume [responsibilities for them]."[53]

Only a few of Cabral's colleagues in the armed forces came to his defense. Two fellow Araguaia combatants echoed Cabral's confession. Another pilot confirmed Cabral's story, with testimony and flight-log evidence, before the Human Rights Commission of the Brazilian Bar Association (OAB) and the 1993 parliamentary commission. Goiamérico Felício, a soldier in Araguaia, recounted details of atrocities, including robbery, sexual assault, and sadism.[54] Cabral sensed that others shared his views, but that they hesitated to make public acts of confession and contrition: "Other colleagues, unfortunately, and I don't know why, don't want to talk about the event. One of them is someone I referred to earlier, Col. Takishita."[55]

Cabral's testimonial novel may have prompted other military officers in Araguaia to make public confessions. In 2004, the journalist Luiz Maklouf Carvalho published Colonel Lício Augusto Ribeiro's account of his involvement in the Araguaia massacre. The account confirmed some of the events Cabral described and added details about the deaths of some militants. Ribeiro, however, referred to Cabral as a "liar," contending that Operation Clean-up had never occurred.[56]

Most of the military reacted to Cabral's account with characteristic silence. The air force brigadier Carlos Baptista, for example, stated, "I can't understand why anyone is interested in delegitimizing an institution that exists, after all, to maintain peace and order." He went on to say that it was time to leave the past in the past and build a new Brazil for the future.[57] The army minister, General Zenildo de Lucena, repeated that sentiment: "The Araguaia guerrilla war belongs in the past and the army is forward-looking."[58] The armed forces minister Benedito Leonel called for a "blanket of forgetting," to "avoid constraints on the democratic process" and protect "individuals involved in this type of war."[59]

Outed by Cabral, Major Curió did not have the luxury of remaining in the shadows. Curió had been a member of the CIE and subsequently became a Partido Democrático Social federal deputy, a colonel in the reserve, and the mayor of Curionópolis (Pará). Based on Cabral's testimony about Curió, the human-rights commission agreed to reopen the case to investigate his role as head of an extermination unit and cover-up operation. Colonel Curió rejected Cabral's story of a cover-up, yet surprisingly confessed that a single tomb in Araguaia held twenty or thirty bodies. He would not, however, reveal the location of that tomb.[60] "I know that I do not have the right to take with me to the grave the truth of what I lived through," he said. "But I'm only going to tell that truth in my memoirs."[61]

Villagers from the region held contradictory views on Cabral's "facts." About Operation Clean-up, for example, a former gravedigger, Osvaldo Rodrigues, stated, "I live in front of the Xambioá cemetery and I never saw the military engaged in nighttime activities there. If graves had been opened up, I would have been able to tell the next day." Another resident, Manuel Leal Lima ("Vanu"), who had been one of the military's principal guides in the area, claimed, "If the army really dug up these bodies, why are they still demanding silence from everyone today?"[62]

On the other hand, after Cabral's confession, more villagers offered eyewitness and personal accounts of the massacre.[63] Ângelo Lopes, imprisoned for ninety days in a tiny jail, stated, "Everyone suffered without deserving it. They hurt a lot of people." Joana Almeida, imprisoned for fifty-two days, says, "I used to cry out of fear. At six o'clock in the evening everyone shut their doors and no one walked on the street. They [the army] picked people up, took them away, held them, and beat them up until they were black and blue."[64]

Opening up debate about the past through Cabral's confessional novel deeply affected the families of the disappeared militants. Not all of them concurred with his version. Sometimes Cabral felt that they objected to petty issues. Cabral's fictitious relationship between an infiltrator and a guerrilla fighter, for example, incensed some family members: "It is true that intelligence units infiltrated the region of Araguaia during the time they prepared for the third [counterinsurgency] campaign, but there isn't any evidence that these infiltrators broke the vigilance of the PC do B and incorporated themselves into their community."[65] A matter of pride was at stake. Sometimes Cabral considered the families' charges against him unfair. He felt that the families discounted his memory lapses as disingenuous: "They even insinuated that I was creating a smokescreen, so that no one would find out what truly happened in Araguaia. I repeat: this is a bald-faced lie."

These objections aside, the community of survivors benefited greatly from the catalyst to memory and debate provided by Cabral's novel. They had failed to bring attention to the issue on their own. A fact-finding caravan to Araguaia in October 1980 had barely received coverage in the media. Survivors' efforts to acquire new information by sharing photographs, describing their family members, and pleading for details had failed. Rumors circulated that the police had reached the village before the caravan to warn against disclosure. But past intimidation may have sufficed to ensure villagers' silence. The families' other objectives—to "remove the negative stigma created by the armed forces regarding these brave and patriotic Brazilians" and to "denounce to the nation and the world the monstrous atrocities, surpassing even Hitler's acts"—also failed.[66] The families did not get enough coverage to diffuse their message.

The families had also sought legal recourse without success. Luiz Eduardo Greenhalgh had represented the families in a lawsuit that demanded government investigation into the circumstances of death and the location of bodies. Greenhalgh had posed five basic questions: who were the prisoners that the military took in the region? What happened to them? Which guerrillas were killed in combat? What documents existed to confirm their deaths? And where were their bodies? A 1985 federal-court proceeding had stalled after only beginning to hold testimony related to the Araguaian disappearances. The families initiated further judicial action to challenge the claim that the amnesty law blocked their right to information. Stymied by local civil courts' inaction, the victims' families and the human-rights community moved the case to the Inter-American Commission in 1995. The executive branch named a special commission in 2001 to conduct an investigation. To date the special commission, the Inter-American Commission, and the United Nations have agreed that the Brazilian military must disclose documents about Araguaia, to no avail.

Cabral's testimony offered the families an opportunity to reenergize the struggle for truth and justice on the Araguaia massacre.[67] He viewed the victims as a nonthreatening, small band of students and young professionals gathered in a remote region of the country with antiquated weapons, inadequate food, deep friendships within the community, and a desire to create a more humanitarian future for all Brazilians.[68] Thus, survivors mined his fictional account and interviewed him for details that they included in their website database. Cabral could only help them with seven of the estimated sixty disappeared in Araguaia. Neither photographs nor verbal descriptions triggered new memories for him. He could not confirm simple details, like whether the pregnant woman he had encountered was Jana Moroni Barroso or Dinalva Oliveira Teixeira. He identified sixty-five perpetrators, but he knew code names and only a few real identities.

Neither Cabral, nor the villagers, nor the commissions of inquiry helped the families discover the truth about their children. As one family member stated, "We collected painful testimonies [from the residents in the region], of atrocities committed there. But I didn't find any proof that my son is dead. They said that he disappeared; no one knows anything about him. We know that a lot of them were shot down. But no one will tell us where our children are buried. They won't even confirm that they are dead."[69] Until the 1995 Law of the Disappeared, the families of the disappeared in Araguaia could not receive indemnity from the government, confirmation of the deaths, the certificates required for bureaucratic processes, or the closure they needed for burial and mourning rituals.[70] Criméia Almeida recounted the impact of silence on her son's life.

> I was a prisoner and General Bandeira de Melo told me that if André was killed, I would be told. But he didn't do this. So, my son who was born in prison, didn't have a father. Today he is fifteen years old and we are still fighting to normalize his situation. This is really difficult. Just to enter into the process I had problems, since I wasn't legally married to André. An alternative would be to ask for a "presumed dead" certificate. But that would mean that we, and not those who killed him, would have to pronounce him dead. I'm not going to do this. . . . I saw the photos of the decapitated people. That was not only meant to intimidate us, it also showed that they [the military] could identify them [the disappeared]. So when they say they killed them and buried them without knowing who was who, they are not telling the truth.[71]

Justice also seems a remote possibility despite the progress jump-started by Cabral's novel. As Cecília Coimbra of Grupo Tortura Nunca Mais states, "No one was ever punished in this country. That breeds today's culture of impunity."[72] She adds, "Extermination and genocide walk hand in hand with impunity. No one has ever been punished. Just as the torturers who killed and hid bodies in the 1960s and 1970s were never punished, today's murderers also go unpunished."[73] Few expect justice in the case of Araguaia. Expressing frustration at the lack of seriousness, one village resident complained, "Nothing's going to happen. It's not that I think so; I know so. In Brazil everything ends in pizza."[74]

The families and human-rights organizations that represent them have persisted in creating public memory projects to debate the past. They identified 12 April as the anniversary of the Araguaia massacre and held memorial acts on that day in Praça Tiradentes in Rio de Janeiro. They document as much about the case as they can and keep the facts in the public eye. They have pressured the Ministry of Education to rewrite history textbooks to recognize the guerrillas of Araguaia and the atrocities committed against them. Family members and nongovernmental organizations working with them are also building an archive that includes documents and writings prepared by the guerrillas and oral accounts about them by those still living in the region.[75] Some survivors and family members of victims have attempted to establish a monument and a museum in Xambioá nearly thirty years after the massacre. When Mayor Wilmar Leite Jr. approved the creation of a memorial, he stated, "The community has lost its fear and understands the importance of the guerrillas for the history and tourism of the region." Plans for the museum included objects related to the guerrilla war, a library, and an exhibition hall, as well as a mausoleum for burying the dead from the massacre. As one journalist writes, "As victims of torture and disappearance, the population [of the region] is interested in showing the rest of the country what they were forced to hide until today."[76]

The search for corpses and documents continues, offering the only possibility of retributive or restorative justice. Excavations in the Xambioá cemetery begun in 1991 produced no results. Subsequent to the publication of Cabral's novel, in 1996, the Ministry of Justice's Commission of Disappeared Political Activists became involved in the search and worked closely with Cabral and the Argentine forensic-anthropology team.[77] In 2001 the government sponsored an official search. Days of circling the Andorinha Mountains in helicopters failed to help Cabral identify the place where the bodies had been burned, nor was the team able to uncover teeth or bone fragments for forensic analysis. Reports of napalm use in the region hinted at a cover-up of the cover-up (Operation Clean-up). Some evidence finally surfaced in 2001, when a gravedigger admitted that he had been ordered by the military to bury two guerrillas' bodies. The excavation team found three bodies at the sites he indicated and positively identified one of them as the corpse of PC do B militant Maria Lucia Petit da Silva. The cadaver showed evidence of torture and execution, consistent with Cabral's account. The other two corpses had deteriorated so badly that they remain unidentified. Bones found by a couple in 1996 and believed to belong to the militants also remain unidentified.

Cabral's confessional novel eroded the military's silence surrounding the Araguaia massacre. It catalyzed a debate. Thus, most of what Brazilians know from perpetrators about authoritarian state violence comes from fiction.[78]

"Anything processed by memory is fiction," claimed Wright Morris.[79] Confessions, in this light, are never *the truth*, but *a truth* from the vantage point of a particular individual and his or her personal and political goals. Confessions invent, replace, borrow, reorder, or omit details to make the past understandable in a particular context. Cabral felt fiction allowed him to tell his story more fully, so that his readers would experience the event and its impact on individuals and the nation. Confessions are fictions—sometimes even lies—that advance a particular interpretation of the past.

"Lying Was a Trait They Had in Common."   Cabral presented a fictional account to own up to his past. But perpetrators produce fictional accounts, passed off as fact, for a variety of different reasons. Graciela Fernández Meijide, discussing her effort to extract confessions from perpetrators for Argentina's National Commission on the Disappeared (CONADEP) report during 1983–1984, describes a criminal personality that seeks revenge, attention, and money by simply inventing stories about the past: "Lying was a trait they had in common, . . . also a need to be in the limelight, and to get revenge on the institution they felt betrayed them. Virtually all of these men had separated from their force. In fact most of them were in jail for stealing more than their 'fair share' of the war booty. They were so intent on peddling testimony (in exchange for immunity from prosecution or leniency in sentencing) that they'd get together in their cells and concoct stories, taking an element from this one's experience, another detail from someone else. It was hair-raising. They were profoundly, essentially criminal."[80]

The temptation to tell a good and convincing story leads to confessional lies, as appeared to be the case with South African apartheid-police perpetrator Joe Mamasela, renowned for his vivid depictions of past violence. Everything about Mamasela's past seemed questionable. He claimed to be a member of the famous "Class of '76" at Morris Isaacson High School and to have been involved in the South African student movement and in the Soweto uprising against Bantu education and Afrikaans as the compulsory medium of instruction. He had subsequently left the country to join the ANC in exile in Botswana, returning to South Africa to mobilize and organize student cells around Johannesburg. Given his reputation, he claimed, the police

The askari Joe Mamasela recounted in Jacques Pauw's documentary film *Prime Evil* the atrocities he and others committed while working for the apartheid death squad Vlakplaas.

had delighted in arresting him at a comrade's house in 1979: "The police asked me who I was, and when I said Joe Mamasela, you could see the excitement written all over their faces."[81] The police tortured and "turned" him into a police collaborator, or askari, who worked for them until the very end of the apartheid era. As Mamasela stated, "There was no way I could resist further, they left no doubt in my mind that they can, and will, and are, eager to kill me. So I said no, I will help you, what do you want?"[82] Mamasela worked for two infamous Vlakplaas death-squad leaders (Dirk Coetzee and Eugene de Kock) and subsequently for the Northern Transvaal Security Branch death squad under Brigadier Jack Cronje's command. He collaborated with the apartheid police in the murder of forty anti-apartheid activists and in petrol-bombing 350 activists' homes.

Despite using Mamasela's colorful descriptions of apartheid-era violence in his documentary *Prime Evil*, the journalist Jacques Pauw doubted Mamasela's version of his past. He doubted Mamasela's commitment to the ANC, his profile among the police as an ANC combatant, and even his torture and "turning." Pauw contended that Mamasela had invented that past for instrumental reasons: "In an effort to avoid a lengthy jail sentence for robbery, Mamasela could have told his interrogators that he was a member of the ANC and that he would co-operate with the police."[83] Vlakplaas Dirk Coetzee agreed that Mamasela had invented his ANC past: "Mamasela hated the ANC as much as we did. He was waging his own war against them."[84]

Mamasela did not disguise his hatred for the ANC. A conversation he had with his son, Lerato, demonstrated that revenge motivated his betrayal of the ANC.

> What did your dad used to do? He [Mamasela] asked.
> You were a policeman, his son answered.
> What kind of policeman? Like the ones you see on the street?
> You were at Vlakplaas.
> And what did I do there?
> You killed people.
> What kind of people?
> Innocent people.
> And why did your dad do that?
> Because the ANC killed your brother.[85]

Once Mamasela began working for the apartheid-police force, his skill at deception proved useful. His capacity to infiltrate and cover up made him an invaluable asset. Mamasela posed as "Bra Solly" and "Mike" to infiltrate the black communities, convincing youths to follow him into exile for military training for the ANC army. In these roles, Mamasela sent fifteen- to twenty-year-old black youths to their death in ambushes by the police or by booby-trapped grenades.[86] Mamasela also disguised police murder of apartheid foes by employing exaggerated and primitive brutality that fed racist notions of "black-on-black" criminal or political violence. Mamasela made the assault on the civil rights lawyer Griffiths Mxenge, for example, look like a common crime by stabbing him repeatedly and stealing his possessions.

The police handsomely rewarded Mamasela for his deception. As one of his apartheid bosses recounted, "Mamasela always wore the most expensive clothes. He would say to me: 'I look like the white man, you look like the *kaffir* [derogatory term for blacks].' I frequently had to submit false claims to keep him happy."[87] At the end of the apartheid era, Vlakplaas paid Mamasela to lie to the Harms Commission investigation into death-squad activity. "He received amounts of R18000, R23000, R27000, he got a state vehicle, we had to pay his children's private school fees and install additional security at his house," including safety lights, a paved footpath, two dogs and dog food, his Vlakplaas commander Eugene de Kock claimed.[88] After the end of apartheid, Mamasela looked for the highest bidder to buy his story. "When I first met Mamasela," wrote Pauw, "he was talking money. He was talking about selling his story for even more to a foreign broadcaster and making money out of writing a book."[89]

That book has not yet materialized, but Mamasela did trade his story for money and protection from the new South Africa's prosecutorial team. He became a state witness to the Transvaal attorney general's office and received protection under its witness-protection program. He complained bitterly that his services for the post-apartheid state did not match what he had earned in the apartheid police. As he stated, "Every month [during the apartheid era] I was earning between R30000 and R40000, now I'm getting a meager five to six thousand a month (from the Transvaal Attorney General). You call that financial benefit?"[90] The attorney general's office, however, cut Mamasela off as a state witness when he repeatedly demanded funds for his children's schooling and security for his home. His testimony became worthless, moreover, when prosecutors realized they could not separate the fact from fiction.[91]

How perpetrators present themselves may help them convince their audience that they are not lying. Mamasela's and Cabral's backgrounds made their stories plausible. Both pointed to their religious experience to further confirm their trustworthiness. Cabral said, "I am evangelical; I don't lie."[92] To a skeptical journalist Mamasela recounted the power and meaning of his baptism and rebirth in a charismatic church: "A man who likes to quote from the Bible, 'The truth shall set you free,' he said there is one thing left he was determined to do. 'I hope to get away from that one day,' Mamasela said pointing at the gun in his lap. 'I want to become a pastor and serve my community. You never know the essence of the truth until you have lived a lie. And I have lived a lie for 15 years.'"[93] Cabral and Mamasela appeared to be telling the truth. But one told his truth through fiction and the other told his fiction as truth. How can one tell the difference?

"He Was Completely Berserk and Totally Uncontrollable." Given the typical lack of material evidence of authoritarian state violence, perpetrators' lies and fictions about their past often remain unverified. Certain narrative structures make perpetrators' lies and fictions seem more accurate than the truth itself. They tend to embellish their stories with vivid, even lurid, details, which make a story seem real even when it is not. One can perhaps explain the success of the journalist and notorious plagiarist Stephen Glass in deceiving all of his colleagues, including fact checkers at the *New Republic*, by the brazen precision of his invented stories, which he passed off as fact.[94]

Verbosity, lurid details, drama, and color made Mamasela's stories feel true. The details he provided, for example, on the murder of three anti-apartheid leaders, known as the Port Elizabeth Black Consciousness Three (PEBCO 3), seemed too gruesome to have been invented: "During the assault on Champion Galela, something brutal happened because warrant officer [Gert] Beeslaar took out the testicles of Champion Galela. He squeezed them very hard until they became the size of almost . . . uh . . . golf balls. And then with his right . . . right hand, he punched them severely, very hard. I saw . . . I saw the man changing the colour of his face, becoming pale and bluish, and there was some yellowish liquid that spurted out from his genitals."[95] Who could make up such details? He must have witnessed them, one might think. Yet regarding his own involvement in the murder, Mamasela kept his words to a minimum: "My role was to choke them, to strangle them. Just to keep them quiet."[96] Similarly, his own role in the murder of civil-rights lawyer Griffiths Mxenge paled in comparison with those of his colleagues in his graphic and dramatic account of the event.

> Nofemela and Tshikalanga started stabbing him . . . he was trying to stand up. He [Mxenge] had a knife, the long knife lodged in his chest, but he pulled it out. He charged Nofemela with his knife, who had to run for his dear life. I grabbed Tshikalanga's pocket knife and chased the deceased. I lunged several times, trying to stab him in the back. He fell, and the knife fell next to him. Nofemela won back the knife, and as I was grappling with him, I felt him becoming weak. I felt warm, liquid-like stuff running down my hands, my arms, and when I looked at my hands I saw it was blood and then I got frightened, and I saw Nofemela cutting his neck with the long knife. Nofemela ran towards

the *bakkie* where he grabbed the wheel spanner. He was completely berserk and totally uncontrollable as he hit the deceased.[97]

Fictional accounts and lies, while providing graphic details about the event itself, often minimize the individual's responsibility for those events. Indeed, the details emerge from their roles as witnesses, rather than as protagonists, in the events. Cabral, for example, revealed dramatic details about the Araguaia massacre, but about his own role he stated simply, "I was just a pilot."

While minimizing their role, perpetrators often use fictional confessions and lies to express remorse for what they did or were forced to do. Cabral was consumed by remorse. Mamasela apologized to his victims: "I'm the only policeman in the whole country who has a dossier that has even the pictures of his victims because these things were troubling me, that I was used to kill my own people. I had sympathy for the innocent victims. I was driven by that sympathy."[98] Speaking to the widows of the PEBCO 3, he stated, "I would just say deeply from the bottom of my heart—this to me is a glorious opportunity to say thank you very much for at least understanding. To me this is a cathartic experience and I would like to extend my apologies to everyone because I see each and every black person as a victim."[99] But those who spent time with him doubted his sincerity, like Pauw, who commented, "I have heard Joe Mamasela speak gleefully and without a shred of remorse about the people he has killed, but whenever he is in public he says: 'No self-respecting human being can feel happy about killing even one person, now if you talk about 30, you will know how I feel. It is terrible. It is a bastard act. It is something that one cannot forgive himself for doing. But under those circumstances, one could do nothing.' "[100] And Pauw wrote, "I have spent many hours with Joe Mamasela, and never have I detected a shred of remorse for anything he has done. He spoke of ways of making money and would talk about the ANC as 'stupid kaffirs' who 'don't have a chance in hell' of ever getting at him."[101] Even his remorse, these observers tell us, represent lies.

The more comfortable perpetrators appear to be with their confession, the more believable their confessions are. Even when lying or inventing facts, perpetrators may convince their audience if they seem relaxed and in control of their story. Mamasela used techniques like smiling and laughing, which suggested he had nothing to hide. One journalist described Mamasela's ease throughout his confession: "No one hurls abuse at Joe Mamasela, even though he goes into horrific details of killings in which he's been involved. Everyone's quiet, almost in awe of the man who seems to have some kind of power over them. Surely, they must hate him for what he's done, for betraying the cause and killing his own people. But it seems they don't. Mamasela, unlike other police killers, constantly makes eye contact with the audience. He appears fearless compared to other amnesty applicants, who sweat, shift uncomfortably in their chairs, and even choke on their words. Mamasela, says one of the lawyers, laughs a lot."[102] Another journalist also referred to Mamasela's humor: "Joe Mamasela smiles at the lawyers who grill him. He smiles at the people in the front row on the floor below the stage."[103] His smile does not appear to be cynical; it exudes satisfaction with who he is. He must be telling the truth, one thinks.

"An Inveterate Liar." The timing and staging of perpetrators' fictional confessions and lies do not appear to follow any set pattern. Cabral's fictional account broke the silence. But in other cases, institutional arrangements and media opportunities encouraged perpetrators to come forward to tell their tales. Mamasela took advantage of the prosecution team's search for information on top officials to tell his story, gain protection, and earn some money.

Institutional opportunities encouraged prisoners in South Africa to invent a story that fit the amnesty criteria to see if they could win their freedom. The TRC's Amnesty Committee did not hear most of these cases, but one stood out in its audacity. The apartheid policeman Michael Bellingan applied for amnesty from jail where he was serving a twenty-five-year sentence for bludgeoning his wife, Janine, to death with a wheel spanner. Bellingan contended that he had been ordered to kill his wife because she had leaked details of his work and stolen secret documents from his briefcase. He claimed that his boss, General Gerrit Erasmus, told him to "solve the Janine problem." His colleagues, Bellingan asserted, would confirm that they knew of the murder and had helped with the cover-up.

No one produced the corroborating testimony Bellingan promised. Instead, all evidence supported the details that had convicted Bellingan: he had staged a robbery-murder to eliminate his wife and free him to marry a woman with whom he was having an extramarital affair. The absence of evidence of a political crime, and Bellingan's pattern of domestic abuse, lies, and extralegal dealings all undermined his case. Calling Bellingan "an inveterate liar" and "one of the best liars [they] had ever met," lawyers in the case supported the TRC's decision to deny Bellingan amnesty.

Other kinds of institutional stages appear to support false confession. The Innocence Projects at the law schools of Northwestern University and the University of Wisconsin, Madison, reveal processes that induce people who are innocent to make false confession to crimes. Mental disability or low intelligence, for example, can explain why some inmates confess to crimes they did not commit. Unable to understand the consequences of pleading guilty, anxious to end the grueling interrogation process, and encouraged to plea-bargain by lawyers and judges as a means to reduce the inevitable sentence, such inmates are prone to produce false confessions. A study of false confessions in Japanese prisons observed that destitute individuals will even offer them up in exchange for a meal that they desperately need.[104]

A Vietnam War veteran who claimed to have been involved in the wholesale slaughter of a village offered a unique twist on false confession. Dying of AIDS, this soldier-cum-dancer choreographed and performed a final autobiographical dance depicting his Vietnam years. The videographers Douglas Rosenberg and Ellen Bromberg filmed his performance, in which he "relived" his experience in Vietnam and recounted the trauma and horror of participating in senseless acts of violence. After he died, and while they were in the throes of finalizing the film, the videographers discovered that the soldier-dancer had never gone to Vietnam. He had been drafted, but spent the war in the United States at a desk job. His friends and family members, as well as the videographers, reflected in the video *Singing Myself a Lullaby* that he bore collective guilt, as an American, for the war, and that he communicated that guilt in the only way he could: as individual responsibility. This generous interpretation ignored the more plausible explanation that confessing to violence he did not commit made his life appear more dramatic and interesting than it truly was. He performed a fictional confession to violence on a media stage to gain attention he would not otherwise have received for his unremarkable life.

Mamasela refused to apply for amnesty for perhaps a similar reason. He stated that he did not consider himself a perpetrator, but rather a victim of the apartheid era, and therefore had no need to confess. Yet by confessing to the media and the state's witness program, he found the expansive stages necessary to perform his fabulous stories.[105]

"They Fell for the Ruse." Cabral's confessional novel suggests that fiction sometimes tells more than fact. Had Cabral presented a factual story, he would have subjected it to the scrutiny of trial testimony and evidence. Defenders of the military regime would have mobilized to discredit it, pointing out all of the gaps in memory and knowledge. But because he presented it as fiction, no one could deny what Cabral had experienced and the impact it had on his life. Indeed, audiences could use his emotional truth to assert the need for investigation and the facts behind his story.

Mamasela played a similar role for some of his victims. One of the widows of his PEBCO 3 murder victims, for example, accepted his apology because it finally told the truth. Her lawyer described her as "fed up with the lies of the [amnesty] applicants" and praised Mamasela for being "prepared to break the long silence and come out with the truth about the killings."[106] His fiction, in other words, provided the details absent in other perpetrators' accounts of the event.

Journalists expressed surprise at the willingness of the black South African community to accept Mamasela's testimony and apology. They wondered why his audience could not see through his insincerity. The journalist Joe Diamini tried to point out Mamasela's betrayal of the very people to whom he subsequently (and cynically) appealed for mercy: "This is the man who still has the gall to say people cry 'crocodile tears,' after causing such untold misery for the entire black nation. This is the man who delayed the liberation of this country through taking orders from the 'white baas' [boss] and killing . . . black people. Do you think that Mamasela ever bothered to tell his wife and children that they were surviving on the money earned through the shedding of blood of their own kind? Mamasela needs to be reminded that the black masses will find it hard to pardon him. . . . I shudder to think that this man should enjoy freedom after all he did. He carried out his crimes in the name of protecting himself and saving his skin."[107]

By linking his life to the life of his black South African audience, Mamasela told a credible story of violence, victimhood, and betrayal. And, in the process, he stood up to his white bosses, as he showed in an encounter with a white lawyer.

MAMASELA: I'm a black person. I was born and brought up in this country. Every black person is a victim of the oppressive regime of the South African Police, of the South African government in the past, and that's a fact. You had a sweet life yourself.

ADVOCATE: Mr. Mamasela, I know that is a fact.

MAMASELA: Thank you very much, if you know. I was a victim and am a double one, of the ANC and the security police.[108]

His problematic relationship to the ANC might have undermined his support among his black South African audience, but Mamasela effectively escaped that criticism by implying that the ANC had forgiven him: "The ANC, more than any other people, they understand that in every war there are casualties, we are the casualties of revolution, we stood up, we tried to pay our humble contribution to the liberation of the emancipation of our people."[109] He referred obliquely to the torture he had endured due to his membership in the ANC and that had forced him to collaborate with the apartheid police: "I will never forget that. No victim can . . . uh . . . can ever forget that torture that he's received from the police. If you were black, you'll understand what I mean. The torture and the constant fear of being killed."[110] Because of this torture, claimed Mamasela, "I was forced to kill my own people, the people I devoted my life into liberating." He made a Faustian bargain that black South Africans understood, even if they did not make or respect his choice: kill for the white masters or be killed by them. A journalist summarized Mamasela's appeal to the black community: "Joe Mamasela seems to be telling the audience: Look at me. I killed your people. But I am black like you. I too was a victim of apartheid. The white police also tortured me."[111]

Yet Mamasela also appeared to be principled. He refused, so he claimed, to deliver poisoned T-shirts to a student leader near Pretoria: "Because I myself was a student [activist], the whole thing did not go well with me, you know with my human compassion. I couldn't deface myself that low to wipe out school children." And he promised to do penance for his deeds: "As a perpetrator, although it was against my will, I must atone in kind, as I'm doing now by testifying and also in cash. Whatever money I have I will share with the victims and hope they will accept that."[112] Mamasela perhaps understood that his community might need his money more than his stories: "When Mamasela arrived in Soweto dusk was falling on the tiny houses and fragile shacks of Mofola South. He said he wanted to come here to show a reporter how popular he was among his people. And as soon as he honked the horn of his car, people approached from all directions asking for money. He handed R50 notes to toothless grownups and silver coins to barefooted children with blackened faces. And every time he asked them to tell a reporter who they wanted for mayor. The answer was always the same: 'Joe.' "[113]

Mamasela's appeal to the audience also involved playing the role of the trickster to invert the balance of power and turn it against the white bosses. He described how he manipulated his "white bosses" to trust him: "They took me as one of them because of the . . . of something that I would call the curative power of humour that I used to entice the white commanders to . . . to love me. I used to even insult myself. I used to call myself a dog! I used to call other askaris dogs. Together we were calling each other dog! Dog! Dog! Dog! And then my white commanders, they fell for the ruse. They loved me! They thought that they've severely and completely . . . uh . . . broke me down! I was calling myself a black, a black Afrikaner. And they loved it! And in the interim, I managed to siphon a lot of data."[114] Mamasela even turned lying into a virtue, a "weapon of the weak."[115] He suggested that whites had invented a language that diminished their own wrongdoing and exaggerated that of blacks. He described this double standard: "Sometimes we tell even our own children little lies to make them happy. And if that makes me a liar, a compulsive liar, so be it. We normally lie! You cannot tell me all your life you never . . . you never told a lie. Because you whites, you believe . . . eh . . . white people don't lie! They only tell a white lie. White people don't steal, they only do white-collar crime. And that's a myth. That's a lie."[116]

Eventually Mamasela's lies caught up with him. The attorney general could no longer support and protect him due to his lying. Despite his colorful performances, the media withdrew interest in him because he could not distinguish fact from fiction. Yet Mamasela's confession, however fictional, remained a vivid account of the kinds of atrocities the regime committed.

Fiction and lies do not exist unproblematically in transitional societies; they can become deeply divisive. Contradictions in perpetrators' confessions pit one version against another. Communities split over which version, if any, of the Scilingo, Astiz, or Romo confessions to believe. Some audiences reject any untruths from perpetrators as damaging to legal processes against them. Thus, even when a perpetrator's message confirms victims' accounts, as in Mamasela's case, or reveals new truths, as in Cabral's, human-rights communities become divided over separating forensic truths from emotional ones. Pragmatic considerations—how fictional confessions and lies advance or undermine legal cases and public acknowledgment of the past—clash with moral and political ones.

CONCLUSION

Advocating fictional confessions or lies is not my purpose in this chapter. Instead, I acknowledge that perpetrators' confessions usually will not provide the whole truth. At times they consciously and deliberately invent their stories. They do not do this necessarily to deceive their audience, however. Quite the contrary, they may feel that the exaggerations and embellishments will give their audiences even better—that is, emotional—understanding of the past than cold and concise factual accounts. John Collins has made the distinction between "stockpiling" and "storytelling" in this regard.[117]

Debates about the past depend largely on catalysts. Fiction and lies successfully catalyze debate in part due to lurid details that unsettle audiences, in part because their audiences try to get the story right. They correct perpetrators' accounts, demanding or filling in details, challenging others, attempting to put together an accurate portrayal of the past. During the process, audiences will also struggle over official history and collective memories.

Through the debate and emotion they generate, fiction and lies may sometimes even produce fuller truths about the past and the possibility for bringing justice that was previously foreclosed. They may make past violence feel real, personal. They may make remorse seem genuine. And they may bring perpetrators onto public stages for the first time, rendering silence and denial impossible.

There are, of course, limitations to the utility of confessional fictions. They do not, for example, hold up well in a court of law without corroborating testimony or supporting evidence. Audiences of human-rights advocates may use them to begin investigating and exposing the past, but they are plagued by problems of verification and reliability. Such efforts may even prove futile. Subjecting them to evidentiary rules and norms in the courtroom or in public opinion may undermine their utility all together. Moreover, audiences who share the goal of exposing past violence come into conflict over how, or whether, to use these invented confessions. Public institutions should not encourage fiction or lies, but audiences can use them to advance their political objectives when they do occur (as they will). Even Bellingan's bald-faced lie about murdering his wife for political reasons turned out to be useful to human-rights groups, which linked his wife's murder to two cultures: violent masculinity and impunity. In doing so, they raised awareness of human-rights issues that extended beyond authoritarian state violence.

CHAPTER EIGHT

AMNESIA

I concede . . . but I can't honestly remember. . . . I cannot remember
it specifically, but I am willing to concede. If you can remember that
aspect, I may concede, yes. . . . I do not recollect this, because I do not
think it happened at all. . . . I am sorry, the finer detail I cannot remember. . . . It is difficult to remember. . . . I am not sure, but I am willing to
concede. Your memory will be better than mine. . . . I honestly cannot
remember. . . . My memory fails me. . . . I can't remember. . . . Sir, I have
done so many heinous deeds in the name of interrogation, that I cannot
remember individually certain aspects. . . . Not as far as I can remember.
Not that I can remember.—Jeffrey T. Benzien, amnesty hearing, 14
July 1997

ALL OF THESE EXPRESSIONS OF AMNESIA, and more, emerged in apartheid
policeman Jeffrey Benzien's confession to the South African Truth
and Reconciliation Commission. But what Benzien had forgotten
seems almost irrelevant, given what he remembered and presented to
the TRC. Benzien reenacted in front of the TRC, and subsequently in
the media, the "wet bag" torture technique he had perfected. There he
was, in the staid TRC chambers, in front of flashing cameras and a
drop-jawed audience, straddling the back of his victim stand-in with a
polka-dotted shirt, suffocating him with a blue bag over his head.
Television and radio news broadcasts captured Benzien in the act of
torture, audibly and visibly shocking his audience, including the Amnesty Committee chairman who futilely attempted to restore order in
the hearing. Through his reenactment, Benzien became the poster boy
for apartheid state violence, and his image appeared everywhere: on
book jackets, in film and TV representations of the TRC, in novels and
poems, and in countless academic papers and books.[1]

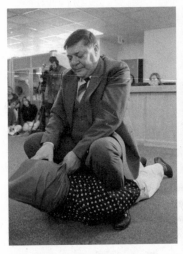

In 1997 the apartheid policeman Jeffrey Benzien reenacted in front of the TRC, and subsequently in the media, the wet-bag torture technique he had perfected. Photos by Benny Gool.

What few remember is that this reenactment—and the public's exposure and debate over apartheid state horrors—only occurred because of what Benzien had omitted from his TRC testimony. Benzien's victims had challenged his sanitized narrative version of the wet bag. Benzien had explained to the TRC that in the police station he would soak a standard-issue bag (used to hold detained prisoners' personal effects) until the fibers swelled and closed off any air holes. He would hold the wet bag over his prisoners' heads, suffocating them. This method guaranteed that he could extract valuable information in thirty minutes from even the most uncooperative prisoner, without leaving a mark or causing permanent damage. His victims rejected Benzien's verbal description of a unitary, benign, yet effective wet-bag method. They elicited details, including the reenactment, to provide a more complete version of apartheid-era torture.

Tony Yengeni, former fighter for the ANC army, Umkhoto we Sizwe (MK), and ANC member of parliament, began the victims' interrogation of Benzien's testimony. He asked to see "what he did to me, with my own eyes."[2] The request threw the hearing into disarray. The committee did not know whether to allow such a display. Benzien resisted the enactment, arguing that he did not have the necessary props and that he no longer had the agility he once possessed to effectively use the technique. Yengeni produced a volunteer willing to play the role of the victim and a blue pillowcase to represent the wet bag. By performing the technique, Benzien unwittingly contradicted his own confession. Nothing about it was benign.[3] Those who lived through it, like Yengeni, continued to suffer from its effects. To underscore his point, Yengeni asked rhetorically, "What kind of man uses a method like this one of the wet bag, to people, to other human beings, repeatedly and listening to those moans and cries and groans and taking each of those people very near to their deaths? What kind of man are you? What kind of man is that, that can do that kind of . . . what kind of human being is that, Mr. Benzien?"[4]

Benzien's victims further challenged his claims about the wet bag's efficiency. Benzien, they contended, did not limit himself to a single thirty-minute session. The wet bag formed part of a "systematic and protracted process" that could last for months and long after prisoners would have had any more valuable information to reveal.[5] Benzien conceded that he had used the wet bag twice in Ashley Forbes's case. Forbes countered that Benzien had used the wet bag to mark each month he had been in detention. In anticipation of one of these "anniversary" sessions, Forbes unsuccessfully tried to commit suicide. His suicide attempt did not protect Forbes; Benzien visited him in the hospital and again threatened to use the wet bag.

Benzien's victims forced him to admit that the wet bag alone did not always produce results, which had led him to add other torture techniques. Forbes recounted Benzien's use of electric shocks from a metal rod inserted into Forbes's anus; physical assaults while Forbes was wrapped in a carpet; beatings that blackened Forbes's eye and broke his eardrum; and breaking his nose by putting both thumbs into his nostrils and pulling until they bled. "Do you remember choking me and then knocking my head against the wall until I . . . lost consciousness?" Forbes asked. Another victim, Gary Kruser, repeated a phrase prisoners learned from Benzien: that they had the choice to be treated like animals or like human beings. According to Kruser, Benzien had beaten him repeatedly in the stomach while he was hanging by handcuffs in the station. Bongani Jonas accused Benzien of depriving him of medical care after he had been shot, and even of jumping on his bullet-shattered leg. Peter Jacobs forced Benzien to admit to prolonged use of the wet-bag technique over several hours and, when failing to get results, resorting to electric shocks. The advocate Michael Donen presented the former victim Niclo Pedro's contention that Benzien had rammed a stick into his anus and searched through his extracted feces for a note he had swallowed. Had the wet bag proved so effective, Benzien would not have had to use such methods to extract information.

In response to each of these claims, Benzien claimed lack of memory. He repeated over and over that he could not confirm or deny their accusations: "I can't honestly remember. . . . I do not recollect. . . . Your memory will be better than mine. . . . My memory fails me." Despite his failure to remember details, however, he often seemed to acknowledge the truth behind his victims' accounts. He seemed to be saying that he could not remember the exact details of each torture session, but that his victims' versions were essentially true. Consider this response, for example: "Sir, if I said to Mr. Jacobs that I put the electrodes in his nose, I may be wrong. If I said I attached it to his genitals, I may be wrong. If I put a probe into his rectum, I may be wrong. . . . I could have used any one of those three."[6]

Benzien accepted responsibility for the range of torture tactics he had forgotten the specifics of, but he would not allow his victims to link his activities to the broader system of repression in apartheid South Africa. Benzien and the police promoted an image of him as a lone perpetrator. He appeared at the TRC hearings without any support from colleagues, friends, or family, leading one news reporter to describe him as "a lonely and pathetic figure."[7] Only General Johannes Lodiwikus Griebenauw, Benzien's former commander, testified on his behalf. Griebenauw, however, took responsibility for failing to reign Benzien and others in, but he made clear that Benzien devised and implemented his interrogation methods on his own. He reinforced the lone-perpetrator image: "I never gave any member an instruction to place a wet bag over anybody's head or to torture them in any other way. I was, however, very much aware of the fact that members' success could be ascribed to the use of unconventional questioning or interrogation methods. It would have been naïve of me to believe that they would extract information in any other way from a well trained terrorist and to do so quite quickly."[8]

To take the blame by himself, Benzien claimed to have forgotten the names of fellow operatives or commanders and of those who had participated in torture sessions and raids with him. When his victims tried to jog his memory with names, Benzien refused to confirm them. When asked about the chain of command and who would have ordered torture, Benzien claimed he could not remember. The TRC chose not to subpoena Benzien's commanders, leaving Benzien holding the (wet) bag by himself.

Most of Benzien's victims were unsatisfied with establishing Benzien's personal accountability for torture and hoped to establish the apartheid regime's responsibility for systematic violations of human rights. Forbes stated, for example, "If I have one reservation with what happened, it is that Benzien did not implicate any of his fellow officers or superiors. It was like he was prepared to sacrifice himself, and maybe that means he still believed in them."[9] Kruser put this theory directly to Benzien, asking him if his commanders still manipulated him to do things their way. Benzien expressed disappointment that more police had not cooperated with the amnesty process and insinuated that he had chosen to do so on his own volition and not under pressure. To his victims, the absences in Benzien's confession and the system he protected with his amnesia revealed more about the apartheid era than his wet-bag disclosure.

By leaving the apartheid repressive apparatus out of his narrative, Benzien turned his confession to torture into a heroic battle between good and evil: "I think even you and the rest of your people sitting there, would admit that I was the person that rightly or wrongly knowing that the information that I could glean from you and your members, could take especially explosives out of the community, which would be used against the public at large. Mr. Yengeni, with my absolutely unorthodox methods and by removing your weaponry from you, I am wholly convinced that I prevented you and any of your colleagues and any one of them that ever had an explosive device in Cape Town, I may have prevented you from being branded murderer nowadays."[10] Benzien exalted his personal power over his adversaries, particularly because of their heroic status within the liberation movement. As one journalist wrote, "In the mind of Benzien, Yengeni, freedom fighter and anti-apartheid operative, is a weakling, a man that breaks easily. . . . I said I am not gonna write no more columns like this, but the torture of Yengeni continues, with some of us regarding him as a traitor to the cause, a sell-out, a cheat and, in some stupid twist of faith and fate, his torturer becomes a hero, the revealer, the brave man who informed us about it all."[11] Yengeni shares this view of Benzien's tactics. Years after the TRC hearing, he remembers not only the permanent psychological damage of Benzien's wet-bag torture, but also the psychological torture that he continued to endure with his humiliation at the TRC hearings.

Benzien used subtle tactics to continue to wrest power away from his former victims during the hearing. He portrayed Yengeni as a squealer, Forbes as a love slave (see chapter 4), and brought the large, hulking Kruser to tears. Benzien's capacity to dominate—through forgetting—these otherwise strong individuals led one reporter to write, "Although he sprinkled his testimony with 'sincere apologies' and at one point wept, he could still psychologically assault his former victims, by revealing information he'd forced out of them which led to the arrest and torture of comrades, by implying they had broken quickly—or simply by failing to remember what he had done to them."[12]

Paradoxically, however, Benzien attributed his loss of memory to his own trauma and victimization, incurred while risking his life to track top MK fighters. He explained his vulnerability when he apologized for his "accidental" killing of MK leader Ashley Kriel.

My purpose was to arrest him and not to kill him. Although his death was a tragedy for his family, I am very, very sorry that he had to die, but the tables could very easily have been turned on that day, the outcome could have easily been very different and it could have left myself and Sergeant Abels being wounded or killed.

And once again, I apologise to the family for his death and I thank God that I, who also have children, also a daughter who is 22 years old, that I was not the person who was killed on that day.[13]

Benzien further explained that he felt threatened by the MK. The MK had targeted members of the security branch for violence, and with Benzien's growing reputation in the western Cape, he and his family felt increasingly vulnerable to assault.

Since my son was in Sub B, he was a little boy of six years old, my daughter was in standard 5, I think she was about 12, for weeks my children could not play in the normal ambit of other children. Because of my work with the Security Branch, they had to travel under police escort to school, they could not play on the playground with the other children. They had to be put in the principal's office all the time, under guard.

My house windows had to be barricaded with cupboards. Every night a wet blanket had to be put in the bath, available where my younger children could get hold of that in the case of grenade attacks. You are surely aware that I was transferred as the Station Commander at Stanford because not only were my nerves shot, my wife threatened divorce if I did not get out of Cape Town.

That was after the African [National Congress] Youth League threatened to have demonstrations on my front lawn. Yes . . . I did terrible things, I did terrible things to members of the ANC, but as God as my witness, believe me, I have also suffered. I may not call myself a victim of apartheid, but yes Sir, I have also been a victim.[14]

Benzien also considered himself a victim of his own hubris. He hinted at how his commanders had taken advantage of his particular level of commitment and dedication to the job: "When it came down to getting the job done, I was the person who did it. Maybe I was too patriotic, too naïve or anything else that you would want to call it."[15] He added that his "false sense of bravado" and effectiveness kept them from "dirtying or bloodying their own hands."[16] One of his commanders commented that Benzien was not the only torturer in the unit, but "one of the best, one of the most effective interrogators."[17] Rather than blame his commanders, Benzien claimed that his own personality led him "to go the extra mile" for the South African Security Branch and thus commit atrocity.

Benzien's psychologist considered his eagerness to please his commanders as the source of his emotional trauma and loss of memory: "He was a good detective who had an excellent record in breaking crime. And because of his success he was recruited to a position that has broken him mentally and physically."[18] His psychologist and his lawyer hoped to portray Benzien as a normal person placed in an extraordinary situation. Benzien did appear fairly normal with his plain suit, his working-class Afrikaner accent, and a background in the police academy and in the murder-and-robbery unit prior to his promotion to the elite Security Branch. He had worked his way up the ladder to the rank of captain by the time of the TRC hearings.

Benzien claimed to have paid dearly for his promotion into the Security Branch. Indeed, he looked and played the part of an individual ravaged by his past. During his performance he cried openly, dropped his face into his hands, and looked down in disgrace. He stated, "The method employed by me is something that I have to live with and no matter how I try to interpret what I did, I still find [it] deplorable. I find it exceptionally difficult, sitting here in front of the news to everybody, I concede that no matter how bad I feel about it, what was done to you and your colleagues, must have been worse. Believe, me, I am not gloating or trying to prove that I am somebody who I am not."[19] He recounted the impact his security-force past had had on his life: a failed marriage, distance from his children, depression, anxiety, addiction, and insomnia. Although his lawyer and psychologist confirmed that Benzien suffered from post-traumatic stress disorder (PTSD), which also explained his memory loss, the team of victims' lawyers remained unconvinced. Benzien's psychologist, they argued, did not have the expertise to diagnose PTSD. Moreover, the disorder applied only to trauma resulting from helplessness. Benzien, in contrast, had had total power over his victims in the police station where he had carried out brutal torture. They viewed the PTSD defense as a cynical attempt on Benzien's part to reverse roles and portray himself as the victim of trauma after he had brutally traumatized his victims.[20]

The Amnesty Committee, however, accepted Benzien's confession and granted him amnesty despite his failure to recall key events and provide full disclosure. Some committee members accepted the psychologist's diagnosis. Others did not necessarily accept a medical diagnosis, but still felt his amnesia was sincere, and not deliberately calculated. They recognized a tendency among perpetrators to dissociate themselves from their acts and to block memories. Benzien had sharp memory of details in which he could appear in a positive—that is, heroic or friendly—light, but he could not remember many specific details about violent acts. In the opinion of many observers, the performance of his job required him to block out negative memories. His addiction to drugs and alcohol further limited his capacity to remember. Still other committee members considered Benzien's testimony an important contribution to truth and reconciliation. He had demonstrated, at an extreme cost to his own public image, the kinds of tactics used by the police. And he had suffered for his past as evidenced by his isolation, emotional breakdown, and the break-up of his family. In the end, Benzien received what he wanted from his confession: amnesty from prosecution.

The committee's decision baffled many observers. How could Benzien, who had become the iconic apartheid torturer, complete with bulging eyes, swollen alcoholic nose, and frightful size, receive amnesty? As Ashley Forbes's mother articulated, "I still see the scars on Ashley, invisible scars. Although he is very brave and trying to disguise it, I still see it on his face and in his demeanor. I can still see the hurt and the pain in the back of his mind and in his soul. . . . I feel his [Benzien's] being given amnesty is unfair and unjust considering all the pain and hurt that he inflicted so mercilessly, without feeling."[21]

Benzien's amnesia, some scoffed, had duped the TRC into foregoing the requirement of full disclosure and allowing Benzien to hide details about his past. Gary Kruser publicly mused that Benzien could not remember his torture methods but recalled "flimsy things like Kentucky [Fried Chicken] and things which I would have thought you had forgotten, but things which stand out more permanently in terms of our interrogation and our experience, you don't seem to remember."[22] Far from bringing truth and reconciliation, these critics felt, Benzien's amnesia further traumatized his victims. His acts of brutality had permanent repercussions for them, and yet they were so insignificant in his own life that he could forget them, or what he did to them.

Not all of Benzien's audiences or victims challenged his amnesty, however. Two of his MK victims told me that in South Africa's political struggle Benzien had played a role very similar to their own, but on the other (wrong) side. He had confessed to his own responsibility, and although he might have said more about the apartheid regime, the Amnesty Committee asked only for individual, not collective, disclosures.

A letter to the *Cape Times* presented a similar acceptance of the committee's amnesty decision but from the opposite political pole. Benzien had disclosed the truth about the past, the letter concurred, but the TRC needed to get at other—more uncomfortable—ones: "Much has been made of Mr. Jeff Benzien and his horrendous wet-bag torture method. Surely, in support of sensational and balanced reporting, your paper could perhaps now show pictures of ANC torture methods on the front page?"[23]

Although Benzien's colleagues might have supported his amnesty, they found his performance at the TRC troubling. His tears and shame, in their view, did not become a professional policeman. More important, he trespassed boundaries of secrecy and acceptable police behavior by admitting to having sodomized men with iron rods and sticks. While these supporters might have accepted torture in the abstract, Benzien's tactics sounded too lurid, too illegitimate. Moreover, rather than adamantly deny such activities, he claimed not to remember them.

Benzien did not lose his job on the police force, but his colleagues made it difficult for him to stay. Demoted to a desk job and publicly humiliated, he no longer had status within the force. Some new members of the police force, former MK cadres, refused to work with the notorious torturer, ostracizing him further. Even his former colleagues distrusted him. Although he had not revealed names or identities, despite efforts by his victims to secure them, he had broken a bond of silence by exposing police secrets. Unable to leave his past behind, Benzien retired from police work with his full pension and benefits and fled from public life.

Benzien's confession eroded public confidence in the TRC since it granted amnesty to a perpetrator without demanding full disclosure. Some blamed that outcome on the understaffed and inexperienced investigation unit. Others attributed it to inconsistencies in the Amnesty Committee decisions. Some perpetrators' lawyers, like François van der Merwe, claimed that the Benzien decision meant that other perpetrators who failed to provide full disclosure should receive amnesty. He contended that his clients, the policemen involved in the murder of the Black Consciousness leader Steve Biko, had expressed their political motive and disclosed as much as Benzien, but without receiving amnesty.[24] The testimony of Benzien, who had used torture to extract information from incarcerated political leaders who had had no recent contact with their organizations, also raised questions about proportionality. When, if ever, is torture proportional to political objectives?

Benzien's hearing also reminded perpetrators of the stigma attached to confession. Benzien received amnesty at a high personal cost to his privacy and reputation. Only those perpetrators already convicted, or facing prosecution, would take such risks. Benzien may have assumed that by torturing high profile ANC leaders he would face prosecution. Most perpetrators bet on the weakness of the cases against them and won. They went on to lead normal lives, hiding their pasts behind silence and denial. Perpetrators sensed that the TRC did not guarantee amnesty for confessions, but it did guarantee public exposure, humiliation, and shunning.

Certainly the Benzien case left much to criticize about the TRC process. But it also pointed to one of the contributions of such an institutional arrangement. Benzien's confessional act made torture real, not an abstraction. He showed it was an inhumane and illegitimate act, used long after it could be arguably effective as a mechanism for extracting information. Nothing about the reenactment of the wet-bag method, or the other perverse forms of torture, looked heroic or admirable. Benzien forced a discussion about what really happened in the name of national security.

Metaphorically, Benzien's amnesia also demonstrated the danger of failing to reveal past atrocities. Forgetting the past erases the damage done to individuals. It allows those who committed crimes to reinvent their past as heroic and brave. Bringing recollections into public debate allows a fuller understanding of the past. Public disclosure, even if only partial, allows others to fill in forgotten details and advance a different political agenda.

COMPARATIVE REFLECTIONS ON AMNESIA

"I can't remember" might appear to be an effective way of ending any discussion about the past. But amnesia did not protect Benzien. If it shielded perpetrators, perhaps more of them would use it. But perpetrators' memory loss invites others—fellow perpetrators, victims, and survivors—to remember, to remind, and to make public events that perpetrators wish to forget. Once in the public eye, perpetrators must respond to events they most want to hide, even from themselves. They lose the control they had enjoyed through forgetting. Thus, ironically, confessional amnesia can advance debate over the forgotten past.

"I Want to Forget." Audiences often interpret amnesia as willful forgetting. Indeed, perpetrators normally only make public what is convenient for them to remember. They omit, or forget, the parts of their past that do not fit their self-images. Benzien offered up a version of himself as an efficient policeman who used a benign form of interrogation to extract valuable information from fierce adversaries. Did he forget, or did he want to forget, those parts of his past that contradicted that image? The Brazilian Army sergeant Antonio Benedito Balbinotti admitted, "I want to forget, I want to live in peace." What Balbinotti hoped to forget were the twelve prisoners who accused him of having tortured them and used electric shocks on a fifteen-year-old boy.

Audiences can overcome willful, or strategic, forgetting. By filling in the forgotten information, they compel perpetrators and others in society to remember. Benzien was forced to concede what his victims remembered: the other torture techniques that he had used and overlooked in his representation of the quick and efficient wet-bag method. Although he never actually confessed to those methods, neither did he deny them. He did admit that victims might possess better memories of their detention experiences than he. Similarly, when confronted by his victim's memory, Balbinotti initially claimed his innocence: "I wasn't guilty of anything. I was just a foot soldier. I followed orders and they didn't send me to do anything." And yet he also admitted to wanting to forget his guilt: "Today we understand more deeply what went on. I didn't think it was right. And I still don't think it was right. What did they do to this country? Yes, I participated, unfortunately. . . . But without any special training to deal with those people, without being aggressive, what could I do? If a prisoner from that era feels harmed by me, I ask forgiveness. These were errors, circumstances, things that happened thirty years ago. It all happened because of the euphoria of those times and because of the context in which I lived. If only I had known, if I had some understanding, if I gave orders to do something. . . . I want to forget, I want to live in peace."[25]

Willful amnesia allows perpetrators to escape their pasts. The Brazilian police sergeant Leo Machado, one of the top torturers listed in *Brasil: Nunca mais*, claimed, "I live one day at a time," and added, "I don't spend time dredging up the past. I don't want to talk about it. I prefer to forget it."[26] He offered no excuses, justifications, or euphemisms, but simply the will to leave it all behind.

Yet the past often haunts perpetrators. In some cases personal demons—insomnia, addiction, anxiety—prevent them from completely forgetting. Even if they escape those demons, victims and survivors often challenge perpetrators' desire to forget. Perpetrators' confessions help audiences in this regard. Because amnesia is rarely total, perpetrators at the very least locate themselves in a particular role, place, and time. In doing so, they put themselves at the site of the criminal act. Witnesses and forensic evidence often fill in the blanks in the amnesia confession and further implicate perpetrators. Forced out of a protective cocoon of unknowing, perpetrators must respond in some way to a past they have willfully or unconsciously forgotten.

As if anticipating this outcome, perpetrators often isolate themselves to avoid remembering what they have chosen to forget. They flee from their pasts, distancing themselves from anything and anyone who might force them to remember who they were and what they did. This often involves divorce, abandoning families, moving to new neighborhoods or new countries, and taking new jobs. This exit option makes it difficult to track them down, as Brazil's news magazine *Veja* discovered. When it eventually found Leo Machado, he had no identifying plaque on his office door, no employees, no neighbors near his home or office who knew him, and no trace of a military career. Shedding his past, Machado remade himself as a lawyer on civil matters. He disconnected himself from his neighborhood and community, leaving his house early in the morning and returning late at night to retreat behind his garden walls. The journalist writing about him called him a "recluse, almost mysterious."[27]

As Machado and others found, however, escaping from their own pasts did not keep the past at bay forever. Institutional processes, the media, and victims may uncover perpetrators' past lives, as well as their own memories of it.

"I Can Remember Lots of Trivialities." For self-preservation, perpetrators may have begun the process of strategic amnesia during the authoritarian regime. Such amnesia may have been necessary so they could continue performing their (violent) jobs. Forgetting the violence even as they commit it allows them to dissociate themselves from it. Military euphemisms facilitate "forgetting" the violence behind the acts by calling them something else. The bond of silence within the security apparatus means that perpetrators never discuss these acts. Without language to describe them, violent acts disappear from memory. Traces of them remain only in the havoc they wreak on perpetrators' daily personal lives: alcohol and drug abuse, insomnia, family and marital problems, depressive withdrawals, suicidal thoughts, violent outbursts, and amnesia itself.

The psychological responses of perpetrators to their violent pasts, like Benzien's PTSD defense, block memory. The medical profession has confirmed the impact of trauma on memory, even though audiences of victims and survivors view perpetrators' memory loss as strategic and cynical. Few in Benzien's audience believed in his loss of memory, seeing it instead as a ruse to avoid confession. The apartheid policeman Jacques Hechter, however, did convince his audience that he had trauma-induced amnesia. Hechter joined fellow security police to apply for amnesty for having kidnapped, assaulted, and murdered political activists while he was part of Vlakplaas and the Northern Transvaal Security Branch in the late 1980s. But Hechter relied on his colleagues to tell him how he had participated in such events. The Amnesty Committee probed Hechter's memory loss, particularly around the torture and murder of the PEBCO 3. Hechter responded, "Mr. Chairman, it's very difficult. Bits and pieces of this information started coming back to me in discussion with [co-amnesty applicant] Warrant Officer Paul van Vuuren." Asked directly if he could remember having electrocuted the activists: "I can remember the electrocution, but only after it was told to me. I can more or less remember the specific place where it happened. It was on a farm. There was a gate. I remember the narrow dirt road. It's a white, white chalk road. I can remember lots of trivialities. There were also guinea fowl. Those are the kind of things I can remember. But the actual serious deeds, I can't remember them." When a committee member expressed surprise that he could not remember the killing of three people, but could remember the guinea fowl, Hechter simply said, "I know it sounds

In 1997 five apartheid security policemen—Warrant Officer Paul van Vuuren, Brigadier Jack Cronje, Colonel Roelf Venter, Captain Wouter Mentz, and Jacques Hechter—applied for amnesty for the kidnapping, assault, and murder of political activists while working for Vlakplaas and the Northern Transvaal Security Branch in the late 1980s. Photo by Jillian Edelstein. Reproduced by permission.

unbelievable, but that's why I say I remember trivialities."[28] When two other police officers implicated Hechter in the assault of a guard in Warmbath in 1987, Hechter again could neither confirm nor dispute the evidence. He acknowledged, however, that the police regularly assaulted those victims who provided insufficient information and tried to convince them to become police informers. In both cases Hechter had been named by colleagues, so he had had to apply for amnesty or face prosecution. And his full disclosure about these events demanded memory of them.

Perhaps Hechter's contention that his memory loss did not result solely from his experience in the apartheid security police assisted his argument. He also described extreme child abuse by his father, who would awaken him and subject him to verbal and physical assaults. Hechter attributed his behavior during the apartheid era to this early trauma and vulnerability. By day he performed the role required of a policeman. By night he became an urban terrorist, pulling on his *balacava* and venturing into townships, seeking violent action.

Remembering "flimsy" details like guinea fowl or Kentucky Fried Chicken can undermine perpetrators' amnesia defenses. To convince their audiences, perpetrators must look the part of individuals deeply troubled by their pasts. They must communicate personal trauma in their confessional act. A preexisting condition, like Hechter's, might also render perpetrators' amnesia more believable. In addition, as long as perpetrators do not benefit from amnesia, and particularly if it might hurt their cases, as with Hechter, they may more easily convince their audience of the veracity of their claims to memory loss.

"To Forget Is a Verb Often Conjugated by Men Accused of Torture." "I don't remember," responded Osvaldo Setorio, a former police commissioner in La Plata, Argentina, and head of one of its largest clandestine torture centers. He did not need to say more when confronted with the case of Clara Analí Mariani. Protected by amnesty laws, he was not forced to remember or make testimony. Indeed, it was in his interest to "forget" as much as possible about the past.[29] Trials often produce confessional amnesia. "I don't know if I am Astiz," read the headlines of an Argentine daily paper after Alfredo Astiz had claimed under oath to not remember any details from his past, including the address of the well-known ESMA where he had worked.[30] During the Trial of the Generals, Admiral Massera's right-hand man, the retired navy lieutenant Jorge Carlos Rádice, appeared to have forgotten all details from his past, responding "following orders" to a question about his specific jobs and "cannot remember" to questions about combat.

Trials offer an incentive to forget that truth commissions do not. Particularly when truth commissions offer amnesty in exchange for truth, as in South Africa, perpetrators have little cause to forget their past. They may only remember it selectively or cast it in a particular light, but total amnesia is rare. When amnesia is used as a defense, as Benzien and Hechter illustrate, it is portrayed as a particular pathology or mental-health issue. Thus, although perpetrators usually do not provide full disclosure in truth commissions, they will usually avoid an amnesia defense and the stigma of mental illness associated with it.

Blanket amnesty, as in the case of Brazil, encourages silence until information is revealed, after which denial and amnesia appear. Perpetrators try to move on in their lives, avoiding both conflict and memory. Some of them create new identities without a past or anything to remind them of it, as is evident in stories of perpetrators who scrubbed themselves vigorously and repeatedly, or drank themselves into a stupor after committing atrocity. They attempt to wash it away. They sometimes succeed, but at other times they are forced into the public arena and often respond with amnesia, as happened with the perpetrators whom *Veja* sought out. As a *Veja* journalist astutely observed, "To forget is a verb often conjugated by men accused of torture during the dictatorship."[31]

Despite attempts by *Veja* and other media outlets to "out" perpetrators and expose their "forgotten" atrocities, the result is often complex. Audiences are exposed not only to past violence and its impact on victims, but also to the ravages of that violence on those who perpetrated it. Perpetrators emerge as more than one-dimensional evildoers. The media, unwittingly perhaps, complicates them and makes them intriguing. Audiences might detest the wrongs committed, but may also feel some empathy with those who committed them.

The events of the Thanh Phong massacre in Vietnam illustrates the role the media play in complicating audiences' understanding of the past. The former senator Bob Kerrey had been the commander of a unit of Navy Seals sent into Thanh Phong to ambush a Vietcong meeting. The zone had been cleared of women and children and non-Vietcong, or so Kerrey and his platoon believed. Kerrey recalled that they had found Vietcong and had fought against them according to instructions. But his former colleague Gerhard Klann recounted a different set of events, specifically acts by Kerrey and his company that would be considered war crimes. In Klann's version Kerrey had restrained an old man while Klann slit his throat. He said that the Navy Seals had gathered women and children together in a cottage and exterminated them. The press reports and media interviews that followed Klann's disclosure tended to credit his account over Kerrey's sanitized one.

Some critics contended that media coverage swayed the public against Kerrey because of the news anchor Dan Rather's interview style. One analyst described this technique as "short, rapid-fire questions that demand yes or no answers, punctuated with the pregnant pause . . . a tawdry star chamber technique designed less to elicit facts than to imply malfeasance."

RATHER: You have no memory of the inhabitants of the main part of the village being lined up . . .

KERREY: No

RATHER: And shot at point-blank range . . .

KERREY: No

RATHER: . . . repeatedly with automatic weapons . . .

KERREY: No

RATHER: . . . and forgive the reference—with literally blood and guts splattering all over everybody.

KERREY: No

RATHER: You have no memory of that?[32]

Rather than stand behind the decorated war hero (Kerrey), the media complicated the past. They cast Klann's memory as the true one, even though they could easily have used Klann's background to discount his story as a fabrication motivated by a desire for public recognition. But rather than challenge Klann's motives or memory, the media interview depicted Kerrey as the one with inaccurate recollections. Kerrey never denied his own memory of events. He simply "did not remember" it in the way Klann did. The media made him out to be shell-shocked at best, or deliberately obfuscating his past for personal and political gain at worst. The media turned Kerrey's amnesia into atrocity, thereby destroying any hopes Kerrey may have had for the presidency. Atrocity, after all, makes better copy than amnesia.

"No to Forgetting!" "No to forgetting!" (¡Que no nos gane el olvido!) read a banner carried by a group of human-rights activists through the streets of Buenos Aires.[33] Organized by the Mothers of the Plaza de Mayo, the group marched to protest the incident in which the police intelligence officer Miguel Osvaldo Etchecolatz had threatened three university students with a gun for having called him "assassin" in a public square. In this case, the perpetrator (Etchecolatz) had not forgotten the past; he had tried to turn it into heroic virtue. What the Mothers of the Plaza de Mayo were protesting was not *his* amnesia, but *public* forgetting, the outcome they anticipated from political processes built on immunity for perpetrators and the prevention of public debate over the past.

"Never Again" has become an international slogan for human-rights groups demanding memory to avoid any repetition of the atrocities of the past. In this sense, all mobilizations by human-rights groups demand political memory and oppose official processes that forget the past.

But amnesia confessions play a unique role for their audiences. Like silence, perpetrators' amnesia provides audiences an opportunity to fill in the gaps left by what is unsaid. But these confessions also provide a way for victims and survivors to equalize their relationships with perpetrators. Their torturer's inabilities to remember offers them power—the power of memory. They can confront perpetrators' hole-ridden stories with the missing details. As one of Benzien's victims stated, "I don't normally talk about my torture. It is not something I am proud of, that I talk about. Benzien was my torturer. I never thought about him. I didn't know what to say, what to do. But at this point he was no longer the arrogant torturer. He was a shadow of himself. The power relationship had changed. I was in a better position to stare at him, shout at him, or whatever."[34]

Staring and shouting may have offered personal healing, but it also played a political role. Many audiences view victims and survivors as seeking revenge through confrontation with perpetrators. But, as one victim suggests, personal revenge is not what most victims want from encountering their perpetrator: "[No one wants to] live again that whole experience. It was demeaning for you to be put through that experience, to hear what had happened in that place. At the end of the day, when they'd done that to you, you had to give them the information that they wanted. No one wanted to relive that experience. Some people decided not to. They decided to sit at home. They preferred not to be reminded . . . and [be] traumatized again." What motivated Benzien's victims to confront him was a political project. They were asked by the ANC to attend the hearing, to legitimize the TRC, and to help South Africans overcome the stigma of victimization. They used their personal stories to fill in the gaps in memory, not only Benzien's but also the nation's. That political agenda, not personal revenge, enabled them to confront their torturer.

Even with this shared political motivation and equalizing power relations, victims and survivors reacted very differently to encounters with their perpetrators. Some felt, for instance, that Benzien had a clear mission to "belittle" and "demean" his victims again. But more important than his personal attacks, these victims/survivors felt, was Benzien "basically giving himself and his technique [the credit] of cracking this cell in minutes. By doing that he suggested that the so-called 'terrorists' were weak; at the drop of a hat they would spill the beans. I needed to fight that, and give that situation more understanding." According to this interpretation, Benzien was continuing the apartheid struggle even in the TRC. He deserved incarceration to pay his debt to society.

Although recognizing Benzien's efforts to maintain his power advantage in encounters with his victims, other victims/survivors interpreted those efforts as less successful. Such survivors had limited political goals and achieved them. As one stated, "You get as much as you can [from the process]. But if you expect too much, you will become demoralized."[35] The process, particularly how the victims/survivors filled in missing information, clarified what had happened in South Africa. But this group of victims/survivors did not really view Benzien as a monster. On the contrary, they saw him in a position equal to their own: "It's context that makes us, it's the structure. If you look at the profile of their side and our side, you see the same thing: conscientiousness, obedience, blind trust. Any one of us could become a torturer in a certain context. I'm a disciplinarian and I follow orders. So I do what I'm told to do. . . . He [Benzien] did his job. I would have done the same."[36] These victims/survivors saw Benzien as part of a hierarchy. In that context, he was no more a monster than anyone else. The important political message was the critique of the apartheid system, not the individuals within it, the goal being to end unequal power relations. In that light, Benzien's participation was a step in the right direction. As one observer stated, "While we are convinced that Benzien did not make a full disclosure, he did—at least—go to the TRC. Others did not."[37]

CONCLUSION

"Oblivion," Jelin claims, "is not an expression of absence or emptiness. Rather it is the presence of that absence, the representation of something that is no longer there, and has been erased, silenced, or denied."[38] That seems to be the perpetrators' wish—to erase their past by failing to remember, to put it out of public discussion, for it to cease to exist even as a memory. But amnesia confessions have distinct limitations.

Amnesia fails to afford perpetrators the control over the past that they seek. As "the presence of the absence," forgetting means *something* happened that is now forgotten. When perpetrators say, "I cannot remember," they hint at a truth. They situate themselves in the realm of the possible: a particular place, in a particular group, at a particular moment, committing particular violent acts. Suspicion mounts because they do not deny, but simply fail to remember. In attempting to explain their memory loss, perpetrators further implicate themselves. Their medical condition links them to a violent world that has created a desire to block out the past. Partial memory or explanations of memory loss without denial, in other words, lead audiences to doubt these confessions.

Because *something* happened, audiences sometimes fill the void in knowledge with their own versions of the past. Some perpetrators may deny security-force violence in the events that their colleagues cannot remember. Democratic governments may also try to use amnesia to end unsettling public debate that can potentially reignite conflict over the past. Victims and survivors, or the lawyers who represent them, often seize the opportunity to produce evidence, material or circumstantial, that links perpetrators or the security apparatus to particular violent events. Rather than erasure, silence, or denial, audiences can transform amnesia into remembering and condemning the past.

Audiences do not have complete control over these processes, however. What perpetrators forget on the one hand and remember on the other is similarly forgotten or remembered by society. South African audiences do not remember Benzien raping men with rods, even though his audience forced him to admit it; their enduring memory of him is the wet-bag treatment. The media faces difficulty in making a story out of what is forgotten. Thus, although *Veja* "outed" Brazilian perpetrators, their amnesia did not turn those individuals into a cause célèbre for exposing the past and demanding justice. Most Brazilian perpetrators remain unknown and protected in their society. Perpetrators gain more legal protection from not remembering than from making admissions. The amnesia strategy failed for Astiz and Scilingo because they had already publicly admitted to the same acts that they subsequently claimed to have forgotten. But blanket amnesia of the simple "I can't remember" kind makes it increasingly difficult to convict perpetrators in the absence of material evidence.

Amnesia sometimes works for perpetrators even when audiences try to undermine them. But for perpetrators to erase, silence, or deny the past, several conditions must prevail: total, not partial, amnesia; a lack of evidence allowing audiences to link them to a violent past; a demobilized human-rights community; and a lack of fellow perpetrators who betray them.

CHAPTER NINE

BETRAYAL

Covert operations . . .was our work. The enemy was the ANC, PAC [Pan African Congress], and SACP [South African Communist Party]. I felt the state had decided to cut us loose. My loyalty towards the government and police was absolute. I would never have sold them out. My opinion is that F. W. de Klerk abdicated the day he unbanned these organisations. I regard him as one of the greatest cowards the country had ever produced. Not because he wanted peace—that is a noble cause—but because, like a small puppy, he turned his back and wet himself. He sold out certain members of the security forces to the ANC. These forces never received the benefit of promises for a general amnesty.—Eugene de Kock, "De Klerk Ordered Attack," 18 September 1996

EUGENE DE KOCK NEVER PLANNED TO TELL HIS STORY about running apartheid South Africa's notorious death squad Vlakplaas. Two life terms and a 212-year prison sentence changed his mind. Applying for amnesty from the Truth and Reconciliation Commission and turning state witness offered him some chance of reducing his jail time. Confession also offered de Kock a way to get back at those who had betrayed him: his men, his commanders, and the apartheid system. He hoped that they might at least share responsibility, and prison time, with him. But de Kock's strategy failed. He remains in jail alone, clinging to the slim hope of a presidential pardon. In the meantime, he has produced a confession that is remarkable for one of South Africa's best-known apartheid assassins.

De Kock's confession exposed the violent acts—including forty murders—that had earned him the nickname "Prime Evil." De Kock, for example, hacked Japie Maponya to death with a spade for failing to disclose information about his brother, an ANC comrade. Maponya, a

The former Vlakplaas commander Eugene de Kock testified in TRC amnesty hearings.
Photo by Benny Gool, Oryx Media Productions, www.africanpictures.net.
Reproduced by permission.

politically disengaged young man, probably did not have the information de Kock sought.[1] De Kock bragged about his "one-armed bandits," student activists who blew themselves up with rigged grenades he had given them. Eleven of them died. Vlakplaas planted weapons on many of the "armed" liberation cells it exterminated. De Kock bombed several buildings, including the South African Council of Churches' Khotso House; the trade-union headquarters, Cosatu House; and the ANC's offices in London. He did not target liberation forces only, but even killed several of his own men who he suspected might betray the unit. And he provided a "third force" of Inkatha Freedom Party (IFP) activists with weapons to wreak havoc in the townships against real and suspected ANC operatives in what became known at the time as "black-on-black" violence.

De Kock's confession resulted from, and formed part of, a cycle of betrayal. The cycle began in 1989 when Almond Nofemela, an askari who had been working at Vlakplaas, was about to be hanged for murdering a white farmer during an attempted robbery. Nofemela had counted on his Vlakplaas bosses to protect him from prison and a death sentence, since he had robbed and murdered in the past without reprisal and with a guaranteed cover-up. He had been reassured by his commanders that if he kept quiet they would make sure the matter would be dropped. But when de Kock sent a message to Nofemela shortly before his execution ordering him to "take the pain," he realized that he would have to fend for himself: "I then realized that I had been betrayed by my superior officers, who had promised to assist me in getting out of the Maximum Security Prison. It was at this stage that I decided to reveal all of the foregoing, and I sent a message to the Lawyers for Human Rights to send someone to me to take a statement accordingly and to apply for a stay of my execution."[2]

In an earlier era Nofemela's story might have withered due to lack of corroboration. Apartheid South Africa's courts would have discounted his claims about a police-sponsored death squad as lunatic rambling by a vengeful and desperate black man on death row. Had de Kock's predecessor at Vlakplaas, Dirk Coetzee, remained quiet, Nofemela might have hanged. Coetzee, however, also felt betrayed. He suspected, based on earlier charges of insubordination and demotions in his rank, that his superiors would claim that he was solely responsible for the crimes Nofemela blamed on Vlakplaas.

Coetzee sought protection through the press. Nofemela's testimony hastened a confessional process he had already initiated with the journalists Max du Preez and Jacques Pauw for the anti-apartheid Afrikaans newspaper *Vrye Weekblad*. In addition to publishing his story, du Preez and Pauw arranged for Coetzee to leave the country and join the ANC in exile for protection from reprisals. With confessions from the white commander, Coetzee, and a black operative, Nofemela, the existence of the police-sponsored death squad Vlakplaas seemed undeniable.

And yet de Kock denied it. "It was still possible to argue that one [Nofemela] was a convicted murderer and the other [Coetzee] a runaway ANC turncoat."[3] The Harms Commission also claimed that no evidence supported Nofemela and Coetzee's claims. Nevertheless, de Kock sensed a shift among the upper echelons of the security community. "After Harms," de Kock recounted, "we at Vlakplaas were no longer golden boys; on the contrary, it was as though we all smelled like skunks."[4] The subsequent Goldstone Commission confirmed de Kock's hunch. It produced evidence that repudiated the earlier Harms Commission, verified some of Nofemela's and Coetzee's claims, and determined that Vlakplaas had become involved in building a "third force," supplying weapons to the IFP to eliminate ANC members. De Kock was arrested.

Despite this change in climate, de Kock still expected absolution. Because he had escaped previous inquiries, trials, and commissions, he planned to "stay on the bus" again, trusting that police cover-up operations and sympathetic judges would protect him.[5] "He [de Kock] never thought it was going to become as serious as this," Coetzee stated. "He thought he had everyone by the balls."[6] His former friend and colleague Craig Williamson suspected that de Kock had not fully appreciated the climate shift: "He wasn't just abandoned by the generals, he was abandoned by the entire political structure. And, therefore, everybody from the top down, when they realised the chips were down and that some unpleasant truths were going to come out, ran for cover. And he was left there, the rabbit in the searchlight."[7]

The prosecuting attorney, Jan D'Oliveira, built a case against de Kock that was supported by the betrayal of his colleagues and subordinates: "The de Kock case was key to our prosecutions. At first de Kock thought he was going to get out and so did all of the people around him. Then they began to realize that we were going to take him down and they began to come to me in confidence to tell what they knew."[8] One by one, his men turned on de Kock, seeking protection as state witnesses. And they received ample compensation. Chappies Klopper allegedly received R90,000 for his testimony against de Kock in the Goldstone Commission. Willie Nortje and Brood van Heerden received jobs in the National Intelligence Agency. De Kock tried to counter some of these claims. He insinuated that Klopper lied for revenge because de Kock had severely beat him after finding him in flagrante delicto with a black prostitute in a bathroom and for trying to bed a fellow policeman's wife. Klopper rejoined that de Kock had launched a plan to "take him out" to keep him from speaking against him.

Even de Kock's superiors betrayed him. Unlike the full-court defense they mounted for their colleague Magnus Malan, they did not help de Kock prepare for trial. They did not even come to his trial. Overwhelmed, de Kock conceded the futility of going after Klopper or anyone else: "The evidence against me was too great for me to attempt to deny it."[9]

De Kock retired from his police position. He divorced his wife and sent her and his two sons into hiding abroad. He attempted to protect himself from violent assaults within and outside the prison walls he inhabited. Prisoners had attacked him with soap bars loaded with razor blades, he claimed. He felt insecure, moreover, because, as he put it, "for two arms of dagga [marijuana] or R100, a member of the 26s or 27s [two notorious gangs in prison] would kill you."[10] The government responded by posting six police-task-force members to protect de Kock. Some speculated that the force might also protect de Kock from taking his own life.[11]

De Kock set out on a long confessional journey, stating, "I have nothing to lose" and "I have no hidden agenda."[12] The media amplified de Kock's confessional performances, making him a regular fixture from his debut at the Harms Commission, to the Goldstone Commission, his lengthy trial, his 4,000-page amnesty application to the TRC, and his testimony in his own and others' TRC hearings. A biography of his life (*Into the Heart of Darkness*), his own autobiography (*A Long Night's Damage*), and a documentary film about him (*Prime Evil*) provided other public confessional venues.

Betrayal became the essence of de Kock's confession: not only how his commanders betrayed him, but also how he would now betray them by speaking out. He attributed his fall to the political negotiations that ended apartheid. "When they start negotiating they have to get rid of the cupboard full of dirty tricks, so instead of being the blue-eyed boy who would be the next general, I'm the leper they must dispose of."[13] Asked how he felt about his superiors' reactions to his trial, he stated: "It was total betrayal. . . . It didn't make me bitter; I felt like vomiting." The committee chairperson scolded him for "playing with words," to which he retorted, "I'm not playing with words. I mean what I say. I can speak Afrikaans." He went on: "I want to mention two names. The one is General Johan Coetzee [former head of the Security Branch] and the other is F. W. de Klerk [former president of South Africa]. They should be put against the wall today. Not only did they mislead people, but they ran away at the first sign of problems. They sold out the white population, except for their own elite group. . . . Those at the top didn't really know what was happening on the ground. They used to sit in the comfort of their air conditioners, work out their pensions and drink glasses of red wine, while we had to lie in the snot and hair and blood in the dust."[14]

De Kock reserves particular vitriol for de Klerk, whom he refers to as the one person that "sticks most in my throat": "He simply did not have the courage to declare: 'Yes, we at the top levels condoned what was done on our behalf by the security forces. What's more, we instructed that it should be implemented. Or—if we did not actually give instructions—we turned a blind eye. We didn't move heaven and earth to stop the ghastliness. Therefore, let the footsoldiers be excused. We who were at the top should take the pain. We who were at the top are sorry.'"[15]

De Kock recognized the practicality of scapegoating him for apartheid violence. He had committed atrocities, after all, often acted independently, and was not particularly well trusted or well liked within the security apparatus. But he was neither the sole nor the worst offender. Vlakplaas, he claimed, did little compared to what "the boys in the Eastern Cape and Natal got up to. . . . [T]hey made Vlakplaas look like a girl scout camp."[16] He characterized Vlakplaas as "almost last in line when it came to cold-blooded and sick murders."[17]

I do not deny that I am guilty of the crimes, many of them horrible, of which I was accused. But I am not the only guilty one. The state chose to give indemnity from prosecution to many of my men simply so that a bulldozer of a case could be assembled against me—and in the process allow other men just as guilty as I to laugh in the face of justice.

But we at Vlakplaas, and in the other covert units, are by no means the guiltiest of all. That dubious honour belongs to those who assembled us into the murderous forces that we became, *and which we were intended to be all along.* And most of them, the generals and the politicians, have got off scot-free.

I received my orders from generals in the South African Police. They in turn . . . got their instructions from the highest levels of government. Few of the generals or the Ministers have faced trial, nor has any former President; and so it would seem that justice has been sufficiently served by turning me, a mere colonel, into a lone demon to explain all the evil of the old regime.[18]

De Kock considered himself a loyal soldier who effectively served his commanders and country: "These men made us believe we were in a just war. They incited security forces and told us we were the last blue line between anarchy and peace."[19] He stated that they had been prepared to win at all costs and by all means "except rape and child molestation."[20] Eager to serve his country, he accepted the post at Vlakplaas—he had not chosen it—and "took the job like a loyal National Party supporter." At Vlakplaas he found others who, like him, were "loyal men who would not hesitate to commit an illegal act in the interest of their country."[21] He did not question his orders, even when he disagreed with them. He doubted the wisdom (but not the legality), for example, of high-profile bombings because he believed they would implicate the regime's involvement in illegal violence. As he stated, "It would then be revealed that the security forces had turned to state-sanctioned terrorism."[22]

Thus, while strategic, de Kock considered his commanders' betrayal to be a cowardly violation of police ethos. De Kock considered himself to be the kind of model officer that he had expected his superiors to be: dedicated to his men and willing to make sacrifices to protect them, the operation, the institution, and the government, even to engage in cover-ups and participate in dirty work rather than foisting it off on subordinates.[23] He turned on his commanders when they did not fulfill these expectations: "I take full responsibility from me downwards for all the actions of my members, but no more from me upwards to the top."[24] He added, "I incorrectly believed that there was integrity and moral fibre in the hierarchy, but I regret this is not the case."[25] He also vowed to become a "thorn in the flesh of his former superiors," since they had proven unwilling to share responsibility for acts carried out under their command.[26] He referred to his commanders as "cowards" who "want to eat lamb, but they do not want to see the blood and guts."[27]

De Kock exposed his superiors' hypocrisy. "If I look at the last two years, it seems as though I was the only white man who fought against the ANC. Everybody is now a reborn supporter of the ANC."[28] He further challenged his commanders' claims that they had not known what Vlakplaas was up to: "Why, if they did not know about these operations, did they hand out medals to me and my unit members?"[29] He referred specifically to the Police Star for Outstanding Service, an award usually reserved for generals, conferred on him by the president shortly after his 1981 bombing of the ANC's offices in London. He recounted having arrived at Johan Coetzee's home after a 1986 raid in Swaziland, where his unit had killed three people and seized ANC documents. Coetzee, in his dressing gown, had offered them coffee and shaken everyone's hand. When he reached de Kock, "he said he did not know whether he should touch my hands since they were covered in blood."[30] De Kock also denounced his commanders' denial: "You could not blow someone up, or kill someone, without clearance—all the way up to commissioner level. I once went over the border without an order to do so, and my action nearly cost me my career. . . . I reiterate: Gen. Coetzee is a liar."[31]

De Kock's superiors rejected his interpretation of events. The former minister of foreign affairs Pik Botha denied de Kock's claims that he had known about and tacitly approved Vlakplaas's cross-border raids on the ANC. De Klerk accused de Kock of being part of a radical fringe element within the security forces, who had fought as vigorously against the political transformation process as they had earlier fought against the ANC.[32] Roelf Meyer, former National Party cabinet member, agreed, attributing de Kock's revenge against his commanders to his rejection of the process of reorganization and political reform begun by de Klerk in 1989.[33] His commanders further portray de Kock as disobedient, a characterization that de Kock relishes. Contradicting de Kock's reputation of "honor midst ignominy," de Kock's commanders and colleagues recounted, was the fact that he had siphoned off Vlakplaas funds for personal enrichment.[34] Captain Wouter Mentz, for example, stated, "I never stole money. I am not Eugene de Kock. I did what I was told and I believed that at the time was necessary."[35] Former president de Klerk asserted that de Kock was autonomous, masterminding all of his atrocities without consultation or detection from his superiors. Asked whether de Kock could have managed all his financial and other resource needs on his own while keeping his actions hidden from his superiors, de Klerk responded, "Yes, I think it is possible."[36]

Some media coverage also cast doubt on de Kock's image of himself as a scapegoat. The journalist Themba Molefe wrote, "Victims of his evil deeds saw an evil murderer being turned into a victim of circumstance. The impression created is that he has been dumped by his masters."[37] Another observer believed that de Kock was "holding back details, trying to make himself look more like a soldier than a monster."[38] By playing the loyal officer, another noted, "he wants to clean it up, to make it look like he was a precision man, an army man in a war."[39] Others challenged the notion that following illegal orders excuses atrocity.

> Eugene de Kock, in defense of his actions, claimed to have been himself a victim, a mere foot soldier following orders, a loyal policeman whose only crime was a misguided patriotism towards the apartheid government. But de Kock was part of a chain of command which led to the highest echelons of political power, whose task was the deliberate and strategic destabilization of the society and who was part of a system which has been recognized as a crime against humanity. De Kock was not a victim of the system, he was a trained assassin who was awarded the highest honours by the apartheid government for the acts he carried out. His defence must be critiqued and reviewed within this context. He cannot be equated with those who were the victims of the human rights atrocities he committed.[40]

Initially, popular sentiment condemned de Kock. He blamed his poor public image on prosecuting attorney Anton Ackerman's efforts to "dehumanize" him and make him out to be a "monster."[41] But his nickname, "Prime Evil," grew out of a reputation for brutality from within, and not outside, the security forces. Survivors of his violence contributed to his negative public reputation. Seipati Mlangeni, the widow of the ANC lawyer Bheki Mlangeni, who was killed by a mail bomb sent by de Kock, said, "I think if I can see him, I can kill him. To me, he is like a vicious animal that won't look twice at its prey. He's a cruel person."[42] Bheki's mother, Catherine Mlangeni, also hoped to see him dead, "like he killed my son."[43] The brother of one of de Kock's victims shared this view: "De Kock is a cruel man, a cruel man. That man, he must suffer. He must suffer. If things go well, they must hang him. He must die." Odirile Maponya, brother of Japie Maponya, declared, "If I was not a Christian, inside the court, I would have killed that man, but because of Christianity, I didn't make it like that. . . . But I know that God is going to punish them. I will forgive them, but God is going to punish them. 'Cause they've done a sin."[44] Protests over his "luxury" cell at Centurion City's Adriaan Vlok prison turned into jubilation when the courts sentenced him to Pretoria's maximum-security prison: "As black people danced and celebrated outside the court building, their fists clenched in the air, Eugene De Kock was driven away to start his sentence in the maximum security section of the Pretoria Central Prison. For the first time, justice was seen to be done to an apartheid killer."[45]

Over time, de Kock's media portrayal became more ambiguous. His signature thick eyeglass lenses, for example, had at first seemed to hide his gaze and veil his emotion, depicting a blank expression without heart or soul, the emotional detachment of a serial killer. Later revelations that the police special task force had barred his admission due to poor eyesight, however, rendered de Kock more vulnerable, almost nerdy.[46] His terse replies had initially marked him as cocky, as when he famously responded that references to him as "South Africa's most effective assassin" were "accurate."[47] He became more sympathetic after revealing that a stutter had caused him to economize on words and permanently scarred him. "By my adolescent years," he stated, "I had pretty much given up taking part in conversations. The therapy helped but I have never lost my inordinate fear of speaking, and I have never forgotten the ridicule to which I was subjected, both to my face and behind my back."[48] His audience began to appreciate the honesty and wry humor in his sparse replies. When asked again whether he was South Africa's most effective assassin, he replied, "I don't know, we have never had an assasin's [sic] conference."[49] He would not say how many people he had killed, stating instead, "It was something you tried to forget."[50] He would not let others put words in his mouth. When the attorney representing the ANC militants massacred in Lesotho in 1985 challenged his version of the story, de Kock responded, "Chairman, I can tell what I recall but if Berger wants me to tell what he wants to hear, tell him to write it down and I will read it to him."[51]

Other bits of de Kock's background provided a more complex image of him. His biographer Jacques Pauw, for example, described de Kock's childhood as devoid of any emotion other than aggression.[52] His overbearing father epitomized the Afrikaner patriarchy that turned out apartheid's killers: heavy drinkers, devout National Party supporters, and members of the secret nationalist Afrikaner Brotherhood (Broederbond). His father's verbal assaults drove his mother out of the home, leaving de Kock and his brother defenseless. De Kock rejects this explanation, however, saying it is "unacceptable to blame my father and my home life for me."[53]

Instead, de Kock and others blame socialization and training within the security forces. According to de Kock, "Members of the security forces, including myself, became brutalised and maladjusted. . . . We were forced to rely more and more on acts of terror—both against our own citizens and against neighbouring states. We started realising that people who felt so strongly about their ideals and rights could be defeated only by fear."[54] His colleagues reinforced the view that de Kock *became* a killer, he was not born one. The police environment and ideology encouraged atrocity against the enemy. "We were literally taught to hate," recounted one of de Kock's colleagues, "If you look at the security course I went on, for five weeks we were subjected to, and we swallowed all of this, the ranting and raving of a person that I'll describe as a cross between Adolf Hitler and Eugene Terre Blanche [South Africa's notorious white supremacist]. About the satanic, godless Communists and their black surrogates that were going to swamp us. Officially we were taught to hate. It was a culture of hatred."[55]

De Kock's participation in South Africa's counterinsurgency border wars exacerbated the effect of this culture of violence. Judge Wilhelm van der Merwe attributed de Kock's "deliberate, coldblooded, and calculated" murder of "innocent people who posed no danger to any member of the police" to the desensitization of protracted guerrilla wars against Robert Mugabe's Zimbabwe African National Union, Joshua Nkomo's African People's Union in former Rhodesia, and the Southwest African People's Organization.[56] Craig Williamson acknowledged that his commanders had selected de Kock to lead Vlakplaas because of the expertise he had developed during his training: "He was part of an élite in the security police. He believed absolutely that he had a mission. The Rhodesian and Koevoet episodes primed him for what he became and for the job he did at Vlakplaas. And let nobody deny that Eugene de Kock's superiors knew who Eugene de Kock was and knew what Eugene de Kock was good at."[57] De Kock's commander at Koevoet, a police counterinsurgency unit in what is now Namibia, reportedly tried to transfer de Kock to a desk job, deeming him unfit to serve in an operational unit since he could not distinguish between right and wrong. De Kock's brother, Vossie, concurred that the bush wars—or, more pointedly, the absence of psychological counseling after them—caused de Kock's emotional breakdown and led to his Vlakplaas atrocities. He stated that de Kock "was going out of his mind."[58]

De Kock denied having any emotional or mental-health problems, attributing his acts, instead, to professional training. He killed for his job and became "a relentless hunter" in pursuit of subversion: "[I stay] on the track until the problem is solved. I act without mercy against the country's enemies and criminals. Many criminals shiver when they hear that I am on their track. The ANC-PAC alliance is haunted by me and I am feared."[59] His colleagues characterized him similarly. Peter Casselton described him as "a soldier . . . a killer. And that's what he was taught by the South African government."[60] Riaan Stander considered him dedicated to his work: "It was immaterial to him whether it was an enemy or not an enemy. It was a question of doing a job. In a certain sense, he is a cold-blooded killer."[61] Krappies Engelbrecht referred to him as "a hunter without mercy, single-minded and nothing deviated him from the job at hand. He frightens members of the ANC/PAC/SACP alliance."[62] His violent exploits led Pauw, among others, to ask, "Did this man enjoy killing people?"[63] De Kock replied with little emotion: "I took no pleasure in what I had to do."

Some of de Kock's strongest supporters attributed his emotional coldness to cultural influences, as hinted at by an Afrikaans-speaking defense lawyer's description of his own police clients: "In one group of clients, all but one lost their wives and children. They drink, gamble. They all need to see psychiatrists. But the Afrikaans people don't show emotions. Boys are taught only one emotion: aggression. There is no fear and no uncertainty, no sorrow, tears, no asking for help. You'd rather just sit in a corner and bleed. . . . Never complain, don't admit to pain, just aggression. . . . We don't allow uncertainty, doubts, fears. Never. We don't say, 'I need assistance.' "[64] De Kock's prison social worker explained his inability to express emotions as a cultural phenomenon: "White men in South Africa don't express their feelings, Afrikaans speaking men even less, and Security Branch people even less . . . you know, cowboys don't cry."[65]

After his conviction, however, de Kock did begin to express emotion, even remorse, for his acts: "I don't think it was necessary for apartheid to hurt and kill. I feel that 95% of our time and energy was used to be destructive and not creative."[66] He further added, "We destroyed lives. Ruined the lives of families of those we killed. It was a futile exercise."[67] He believed that the apartheid regime created the same beast it had fought against: "I did not know then that, in fighting terrorism, we South Africans would become terrorists ourselves; that we would end up violating the very things we were fighting for." This occurred, he claimed, because "we began to believe we were supermen who could behave ruthlessly in the name of patriotism and state security. The state had made torture legitimate."[68]

De Kock's amnesty application for over 100 crimes reflected this sentiment about state-sponsored violence: "We wasted the most precious gift, which is life. . . . I would like to tell those families that I am very sorry about it."[69] Several other apologies followed. Pauw's biography quoted de Kock: "There are times when I wish I wasn't born. I can't tell you how dirty I feel. I shouldn't have joined the South African Police. We achieved nothing. We just left hatred behind us. There are children who will never know their parents and I will have to carry this burden for ever. I'm a very private person and I don't like to show emotion, but I sympathise with my victims as if they were my own children. This is all I can say."[70] *Cape Argus* reported de Kock to have said, "There have been so many times that I thought: 'How is it possible? How could I sink to that level?' Until this day I cannot reconcile [the murders] with my religious beliefs. There is no justification. If it were within my power I would bring back those who were killed. But this is how God is punishing me—you can never go back and change things. I will have to bear this cross for the rest of my life. In my own case, I believe I became blunted to physical danger and to my fellow humans. I could also easily justify doing the things I did."[71] De Kock apologized to the South African Council of Churches and to the Congress of South African Trade Unions, whose headquarters he had bombed. He asked them to accept his apology on behalf of himself and all of those who had served under him, but he refused to speak on behalf of those who had given the orders.[72] Gestures of atonement accompanied de Kock's apologies. He promised to distribute the proceeds from his autobiography to victims of apartheid and their families.[73] He offered to make amends through public service by training soldiers in another "black state" to clear land mines.[74] His frequent apologies led one journalist to include him in South Africa's "category of remorseful converts."[75]

The new, post-apartheid de Kock also denounced racism and embraced racial harmony. He claimed that he had fought not a racial war, but a war against communism. He produced evidence from his past suggesting that he had fought for equality for black South Africans. He had tried, he claimed, to distribute equal food rations for black and white soldiers while stationed in Rhodesia. His Koevoet superiors had assigned him to lead black troops because of his rapport: "Let De Kock work with the kaffirs because he gets along well with them."[76] He provided examples of generosity toward blacks, such as paying for his gardener's visit to his own doctor. A black police subordinate had even named his son Eugene de Kock to honor him.[77] Indeed, he attributed his survival in prison to protection by black prisoners.[78]

De Kock also abandoned the National Party and joined the Inkatha Freedom Party to participate in the new South Africa. He considered the IFP a friend since it had also fought the ANC. "They fought their hearts out (in the army and police) but did not have the vote."[79] De Kock had developed ties in the IFP when he was "convinced that South Africa was on the verge of a civil war and I knew that the white people would not be prepared to fight for their existence. The only way out was to help Inkatha."[80] But he only joined the party, he said, after the ANC offered to include him in their intelligence apparatus, prior to the 1994 elections: "I could not walk over [to the opposition], but I knew that South Africa would have a black government soon and, therefore, I joined the Inkatha Freedom Party."[81]

Although he would not join the ANC, de Kock expressed admiration for the party. He praised the courage of those who had died at his hands with ANC secrets on their lips. Mentioning Glory Sidebe in particular, he remarked, "We were equals. Sidebe was a blue-blooded member of the ANC and Africa, who was fighting for the freedom of his people. I was combating terrorism."[82] De Kock also expressed admiration for the leadership of the ANC, which, unlike that of the National Party, stood behind its foot soldiers and took responsibility for their actions, however abhorrent it thereby appeared in postconflict judgment. De

Kock further asserted that he, too, would have fought for liberation had he been a black man during apartheid."[83]

As de Kock's image shifted, so, too, did public response to him. The media captured growing admiration for him. The *Cape Times* reported, "Eugene De Kock yesterday seemed to win over large segments of the audience in the Centenary Hall with his forthright evidence to the Truth and Reconciliation Commission. Even family members of the Motherwell Bombing victims were impressed."[84] According to the *Cape Argus*, "De Kock is often portrayed as driven by embitterment for having been hung out to dry by the spineless retraction of his masters. But this week the apartheid state's top gun came across in his naked determination to tell the truth . . . as relentless as the honey badger he once chose as the Vlakplas [*sic*] unit emblem."[85]

Victims of apartheid violence expressed respect for de Kock's admissions. A widow of one of the famous Cradock Four political activists said, "No one wanted to cross examine de Kock. You just had the sense that he has nothing to hide. Even though he is a killer—the worst—the angel of death—still you respect him because he is telling the truth."[86] Another observer stated, "He impressed me from day one of the trial because he speaks the truth."[87] Some even linked his confession to reconciliation. Anna Mohatle, whose sister Mankaelang was killed in de Kock's 1985 raid in Lesotho, stated, "It is better now that we know who killed them. Before we just knew that they were killed by the Boers and I hated all Boers. I do not do that any longer."[88] Other victims described de Kock more favorably than other apartheid perpetrators, as did a woman widowed by the Motherwell bombing incident, which killed four black members of the security police: "He [de Kock] has expressed sympathy and apologized. We have been sitting here the whole week and Niewoudt hasn't even looked at us. . . . I think his [de Kock's] apology is from the bottom of his heart."[89] The psychologist Pumla Gobodo-Madikizela characterized de Kock's confession as a "determination to bring everything into the open, and to spare no one." Gobodo-Madikizela described de Kock's behavior regarding his superiors: "He confronts and he questions. They cannot silence him. . . . [T]he unstoppable De Kock [is] talking back to his masters."[90]

De Kock developed a near-cult following. He appealed in particular to women, a coterie of whom religiously attended his hearings and even professed their love for him in letters to prison and during visits.

TRC staff claimed that the commission's "tea matron" warmed to de Kock as if he were her son. He touched people, as the sister of one of his fellow prisoners expressed to me: "You'll really like him. He's such a gentleman, but very, very misunderstood." An observer at his amnesty hearing noted, "I feel terrible for de Kock, you know, because I can hear that he feels so sorry about everything he has done."[91] The journalist Jann Turner, looking for the man who had murdered her father, the political activist Ric Turner, wrote in the *Mail and Guardian* about her transformed feelings toward this apartheid killer. He disarmed her by greeting her and apologizing for failing to shave before their meeting in the prison. He tried to help her locate her father's killer, even though none of his clues panned out. She described a sweet, sensitive man unable to request forgiveness because he did not believe his acts deserved forgiveness. The warmth de Kock received led him to remark, "The only friends I have now are my former enemies."[92]

Cynics doubted the sincerity of de Kock's post-incarceration transformation. His prosecuting attorney, for example, referred to him as a "megalomaniac . . . with a special talent for deception."[93] A prison guard echoed the view that de Kock was a master of disguise, capable of maintaining charm and a gentle demeanor to achieve his goals: "If you could only see him late at night when all of the anger starts to come out. You'd see a very different de Kock then."[94] His charm seemed rehearsed; for example, he used the same apology about failing to shave not only with Turner but also with Gobodo-Madikizela, me, and presumably other women interviewers.[95]

Some of de Kock's former subordinates who testified against him feared retaliation. Almond Nofemela requested that he be placed in a section of the prison separate from de Kock for fear of violent reprisal.[96] One of de Kock's friends stated, "He is a very dangerous man who will murder potential witnesses. I fear the man. He had threatened to kill Willie Nortje after it became known that he had spoken."[97] Others viewed his timing skeptically, as did Pauw: "He was very arrogant until he was convicted. On that very day De Kock changed his whole strategy. Then he became a man obsessed by remorse."[98] Pauw doubted de Kock's sincerity: "He knows he's *supposed* to say 'I'm sorry,' but there is a difference between that and realizing that what he did was wrong."[99] Some survivors similarly questioned his sincerity. Dawn Botha, whose brother, Leon Meyer, was killed in de Kock's Lesotho raid, stated, "I am angry with all of them but especially with De Kock. They are very calm when they describe the murder, it is just another style of living. I do not believe it when they say they are sorry."[100] Japie Maponya's brother claimed that de Kock went through the motions of apology, but without any feeling: "He was reading [his statement]. When you look at him, he didn't have any sorry. He was not having that shame."[101] Although de Kock informed Joyce Leballo about the death of her son, Tisetso, she could not forgive him for the killing, regardless of his words: "I'm happy that the truth has come out, but as for De Kock he should rot in jail. . . . I saw De Kock once in the Supreme Court during his trial. He is a devil. He is cruel and insensitive to people's feelings. He should just be kept in jail where his horrendous deeds will eat him up."[102] Lawyers for human rights and some of de Kock's victims wanted more evidence of his commitment to those he had harmed, as the victim advocate Laura Pollecut stated: "We would like to see some civil claims by the victims against De Kock who has millions of Rands tied up in foreign accounts. We think it would be good if they could be frozen and an inquiry be launched into where the money came from."[103]

Little consensus emerged about de Kock, except that he advanced public knowledge of the violent past. Because he named names and detailed events, de Kock generated a "rippling effect leading to further applications" for amnesty.[104] De Kock's testimony prompted confessions by five of Vlakplaas's most brutal killers—Brig. Jack Cronje, Col. Roelf Venter, Capt. Wouter Mentz, Capt. Jacques Hechter, Warrant Officer Paul van Vuuren—among others. As a prosecuting attorney stated, "De Kock started the whole process. Through his statements we were able to gather seminal evidence which we then had to corroborate. We realized that we could not pursue all of the cases he opened up. There simply were not enough resources. So we had to start setting priorities. I call them shelves. Some became top shelf items and others fell to the lower shelves. I asked for an increase in staff to help me get through some of this material, but I didn't get it."[105] Although he did not produce any additional convictions, de Kock unlocked the TRC amnesty process. One truth commissioner acknowledged the "great, great favor" de Kock's confession was for the TRC.

> The security forces had spent all that time preparing alibis, creating their watertight defenses. There was very little an amnesty process and investigative committee could do. It was very, very limited. They

needed to persuade one of the perpetrators to disclose. That was the value of de Kock. Since he had been thrown to the dogs, he had nothing to lose. He became a useful source for the process. You couldn't conceivably crack these things without someone like him.

The real threat of prosecution did bring them to the commission. You had to be fairly confident that the chances of prosecution were high to go forward, and there were very few eyewitnesses or other evidence. What evidence that existed had been destroyed. Or no records had been kept. It was the "need to know" basis which allowed the Security Branch to wipe everything clean. It was like looking for a needle in the haystack. Investigations had real limitations. . . . We were dealing with expert people, "accomplished liars," who had learned their tricks after years of avoiding prosecution. De Kock was indispensable to crack open the case.[106]

George Bizos, representing anti-apartheid activists in their cases against amnesty, agreed that de Kock's testimony proved indispensable for bearing out the truth.

The rush for amnesty was not born of remorse or even regret, but as a result of Attorney-General Jan D'Oliveira's successful prosecution of Eugene de Kock. It was the thought of sharing the dock with him that drove the flood of applications. Once de Kock was convicted and received two life sentences plus 212 years' imprisonment, his declaration that he would tell all forced many to apply for amnesty who would otherwise not have done so. De Kock gave notice that he would submit his application for amnesty at the very last minute. He did not want to be in this alone; he wanted all to come forward and, in particular, he wanted to implicate the politicians and the generals who had abandoned him. His submission ran to over a thousand pages. Those who suspected that they may have been implicated could not afford to take the chance, and applications flooded in.[107]

De Kock did not get what he hoped from confession. He received amnesty for some, but not all, of his crimes, and thus remains in jail, serving his 212-year sentence. He dented the top commanders' armor, but not enough to put them on trial or in prison. Nevertheless, de Kock became a potent symbol of the apartheid era, stimulating national debate that made it impossible for South Africans to ignore the regime's violence.

Betrayal confessions hold great promise for revealing and debating past authoritarian state violence. Perpetrators implicate others, rather than simply confess to their own acts. They sometimes unravel the mystery of violence all the way to the top of the chain of command. Rather than focusing on individual guilt, betrayal confessions explore the systematic nature of past violence and the orders from above that demanded it. The authoritarian regime's house of cards thus begins to shake, if not crumble and collapse.

Betrayal confessions have their limitations, as de Kock's experience shows. The perpetrators who betray their colleagues or superiors often have dodgy records. Their credibility is further compromised by the conditions that lead them to betray the forces. Ulterior motives, such as release from prison, can damage the credibility of these confessions. And superiors often count on the prestige of the high command to duck charges made by these lower-ranking officials. Thus, the former military president João Figueiredo, nearly ten years after the end of the Brazilian dictatorship, asserted, "If there was torture during the military regime, then it was done by the lower ranks, because I do not believe that a general is capable of something as dirty as that. I just don't believe it."[108] Conflict erupts as societies grapple with what and whom to believe about the past and what action to take as a result.

"Conditions Are Right to Face the Monster." "Getting caught" seems to be a reasonable motive for perpetrators to make betrayal confessions. It certainly worked in the de Kock and Nofemela cases. Neither won his release from prison through confession, but Nofemela at least escaped the gallows, and de Kock restored a bit of his dignity. The Chilean intelligence agent Carlos Herrera Jiménez also abandoned the regime and the armed forces only after his indictment and ten-year prison sentence for the murders of Mario Fernández, Tucapel Jiménez, and Juan Alegría. He claimed he had followed his general's orders and questioned why he, and not the general, faced incarceration. He expressed regret for having served in the CNI not because of the crimes attributed to him, but because of his superiors and colleagues' "lack of commitment" to him.[109]

Despite these cases, indictment does not guarantee betrayal confessions. Alfredo Astiz, in Argentina, did not turn on his colleagues despite his conviction. He had little to gain, and potentially his only remaining support to lose from such a betrayal. Manuel Contreras, in Chile, eventually blamed President Pinochet for his orders, but he did so only after the courts removed Pinochet's immunity and began investigations and prosecutions. Unless betrayal accrues clear benefits, or at least comes with low costs, even indicted perpetrators will remain loyal.

On the other hand, indictment is not a necessary condition for betrayal confessions either. Dirk Coetzee never faced indictment, but his anticipation of it led to his betrayal confession.[110] A primary motive behind betrayal confession, therefore, involves restoring the personal and institutional dignity robbed from peerpetrators by their commanders' silence, denial, or blame.

Tangible benefits from betrayal, including protection from prosecution, sentence reduction, and material gain, are not always as obvious as they were in the cases of de Kock or Nofemela. The Chilean collaborator Juan René Muñoz Alarcón betrayed the regime by simply stating, "I believe that the conditions are right to face the monster that is DINA."[111] But Muñoz had a history and pattern of betrayal: just as he had earlier sought to protect himself by avenging his Socialist Party comrades-cum-enemies by collaborating with the "monster," he subsequently sought revenge against DINA for detaining and torturing him for his disobedience. Having betrayed the regime and its opponents, Muñoz's only source of support was his confession to the Vicaría de Solidaridad.

Coetzee made a similar pact with his former enemies by betraying his commanders and joining the ANC. "Instead of the brutal savages about whom we were taught by the South African regime," Coetzee recounted, "I found highly intelligent, extremely well-informed, and civilized gentlemen for whom I soon felt nothing but admiration and respect."[112] He, no doubt, also hoped that he could parlay his betrayal of Vlakplaas and his membership in the ANC into a prestigious position within the new South Africa's police or intelligence forces.

When and why perpetrators make betrayal confessions dictates where they confess. Indicted perpetrators, like de Kock and Nofemela, rarely have any forum other than the legal system for defending themselves through betrayal. De Kock added the TRC and media as venues. The media outlets likely to produce betrayal confessions are those most critical of the perpetrators making them. Adolfo Scilingo told his story to the famously anti-authoritarian Horacio Verbitsky and *Página/12*. Coetzee produced his confession for the only Afrikaans-language anti-apartheid newspaper, *Vrye Weekblad*. Opposition presses seize opportunities to expose authoritarian-regime crimes, even if it means taking sides with a past perpetrator of those crimes. Sometimes such opposition presses do not exist, or they lack the power to guarantee the safety of perpetrators. Thus, Andrés Antonio Valenzuela Morales, a security agent for the Chilean Air Force, left Chile and told his story to a Venezuelan newspaper journalist whose exposés of the Chilean regime he had read. Only after its printing in Venezuela did the confession filter back to Chile through human-rights organizations' reprints.

"I Feel Like a Traitor." Betrayal confessions offer only one role to perpetrators: the loyal, patriotic, duty-bound, and effective soldier. These perpetrators killed and tortured out of a sense of duty to their commanders and country. Now those who made the policies remain free, while those who implemented them face reprisals.

Betrayal by their superiors provides perpetrators with an acceptable image, but counter-evidence undermines it. Most of these perpetrators have histories of disloyalty, autonomy, insubordination, and misconduct that belie the image they hope to project. The very act of betraying their commanders itself casts doubt on their degree of loyalty and subordination, and the instrumentality of betrayal raises questions about motives. Few perpetrators would risk the honesty expressed by Leonardo Schneider, a former MIR leader who became a SIFA intelligence agent: "I feel like a traitor. That's what I am, aren't I? . . . I try to employ correct categories and the words traitor and criminal don't shock me. These are things I did and I have always been clear about them. This is my past and I take myself as I am."[113]

De Kock's unfair treatment enhanced his capacity to vitiate his negative image in South Africa. While most of his audience would agree that he should serve time in jail, few would think that he should be the only apartheid official to do so. In addition, de Kock provided a service to the new South Africa: by revealing information, he forced others to tell their stories. Finally, those stories pointed to orders and complicity at the top of the apartheid apparatus and yet his superiors refused to assume their responsibility. De Kock's scapegoat status thus improved his public image, but he alone paid with his freedom for his role in the apartheid regime.

"The Hidden Weapon in a War without Rules." The advocate George Bizos, who represented families of victims at the TRC, expressed his frustration with the quality of perpetrators' confessions: "Many [amnesty] applicants have said no more than what they knew was known to the victims, their relatives and the amnesty committee, thereby protecting their comrades who have not applied within the prescribed period. Many applicants have not been prepared to say that they received direct instructions from above, preferring to rely on the implied authority of political speeches exhorting them to battle. At times it is clear that their loyalty lies not with the truth but with their partners in crime."[114]

The content of betrayal confessions often contains potent images that imprint in collective memory, like Scilingo's death flights. Coetzee's disclosure of a cold-blooded *braai* (barbecue) and beer fest had a similar impact.

> One of Major Archie Flemington's men took a Makarov pistol with a silencer on and whilst Mr Kondile was lying on his back, shot him on top of the head. There was a short jerk and that was it. The four junior, non-commissioned officers—Paul van Dyk, Sergeant Jan from Colonel Nic van Rensburg's branch, and the two Ermelo men—each grabbed a hand and a foot, put it on to the pyre of tyre and wood, poured petrol on it and set it alight. Whilst that happened, we were drinking and even having a braai next to the fire.
>
> . . .
>
> Now that I don't say to show our braveness, I just . . . uh . . . shh . . . tell it to the commission to show the . . . the callousness of it and to what extremes we have gone in those days. And the body takes about seven hours to . . . to burn to ashes completely and the chunks of meat, especially the . . . the . . . the buttocks and the upper parts of the legs, had to be turned frequently during the night to make sure that everything burnt to ashes. And the next morning, after raking through the rubble to make sure that there was no big pieces of . . . uh . . . meat or bone left at all, we all went our own way.[115]

Nevertheless, some of the most effective betrayal confessions were never intended to reveal secrets. When the Argentine captains Antonio Pernías and Juan Carlos Rolón confessed, they hoped only for confirmation of their promotion through the Senate's public hearings. The media surrounding the hearings, however, implicated the officers in past abuses. Pernías had reputedly developed poison darts that he tested on prisoners, participated in the Santa Cruz church attack that ended in the disappearance of Mothers of the Plaza de Mayo members and affiliates (including two French nuns), executed five priests (*padres palotinos*), and infiltrated exile organizations abroad. Rolón, who was decorated with the Medal for Heroic Bravery in Combat (*Medalla al Heroico Valor en Combate*) in 1978, indicated his own role in the military's "war against subversion." Under questioning, both captains admitted to widespread use of torture by the regime, including themselves. Pernías called it "the hidden weapon in a war without rules" and confessed, "I did my part just like many others."[116] Rolón also admitted to torture, claiming that it had involved nearly everyone in the navy: "All officers rotated into the task forces that were formed to carry out what was called the antisubversive struggle." Rolón further admitted, "We didn't have any choice. The only choice was to quit."[117] Pernías clarified that, as loyal officers, they would have carried out any order, whether issued by an authoritarian regime or a democratic one. He cynically questioned whether he should disobey the orders of commanding officers appointed by the Senate, the same body he was testifying to for his own promotion.

The Senate extracted betrayal confessions from loyal but unwitting officers, not individuals seeking revenge. These officers seemed unaware of the revelations they were making. In their view, they had done everything asked of them. They maintained their loyalty to the institution, received promotions and rewards from it, and expected that trajectory to continue. They felt no remorse for their acts and no need to deny or hide them. Pernías seemed to approximate remorse when he stated, "What bothers me is the death of innocent people," but he did not include victims of military violence in his list of innocents, which comprised "Lieutenant Mayol, petty officers, and also civilians."[118] Rolón justified the violence as part of an unconventional war against "the largest urban guerrilla movement in the history of the world."[119] He stated, "This was really unprecedented and we were unprepared. We received very little training and then we were sent off to participate in these urban operations."[120] He added that "Argentina had lived through a very traumatic event that had a traumatic solution that no one liked, least of all those of us who had to act. These were historical circumstances."[121] Pernías, moreover, considered himself innocent, arguing that the navy had purged officers who had used excessive force in the antisubversion war. While he refused to "name names" of such officers, Pernías emphasized that he had remained on active duty, implying that he had maintained a good record. Pernías further claimed that the war avoided "unnecessary deaths."[122] Rolón described his involvement as "service . . . to re-establish a democratic style of life in Argentina."[123] Their confessions, in other words, justified their acts and asserted their innocence. But in admitting that torture had formed part of a systematic and repressive apparatus that involved all members of the service, they undermined the regime's claims of "errors and excesses" by a few unstable individuals.

To be effective, betrayal confessions must not only reveal institutional secrets, but also demonstrate that the confessor can adapt to the new democratic system. Remorse provides a narrative device, employed by perpetrators like de Kock and Scilingo, that suggests that the confessor has severed ties to his commanders and the ideology that guided them. When Herrera Jiménez apologized to Chilean society, he reached out "particularly to the people whose relatives might have been harmed by my fanatic acts."[124] De Kock and Coetzee expressed their capacity to adapt to the new South Africa by abandoning the National Party and joining the IFP and ANC, respectively. Pernías and Rolón offered institutionally prescribed, but mechanical expressions of their capacity to adapt. Pernías stated, "I believe that this was an unprecedented experience and that the situation will never occur again."[125] Rolón added, "If it is my turn to be here today, I insist that this is an honor and a privilege, [and] I will accept whatever the Senate decides with a republican spirit, and I will respect the decision and continue believing in democracy."[126]

"A Question of Revenge." When perpetrators make betrayal confessions, they are alone. As one witness acknowledged, "They are speaking about acts they committed, that not one of their accomplices can acknowledge, because they are not acts that extol them, but rather ones that defame them."[127] Their commanders and colleagues deny and attempt to silence their confessions, or simply distance themselves from these perpetrators. Colleagues of Captains Pernías and Rolón asked, "Why didn't any admirals accompany them [to the Senate hearings], why were journalists allowed into the hearing, and why didn't they wear their uniforms?"[128] This distancing by superiors and

institutions, which gives the impression that the confessors have been hung out to dry, can lead to public sympathy for these individuals. The Peronist senator Deolindo Bittel, although he ultimately voted against their promotion, considered Pernías and Rolón loyal officers who had effectively performed their duties: "These boys are having to pay the price for something that is not their fault."[129]

However, even audiences who feel these perpetrators have been scapegoated and who recognize the value in their confessions often find it difficult to support them because of past violence. Pernías and Rolón, for example, had already received four promotions, and seven naval captains with backgrounds in the "dirty war" had received confirmation for their promotions from the Senate.[130] Mobilization by the human-rights community and the media pressured the senate committee to raise questions not asked during earlier hearings. The revelations that perpetrators made in response to those questions created an outcry in Argentine society, making it nearly impossible for the Senate to promote them. Emilio Mignone, former director of the Center for Legal and Social Studies (CELS), expressed the view of the human-rights community and its echo throughout Argentina when he rhetorically asked: "Is it acceptable to Argentine society today that the armed forces become governed by morally debased officials who tortured and assassinated prisoners, whether or not they faced judicial sentence?"[131] Instead of promotion, Pernías and Rolón faced charges for justifying a crime (*apología del delito*).[132]

Some observers defended Pernías and Rolón. The politician Álvaro Alsogaray, for example, claimed on a television talk show that Pernías and Rolón had not admitted to using torture. When another guest on the show identified herself as a victim of Pernías's torture, Alsogaray first questioned her honesty and then attacked the talk-show host for "giving her the space to continue her campaign [against the military regime] here and abroad."[133]

Even planned betrayal confessions do not necessarily benefit the confessing perpetrators. Dirk Coetzee expected to be rewarded for his confession with a high-level position within the intelligence branch or police force. However, he ended up being assigned instead to a low-level intelligence position, and he expressed his frustration by warning others to keep quiet: "I can tell you . . . my message to the rest of the Dirk Coetzee's still sitting out there that didn't stand up so far is 'Wait! Look at what happened to Dirk Coetzee. Watch me close. See

Dirk Coetzee, former commander of Vlakplaas. Photo by Jillian Edelstein.
Reproduced by permission.

what's happening in the next few weeks and months and then make your decision. Then decide for yourself whether it's really truth and reconciliation, whether it is really transparency, whether there is really a will in the new government's new South Africa towards peace and reconciliation and whether it's a question of revenge.' "[134]

Perpetrators who make betrayal confessions can face violent retribution. Muñoz predicted his own murder in Chile. Scilingo suffered violent reprisals in Argentina. Both Nofemela and de Kock asked for personal protection in jail to avoid assaults. Coetzee feels that his life is in danger and requires visitors to pass through several metal detectors and body searches to reach his office. He claims to carry a gun strapped to his body at all times, to sleep with a gun under his pillow, and to store one in his bathroom to make sure that he is not caught unprotected.

Betrayal confessions cost perpetrators their former sources of support. They usually fail to develop new sources of support, even when audiences appreciate the value of their revelations. What they achieve is a political dialogue over the past that challenges tired denials and hegemonic silence. An opinion published in *Página/12* about Pernías and Rolón could be extended to other perpetrators who betray their institutions and commanders: "[They revealed] a new social monstrosity: torture as an institution. The institution as pathology. . . . [T]hey interiorized [torture] as normal, as obvious, and as common practice among professionals . . . as an interrogation instrument taught in the Argentine Navy's educational programs . . . [and they carried out] a system of rotation in which all became accomplices."[135] Their confessions made the "errors and excesses" excuse untenable.

CONCLUSION

Betrayal confessions arguably advance exposure and debate over the authoritarian past more than any other type of confession. They reveal the deliberate, methodical, and targeted nature of the violence, the source of orders to carry it out, and the knowledge of it by the top echelons of the security apparatus and the authoritarian regime itself. They discredit suggestions of isolated incidents, excesses or errors by rogue forces. They implicate not only the confessor but also the regime in the systematic violation of human rights.

Institutional mechanisms, however, only weakly encourage betrayal confessions. Most perpetrators, even when induced to speak out about their pasts, tend to provide only partial details, protecting their security institutions, colleagues, commanders, or themselves from reprisals. Only perpetrators who seek some protection or gain from betrayal, without risk, are likely to produce such confessions. Given the high costs of betrayal, such confessions are rare, used only as last resorts, when no other alternative exists for resolving a desperate situation. Thus, one might expect betrayal confessions only in the cases of life imprisonment, death sentences, or death threats.

Retributive justice, in other words, is more likely than other forms of transitional justice to encourage betrayal confessions. Witness-protection programs, for example, allow perpetrators to reveal secrets and avoid prosecution while receiving protection from violent reprisals. Such programs encouraged de Kock's colleagues and subordinates to divulge information about his Vlakplaas leadership and exploits. Plea-bargaining also offers perpetrators the means to reduce their expected sentences. Almond Nofemela used such a tactic to commute his death sentence into life imprisonment. Journalists, such as du Preez and Pauw, negotiated arrangements in which Coetzee would receive protection outside the country in exchange for his confession. Once the breach in silence and denial occurred, a spate of confessions followed, each perpetrator seeking protection through betrayal confessions.

These arrangements do not evolve without conflict. De Kock attained a positive image among a part of the South African audience, only because he alone faced punishment for violence. Those who escape punishment through witness protection or pleas do not enjoy the same respect. Instead, audiences may question the justice of granting amnesty to those who engaged in the same kinds of violence, but spoke out first against their colleagues.

CONCLUSION

CONTENTIOUS COEXISTENCE

People can die of an excessive dose of the truth, you know.
—Ariel Dorfman, *Death and the Maiden*

DEMOCRATIC THEORISTS AND GOVERNMENTS alike endorse the above-stated
claim by Gerardo in Ariel Dorfman's play *Death and the Maiden*. The
scholar Stephen Holmes quips, "Repression can be perfectly healthy
for democracy" and "Tongue-tying . . . may be one of constitutional-
ism's main gifts to democracy."[1] With the exception of South Africa,
the democracies analyzed in this book generally concurred with Gerardo and Holmes. Argentina, Brazil, and Chile have tried, mainly unsuccessfully, to keep contentious issues off the public agenda in order
to protect fragile political systems from polarizing debate and to avoid
provoking authoritarian reversals. Despite their failure to silence the
past, these democracies have survived and flourished.

In *Unsettling Accounts* I have thus challenged the "fatal overdose of
truth" notion prevalent in democratic theory and practice. But I have
also disputed the opposite claim, espoused by Paulina in *Death and the
Maiden* and some theorists and practitioners of transitional justice,

A bench sitting next to the Argentine dictatorship's former clandestine torture center Club Atlético calls on people to "never forget." Photo by author.

that the truth sets one free and settles accounts with the past. "Healing truths" have proved equally elusive. Most countries emerging from authoritarian rule have not adopted South Africa's model of reconciliation through truth, because they recognize the unlikelihood of establishing one truth about the past that will resolve the deep and enduring political divisions they confront.

Between the cautionary and utopian extremes of conflict resolution lies a more practical model: contentious coexistence. Contentious coexistence rejects ineffective gag orders and embraces democratic dialogue, even over highly factious issues, as healthy for democracies. It rejects infeasible official and healing truth in favor of multiple and contending truths that reflect different political viewpoints in society. Contentious coexistence does not require elaborate institutional mechanisms, but rather is stimulated by dramatic stories, acts, or images that provoke widespread participation, contestation over prevailing political viewpoints, and competition over ideas. Contentious coexistence, in other words, is democracy in practice.[2]

This book has explored unsettling accounts and the contentious coexistence they have spawned through perpetrators' confessions. Similar processes have unfolded in other countries at different stages of democratic development, suggesting the absence of inoculation from the assumed fatal dose of truth. Consider, for example, the dramatic accounts of honor killings and stoning of allegedly adulterous women in Iran, Jordan, Nigeria, Pakistan, and elsewhere. These stories did not initiate friction over the interpretation and application of Sharia laws, which regulate public and aspects of private life, in contemporary Muslim societies. But nongovernmental organizations within and outside these countries used these stories to mobilize broad participation and debate and to demand political change. Similarly, while the banning of Muslim girls from French public schools did not instigate conflict over the secular state and religious freedom, it did heighten the political drama surrounding the debate and drew in a surprising range of perspectives. These examples of deep and seemingly unresolvable conflicts occurred without undermining democracy, but also without establishing a reconciling truth. Unsettling accounts unleash a society-wide probing into how to interpret the stories and what they mean for contemporary political life. Response to the photographs that exposed U.S. abuses in the Abu Ghraib prison in Iraq extends the arguments in this book to established democracies. These photographs and perpetrators' confessions sparked contentious coexistence in different political contexts and affected democratic practice and outcomes.

"THE PHOTOGRAPHS DID NOT LIE"

After the September 11, 2001 bombing of the World Trade Center, preventing another terrorist attack obsessed the U.S. government and public. The scholar Alfred McCoy noted that "a growing public consensus . . . in favor of torture" prevailed at the time.[3] That consensus hinged on a "ticking bomb" theory: torture provided an effective and necessary means of extracting information from terrorists to prevent planned attacks on civilian populations.[4] The photographs from Abu Ghraib prison, however, changed that perception. They revealed depraved behavior by U.S. prison guards:

> The photographs did not lie.
>
> American soldiers, male and female, grinning and pointing at the genitals of naked, frightened Iraqi prisoners; an Iraqi man, unclothed and leashed like a dog, groveling on the floor in front of his female guard; a prisoner standing on a box with a sandbag over his head and wires attached to his body beneath a poncho. These were not enemy propaganda pictures; these showed real atrocities actually inflicted by Americans.[5]

Eroding the previous consensus, the images catalyzed a "serious nationwide political debate" and an "epic political struggle" that involved "ordinary Americans" among "a surprisingly diverse range of voices . . . breaking the public climate of timid compliance."[6] The journalist Mark Danner attributed outrage not only to the photographs but also to the context in which they emerged: "Details of the methods of interrogation applied in Guantánamo and at Bagram Air Base, began to emerge more than a year ago. It took the Abu Ghraib photographs, however, set against the violence and chaos of an increasingly unpopular war in Iraq, to bring Americans' torture of prisoners up for public discussion."[7] The public reaction to the photographs eroded consensus and challenged the Bush administration's strategies. As the essayist Susan Sontag wrote, "Apparently it took the photographs to get their attention, when it became clear they could not be suppressed; it was the photographs that made all this 'real' to Bush and his associates."[8]

The photographs from Abu Ghraib fit the definition of unsettling accounts: dramatic performances, speech, or events that rupture political silence or prevailing political consensus and engage a broad sector of society in the democratic practices of participation, contestation, and competition. These dramatic political spectacles prompt even cautious or complicit media outlets to cover them. By widely disseminating emotionally charged images and narratives, media portrayals draw out a diverse range of perspectives. Unsettling accounts obliterate passivity even among audiences otherwise reluctant to discuss politics. They spark debate in public and private sites: families, schools, barbershops, coffee shops, churches, neighborhoods, communities, blogs, on television, on the radio, and in the newspapers. Controversies, normally limited to a small, specialized sector of society, now reach individuals without any personal or direct connection to the underlying events. Moral outrage and political challenges to prevailing political views are aired publicly, sometimes for the first time. The unsettling photographs from Abu Ghraib have even prompted former prisoners of U.S. detention centers to speak out—voices not previously heard.[9]

Unsettling accounts do not merely amplify existing political views in society; they provoke new ways of thinking about politics among newly engaged sectors. Perpetrators' confessions, for example, did not only magnify the existing political demands of victims and survivors; they also presented new views from within the security apparatus and among former regime supporters. They challenged a prevailing view. Whether perpetrators confessed their remorse for past atrocities, bragged about their heroic accomplishments, or expressed salacious pleasure at having inflicted pain, they broke the regime's silence and denial of violence. Regime supporters who had previously believed, or wanted to believe, that victims and survivors had invented stories of atrocity for political gain could not easily ignore evidence to the contrary presented by the perpetrators of that violence.

Similarly, the Abu Ghraib photographs graphically revealed what the formerly abstract consensus around torture really meant. The Bush administration refused to label the acts portrayed in the photographs as "torture," using the language of "humiliation" instead. But even the administration's defenders ignored the euphemism. Senator Bill Frist (Republican, Tennessee) remarked, "What we saw is appalling."[10] Rejecting President Bush's notion that only a "few rotten apples" had committed the abuses, Senator Lindsey Graham (Republican, South Carolina) asserted, "Some of it has an elaborate nature to it that makes me very suspicious of whether or not others were directors or encouraging [the acts]."[11] Senator John McCain (Republican, Arizona) blamed the photographs, and presumably what they depicted, for weakening national security: "I would argue the pictures, terrible pictures from Abu Ghraib, harmed us not only in the Arab World, . . . but . . . also harmed us dramatically amongst friendly nations, the Europeans, many of our allies."[12] As a result of the photographs, McCain sponsored a "torture amendment" that would firmly ally the United States with the international ban on torture. President Bush, responding to pressure from within and outside his party, backed down from his initial decision to veto the amendment. As one journalist noted, "The American people spoke. Both chambers overwhelmingly passed this law [the torture amendment] by veto-proof majorities. It's shameful Bush had to be bullied into supporting it.[13]

Perpetrators' confessions and the Abu Ghraib photographs demonstrate that deeply contentious issues provoke debate without destroying or even threatening democracies. Unsettling accounts, while they do contest prevailing political views, do not replace them with an alternative, "healing" truth, however. Instead, political groups clash over how to interpret unsettling accounts and their meanings for contemporary political life.

"WITHHOLDING PANCAKES"

Unsettling accounts break down consensus because individuals dissociate themselves from the viewpoints represented in them. Not all audiences, however, reject the viewpoints represented in the unsettling accounts. Indeed, debate erupts because some individuals and groups maintain the prevailing view. These individuals and groups reinterpret unsettling accounts, trying to give them new political meaning in the hope of rebuilding political consensus. Political groups, in other words, compete over the interpretation of unsettling accounts. Reflecting on the Abu Ghraib photographs, a journalist remarked that their "ubiquity . . . suggests not only their potency but their usefulness and their adaptability."[14] Unsettling accounts do not replace one consensus with another, but rather intensify public debate over political events and their meaning for contemporary life.

Regime supporters, therefore, neither defend nor endorse atrocities or sadism; they reframe the confessions that depicted such acts using a variety of narrative techniques. They denigrate some perpetrators—particularly those who issue betrayal, remorseful, and sadistic confessions—as opportunists, liars, and psychopaths. If the confessed acts did occur, so they argue, they were carried out by a few rotten apples and did not represent either the noble security forces who defended the country or the regime's war strategy. Regime supporters publicly defend human rights, arguing that the regime had to protect the country from "terrorists." They use the language of "never again" to call on the country to remain vigilant against subsequent national threats. They also accuse the media and the left wing of misrepresenting, misinterpreting, or staging obscene confessions to slander the previous regime and its heroic accomplishments.

These narrative techniques rarely persuade objective observers. They do provide rhetorical cover, however, for individuals seeking an excuse to defend prevailing political views against the damaging evidence provided by unsettling accounts. President Bush's approach to the Abu Ghraib photographs, Sontag argued, aimed to "limit a public-relations disaster . . . rather than deal with the complex crimes of leadership and of policy revealed by the pictures."[15] Bush-administration supporters tried to reframe the images as "pranks," rather than as abuses, as did the talk-radio host Rush Limbaugh: "This is no different than what happens at the Skull and Bones initiation, and we're going to ruin people's lives over it, and we're going to hamper our military effort, and then we are going to really hammer them because they had a good time."[16] Another reframing device used by Bush-administration supporters involved emphasizing the threat of a terrorist attack and the importance in protecting U.S. citizens with "coercive interrogations," "tough measures," or other euphemisms for what the photographs depicted. Senator Trent Lott (Republican, Mississippi), for example, quipped, "Interrogation is not a Sunday-school class. . . . You don't get information that will save American lives by withholding pancakes."[17]

Unsettling accounts do not replace one prevailing political view with another. Instead, they generate political competition over how to interpret dramatic political events, how to use them, and what they mean for contemporary political life. Such a rhetorical war does not end by killing off democracy or saving it. Instead, it puts into practice the art of competition over ideas and the possibility of building consensus around democratic values.

Political groups feel compelled to publicly associate or, more likely, disassociate, themselves from the repulsive acts represented in unsettling accounts. For those groups that had failed to successfully oppose prevailing opinion, unsettling accounts provide an opportunity to do so and thereby strengthen their political claims. Perpetrators' confessions, therefore, help victim and survivor groups raise public awareness of a regime's atrocities and the need for building rule of law to end impunity. Similarly, human-rights groups who condemned the use of torture by the United States employed the Abu Ghraib photographs to show the American public what torture looked like and why it should be outlawed. Such groups use unsettling accounts to persuade audiences to accept their political perspectives; they may even win over former opponents.

This is not, however, a one-sided battle: groups must compete with others' efforts to reframe unsettling accounts. The ensuing debate forces both sides to make more persuasive arguments in vying for political power. The result is often what McCoy described in the aftermath of the Abu Ghraib photographs: "a substantive public discussion . . . marked by nuance, passion, and even, at times, erudition."[18] Unsettling accounts thus render old shibboleths obsolete and demand new arguments to address a new reality.

Sometimes this process involves simply repackaging old ideas in new ways. That effort, however, requires understanding how various perspectives on politics will resonate with a society stunned by unsettling accounts. Groups thus weed out language that legitimates the atrocities depicted, even when those groups concur with the political perspective behind the unsettling accounts. To maintain their base of support, they must show that what they defend differs from atrocity. That process involves a capacity for nuance and rhetorical sophistication.

Simply coding language to hide support for atrocity will maintain support for the group among its most ideologically committed members. Others will see the coded language for what it is and withdraw their support. The latter implicitly endorse the perspectives held by their political enemies, building a broader public consensus around those viewpoints.

Perpetrators' confessions illustrate this process, with former regime supporters, scandalized by tales of atrocity, aligning themselves in support of the protection of human rights. However, these groups do not always, or necessarily, condemn the authoritarian regime as a whole. In Chile, for example, some of Pinochet's former supporters condemned the human-rights violations committed by the regime, but endorsed the regime's economic strategies. In Argentina, the head of the navy decried officers who made, and soldiers who followed, illegal orders, but he did not condemn the "war against subversion."

Similarly, two years after the fact, President Bush declared Abu Ghraib the "biggest mistake" in the war on global terror, stating, "We've been paying for that for a long period of time."[19] The fog of war—a strategy Vice President Dick Cheney advocated five days after 9/11, when he said, "A lot of what needs to be done here will have to be done quietly, without any discussion"—failed to shield the administration's policies from public scrutiny.[20] The Pentagon and the Defense Department rejected Cheney's strategy of creating secret manuals on interrogation techniques, a move that implicitly allied them with the position on torture held by human-rights groups. As Elisa Massimino, the Washington director of Human Rights First, stated, "If the Pentagon is stepping back from that, it's a welcome sign that they now understand the need for transparency and clarity."[21] The unsettling photographs from Abu Ghraib and resulting widespread outrage no doubt contributed to this policy shift.

The understanding generated by unsettling accounts and contentious coexistence, in turn, leads to fragmentation within formerly entrenched political poles. Thus, rather than there being only two contending perspectives in society, a range of views and cross-cutting alliances develop. Some authoritarian-regime supporters in South Africa and Latin America, for example, unambiguously condemn the atrocities those regimes committed, thereby allying themselves with victims and survivors. On the other hand, some victims and survivors share with authoritarian security forces the desire to censor perpetrators' confessions. Still others persist in their original condemnation of or support for those regimes. But all of these political perspectives reflect growing consensus around the importance of protecting human rights, even as they diverge on how to define those rights and who has historically abused them.

Unsettling accounts and contentious coexistence lead to political transformations. Perpetrators' confessions contributed to the reversal of amnesty laws in Argentina and Chile, thus eroding the culture of impunity by making those criminal abuses undeniable. Perpetrators' confessions in South Africa's TRC also erased previous denials of apartheid state violence. The Abu Ghraib photographs compelled the White House to retract its earlier definition of torture as only "serious physical injury, such as organ failure, impairment of bodily function, or even death."[22] It also investigated, tried, and found guilty those who had committed the Abu Ghraib abuses. It signed the torture amendment. The uproar over the photographs no doubt contributed significantly to these developments.

Some contend, however, that these political changes mark only superficial, and not fundamental transformations of policies. Unsettling accounts in Brazil, for example, have not contributed to any changes in its amnesty laws. Perpetrators denied amnesty by the TRC have not faced prosecution in South Africa. Changes in amnesty laws have brought few perpetrators to prison for their violations in Argentina and Chile. And the Bush administration has found ways to circumvent the constraints on its policies imposed in the aftermath of the debate over the Abu Ghraib photographs. Specifically, none of those responsible for preparing the legal memos bypassing international bans on torture have lost their positions in the Bush administration, and some have even received promotions.[23] The commanders of those who committed the atrocities have avoided investigation, trial, or even criticism. President Bush tried to sneak past the U.S. public a measure granting him the power to interpret the torture amendment as needed.[24] The new consensus that emerged from the Abu Ghraib photographs, some cynics contend, was to hide torture better, not ban its use. Even without such cynicism, evidence suggests that the uproar over the Abu Ghraib photographs failed to end the use of torture in prisons in Guantánamo Bay, Afghanistan, and third-party accomplice states as part of the war on terror.[25] Danner asks, "Is what has changed only what we know, or what we are willing to accept?"[26]

Unsettling accounts and contentious coexistence do not heal democracies. Indeed, they cannot even guarantee particular policy changes. What they do is change the political context and put into practice the democratic art of participation, contestation, and competition. The political scientist David Art concisely summarizes the ambiguous results of the democratic processes they engender: "Public debates create new frames for interpreting political issues, change the ideas and interests of political actors, restructure the relationships between them, and redefine the limits of legitimate political space. These changes do not occur because the better argument carries the day, but rather because public debates set in motion a series of processes that reshape the political environment in which they occur."[27]

In other words, some unsettling accounts and forms of contentious coexistence may prove more successful than others in transforming the political landscape. The performative analysis I have adopted in this book identifies the factors that constrain and enhance the role of unsettling accounts and contentious coexistence in democracies. Some performances fare better than others in catalyzing responses from individuals. Thus, any response to the fictional text written by an unknown pilot who witnessed, but did not commit, violence and who could not remember key details in Brazil cannot compare with the outrage when someone confesses to having killed thirty people by dropping them from a plane in Argentina, or expresses pleasure at sexually torturing women in Chile, or demonstrates the wet-bag torture technique in a media circus in South Africa. The power of unsettling accounts varies with the power of the performance: who makes it (actor), what they recount (script), and how they recount it (acting).

Factors external to the perpetrators' confessional speech—institutional mechanisms (staging), political context (timing), and public response (audience)—also shape the power of unsettling accounts to stimulate debate and engender political change. Governments that control the staging of unsettling accounts may also limit the participation and contestation they create. These controls take the form of censorship, speech laws, and limiting access to information. In addition, media that share political perspective with the government or political actors challenged by unsettling accounts tend to provide thin and highly edited coverage of those accounts, thus dampening their political impact. The Chilean media fits this description, with its limited coverage of perpetrators' confessions and its decision to present an edited version of Romo's only after it had provoked an uproar outside the country. The success of the Bush administration in keeping the unedited file of photographs from Abu Ghraib out of the mainstream media helped its efforts in minimizing the acts portrayed as "humiliations," rather than torture.

Others blame the public's preoccupation with another terrorist attack on U.S. soil for its acceptance of the Bush administration's strategy in the "war on terror." The journalist Joseph Lelyveld, for example, argues that "when it comes to imminent threats of terrorism, the democratic process doesn't demand open debate."[28] Danner, however, remains baffled by the muted response from U.S. audiences to the Abu Ghraib photographs: "It is not about revelation or disclosure but about the failure, once wrongdoing is disclosed, of politicians, officials, the press, and, ultimately, citizens to act. The scandal is not about uncovering what is hidden, it is about seeing what is already there—and acting on it. It is not about information; it is about politics."[29] Abu Ghraib suggests that political timing, particularly when more pressing political issues prevail, limits the power of unsettling accounts to catalyze political participation and contestation. Similarly, perpetrators' confessions that occur long after the end of the abuses, as in Brazil, may shock audiences without mobilizing them behind political change.

This is particularly true if there are few politically mobilized sectors in society capable of keeping unsettling accounts on the democratic agenda. The further back in time the political events occurred, and the fewer the sectors of the population they affected, the harder it will be to keep political actors mobilized to fight for political change. Sontag wrote, "The pictures will not go away," referring to the enduring images from Abu Ghraib.[30] But for those pictures to be used effectively to promote specific political ends, an organized group or set of individuals must use them. Mobilized groups, as perpetrators' confessions have illustrated, can transform even inauspicious unsettling accounts into catalysts for political action. In Argentina human-rights activists turned heroic confessions into evidence of atrocities committed and thus were able to demand justice. In Chile and in South Africa they filled in details missing from denials and amnesia confessions to challenge impunity. They even overcame silence in Brazil, using a mere whisper of a confession to reveal hidden atrocities.

The success of these groups also depends on their ability to overcome other organized sectors of society poised to combat the political change they advocate. In this battle, the best, most ethical, democratic, or even legal argument will not necessarily win. Unsettling accounts may bring forth previously silenced views, but they do not guarantee that those views will prevail in a power struggle with the opposition.

"GOOD COUNTERSPEECH IS ONE REMEDY FOR BAD SPEECH"

In *Unsettling Accounts* I advocate political participation to contest prevailing views that have impeded the promotion of democratic values, like human rights and rule of law. I recognize that political competition means that groups advocating those values will not always succeed in achieving the specific policy outcomes they desire. But by provoking participation, contestation, and competition, unsettling accounts contribute to building stronger democratic practices, if not policies.

The contentious-coexistence model, moreover, proves more realistic and effective than its alternatives. Both the "fatal overdose of truth" and "healing truth" theories suffer from the same utopian assumption that democracies can successfully gag contentious issues. Little evidence supports this assumption. Efforts by the Bush administration to run the global war on terror in secret failed to stifle the photographs from Abu Ghraib or other abhorrent tales of U.S. abuses. Strategies to impose one official truth to reconcile conflict over the apartheid state in South Africa or military regimes in Latin America also failed. Perpetrators' confessions broke the pact of silence among the military in Latin America. They even defied speech laws aimed at protecting society from harmful justifications by perpetrators for their past crimes. South African government officials, most famously the former president P. W. Botha, publicly denounced the TRC and the healing truth it imposed. A reluctant media in the United States and in Chile, wary of exposing an unfavorable view of past and present governments and their policies, still presented enough of the unsettling accounts to unleash outrage. Powerful political groups defending the status quo—like the militaries in Latin America—could not even keep their own members from defying gag rules.

Not only are such efforts at stifling debate infeasible, but they also prove dangerous. They drive strongly held, but silenced, views underground and beyond the scrutiny and judgment of public debate. Certainly some forms of speech require prohibition, specifically direct and credible threats of violence aimed at specific individuals, or injurious speech that violates individuals' right not to listen.[31] For other kinds of speech, however, democracies benefit most from unfettering them, compelling them to compete with better—more democratic— ideas. As the adage goes, "Good counterspeech is one remedy for bad speech."[32]

What I have described is a messy process. It involves coping with heightened tensions, sometimes at very early stages of democratic development. It exposes citizens to uncomfortable facts and perspectives that they would rather avoid, and indeed have sometimes managed to avoid for some time. And the outcomes, at least in terms of specific policies, are uncertain. But this messy process is unavoidable and healthy in new and established democracies.

All translations of material in other languages are my own, unless otherwise specified.

INTRODUCTION

Epigraph from Dorfman, *Death and the Maiden*, 41.

1. "By an account, then, we mean a statement made by a social actor to explain unanticipated or untoward behavior—whether that behavior is his own or that of others, and whether the proximate cause for the statement arises from the actor himself or from someone else. An account is not called for when people engage in routine, common-sense behavior in a cultural environment that recognizes that behavior as such." Scott and Lyman, "Accounts," 46–47.
2. Elster, *Deliberative Democracy*, 1, 8.
3. Holmes, "Gag Rules," 202.

1. CONFESSIONAL PERFORMANCE

1. Edelman, *Constructing the Political Spectacle*, 5.
2. Palmer, "Toward a Postmodern Hermeneutics of Performance," 20. Diana Taylor refers to *doing* as performance, "*carrying through*, actualizing, making something happen" ("Performing Gender," 276). Victor Turner defines acting as "doing things in everyday life, or performing on the stage . . . the essence of sincerity—the commitment of the self to a line of action for ethical motives perhaps to achieve 'personal truth,' or it may be the essence of pretense—when one 'plays a part' in order to conceal or dissimulate" (*From Ritual to Theatre*, 102). Perpetrators' public confessions also fit J. L. Austin's notion of perlocutionary speech acts (*How to Do Things with Words*).
3. Feldman, *Strategies for Interpreting Qualitative Data*, 42.

4. Ibid., 66.

5. Burke, *A Grammar of Motives*.

6. Messinger, Sampson, and Towne, "Life as Theater."

7. Turner, *From Ritual to Theatre*, 92.

8. "Who the actors might be performing for," Martha S. Feldman contends, "is important for attributing meaning to the performance" (*Strategies for Interpreting Qualitative Data*, 49). She ignores, however, the role audience plays in the performance itself. She further ignores the importance of timing, or political context, to the performance. For this insight on timing, I thank Craig Calhoun.

9. Taylor, *Ubu and the Truth Commission*, v.

10. Bird and Garda, "Reporting the Truth Commission," 338.

11. Jane Taylor, "Truth or Reconciliation?" *Rhodes Journalism Review*, no. 14 (May 1997), special ed., http://jms.ru.ac.za/.

12. Martin Snodden, comments at the Interrogating Reconciliation conference, Ateneo University, Manila, Philippines, 15–18 August 2001.

13. Huggins, Haritos-Fatouros, and Zimbardo, *Violence Workers*.

14. Some observers consider the term *perpetrator* benign because it implies nothing more than "making things happen." The psychologist Brandon Hamber notes that the term's etymology would suggest only the capacity to accomplish, achieve, bring about, and effect things. Brandon Hamber, "Language Words: Journalists Talk About Translations, Terms, and Meanings," *Rhodes Journalism Review*, no. 14 (May 1997), special ed., http://jms.ru.ac.za/.

15. Dan Bar-On, *Special Report on the Truth and Reconciliation Commission*, SABC-TV, 1 March 1998; Milgram, *Obedience to Authority*; Philip Zimbardo, Stanford Prison Experiment, http://www.prisonexp.org; Huggins, Haritos-Fatouros, and Zimbardo, *Violence Workers*; and Sullivan, Piereson, and Marcus, "An Alternative Conceptualization of Political Tolerance." According to the research of Theodor Adorno, Else Frenkel-Brunswik, Daniel Levinson, and Nevitt Sanford, socialization in the family explains how some individuals rank high on "f-test" measures of fascist tendencies: members of repressive families with strong authoritarian fathers have higher propensities toward fascist behavior, since powerful leaders attract them and authorize them to act out their repressed aggression against marginalized groups. Adorno et al., *The Authoritarian Personality*. Subsequent studies have refuted these findings; see, for example, Altemeyer, *Enemies of Freedom*.

16. Rosenberg, *Children of Cain*, 18.

17. Jann Turner, "Eugene: From Apocalypse Now," *Mail and Guardian*, 28 May 1999.

18. Goffman, "Performances," 91.

19. Lincoln, *Authority*, 5.

20. Carlson, *Performance*, 49.

21. Goffman, *The Presentation of Self in Everyday Life*, 19.

22. Goffman, "Performances," 89–90.

23. Lifton, *The Nazi Doctors*.

24. John J. MacAloon, cited in Roach, "Kinship, Intelligence, and Memory as Improvisation," 219.

25. Goffman, *Encounters*, 80.

26. Ndebele, "Memory, Metaphor, and the Triumph of Narrative," 27.

27. Phelan, *Unmarked*, 165. See also Jelin, *Los trabajos de la memoria*, 12–13, 43.

28. Goleman, *Vital Lies, Simple Truths*.

29. Crownshaw, "Performing Memory in Holocaust Museums," 20–23.

30. Goffman, *The Presentation of Self in Everyday Life*, 35.

31. Jelin, *State Repression and the Labors of Memory*, 36.

32. Cohn, "Sex and Death in the Rational World of Defense Intellectuals"; Feitlowitz, *A Lexicon of Terror*.

33. Osiel, *Mass Atrocity, Ordinary Evil, and Hannah Arendt*.

34. Retired air force general Fernando Matthei, quoted in Guzmán, *Romo*, 13.

35. Osiel, *Mass Atrocity, Ordinary Evil, and Hannah Arendt*.

36. Edelman, *The Symbolic Uses of Politics*, 103.

37. Patraka, "Spectacles of Suffering," 100.

38. Ibid.

39. Edelman, *The Symbolic Uses of Politics*, 108. To modify a statement by Bruce Lincoln, confessional stages are not where performance is authorized, but where struggles play out over who does the authorizing, what is authorized, and how (*Authority*, 142).

40. Avslander, *Liveness*, 5.

41. Fair and Parks, "Africa on Camera," 50.

42. Auslander, *Liveness*, 118.

43. Peggy Phelan does not consider mediatized events performances at all: "Performance's only life is in the present. Performance cannot be saved, recorded, documented, or otherwise participate in the circulation of representations *of* representations: once it does so, it becomes something other than performance. . . . [Performance] becomes itself through disappearance." She further values mediatized venues only as a tool to remember the performance itself: "The document of a performance then is only a spur to memory, an encouragement of memory to become present" (*Unmarked*, 146). Philip Auslander, claiming that the purity of the live performance grows out of a sense of nostalgia and paranoia, questions the separation of the two (live and mediated) forms of performance. Liveness, he asserts, could not exist without its opposite: the reproducible. Auslander, "Liveness," 210n2.

44. Fuoss, "Lynching Performances, Theatres of Violence."

45. Jelin, *State Repression and the Labors of Memory*, 40.

46. Beverley, "The Real Thing," 276; Laub, "Bearing Witness or the Vicissitudes of Listening," 59–63.

47. Fish, *Is There a Text in This Class?*

48. Boal, "The Theatre as Discourse," 97.

49. Jarry, "Of the Futility of the 'Theatrical' in Theater," 210.

50. Fish claims that interpretive communities extract meaning from prevailing norms and interpretations, creating a convergence of norms (*Is There a Text in This Class?*). Susan Bennett views a spectator "as a member of an already constituted interpretive community . . . [who] brings a horizon of expectations shaped by the pre-performance elements" (*Theatre Audiences*, 139). She explores this notion through Brecht's doubts about a fixed or universally shared perception of the same performance within an audience. Edelman suggests that political spectacles give rise to "uncertainties, interpretations, and contradictions" and not to "conclusive generalizations. Political understanding lies in awareness of the range of meanings political phenomena present and in appreciation of their potentialities for generating change in actions and beliefs. It does not spring from designating some one interpretation as fact, truth, or scientific finding" (*Constructing the Political Spectacle*, 123).

51. Van Zyl presents an "instrumental" approach when he states that "international experience indicates that perpetrators tend to disclose wrongdoing only when they believe that failing to do so puts them at risk, and that this risk is significantly greater than the consequences of confessing to their crimes" ("Transitional Justice in Iraq," 6).

52. Ignatieff, "Articles of Faith."

53. "Aggressors have their own defence against truth, but so do victims. People who believe themselves to be victims of aggression have an understandable incapacity to believe that they also committed atrocities. Myths of innocence and victimhood are a powerful obstacle in the way of confronting unwelcome facts" (ibid.).

54. O'Donnell and Schmitter, *Transitions from Authoritarian Rule*; Zalaquett, "Balancing Ethical Imperatives and Political Constraints."

55. Jelin, *State Repression and the Labors of Memory*, 43. See also Jelin, *Los trabajos de la memoria*.

56. Elizabeth Jelin explores how silence prevents victims' memories from circulating, isolating and trapping victims in a ritualized repetition of their pain. Social expression, in contrast, allows for the search for political meaning out of past experiences. Jelin, *Los trabajos de la memoria*, 62.

57. Flanigan, *Forgiving the Unforgivable*, 106.

58. *Special Report on the Truth and Reconciliation Commission*, SABC-TV, 16 March 1998.

59. While some forgiveness advocates recognize the need for victims to forgive even without apology, others hinge the capacity to forgive on perpetrators recognizing the gravity of their acts, as expressed through remorseful confes-

sions. Archbishop Próspero Penados del Barrio, of Guatemala City, suggests that the burden of forgiveness rests with the perpetrators, not the victims. For personal reconciliation they must repent, recognize their guilt, and seek pardon. Jeffrey, "Guatemala," 8.

60. Paul van Zyl notes that in Sierra Leone and East Timor "some perpetrators have provided truth commissions with evidence primarily because of a desire to be reintegrated into their communities, not because they fear prosecutions and wish to have their criminal liability extinguished" ("Transitional Justice in Iraq").

Goffman remarks, "Remorse, apologies, asking forgiveness, and generally, making symbolic amends are a more vital element in almost any process of domination than punishment itself." Quoted in Scott, *Domination and the Arts of Resistance*, 58.

61. *Special Report on the Truth and Reconciliation Commission*, SABC-TV, 16 March 1998.

62. As Ignatieff states, "The past continues to torment because it is *not* past. These places are not living in a serial order of time, but in a simultaneous one, in which the past and present are a continuous, agglutinated mass of fantasies, distortions, myths and lies. . . . For the tellers of the tale, yesterday and today were the same" ("Articles of Faith," 119–21).

63. Malamud Goti, "Trials from Within and from Without."

64. Van Zyl, "Transitional Justice in Iraq."

65. Malamud Goti, "Trials from Within and from Without"; Méndez, "Accountability for Past Abuses"; Orentlicher, "Settling Accounts."

66. By establishing individual responsibility, courts avoid the attribution of collective guilt, which often fuels further conflict. May, "Memo for Workshop on International Criminal Accountability."

67. Michael Johnson made the observation at the Social Science Research Council Program on Global Security and Cooperation, International Law, and International Relations, Workshop on International Criminal Accountability, Washington, 6–7 November 2003. See also Morris, "International Humanitarian Law." Mark Osiel persuasively argues that most perpetrators lack either the autonomy, the information, or the desire to determine whether the orders they receive are lawful or not. They trust their commanders, a trust bolstered by cuing from their colleagues, family, church, and the media that affirms what they are doing. Expecting soldiers to disobey orders from trusted superiors to uphold laws during a state of emergency may be unrealistic. Osiel, *Mass Atrocity, Ordinary Evil, and Hannah Arendt.*

68. Judge Richard May commented that deterrence results from social thinking in which committing state violence is as unimaginable as "going into the bath with one's socks on. You just don't do it." Comment made at the Social Science Research Council Program on Global Security and Cooperation, In-

ternational Law, and International Relations, Workshop on International Criminal Accountability, Washington, 6–7 November 2003.

69. "To discover that their heroes were guilty of war crimes," Ignatieff writes, "is to admit that the identities they defended were themselves tarnished. Which is why societies are often so reluctant to surrender their own to war crimes tribunals, why societies are so vehemently 'in denial' about facts evident to everyone outside the society. War crimes challenge collective moral identities, and when these identities are threatened, denial is actually a defence of everything one holds dear" ("Articles of Faith," 118).

70. Wolin, "Fugitive Democracy," 37.

71. Ackerman, "Why Dialogue?" 8, 12.

72. Ibid., 16.

73. Ibid., 6.

74. Ibid., 16.

75. Benhabib, "Toward a Deliberative Model of Democratic Legitimacy," 72.

76. Jelin, *Los trabajos de la memoria*, 51–62. Jelin admits that there is a dual danger of "an 'excessive' presence of the past in ritualized repetition and in the compulsion to act out, and the menace of selective forgetting" (Jelin, *State Repression and the Labors of Memory*, 6).

77. Mansbridge, "Using Power/Fighting Power."

78. Young, "Communication and the Other," 122.

79. Ibid., 124.

80. Ibid., 120.

2. REMORSE

Epigraph from "De Scilingo para Neustadt," *Página/12*, 17 December 1995.

1. Comisión Nacional Sobre la Desaparición de Personas, *Nunca más*; Acuña and Smulovitz, "Ni olvido, ni perdón"; Brysk, *The Politics of Human Rights in Argentina*; Graziano, *Divine Violence*. Americas Watch and Amnesty International published their reports based largely on archives collected by Argentine human-rights groups such as the Center for Legal and Social Studies and the Mothers of the Plaza de Mayo. Testimonies include Timerman's *Prisoner without a Name, Cell without a Number* and Partnoy's *The Little School*, and testimonial novels include Valenzuela's *Other Weapons*.

2. In response to Scilingo's confession, a spokeswoman for the Mothers of the Plaza de Mayo stated, "We knew all this a long time ago. We also knew that the Catholic Church was deeply involved with the *desaparecidos*. What we don't understand is why one of their own people came forward." Rosa Pantaleón of the Permanent Assembly for Human Rights added, "We are not surprised. In 1979 bodies were being found in Uruguay . . . but the explanation never came. And in fact we always knew of these atrocities, but the truth

seems to be coming out only now." "ESMA Accuser Under Fire," *Buenos Aires Herald*, 4 March 1995.

3. "La primera confesión," *Página/12*, 4 March 1995.

4. *Hora Clave*, 2 March 1995. The journalist Horacio Verbitsky played tapes of his interviews with Adolfo Scilingo on this program. Scilingo himself appeared on the program on 9 March 1995.

5. Adolfo Scilingo, interview by Mike Wallace, "Tales from the Dirty War," *60 Minutes*, CBS, 2 April 1995.

6. Ibid.

7. Blixen, "Para que no haya mas Scilingos."

8. Ibid.

9. Verbitsky, *The Flight*, 35–36.

10. Ibid., 31.

11. Ibid., 49.

12. Blixen, "Para que no haya mas Scilingos."

13. Verbitsky, *The Flight*, 153.

14. Horacio Verbitsky, " 'Comence a romper el caparazón,' " *Página/12*, 4 April 1995.

15. *Hora Clave*, 2 March 1995, tapes of Verbitsky interviews with Scilingo.

16. Verbitsky, " 'Comence a romper el caparazón.' "

17. Ibid.

18. Verbitsky, *The Flight*, 153.

19. "Más que Watergate," *Página/12*, 26 March 1995.

20. Raúl Alberto Guarú admitted that during his military service in 1976 he witnessed firing squads at the ESMA and knew that many people were buried there. He added, "I found out that they threw living people into the sea from comments that many subofficials made to me." "Hubo entierros en la ESMA," *Clarín*, 11 March 1995.

21. Victor A. Nuccetelli, "Scilingo" (letter to the editor), *Página/12*, 11 June 1996.

22. Blixen, "Para que no haya mas Scilingos."

23. "Scilingo apunta a Camilión," *Página/12*, 15 March 1995.

24. "El fin nunca justifica los medios: texto completo del mensaje del jefe del estado," *Página/12*, 26 April 1995.

25. Horacio Verbitsky, "El ídolo caido," *Página/12*, 6 August 1995.

26. Not surprisingly, Balza's audience split with regard to his statement. The human-rights community criticized it as tepid and unwilling to break with the regime's "two demons" thesis in which both "subversives" and the military shared responsibility for violence. Members of the armed forces, in contrast, believed that Balza had gone too far in criticizing the military. In one notable attack, General Luciano Benjamín Menéndez, who had run the La Perla concentration camp, criticized Balza for referring to "repression" instead of "military operations" and for failing to use the terminology of

"Marxist aggression" in describing the guerrilla movement. Gabriel Paquini, "Un grave error," *Página/12*, 28 April 1995.

27. Jason Webb, "Human Rights Group Says Priests Collaborated," *Reuters*, 8 March 1995.

28. "La iglesia no abre sus actas secretas," *Clarín*, 11 March 1995.

29. Both the bishop of Morón, Justo Laguna, and the bishop of Puerto Iguazú, Joaquín Piña, offered apologies for individual leaders' mistakes during the dictatorship. Laguna emphasized that the church is holy, but that individuals within it may err. Piña suggested that asking forgiveness is the Christian way and that the church should not hold itself above the process of reconciliation. "Con veinte puntazos," *Página/12*, 7 March 1995.

30. General Albano Harguindeguy, minister of the interior under General Jorge Videla, allegedly made the speech to the clerics. "Los represores no comulgan en Viedma," *Página/12*, 6 May 1995.

31. Scilingo remained in jail from 1995 until 1997, when documentation proved that he had not committed fraud; the case amounted to writing a bad check for seven videos. Horacio Verbitsky, "Los pecados capitales," *Página/12*, 5 May 1996. As the activist Martín Abregú states, "I don't think that the goal was to silence him, because it was clear that Scilingo wanted to continue talking. . . . I think his jailing was a way of discouraging others from confessing." Calvin Sims, "In Exposing Abuses, Argentine Earns Hate," *New York Times*, 29 October 1995.

32. Horacio Verbitsky, "Una generación después," *Página/12*, 30 April 1995.

33. Blixen, "Para que no haya mas Scilingos."

34. In contrast to Pierini, Julio César Strassera, the prosecutor at the Trial of the Generals, viewed Scilingo in this way: "The man is remorseful and tormented. . . . The grave thing is the lack of interest on the part of the Argentine Government in clarifying these events. . . . There isn't profit-making behind Scilingo's testimony. There are no ulterior motives." Verbitsky confirmed Strassera's view, adding details like his refusal to accept compensation for interviews, his lack of salary from the navy, his joblessness, his inability to pay his bills, and his rejection of an offer from Hollywood to make a film of his story because it did not treat it seriously enough. Horacio Verbitsky, "Saber o no saber," *Página/12*, 12 October 1997.

35. Minister of Defense Oscar Camilión also accused Scilingo of using his testimony for electoral ends because of its timing. "Scilingo ratificó su denuncia contra el jefe de la Armada," *Clarín*, 11 March 1995.

36. His kidnappers knifed into his cheeks and his forehead the letters M, G, and V, indicating the journalists Magdalena Ruiz Guiñazú, Mariano Grondona, and Horacio Verbitsky.

37. Horacio Verbitsky, "Gente nerviosa que no deberia andar suelta," *Página/12*, 7 July 1995.

38. "Scilingo bajo amenaza," *Página/12*, 9 November 1995.

39. "Por una nueva CONADEP," *Página/12*, 22 March 1995.

40. Andrea Rodríquez, "Que haya otros que cuenten," *Página/12*, 5 March 1995.

41. Sims, "In Exposing Abuses, Argentine Earns Hate."

42. "El turno de el Olimpo," *Página/12*, 28 April 1995.

43. Horacio Verbitsky, "Y Brown se quedó solo," *Página/12*, 4 March 1995.

44. Two Spanish judges—Manuel García Castellón and Baltasar Garzón—have used universal jurisdiction claims to investigate, extradite, and try amnestied military officers in Chile and Argentina. Marlise Simons, "Madrid Throws Cold Water into Latin Atrocities," *New York Times*, 4 January 1998. The most famous case involved the unsuccessful 1998 attempt to extradite General Augusto Pinochet from England to Spain to stand trial for human-rights abuses. The judges succeeded in 2003 in extraditing Ricardo Miguel Cavallo, a former Argentine Navy lieutenant at the ESMA, from Mexico to Spain. In December 2005 Cavallo faced charges for kidnapping 227 (including 16 babies) and torturing 110 people.

45. Juan Carlos Algañaraz, "Scilingo quiere medios para vivir en España," *Clarín*, 14 November 1997.

46. Verbitsky claims that Judge Garzón's cases, particularly those of Carlos Daviou, Navy Intelligence, Carlos José Pazo, and Gonzalo Torres de Tolosa, have depended on Scilingo's testimony.

47. Fernando Mas, "Scilingo reta a un almirante para que testifique en España," *La Nación*, 3 November 1997.

48. "Scilingo bajo amenazas," *Diario Popular*, 14 January 1998.

49. Juan Carlos Algañaraz, "Liberan a Scilingo bajo fianza," *Clarín*, 19 November 1997. By May 1999, Scilingo owed $10,000 for his lodging; restaurants he once frequented refused to serve him because he did not pay his bills; his lawyer in Spain, Fernando de Gallo, ended his services without collecting the $51,000 Scilingo owed him; he owed $150 in emergency medical bills; and he claimed that he could not purchase the X-rays his dentist had ordered because he could not pay the $40 bill for them. He lived primarily on Catholic and Spanish charity support.

50. Only a week after his release to house arrest, Scilingo was attacked by an Argentine relative of a disappeared person who recognized him in his hotel. He began to change his hotel every two days to avoid assaults. After a leader of the Spanish support group for the Mothers of the Plaza de Mayo, Andrea Benítez, yelled at him in the street, he tried to physically assault her, after which his bodyguards pushed and kicked her. She ended up in the hospital and later brought a suit against Scilingo. People yelled "Assassin!" at him as he walked through the corridors to the hearing.

51. Mariano Gondar, "Scilingo ayuda al Gobierno por el juicio de España," *Perfil*, 14 June 1998, 10.

52. Scilingo has launched a number of legal attacks over time. In 1995 he denounced the naval chief Admiral Enrique Molina Pico for cover-up and failure to assume responsibility. He filed a defamation case against President Menem, Guido DiTella (Exterior Relations), and Alicia Pierini (subsecretary of human rights for the Interior Ministry). He also charged Judge Miguel Solimine for ordering his arrest for alleged fraud, which led him to remain in jail for two years, until the San Isidro court ruled the case null and void. In 2001 he brought an unsuccessful conflict-of-interest case against Judge Garzón. He also attempted to bring charges against Garzón for kidnapping him, tricking him into going to Spain, lacking jurisdiction over him, violating international law for holding him, and releasing information about his whereabouts, which led to attacks against him. He used Argentine military law to argue that soldiers (instead of their commanders) were legally responsible for fulfilling orders only if they exceeded the orders in some way.

53. Juan Carlos Algañaraz, "Reclaman el arresto de Scilingo," *Clarín*, 6 November 1999.

54. Behr, "Living in the Fault Lines," 118–19. Behr posed as a prominent leader of National Union of South African Students at Stellenbosch University from 1986–1990 while he fed information about the anti-apartheid student movement to his bosses in the security force.

55. *Special Report on the Truth and Reconciliation Commission*, SABC-TV, 23 November 1997.

56. Ibid., 8 June 1997.

57. Notable among the "born again" perpetrators is "Duch," or Kang Kek Ieu, the former director of the Khmer Rouge's Tuol Sleng prison and responsible for the 14,000 murders that took place there. Chandler, *Voices from S-21*, 20–23.

58. Virgilio Paz Romero made this comment in a press conference in Miami in August 2001, after the Immigration and Naturalization Service had released him from his prison sentence. Arrested in 1991, he had pleaded guilty to and been sentenced for the charge of conspiracy to assassinate Letelier. Alex Veiga, "Cuban Exile Regrets Role in Chilean Diplomats' Death in 1976," *Associated Press*, 1 August 2001.

59. Despite the invaluable perspective they provided from within the security apparatus, Arce and Merino never fully reintegrated themselves into the Chilean community. Merino secluded herself from public attention, retreating to the life of a "believer." Arce left Chile to join her son in Mexico.

60. *South Africa's Human Spirit* (CD-ROM set), vol. 5 (*Windows of History*), track 5 ("Tell Us about It").

61. Monica Nquabakazi Godolizi testimony to the Truth and Reconciliation

Commission: Human Rights Committee, East London, 15 April 1996. Cases EC0003/96, EC0004/96, EC0005/96.

62. *South Africa's Human Spirit* (CD-ROM set), vol. 3 (*Worlds of License*), disc 2, track 4 ("Fires of Revolution").

63. *Special Report on the Truth and Reconciliation Commission*, SABC-TV, 22 March 1998.

64. Testimony by Biljana Plavšić to the International Criminal Tribunal for the former Yugoslavia (ICTY), 17 December 2002, 609–10 (transcript).

65. Ibid., 610.

66. Jelin, *Los trabajos de la memoria*, 109–10.

67. Pete Rose, interview by Terry Gross, "Baseball Legend Pete Rose," *Fresh Air*, National Public Radio, 28 January 2004.

68. Stephané Bothma, "Child's Death Is Spy's 'Biggest Regret,'" *Business Day*, 15 September 1998.

69. Krog, *Country of My Skull*, 73.

70. Nic Borain, "The Smell of Rotten Apples," *Mail and Guardian*, 12 July 1996.

71. Ibid.

72. Brian Mitchell had been the station commander at New Hanover Police Station. He ordered four "special constables," linked to the Inkatha Freedom Party, to attack United Democratic Front activists in the area. Although the participants in the rampage disagree over the details, it ended with homes and businesses afire and eleven people attending a vigil dead. On 30 April 1992 Mitchell was sentenced to death on eleven counts of murder and to imprisonment for three years on each of two counts of attempted murder. In 1994, after he had served two years on death row, his sentence was changed to thirty years imprisonment. In 1996 Mitchell received amnesty from the TRC for his confession.

73. *South Africa's Human Spirit* (CD-ROM set), vol. 3 (*Worlds of License*), disc 1, track 3 ("Return to Their Land").

74. *Special Report on the Truth and Reconciliation Commission*, SABC-TV, 20 October 1996.

75. *Where Truth Lies*, VHS, directed by Mark J. Kaplan (Oley, Penn.: Bullfrog Films, 1999).

76. Arce, *El infierno*, 19.

77. *South Africa's Human Spirit* (CD-ROM set), vol. 3 (*Worlds of License*), disc 1, track 5 ("Till the Day I Die"). On that broadcast, Mhleli Mxenge, Griffiths Mxenge's brother stated, "In fact, I don't expect remorse. In fact, I could answer that question if he has been to a court of law, if he has been convicted and charged, you know. I'm therefore totally opposed to granting amnesty to Dirk Coetzee." Another brother, Fumbatha, stated, "My brother was butchered like a beast in a butchery, you know, for doing nothing. An innocent

victim. So you can just imagine, I mean the word forgiveness in as far as Dirk Coetzee is concerned does not exist in our dictionary." Coetzee responded, "There is one thing that I will have to live [with] 'til the day that I die: it's the corpses that I will have to drag with me to my grave of the people whom I've killed. Remorse? I can assure you a lot—a helluva lot." *Special Report on the Truth and Reconciliation Commission*, SABC-TV, 22 March 1998.

78. Institute for Justice and Reconciliation, "Brian Mitchell: Staying Power," 1.

79. The plan, still in blueprint, involved a community resource center that would include an arts and crafts center, a museum, library and computer center, and an adult-education center.

80. Trust and resources are the primary barriers Mitchell faces in effectively working with the community. IJR and its links to donors might help Mitchell and Trust Feed overcome the resources barrier, but trust remains a problem. In my interview with him, Mitchell claimed to have helped, protected, and encouraged blacks within the community to no avail, yet he made racist slurs like "The Zulu are lazy," even when surrounded by hardworking Zulu waiters. He still ignores how the legacy of racism, unemployment, and illiteracy plague the community. Interview with the author, Zululand, Kwa Zulu-Natal, South Africa, 16 October 1996.

81. Institute for Justice and Reconciliation, "Brian Mitchell: Staying Power," 1.

82. *South Africa's Human Spirit* (CD-ROM set), vol. 3 (*Worlds of License*), disc 2, track 3 ("I Can't Forgive Them").

83. Ibid.

84. Ibid.

85. Anthony Holiday, "Behr Adds to Fears of Informers," *Cape Times*, 22 July 1996.

86. Behr, "Living in the Fault Lines," 117.

87. Ibid, 119.

88. Ibid.

89. Ibid., 115; Behr is citing an unspecified *City Press* review. Behr's *The Smell of Apples* had received the M-Net award for fiction in 1996, the 1994 CNA debut award, the 1994 Eugene Marais prize, and the 1995 British Betty Trask award.

90. Justin Pearce, "How Author Was Forced to Confess," *Mail and Guardian*, 12 July 1996.

91. *Special Report on the Truth and Reconciliation Commission*, SABC-TV, 14 July 1996.

92. *South Africa's Human Spirit* (CD-ROM set), vol. 4 (*Portraits of Truth*), track 10 ("I Beg You!").

93. The French general Jacques Massu, at the age of ninety-two, confessed to the atrocities he committed in the Battle of Algiers nearly half a century earlier. Time and age convinced Massu that "torture is not indispensable during

wartime. We could have done it without it. When I think about Algiers, I am saddened. We could have done things differently." Florence Beaugé, "Torture en Algérie: Le remords du général Jacques Massu," *Le Monde*, 22 June 2000, reprinted in Gaspari, *A ditadura escancarada*, 44.

94. *South Africa's Human Spirit* (CD-ROM set), vol. 3 (*Worlds of License*), disc 1, track 7 ("In the Eye").

95. Interview with Joe Slovo in *Need to Know*, directed by Jann Turner, Channel 4, UK Television, 1993, rebroadcast on *Special Report on the Truth and Reconciliation Commission*, SABC-TV, 7 July 1996.

96. Cynthia Ngewu, quoted in Krog, *Country of My Skull*, 142.

97. Velile Goniwe, *Special Report on the Truth and Reconciliation Commission*, SABC-TV, 22 March 1998.

98. Mbuyi Mhlawuli, *Special Report on the Truth and Reconciliation Commission*, SABC-TV, 22 March 1998.

99. Ana Maria Careaga, interview by author, Buenos Aires, Argentina, 2 August 2002.

100. Martin Abregú, quoted in *Página/12*, 18 March 1995, and reprinted in Feitlowitz, *A Lexicon of Terror*, 224.

101. Mark Gevisser, "Sandile Dikeni, Poet and Radio Broadcaster: A Voice of Truth and Dissent," *Mail and Guardian*, 26 July 1996.

3. HEROIC CONFESSIONS

Epigraph from Cerruti, "El asesino está entre nosotros 6–9."

1. Those disappeared included a founder of the Mothers of the Plaza de Mayo, two French nuns, young supporters from Vanguardia Comunista, human-rights activists, and "innocent bystanders."

2. On a visit to Argentina, Jacques Chirac referred to Astiz as an "assassin." Eduardo Febbro, "Francia sigue sin olvidar," *Página/12*, 16 January 1998. Italy asked for Astiz's extradition for the murder of three Italian citizens: Angela Maria Aietta, born in Italy and the mother of Dante Gullo, a Peronist leader; Susana Pegoraro, of Italian descent, whose daughter was born in captivity and illegally adopted; and Susana's father, Juan Pegoraro.

3. Hebe de Bonafini, of the Mothers of the Plaza de Mayo Association, considered President Carlos Menem's reaction to Astiz as a strategy to distract citizens from the other polemical political issues and the justification for an "autogolpe." "Reclamos y denuncias judiciales," *Clarín*, 16 January 1998.

4. One of the Spanish court cases was brought by Federico Gómez for the disappearance of his father, Conrado Higinio Gómez, and the robbery of his goods by ESMA personnel. A panel of judges determined that civil courts needed to investigate whether the robbery of Gómez's property formed

"part of the terrorism repression strategy" or if it constituted disobedience on the part of those involved. The judges also determined that the elder Gómez was apprehended on 10 January 1977, seen in the ESMA, and subsequently disappeared. His disappearance constituted a crime against humanity. Argentina was therefore obligated by international law to try or extradite the perpetrator for trial.

5. One of the interim presidents, Adolfo Rodríguez Saá, agreed to reconsider President Fernando de la Rúa's extradition policy. Unfortunately for the international courts and local human-rights activists, Saá left office quickly, and his successor, President Eduardo Duhalde, clamped down once again on bringing Astiz to justice through foreign courts.

6. Rosenberg, *Children of Cain*, 79.

7. Gabriela Cerruti, "La conversación," *Trespuntos*, 21 January 1998, 9.

8. Cerruti, "El asesino está entre nosotros," 6.

9. Gabriela Cerruti, "Astiz en el banquillo," *Trespuntos*, 8 April 1998, 20.

10. Rosenberg, *Children of Cain*, 141.

11. Cerruti, "El asesino está entre nosotros," 11.

12. Ibid., 8.

13. The journalist Miguel Bonasso, however, raised doubts about Astiz's version, contending instead that Roqué had holed up alone in his house and begun shooting for his life against Astiz and his colleagues. Recognizing that he would not come out alive, Roqué blew himself up. Bonasso's implication, therefore, was that Astiz took credit for murders he did not commit and for surviving threats to his life that did not exist. Miguel Bonasso, "Las mentiras de Astiz," *Página/12*, 20 January 1998.

14. Cerruti, "El asesino está entre nosotros," 9.

15. Luis Bruschtein, "La marina me enseñó a matar," *Página/12*, 15 January 1998.

16. Cerruti, "El asesino está entre nosotros," 7.

17. Sajón, for example, who had served as press secretary during General Alejandro A. Lanusse's dictatorship, had never taken up arms against the regime nor had he joined a left-wing movement. Since Sajón's murder had previously been attributed to the police, Astiz's revelations opened up for survivors another avenue for investigation and prosecution.

18. Cerruti, "El asesino está entre nosotros," 11.

19. Astiz also considered dangerous the Vanguardia Comunista, an idealistic Maoist group that believed in passive resistance and the long struggle, and he orchestrated raids that disappeared most of that group.

20. Cerruti, "El asesino está entre nosotros," 7.

21. Ibid., 9.

22. Ibid., 11.

23. Ibid.

24. According to Cerruti, however, Astiz had not declined to be interviewed by

Mauro Viale, but only negotiated payment. Gabriela Cerruti, "Astiz del dicho al hecho," *Trespuntos*, 28 January 1998.

25. As a relative indicator of the media obsession with Astiz, news articles from a variety of Argentine newspapers filled twenty-three diskettes, while stories regarding Scilingo filled only three. No other Argentine perpetrator came even close to matching Astiz's notoriety.

26. Cerruti, "El asesino está entre nosotros," 11.

27. Cerruti connected the Commando Cueva (Cave Commando) to Massera, since he formed a secret society that met in a room in the Círculo Naval that they called the Cave. Cerruti, "Astiz del dicho al hecho."

28. "Las lecciones de muerte," *Clarín*, 21 January 1998. The appearance of a swastika bearing Astiz's name on a memorial to the disappeared in San Justo, Matanza, was widely interpreted as a similar threat to human-rights activists.

29. In contrast to the Menem government, Minister of Justice Raúl Granillo Ocampo believed that Astiz ultimately supported democracy, as evidenced by other lines in Astiz's interview: "I am betting on this system even though it doesn't benefit me. I thrive on chaos. I know how to move better in chaos. But I believe in democracy. And I believe that during a democratic government the armed forces should be democratic" (Cerruti, "El asesino está entre nosotros," 9). Granillo faced harsh criticism in *Página/12* and from Aníbal Ibarra, the vice-president of the Buenos Aires legislature, for his statements in Astiz's defense. These critics believed Granillo focused only on the thin veil that disguised Astiz's call for military intervention if the democratic government eroded immunity laws or destroyed the ESMA. In their opinion, Granillo ignored the reassertion of military tutelage over the democratic system. "Granillo cree que Astiz es, al menos, un demócrata," *Página/12*, 18 January 1998.

30. Federico Polak, quoted in "La voz de un asesino," *Página/12*, 16 January 1998.

31. Cristian Alarcón, "Otra vez monumento al indulto," *Página/12*, 18 January 1998.

32. Ramón "Palito" Ortega, former presidential candidate, quoted in "Astiz prefiere el auxilio de la defensora oficial," *La Nación*, 29 January 1998.

33. Bartolomé de Vedia, "El límite del perdón," *La Nación*, 25 January 1998.

34. Bonasso, "Las mentiras de Astiz."

35. Ibid.

36. Goñi, *Judas*, 166–67.

37. Among the municipalities are Monte Hermoso, Gualeguay, the City of Buenos Aires, San Carlos de Bariloche, Bahía Blanca, Luján, and Azul.

38. Captain Pedro Taramasco and the federal judge Luis Dardanelli Alsina walked out of the wedding reception. "Otro repudio a Astiz," *Clarín*, 24 December 1997.

39. "Rico y Bussi, en contra del marino," *La Nación*, 21 January 1998.

40. "Chávez ya se prepara contra Astiz," *Página/12*, 17 September 1995.

41. "El ángel de la muerte viene golpeado," *Página/12*, 6 October 1995. In 1997 teenagers in Gualeguay (Entre Rios) attacked Astiz in a dance club after he strutted in announcing "I am Captain Astiz and I want to visit this place." After trying to convince the owners to eject him, a young woman spit in Astiz's face. He grabbed her arm, she twisted away, and a brawl broke out. Graciela Mochkofsky, "Por el derecho de admisión," *Página/12*, 5 August 1997.

42. "El ángel de la muerte viene golpeado."

43. "Que la gente reaccione" and "Van a repetirse," *Página/12*, 6 October 1995.

44. These included the Peace and Justice Service (SERPAJ); Ecumenical Human Rights Movement (MEDH); Mothers of the Plaza de Mayo, Founding Group; Association of the Families of the Detained and Disappeared (AFDD); Permanent Assembly for Human Rights (APDH), La Plata; Argentine League for the Rights of Men; and the Argentine Labor Confederation (CGT).

45. Elisa Tokar, quoted in Rosenberg, *Children of Cain*, 99.

46. Apparently, the navy considered Acosta a danger and dishonorably discharged him after he posed for a magazine spread, wearing his navy uniform and passing his cap to a woman in an "indecorous manner." Ibid., 139.

47. Pablo J. Gaggero, "Sus amigos aseguran que seguirán amparándolo," *La Nación*, 28 January 1998.

48. Goñi, *Judas*, 106.

49. Sara Solarz de Osatinsky, quoted in ibid., 166.

50. Ibid., 167.

51. "Para el último preso en la ESMA, Astiz es 'una persona siniestra.' " *La Nación*, 19 January 1998.

52. Juan Castro Olivera, "La influencia de Massera," *La Nación*, 18 January 1998.

53. Goñi, *Judas*, 173.

54. "Las pericias no ayudan a Astiz," *Clarín*, 6 February 1998.

55. Cerruti, "La conversación."

56. "Bravo ve una maniobra del masserismo," *Clarín*, 19 January 1998.

57. Juan Castro Olivera, "La Armada, en busca de una depuración," *La Nación*, 20 January 1998. The alleged plot would have possibly had to involve a middle-man, like Martínez, since Astiz apparently had a long-standing grievance about Massera's failure to promote Astiz's father to the rank of admiral.

58. "Astiz quedó libre y prepara su defensa ante once denuncias," *Clarín*, 28 January 1998.

59. Sergio Moreno, "Una conspiración muy funcional a los planes de la Marina de Guerra," *Página/12*, 21 January 1998.

60. Rosenberg, *Children of Cain*, 140.

61. Cerruti, "Astiz en el banquillo," 22.

62. Cerruti, "El asesino está entre nosotros," 11.

63. Ibid., 9.

64. "Las 'bromas' pesadas del señor Astiz," *Página/12*, 4 April 1998.

65. "Jamás hablé de matar," *Página/12*, 10 March 1998. Astiz demanded the recording of the interview. Cerruti, however, could only produce post-interview notes, contending that she preferred to avoid the intimidation of informants that tapes and interview notes might cause.

66. Victoria Ginzberg, "Estuve en el lado adecuado," *Página/12*, 4 March 2000. Astiz's court-appointed lawyer, Perla Martínez de Buck, inadvertently bolstered the credibility of Cerruti's report by emphasizing Astiz's deep respect for political power, subordination to the constitution, love for his country, political apathy, spirit of sacrifice, steadfast devotion, and willingness to die for his ideals.

67. Daniel Gutman, "Condenaron a Astiz por apología del delito, pero no va a la carcel," *Clarín*, 9 March 2000.

68. David Cox, "El hombre que sabe demasiado," *Trespuntos*, 14 January 1998.

69. Juan Aberg Cobo, quoted in Goñi, *Judas*, 208.

70. "Varios almirantes defendieron a Astiz en el juicio," *La Nación*, 29 February 2000; Gabriela Cerruti, "Cinco opiniones sobre un fallo polémico," *Página/12*, 9 March 2000.

71. Cerruti, "Cinco opiniones sobre un fallo polémico." She notes: "It was impressive seeing how the witnesses from the navy would react as a block, presenting Astiz as a mythic figure. Although men committed crimes, an institutional ideology still allows them to see each other in this [admirable] light."

72. Cerruti, "El asesino está entre nosotros," 8.

73. Silvina Labayrú chose a different "protector" within the torture center, but testified about her experiences as a prisoner at the ESMA to the National Commission on the Disappeared (CONADEP). Labayrú had posed as Astiz's sister when he infiltrated the Mothers of the Plaza de Mayo. Goñi, *Judas*.

74. Cerruti, "El asesino está entre nosotros," 8.

75. Ibid., 9–10.

76. Ibid., 7.

77. Ibid., 8.

78. "Astiz dejó sin respuesta las preguntas sobre personas desaparecidas," *Clarín*, 20 January 1998.

79. Carlos Pacheco, "Uki Goñi: Alfredo Astiz es el inconsciente colectivo de la ESMA," *La Maga*, 28 January 1998, 46–47.

80. "Cinco opiniones sobre un fallo polémico," *Página/12*, 9 March 2000.

81. Gabriela Cerruti, quoted in ibid.

82. Martín Roqué, quoted in Diego Rosemberg and Patricia Rojas, "La hora de la verdad," *Trespuntos*, 28 January 1998.

83. Cerruti, "La conversación," 10.

84. "La voz de un asesino," *Página/12*, 16 January 1998.

85. Horacio Verbitsky, "De la verdad a la justicia," *Página/12*, 5 May 2000.

86. "The Generals Deserted Us: Former Security Policemen," *South African Press Association*, 21 October 1996.

87. "Williamson Had Qualms about Killing Woman He Knew as Friend," *Cape Times*, 16 September 1998.

88. John Yeld, "I Can't Justify Killing a Child, Admits 'Superspy,'" *Cape Argus*, 17 September 1998.

89. Ibid.

90. Ruth First's resignation from the Communist Party in 1964 (eighteen years before her murder) and her well-known disagreements with the ANC over the position of women in its ranks cast doubts on Williamson's claim that she was a political target.

91. The lawyer for First's and Schoon's families, George Bizos, attempted to show the TRC Amnesty Committee that Williamson had targeted Schoon for personal revenge because the Schoons had suspected Williamson's role as an infiltrator and had begun to blow his cover. To receive amnesty from the TRC, applicants must have a political, rather than a personal, motive.

92. Stephen Laufer, "An Anomaly Who Still Sees Himself as a White Knight," *Business Day*, 17 September 1998.

93. Ibid.

94. David Beresford, "Coetzee's 'Fairy Tales,'" *Weekly Mail and Guardian*, 11–17 September 1998.

95. Laufer, "An Anomaly Who Still Sees Himself as a White Knight."

96. Ibid.

97. Allen Levin, quoted in Maureen Isaacson, "First's Friend Gives Chilling Testimony," *Sunday Independent*, 28 February 1999.

98. Stephané Bothma, "Spying 'Is like Prostitution,'" *Business Day*, 17 September 1998.

99. Quoted in d'Araujo and Castro, eds., *Ernesto Geisel*, 225, reprinted in Gaspari, *A ditadura escancarada*, 37.

100. Gaspari, *A ditadura escancarada*, 37.

101. Interview with Marcelo Paixão de Araújo in Alexandre Oltramari, "Torturei uns trinta," *Veja*, 9 December 1998, 49.

102. Rian Malan, "Crises Show Up Demise of Rainbow Nation," *Business Day*, 21 April 1998.

103. *South Africa's Human Spirit* (CD-ROM set), vol. 2 (*Slices of Life*), track 12 ("Salute Me!").

104. Testimony by Slobodan Milosevic to the International Criminal Tribunal for the Former Yugoslavia (ICTY), 26 September 2002, 10, 247 (transcript).

105. Ibid., 10, 314 (transcript).

106. Ciancaglini and Granovsky, *Nada más que la verdad*, 203.

Gaspari, *A ditadura escancarada*, 42.

108. Scartezini, *Segredos de Médici*, 36.

109. *South Africa's Human Spirit* (CD-ROM set), vol. 2 (*Slices of Life*), track 12 ("Salute Me!").

110. The Communist Party leaders included Manuel Guerrero, Santiago Nattino, and José Manuel Parada.

111. Estay chose not to explain his collaboration with the regime as a result of torture. Indeed, he denied that he had been tortured, stating instead that he was "questioned by various methods." "Confessions of Former Secret Service Agent 'El Fanta,'" 24 January 1993, 1, http://derechoschile.com/.

112. Ibid.

113. When first asked how he felt about the murders, he deflected the question stating, "I think you can imagine what any person would feel in a situation like that." Ibid., 3.

114. Robb Northey, "No Reconciliation without Truth, Says Schoon," *Star*, 6 November 1998.

115. Schoon's son and First's daughters have appealed Williamson's amnesty.

116. The precarious legal situation has led perpetrators' lawyers to urge silence. Williamson and I had spoken on the phone and even agreed to an interview until his lawyer intervened to prevent him from jeopardizing his amnesty.

117. Young, *The Texture of Memory*, 2.

118. Scott, *Domination and the Arts of Resistance*, 45.

119. Ibid., 49.

120. Ibid., 45.

4. SADISM

Epigraph from Osvaldo Romo Mena, interview by Mercedes Soler on 11 April 1995, broadcast on "En Confianza," *Primer Impacto*, Univision, 17 May 1998. Quote in transcript in Soto, *Voces de muerte*, 2:70–71.

1. "Justicia miltar absolvió al 'Guatón Romo,'" *La Cuarta*, 7 October 2000.

2. Guzmán, *Romo*, 95. Gladys Díaz, "¿Dónde están hoy los dinos de ayer?" *Gente Gris de Miranda Torva*, http://www.sech.cl/, reprinted in *Análisis*, October 1991.

3. Guzmán referred to his smell no less than four times in her book (*Romo*, 23, 24, 65, 227). Nearly every victim interviewed mentioned his odor. Gladys Díaz described it as the "smell of grease and perspiration despite having bathed himself in Flaño cologne" ("¿Dónde están hoy los dinos de ayer?").

4. Catherine Jagoe, "Confessing Evil," paper presented at the Center for the Humanities, Stoughton Public Library, Stoughton, Wisconsin, 23 March 2004.

5. Romo denies involvement in the murder of Castillo's partner, Miguel Enríquez, but identifies his superior officer Miguel Krassnoff as responsible. Castillo and Girard, *La flaca Alejandra*.

6. E.O.G., "Diabetes no perdona al 'Guatón Romo,'" *La Nación*, 11 September 2000.

7. This was a well-known land invasion in the Lo Hermida zone that ended in a violent confrontation, the death of a militant, and many wounded. President Allende sided with the Lo Hermida residents and protesters and not with the police who invaded.

8. Most accounts attribute Romo's position in DINA to his link to Julio Rada, who had arrested Romo in the late 1960s for petty crimes. Rada, along with Romo, subsequently helped investigate a death that had occurred during the Lo Hermida land invasion. When Rada became the new director of criminal investigations under the Pinochet government, he allegedly pulled Romo out of a line of MIR detainees and convinced him that he could save his life by collaborating.

9. News of the Univision broadcast arrived in Chile through a review—"Torture on Television"—written by Mauricio Montaldo, the Miami correspondent for Chile's *Últimas Noticias*. In June 1995 Chilevisión reproduced part of the Univision program, but it "suppressed the most lurid parts, the particularly crude ones, to avoid offending the memories of the victims or harming the sensibilities of the television audience" (Soto, *Voces de muerte*, 2:70). The Chilean magazine *Punto Final* published the interview, but no other print media followed suit because of the uproar over the broadcast. *Punto Final*, 11–24 June 1995. The intense public reaction to so little coverage led one observer to refer to the media event as a "reduced and censored scandal" (Roberto Contreras, "Exijo ser un héroe [o el silencio de inocentes]," http://www.critica.uchile.cl/memoria/romo.htm).

10. Romo specifically referred to methods including "the grill," the "parrot's perch," the wet and dry "submarine," and driving a truck over prisoners' legs. Guzmán, *Romo*, 165–69.

11. Soto, *Voces de muerte*, 2:73.

12. Guzmán, *Romo*, 155.

13. Ibid.

14. Ibid., 69–70.

15. Ibid., 150.

16. Ibid., 145.

17. Ibid., 146.

18. Ibid., 210. Romo admitted to killing the MIR leader Dagoberto Perez, saying, "I fired and so did everybody else. That's war for you, that was what the Dirty War was like. It was me first, me second, and me third." Soto, *Voces de muerte*, 2:72.

19. Guzmán, *Romo*, 153.

20. Ibid., 202–3.

21. Ibid., 155. See also pp. 145 and 209.

22. Ibid., 209.

23. Ibid., 109. Another example of Romo's contradictions involves the disappearances of women prisoners. He denied any knowledge of how women disappeared from the torture centers stating, "I don't know because I saw them healthy. Look, I went home in the afternoon and the next day I'd ask, 'Where is Jane Doe?' They told me that she had been transported. I don't know." Ibid., 160. But clearly he did know, and he wanted his interviewer to know he knew. So he told Guzmán that he could not tell her where the prisoners were taken on the "transports," but suggested that she think of "German names." This statement confirmed rumors that many of the disappeared had last been seen at a detention center in a German community, Colonia Dignidad. Ibid., 161. Romo subsequently testified in trials that Colonia Dignidad "was used to detain people who were to later disappear," although the German community's lawyer dismissed Romo as "mentally disturbed." "Former DINA Agent Incriminates Colonia Dignidad," *Global News Wire–CHIP News*, 10 August 2001.

24. Jorge Escalante, "Romo describió nexo de la DINA con Colonia Dignidad." *La Nación*, 7 August 2001.

25. Patricia Bravo, "Cara a cara con el Guatón Romo," *Punto Final*, 7–20 December 2001.

26. Guzmán, *Romo*, 220.

27. "Confronting the Villa Grimaldi Torturers: The Court Encounter between Torture Victims and DINA Agents," *Global News Wire–Santiago Times*, 23 August 2001.

28. Arce, *El infierno*, 169.

29. Guzmán, *Romo*, 200.

30. Ibid., 174. See also Arce, *El infierno*, 142.

31. Ibid., 156.

32. Ibid., 172.

33. Ibid., 156–57.

34. Ibid., 194–95.

35. Ibid., 160.

36. Ibid., 146.

37. Ibid.

38. Ibid., 112.

39. Ibid., 151–52.

40. Ibid., 151.

41. Ibid., 154.

42. Ibid., 161.

43. Ibid., 172.

44. Ibid., 212.

45. Soto, *Voces de muerte*, 2:74.

46. Ibid., 66, 172, and 222. Romo seemed to lie even when it would not enhance his reputation and even when he could easily be caught in the lie. He bragged to Guzmán, for example, about having written a popular song (about the disappointment of having a daughter) for which he had no authorship. Ibid., 66.

47. Guzmán, *Romo*, 172.

48. Ibid., 222.

49. Soto, *Voces de muerte*, 2:71.

50. Guzmán, *Romo*, 175.

51. Ibid., 179.

52. "La impunidad es ante todo un problema político," *Angel Fire*, http://www.angelfire.com/.

53. Guzmán, *Romo*, 181–82.

54. Ibid., 40.

55. Ibid., 181.

56. The callers warned her that they knew how to find her, including her address, car, and other details about her life. Ibid., 231.

57. The journalist Vivian Lavín reported that Romo had prepared his retraction with the help of Ibarra, who silently watched while Romo had it notarized by a military judge and a court secretary. Other news sources confirmed Ibarra's role in the retraction. "Osvaldo Romo, la entrevista que generó intensa polémica," *El Mercurio Online*, July 4, 2007 (http://www.emol.com/noticias/nacional/detalle/).

58. "Justicia militar absolvió al 'Guatón Romo,'" *La Cuarta*, 7 October 2000.

59. *La Tercera*, 21 May 1995, reprinted in Guzmán, *Romo*, 26.

60. Guzmán, *Romo*, 181.

61. *El Mercurio*, 23 May 1995, reprinted in Guzmán, *Romo*, 26. Minister of Justice Soledad Alvear did take the commentary seriously enough to charge Romo with "justifying violence" and "threatening and obstructing justice."

62. "Hacen dibujos para que Romo vuelva a canasta," *La Cuarta*, 14 October 2000.

63. "Confesiones de Romo: Locura del verdugo o locura de la sociedad?" *Rocinante*, 2 March 2001, 24.

64. Ibid.

65. Ibid., 24–25.

66. Ibid., 25.

67. Juan Salinas, "Osvaldo 'Guatón' Romo: Un traidor, torturador y asesino, en libertad," *El Siglo*, 13–19 October 2000.

68. Alejandra Holzapfel Picarte, in Bravo, "Cara a cara con el Guatón Romo."

69. "Confesiones de Romo: Locura del verdugo o locura de la sociedad?" *Rocinante*, 2 March 2001, 25.

70. Foreign journalists from Holland and France had interviewed Romo previously, and taped and broadcast those interviews on foreign television with local coverage, without provoking outrage over prison access.

71. Guzmán, *Romo*, 17.

72. Ibid., 16–17.

73. Ibid., 229.

74. Ibid., 232.

75. Ibid., 230.

76. These included nongovernmental organizations from Belgium, England, France, Germany, Spain, and Sweden. See "Carta abierta a los gobernantes chilenos," signed by Colectivo Chileno Europeo contra la Impunidad (CCECI), 8 October 2000, http://www.noticias.nl/. Also available on www.correodel sur.ch.

77. "Agrupaciones de derechos humanos rechazan libertad de Osvaldo Romo," *El Metropolitano*, 8 October 2000.

78. Arce, *El infierno*, 141–42.

79. Nancy Guzmán, quoted in Willy Haltenhoff, "Me dio mucho miedo ver libre a Romo," *La Nación*, 13 November 2000; Guzmán, *Romo*, 27.

80. They were charged in the death of MIR leaders Alfonso Chanfreau and Miguel Enríquez. "Funcionamiento de estructura operativa," *La Nación*, 7 August 2001. See also Robert J. Quinn, "Will the Rule of Law End? Challenging Grants of Amnesty for the Human Rights Violations of a Prior Regime: Chile's New Model," *Fordham Law Review* 62 (February 1994): 905–60.

81. Arce, *El infierno*, 142; Haltenhoff, "Me dio mucho miedo ver libre a Romo."

82. Bravo, "Cara a cara con el Guatón Romo." For a discussion of the *funas*, or the public "outing" of Romo, see "Careo," *Últimas Noticias*, 28 July 2001.

83. Malcolm Coad, "The Healing Pain through Purgatory Fire," *Guardian* (London), 6 February 1993.

84. Dorfman, *Death and the Maiden*, 59.

85. See Lieutenant General Anthony R. Jones, "AR 15-6 Investigation of the Abu Ghraib Prison and 205th Military Intelligence Brigade," *Investigation of Intelligence Activities at Abu Ghraib*, 23 August 2004, 6–33.

86. Alexandre Oltramari, "Torturei uns trinta," *Veja*, 9 December 1998, 44–46. Araújo was named by more victims (twenty-two) than any other single torturer. He admitted to *Veja* that he did not know how many people he had tortured while he was the lieutenant of the Belo Horizonte Infantry Regiment (1968–1971), but he estimated the number to be around thirty. He confirmed that his victims had presented "essentially correct" descriptions of his torture methods.

87. Bravo, "Cara a cara con el Guatón Romo."

88. Paul van Vuuren, *Special Report on the Truth and Reconciliation Commission*, SABC-TV, 22 February 1998.

89. Oltramari, "Torturei uns trinta," 45.

90. Ibid., 44–49.

91. Ibid., 48.

92. See Truth and Reconciliation Commission, Amnesty Hearing for Jeffrey T. Benzien, Cape Town, South Africa, 14 July 1997, 96–117.

93. Feitlowitz, *A Lexicon of Terror*, 212.

94. Ibid.

95. *Mediodía con Mauro*, Argentina Televisora Color (ATC), 15 and 25 August 1997, 15 September 1997, and 13 and 21 November 1997.

96. One of the few interesting exchanges in this program involved a young Peronist militant who questioned Simón's hero status: "None of his commanders will defend him. Do you know what it means to put someone like this on the same level as the soldiers in Malvinas?" Ibid.

97. Stiglmayer, "The Rapes in Bosnia-Herzegovina," 153–54.

98. Oltramari, "Torturei uns trinta," 48.

99. Jay Mariotti, "Tyson-Golata: Shameless Sham," *Chicago Sun-Times*, 19 October 2000, Sports section, 134.

100. Gaspari, *A ditadura escancarada*, 24.

101. "Aislarlos es un deber," *Página/12*, 4 December 1996.

102. André Petry, "Porão iluminado," *Veja*, 9 December 1998, 42.

103. Interview by the author, 7 February 2002, Cape Town, South Africa.

104. Carlos de la Rúa, on *Mediodía con Mauro*, Argentina Televisora Color, 15 and 25 August 1997, 15 September 1997, and 13 and 21 November 1997.

5. DENIAL

Epigraph from Contreras Sepúlveda, *La verdad histórica*, 120–21.

1. Contreras lost two appeals on the Sandoval case, despite efforts by the defense to call his disappearance a murder (and, thus, protected under the amnesty law). Contreras found more support from Judge Victor Montiglio, who in 2005 overturned Judge Juan Guzmán's earlier decision and applied amnesty to Contreras in the Operation Colombo case.

2. Branch and Propper, *Labyrinth*, 503.

3. Ibid., 147–48.

4. "Lanzaran biografía de 760 páginas sobre ex dictador Pinochet," *Deutsche Presse-Agentur*, 18 October 2002.

5. Branch and Propper, *Labyrinth*, 129.

6. Peter Kornbluh, "CIA Outrages in Chile," *Nation*, 16 October 2000.

7. Ana María Yévenes, "Yo también tengo documentos," *Ercilla*, 2 October 2000.

8. Alfonso Loya, "Pinochet situación Chile," *Servicio Universal de Noticias–Info-Latina*, 21 October 1998.

9. Suffering from a terminal illness, this individual decided to tell his story. "Ex agente sostiene que Manuel Contreras decidió qué detenidos eran lazados al mar," *La Tercera*, 1 February 2001.

10. "Carta abierta a Contreras," *Punto Final*, 11–24 June 1995, 4.

11. Among these television appearances were those that occurred on 25 March 1991, 17 August 1993, 31 May 1995, 28 May 2001, and 7 October 2001.

12. Polifemo, "Grititos de gato mojado," *Punto Final*, 24 June 1995, 23.

13. "La respuesta de Manuel Contreras a Odlanier Mena," *La Tercera*, 14 March 1998.

14. "La palabra de Contreras," *Qué Pasa*, 7 March 1998, 20.

15. "Las afirmaciones del General Contreras que nadie desmiente," *Despierta Chile* 1, no. 1 (September 2001) (documentos desclasificados), http://www.despiertachile.cl/.

16. "Ex-Jefe de la DINA dice que no tiene nada de que arrepentirse," *Efe*, 29 May 2001.

17. Contreras Sepúlveda, *La verdad histórica II*, 3.

18. Contreras Sepúlveda, *La verdad histórica*, 137.

19. "No hay detenidos despararecidos," *Caras*, 29 September 2000, 19.

20. Ibid., 22.

21. Contreras Sepúlveda, *La verdad histórica II*, 4.

22. Ibid., 9.

23. Ibid., 6.

24. "Pinochet's Police Chief Says Will Hand Over Information on Disappeared," *Agence France-Presse*, 2 December 1999. Contreras would literally and figuratively disappear a detainee by calling him or her "this extremist," and not "this citizen," or even "this person." The DINA agent revealing the use of documents is Luz Arce; see Arce, *El infierno*.

25. Contreras Sepúlveda, *La verdad histórica*, 17.

26. Contreras Sepúlveda, *La verdad histórica II*, 7.

27. Contreras Sepúlveda, *La verdad histórica*, 120. Contreras made a similar reference in his second book to "the same Marxists who yesterday raced to find refuge in embassies and fled the country in September '73," and who subsequently returned to Chile to "find themselves in elevated posts in every area of national life," which granted them "immunity from their own past acts," and who "without hiding their hatred, without hiding their resentment, and without hiding their desire for revenge," "denigrate[d] yesterday's victors, the ones who saved Chile from destruction and death, by treating them like criminals and assassins" and turning "popular opinion against them" (ibid., 3).

28. Contreras Sepúlveda, *La verdad histórica II*, 2.

29. Contreras Sepúlveda, *La verdad histórica*, 120.
30. Contreras Sepúlveda, *La verdad histórica II*, 4.
31. Contreras, countering charges of sexual abuse within the secret detention centers, blamed "the Marxists" for disrespecting women. "Women," he claimed, "could not be your own because of the need for secrecy and security. If he lived with his own wife and she was recognized by someone, she would be followed, and they'd capture the MIRista right away. So there was an exchange of women, according to the machismo of the MIRistas, only to 'trick the enemy' " (*La verdad histórica*, 45).
32. Contreras Sepúlveda, *La verdad histórica*, 129; Contreras Sepúlveda, *La verdad histórica II*, 10.
33. Contreras Sepúlveda, *La verdad histórica II*, 279.
34. His explanation begins with Vernon Walters, the deputy director of the CIA, who sent instructors to Chile to teach national intelligence in 1974. Following orders from Pinochet, Contreras accepted the instructors. (Chile had previously relied on military, not national, intelligence.) When the training period came to an end, the head of the team told Contreras that he had instructions to remain and even to fill key positions within DINA. "I asked them if they were crazy, because this was a military institution and no civilians could take positions, even less so foreigners." Walters intervened, suggesting that Chile accept the same relationship the CIA had with Venezuela: seven CIA agents working in the Venezuelan security agency, DISIP. Contreras refused to accept the condition and the unhappy instructors left. Contreras interpreted their parting words—that "we'd soon hear from them"—as evidence of the CIA's subsequent involvement in framing DINA in murder: "And this is what occurred," wrote Contreras, "because on the 30th of September of 1974 Michael Townley, an acknowledged CIA agent, murdered General Prats in Buenos Aires." Contreras claimed that Townley then became involved in the attempted murder of Bernardo Leighton in Italy and the successful murder of Orlando Letelier in the U.S., "all because we did not want to become partners." Yévenes, "Yo también tengo documentos."
35. Contreras, *La verdad histórica II*.
36. "Pinochet (Scheduled) Former DINA Chief's Book Offers Proof Chile's Military Has Info," *Efe*, 30 September 2000. Contreras rebutted, stating, "I deny categorically those false, deceptive, and ridiculous versions that I sent a large quantity of DINA documents to some other part of the world. The reality is that I didn't take with me to my new location, nor any other place, any documents from the National Intelligence Division" (*La verdad histórica II*, 1).
37. "Carta abierta a Contreras," 4.
38. Contreras claimed that Bussi had sent a friend to beg him and DINA to release her from the "veritable prison" in which Fidel Castro kept her in Cuba and to

allow her to return to Chile. When Castro discovered Bussi's betrayal, however, he killed her daughter, Beatriz, and circulated the rumor that she had committed suicide. Rather than engage in a battle with Contreras about historical evidence, Bussi merely rejected his [Contreras's] obscene fiction. "Viuda de Allende desmiente a jefe de la policía secreta de Pinochet," *Agence France-Presse*, 4 September 2001. Contreras further claimed that Castro visited Allende's tomb in Chile, but without Bussi. When Castro discovered that Beatriz was buried there, too, he "left the mausoleum rapidly. That is the real reason Doña Hortensia did not join him [at the cemetery], Contreras contended, since she didn't want to be together with the Cuban dictator in front of her daughter's tomb, knowing that he had ordered her assassination" (*La verdad histórica II*, 20).

39. Noll Scott, "Court Upholds Sentence on Chilean Army Torture Chief," *Guardian* (London), 31 May 1995.

40. Calvin Sims, "Chilean Vows to Avoid Prison in Letelier Case," *New York Times*, 31 May 1995. Contreras also famously avowed, "I will not go to any jail as long as there is no real justice." "Chilean Army Accepts Letelier Case Verdicts," *Agence France-Presse*, 1 June 1995.

41. The Catalan Brigade played the verse of the national anthem that referred to the "brave" military and that had been excised after the end of the dictatorship. The group protested what they perceived to be "pressure [to prosecute] in the Letelier case" and called on Chileans to join the struggle against "new acts of corruption" and "disregard" forthe armed forces' authority. The army denied knowledge of the brigade. "Chile: Letelier Case Heats Up as Verdict Approaches," *Inter Press Service*, 19 May 1995.

42. Gabriel Escobar, "Chilean Vigil for Arrest of an Ex-General; Convict in Letelier Case Joining Trend: Rank Has Fewer Privileges," *Washington Post*, 13 June 1995.

43. "Comunistas califican de 'tortura' liberación de General Contreras," *Efe*, 20 January 2001.

44. Branch and Propper, *Labyrinth*, 155.

45. Ibid.

46. "El general y su laberinto," *La Tercera*, 24 September 2000.

47. Oscar Sepúlveda, "Desgraciadamente, las platas de la CIA no me llegaron," *Cosas*, 29 October 2000. After he left Punta Peuco, Contreras began house arrest in a condominium unit. His neighbors did not greet his arrival warmly, but instead joined left-wing politicians and human-rights activists in protest, burning candles in a vigil and carrying posters demanding that he leave the residential community. "Protesta contra M. Contreras," *El Mercurio*, 27 January 2001.

48. "La respuesta de Manuel Contreras a Odlanier Mena," *La Tercera*, 14 March 1998.

49. "No hay detenidos despararecidos," *Caras*, 29 September 2000, 22.

50. Organizations like Comité de Defensa de los Derechos del Pueblo (CODEPU), Association of the Families of the Detained and Disappeared (AFDD), and the Communist Party thought Contreras might feel sufficiently abandoned and scapegoated and reveal information that would indict Pinochet and other top leaders in the regime.

51. Hitchens, *The Trial of Henry Kissinger*, 70.

52. "Proceso contra Pinochet," *Servicio Universal de Noticias–InfoLatina*, April 1999.

53. "El recurso que ocasionó controversia de generales," *La Tercera*, 14 March 1998.

54. Cristian Bofill R., "Amenaza y venganza," *Qué Pasa*, 7 March 1998, 21.

55. The document was alleged to be part of the materials Contreras sent to the Supreme Court of Chile to consider in its review of his prison sentence. But it may have formed part of the case developing in Spain against Pinochet and intended for the Spanish news media. Ibid., 18.

56. "Pinochet: Contreras habla 'Como si me acusara,'" *La Nación*, 14 March 1998.

57. "Reafirma dependencia de Pinochet," *La Tercera*, 4 April 2000.

58. "Sobrino General: Tampoco nosotros tendremos ni olvido ni perdón," *Efe*, 8 October 1999. He went on to reflect, "We will not pardon or forget those who have sold out our country and kidnapped General Pinochet. We claim September 11 [the coup d'etat] as the only valid alternative to get out of the situation in which we found ourselves." He ominously warned that "new movements of the extreme right or nationalist groups" might emerge to defend the armed forces. And he ended with a call to arms: "Chile must begin to wake up. There can't be so much forgetting and ingratitude. . . . This [detention of Pinochet] is not something we are going to forget. Spaniards should not even consider coming to Chile, because their visit would not be pleasant for them. We are writing down in a notebook, all of the people who have contributed to this act of revenge." Ibid.

59. "Las afirmaciones del General Contreras que nadie desmiente," *Despierta Chile* 1, no. 1 (September 2001) (documentos desclasificados), http://www .despiertachile.cl/.

60. Ibid.

61. "Chile: President and Army Disagree over Impact of Ruling," *Inter Press Service*, 31 May 1995.

62. "Molestia en ejército por las acciones del general (R) Contreras," *Últimas Noticias*, 5 March 1998.

63. "Ex-Agente acusa ejército no reconocer responsabilidad abusos," *Efe*, 5 April 1999. Carlos Herrera Jiménez was charged with murdering the union leaders Mario Fernández and Tucapel Jiménez and the carpenter Juan Alegría in the early 1980s.

64. Ibid.

65. Manuel Delano, "El ex 'numero dos' de la DINA culpa a Pinochet del asesinato de Letelier: EE.UU. reanuda la investigación del caso," *El País*, 24 March 2000.

66. "Esperando la lista," *Hoy*, 28 September 1998.

67. Cherie Zalaquett, "No soy hijo de un criminal," *Caras*, 20 March 1998. See also " 'Mamito' volvió a agitar las aguas," *Últimas Noticias*, 24 July 1999.

68. Sims, "Chilean Vows to Avoid Prison in Letelier Case."

69. "Chile Ex-Head of DINA Says Former DINA Agents Hold Senior Government Posts," BBC Summary of World Broadcasts, 28 March 1991.

70. Rodrigo Eitel, "Yo soy pinochetista, no contrerista," *La Hora*, 9 March 1998.

71. "Lanzaran biografía de 760 paginas sobre ex dictador Pinochet," *Deutsche Presse-Agentur*, 18 October 2002.

72. "Molestia en ejército por las acciones del general (R) Contreras," *Últimas Noticias*, 5 March 1998.

73. "Sacerdote niega vinculación con policía política de Pinochet," *Efe*, 20 December 2000.

74. Jonathan Franklin and Monte Reel, "Former Secret Police Chief Blames Pinochet for Abuses," *Washington Post*, 15 May 2005.

75. Manuel Contreras Sepúlveda, "Introducción a la entrega de documentos que demuestran las verdaderas responsabilidades de las instituciones de la defensa nacional en la lucha contra el terrorismo en Chile," Santiago, 13 May 2005, www.lanacion.cl.

76. "Pinochet and Ex-Police Chief Meet," *BBC News*, 18 November 2005, http://news.bbc.co.uk.

77. Originally quoted in *Sur* in 1989, reproduced in "La Perla es mi obra, mi hija," *Página/12*, 21 March 1995.

78. Carlos Dutil, "Política nacional," *Noticias*, 2 April 1995.

79. Alejandro Agostinelli, "Me duele que hablen de la conexión local," *La Prensa*, 18 July 1995.

80. Etchecolatz, *La otra campana del nunca más*, 178.

81. "Los seguidores del ex-represor, con violencia," *Clarín*, 7 April 2001.

82. Etchecolatz, *La otra campana del nunca más*, 17.

83. Ibid., 124.

84. Ibid., 9–10. Etchecolatz is quoting from the Israeli Supreme Court.

85. Ibid., 20.

86. "Chile Torture Victims Win Payout," *BBC News*, 29 November 2004, http://news.bbc.co.uk.

87. Ibid., 150.

88. Ibid., 7, 186.

89. *South Africa's Human Spirit* (CD-ROM set), vol. 2 (*Slices of Life*), track 4 ("The Call for Blood").

90. *South Africa's Human Spirit*, vol. 2 (*Slices of Life*), track 8 ("In the Corridors").

91. Ibid.

92. Ibid.

93. Etchecolatz, *La otra campana del nunca más*, 169. Etchecolatz—who presented himself as one of ten children raised in relative rural poverty, with a ten-kilometer walk to school and insufficient food to eat—claimed to know the "meaning of sacrifice." Ibid., 14.

94. Although seemingly from a middle-class background in La Pampa, Etchecolatz described himself as someone who had had no toys and very little money until the Eva Perón Foundation provided him with his own soccer ball. His deprivation uniquely prepared him for a role in intelligence, he claimed, since he could note subtle changes in environment from having grown up in the homogeneous landscape of La Pampa. Ibid.

95. Vergez abandoned his political pretensions, but maintained links to the security services. He became an agent for SIDE, the army's national intelligence, to investigate the AMIA bombing.

96. Testimony by Milorad Krnojelac to the International Criminal Tribunal for the Former Yugoslavia, 26 June 2001, 7,677–80, 7,698 (transcript).

97. "El escandalo," *Página/12*, 2 May 1998.

98. "Testimonio," *Página/12*, 21 March 1995.

99. J. M. Pasquini Durán, "Espejos de horror," *Página/12*, 21 March 1995. The media also picked up an offstage encounter between Vergez and the mothers and grandmothers of the Plaza de Mayo. Vergez had volunteered to organize a meeting between perpetrators and the human-rights community to reconstruct the lists of the disappeared. The mothers and the grandmothers refused to meet with murderers and torturers who they felt belonged in jail. Their response, reported by the press, undermined the image Vergez may have hoped to create with his gesture of reconciliation.

100. Victoria Ginzberg, "El represor dice ser víctima," *Página/12*, 27 October 1998. Etchecolatz appeared on *Hora Clave* on 28 August and 4 September 1997.

101. *South Africa's Human Spirit*, vol. 2 (*Slices of Life*), track 4 ("The Call for Blood").

102. Ibid.

103. Ibid.

104. Ibid. At the time of this broadcast, Antjie Krog used the name Antjie Samuel.

105. De Kock, *A Long Night's Damage*, 279.

106. "Crimen," *Página/12*, 6 August 1998.

107. Vergez, *Yo fui Vargas*, 246.

108. Raquel Robes, quoted in Victoria Ginzberg, "El accionar de los viejos tiempos," *Página/12*, 10 September 1998.

6. SILENCE

Epigraph from William França, "Anistia se sobrepõe a dor das famílias, diz general," *Folha de São Paulo*, 4 September 1995, Caderno Brasil, 8; reprinted in Mezarobba, *Um acerto de contas com o futuro*, 89.

1. Brandon Hamber, "Living with the Legacy of Impunity: Lessons for South Africa About Truth, Justice, and Crime in Brazil," *Latin American Report* 13, no. 3 (July–December 1997): 4–16.
2. D'Araujo and Castro, *Ernesto Geisel*, 223, reprinted in Martins Filho, "A memória militar sobre a tortura," 91.
3. Gaspari claims that the Center for Army Intelligence (CIE) tripled its number of officials in just a little over two years, allowing it to take control of the conventional forces. Gaspari, *A ditadura escancarada*, 36.
4. Archdiocese of São Paulo, *Torture in Brazil*, 104.
5. Ibid., 106.
6. Ibid.
7. Comissão de familiares de mortos e desaparecidos politicos, Instituto de Estudos da Violência do Estado (IEVE), Grupo Tortura Nunca Mais (RJ/PE), *Dossiê dos mortos e desaparecidos políticos a partir de 1964.*
8. Renato Brilhante Ustra, quoted in Alexandre Oltamari, "Esse maldito passado," *Veja*, 9 December 1998, 52. Ustra eventually ended his silence and published his memoirs, appropriately titled *Rompendo o silêncio* (Breaking the silence).
9. Mezarobba, *Um acerto de contas com o futuro*; González, "Brazil."
10. Carvalho and Catela, "31 de marzo de 1964 en Brasil."
11. *Veja*, 11 June 1997, reprinted in Carvalho and Catela, "31 de marzo de 1964 en Brasil," 228.
12. Admiral Mauro César Pereira, quoted in *Veja*, 12 April 1995, 37, reprinted in Carvalho and Catela, "31 de marzo de 1964 en Brasil," 227.
13. Carvalho and Catela, "31 de marzo de 1964 en Brasil," 228.
14. Ibid., 212.
15. *Veja*, 11 June 1997, reprinted in Carvalho and Catela, "31 de marzo de 1964 en Brasil," 228.
16. *Folha de São Paulo*, 1 April 2000, 1–7, reprinted in Carvalho and Catela, "31 de marzo de 1964 en Brasil," 228–29.
17. Andréa Michael, "General do Exército decide se calar sobre aniversário do golpe," *Folha de São Paulo*, 29 March 2007.
18. Scartezini, *Segredos de Médici*, 36.
19. Contreiras, *Militares*.
20. See d'Araujo et al., *Os anos de chumbo*; d'Araujo et al., *Visões do golpe*; www.ternuma.com.br.
21. Colonel Carlos Alberto Brilhante Ustra in March 1988, quoted in Gaspari, *A ditadura escancarada*, 30.

22. João Quartim de Moraes, Wilma Peres Costa, and Eliézer Rizzo de Oliveira, *A tutela militar*, reprinted in Martins Filho, "A memória militar sobre a tortura," 93.

23. "O silêncio conspira contra os militares," *Amazônia revista*, http://www.ama zonpress.com.br/.

24. Ustra, *Rompendo o silêncio*, 161.

25. Interview by the author with Aníbal Castro de Sousa, São Paulo, 29 March 2007. This is the first case brought in Brazil against a torturer in the nearly thirty years since the adoption of the Amnesty Law. It is a civil case and involves neither a prison term nor a fine. If successful, it will simply officially declare that Ustra tortured the Teles family. Many consider the trial to be the first challenge to the Amnesty Law and the opening of subsequent criminal and civil trials of authoritarian regime perpetrators. Larry Rohter, "Groups in Brazil Aim to Call Military Torturers to Account," *New York Times*, 16 March 2007, A12.

26. Carvalho and Catela, "31 de marzo de 1964 en Brasil," 238–42.

27. Ibid., 214.

28. Ibid., 229–33. As Elio Gaspari suggests, the award was intended to demonstrate acts of bravery. But in the 1975 *Almanaque do pessoal militar do Exército* (Army personnel almanac), six of the seven recipients had been involved in the Araguaia massacre. The seventh, Lt. Ailton Joaquim, was an infamous torturer.

29. Elizabeth Silveira e Silva, president of Torture Never Again, in ibid., 233.

30. Ibid., 235–38.

31. Feitlowitz, *A Lexicon of Terror*, 34.

32. "A otra cosa, Mariposa," *Página/12*, 29 March 1995.

33. Oltramari, "Esse maldito passado," 53.

34. General Sílvio da Silva, quoted in "O silêncio e a fala dos militares."

35. Colonel Antônio, General Sílvio da Silva's advisor, quoted in ibid.

36. "De eso no hablo," *Página/12*, 9 March 1995.

37. Colonel Hilton Paulo da Cunha Portela, alias "Dr. Joaquim," listed by eighteen prisoners as their torturer in *Brasil: Nunca mais*. Oltramari, "Esse maldito passado," 53.

38. "De ida y de vuelta," *Hoy*, 9–15 March 1998.

39. "Pinochet asegura que no tuvo nada que ver con las violaciones a los derechos humanos en su regimen," *Efe*, 7 September 1998.

40. Horacio Verbitsky, "Y Brown se quedó sólo," *Página/12*, 4 March 1995.

41. Simon Zwane, "Commissioner of Terror and Lies," *Cape Times*, 3 June 1998.

42. Foster, Haupt, and de Beer, *The Theatre of Violence*, 105–25.

43. Interview by author, Pretoria, South Africa, 15 May 2002.

44. Maureen Isaacson, "Has de Kock Lost His Nerve?" *Cape Argus*, 11 June 2000.

45. Constand Viljoen believed that the TRC would become a "witch hunt against the Afrikaner," and he therefore advocated collective, over individual, responsibility for apartheid. Boraine, *A Country Unmasked*, 45, 56–57.

46. John Daniel, "Editorial: The Truth and Reconciliation Commission," *Transformation* 42 (2000): 5–6.

47. Muñoz stated that while at cavalry school he had carried to the commander of military institutes the list of individuals kidnapped that day. The military has repeatedly denied the existence of any list of prisoners or disappeared. "El turno de el Olimpo," *Página/12*, 28 April 1995.

48. Valenzuela quoted in Soto, *Voces de muerte*, 2:8–9.

49. Quotes from González and Valenzuela reprinted in Soto, *Voces de muerte*, 1:61. Valenzuela deserted SIFA in 1984, fled Chile, and told his story to *El diario de Caracas*, 8–10 December 1984; reprinted in Soto, *Voces de muerte*, 1:59–73, 2:5–40. Valenzuela's confession appears almost as a death wish, not only because of the risks he ran in making it, but also because of his expressions of self-hatred: "I don't want my children to love me. I know that any day now they're going to kill me and I don't want them to suffer. . . . My children love their uncles more [than me]. When they arrive, my children run to them, hug them and greet them. When I arrive, sometimes they run [to me] and I don't pay much attention to them. I love them, but not the way I should. . . . I have a very strange way of loving people. I don't know how to explain it. . . . I prefer that they don't love me back. With my family I am very different [than I used to be]. I never see my parents [any more]." Soto, *Voces de muerte*, 2:34.

50. Samuel Enrique Fuenzalida Devia, testimony before the Comisión Nacional de Verdad y Reconciliación, Hamburg, Germany, 6–7 November 1990, Vicaría de la Solidaridad Archives.

51. Ibid.

52. For a discussion of the media broadcast of the Trial of the Generals, see Feld, *Del estrado a la pantalla*.

53. *Chile, Borreaux en Liberte*, directed by Tony Comiti and Emmanuel D'Arthuys (Paris: Tony Comiti and Canal M6, 1999).

54. Martins Filho, "A memória militar sobre a tortura," 97.

55. Nancy Gates Madsen, personal correspondence, 19 May 2003.

7. FICTION AND LIES

Epigraph from Cabral, *Xambioá*, 248.

1. Archdiocese of São Paulo, *Torture in Brazil*, 235–38.

2. Joana Almeida, quoted in Sônia Zaghetto, "Guerrilha ainda tortura lembranças," *O Liberal*, 5 June 2001.

3. "Relatório: Caravana dos familiares dos mortos e desaparecidos na guerrilha do Araguaia," Letter to the President of the Brazilian Bar Association (OAB), Dr. Joaquim Lemos Gomes de Souza, by Paulo César Fonteles de Lima from the OAB-PA, 15 January 1981, published in *Ordem dos Advogados do Brasil* 27/28 (September–December 1980, January–April 1981).

4. Most studies assume that PC do B militants gave up information on the movement in Araguaia after interrogation under torture, but debate exists over who gave that information up first and launched the military offensive. Carvalho, *O colonel rompe o silêncio*, 63–102.

5. Several books have attempted to recount the events leading up to and including the Araguaia massacre, deriving information from scant documents, few survivors among the militants and villagers who are willing to speak, and even fewer perpetrators' testimonies. See, in particular, Campos Filho, *Guerrilha do Araguaia*; Carvalho, *O colonel rompe o silêncio*; Gaspari, *A ditadura escancarada*, 399–464; and Morais and Silva, *Operação Araguaia*.

6. Goiamérico Felício, a paid guide for the military, described a soldier who took ears off the guerrillas he had killed and wore them in his belt as souvenirs. Euler Belém, "Diário de uma guerra suja" and "Memória desbloqueada," *Jornal Opção*, 14–20 September 1997, 12–14, reprinted in "O silêncio e a fala dos militares."

7. In 1995 army colonel Álvaro de Souza Pinheiro wrote in the U.S. magazine *Airpower* that the Brazilian Air Force (FAB) had used napalm in the fight against guerrillas in Araguaia. Luiz Maklouf Carvalho, "FAB usou napalm no Araguaia, diz Colonel," *Folha de São Paulo*, 20 April 1998.

8. Morais and Silva, *Operação Araguaia*, 596–99. Interviews by the author with Victoria Grabois and Danilo Carneiro, Rio de Janeiro, 31 March 2007.

9. "Sombras do presente," *Veja*, 13 October 1993, 26.

10. Rinaldo Gama, "O fim da guerra no fim do mundo," *Veja*, 13 October 1993, 17.

11. "As guerras secretas," *Veja*, 6 September 1978, 52–53.

12. Ibid. The lack of documentation confirmed some officials' view that the event never occurred. As General Nialdo stated, "Everything that the military does involves a report. This is the norm. In theory, whatever army activity, even if it falls outside normal events, is registered in a report." The army minister Carlos Tinoco denied the existence of documents. The armed-forces minister Benedito Leonel contended that the documents had been destroyed after ratification of the 1979 amnesty law, but later reported to the press that the documents had not been destroyed but turned over to Governor Itamar Franco. No one has recovered these documents. Etevaldo Dias and Ronaldo Brasiliense, "Exército atacou Igreja após vencer luta no Araguaia," *Jornal do Brasil*, 23 March 1992, reprinted in "O silêncio e a fala dos militares."

13. "A guerrilha do Araguaia," *Movimento*, 17 July 1978, reprinted in "O silêncio e a fala dos militares."

14. General Zenildo Lucena, quoted in "Sombras do presente," *Veja*, 13 October 1993, 26.

15. "Guerrilha do Araguaia," *Militante: O portal revolucionario brasileiro*, http://www.militantehp.hpg.ig.com.br/araguaia.htm.

16. Ari Cipola, "Guerrilheiros do Araguaia podem estar enterrados na sede do DNER," "Comissão procura restos mortais de vítimas da guerrilha do Araguaia," and "Coronel da reserva escreveu livro coplando detalhes da guerrilha," *Correio do Tocantins*, 10–16 May 1996, 1, 5, reprinted in "O silêncio e a fala dos militares."

17. "Especialistas argentinos concluem hoje relatório sobre ossadas do Araguaia." *O Estado de São Paulo*, 23 July 1996, http://www.estado.com.br/.

18. Cabral, *Xambioá*, 166.

19. Deputy Luiz Eduardo Greenhalgh (PT-SP), a lawyer for the families of sixty-eight disappeared guerrilla fighters for the PC do B, called for a reopening of the investigation into the role of the military police in counterinsurgency operations. Carlos Mendes, "Quintão vai falar sobre guerrilha do Araguaia," *O Estado de São Paulo*, 25 May 2001, http://www.estado.com.br/.

20. "Depoimento do Coronel Aviador Pedro Corrêa Cabral."

21. Cabral, *Xambioá*, 5.

22. "Depoimento do Coronel Aviador Pedro Corrêa Cabral."

23. Cabral, *Xambioá*, 166.

24. Ibid., 23.

25. Ibid., 182–83.

26. "Romance da memória," *Veja*, 13 October 1993, 27.

27. "Depoimento do Coronel Aviador Pedro Corrêa Cabral."

28. Gama, "O fim da guerra no fim do mundo," 19.

29. "Depoimento do Coronel Aviador Pedro Corrêa Cabral."

30. Cabral, *Xambioá*, 247.

31. Ibid., 251.

32. Ibid., 252.

33. "Depoimento do Coronel Aviador Pedro Corrêa Cabral."

34. Ibid.

35. Cabral, *Xambioá*, 6.

36. "Depoimento do Coronel Aviador Pedro Corrêa Cabral."

37. Ibid.

38. Ibid.

39. Ibid.

40. Gama, "O fim da guerra no fim do mundo," 16.

41. "Coronel falará de guerrilha na Câmara," *Jornal do Brasil*, 11 October 1993, 2.

42. "Depoimento do Coronel Aviador Pedro Corrêa Cabral."

43. Ibid.

44. Ibid.

45. Ibid.

46. Ibid.

47. Jarbas Passarinho, quoted in "O silêncio conspira contra os militares," www
.amazonpress.com.br. Antônio Bandeira, although never mentioned by
Cabral, and suffering from memory loss and severe depression, spoke out
through his daughter. Marcia Bandeira used the attention Cabral's confession brought to the Araguaia case to challenge the *Brasil: Nunca mais* indictment of her father as a torturer. Her father, she claimed, had never himself
tortured, but had known that lower-ranking officers had done so "to show
their loyalty." She wrote, "In his hours of clarity my father only repeats that
he does not regret anything that he did and he has nothing to hide." Juliana
De Mari and Vladimir Netto, "Uma história sem fim," *Veja*, 15 April 1998.
Bandeira concurs with Passarinho that her father formed part of the "moderate line" within the military along with his personal friend President Castello
Branco: "For him, the revolution was supposed to be for a short period of
time." "O silêncio conspira contra os militares." She did not, however, dissociate the hardliners in Araguaia from the military, but simply as advocates
of a different approach within the military.

48. Jarbas Passarinho, quoted in "O silêncio e a fala dos militares."

49. Ibid.

50. General Hugo Abreu, "Terceira campanha–a guerra suja," www.desaparec
idospoliticos.org.

51. "Hugo Abreu nega ter admitido torturas," *O Estado de São Paulo*, 13 September 1978, 15.

52. "O silêncio e a fala dos militares."

53. Ibid.

54. Ibid. The military denounced Napoleão, a Cabral supporter, as mentally
disturbed, an alcoholic, and allegedly institutionalized him with agents disguised as attending nurses. "Porões da ditadura (2): Internação para evitar
denúncias," *Diário Catarinense*, 30 July 1995, reprinted in ibid.

55. "Depoimento do Coronel Aviador Pedro Corrêa Cabral."

56. Carvalho, *O colonel rompe o silêncio*, 210. Another officer also wrote his testimonial account on Araguaia after the publication of Cabral's novel. See
Aluísio Madruga de Moura e Souza, *Guerrilha do Araguaia: revanchismo: a
grande verdade* (Brasília: 2002).

57. Tânia Monteiro e João Domingos, "Crítica ao MP é elogiada pela Aeronáutica
e pelo STM," *O Estado de São Paulo*, 25 August 2001, http://www.estado
.com.br/.

58. "O silêncio e a fala dos militares."

59. Ibid.

60. "O mistério da serra," *Veja*, 13 October 1993, 22.

61. Larry Rohter, "A Man of Many Names but One Legacy in the Amazon," *New York Times*, 11 September 2004, A4.

62. Amaury Ribeiro Jr., "Ex-guia mostra onde os corpos foram enterrados," "De Xambioá a Marabá, o roteiro dos cemetérios," and "Moradores contam prisão e a morte de guerrilheiros," *O Globo*, 2 May 1996, 8–10, reprinted in "A ocultação dos mortos."

63. Eumano Silva, "Guerrilha do Araguaia: 30 anos," published in *Correio Braziliense*, reprinted in www.vermelho.org.br.

64. Zaghetto, "Guerrilha ainda tortura lembranças."

65. "Romance da memória," 27.

66. "Relatório: Caravana dos familiares dos mortos e desaparecidos na guerrilha do Araguaia."

67. Tânia Monteiro, "Exército apura denúncias sobre ação no Araguaia," *O Estado de São Paulo*, 3 August 2001, http://www.estado.com.br/.

68. Paulinho Fontelles identifies the orientation of the PC do B cell in Araguaia as part of a struggle against the dictatorship and not an effort to impose a socialist revolution in the country.

69. "Tortura en julgamento," *Afinal*, 21 May 1985.

70. Mezarobba, *Um acerto de contas com o futuro*, 65–106. The indemnity law (no. 9.140) provided between $100,000 and $150,000 to families of the disappeared guerrilla fighters once the government officially recognized their deaths. Because of the success in finding bodies and the possibilities of locating more in different locales, the law had to be extended. See "Comissão estende prazo para famílias de desaparecidos," *O Estado de São Paulo*, 14 May 1996, http://www.estado.com.br/.

71. "Uma arma contra as forças ocultas," *Jornal da Tarde*, 12 September 1988.

72. Cecília Coimbra, in "Brazil 1995: Government to Pay Compensation to Families of Victims of the Repression Suffered During Dictatorship," *Notisur*, 29 September 1995, http://ssdc.ucsd.edu.

73. Coimbra, "Torture in Brazil," 90; Hamber, "Living with the Legacy of Impunity," 4–16.

74. C. S., quoted in Zaghetto, "Guerrilha ainda tortura lembranças."

75. Claudio Renato, "Famílias querem que escola lembre guerrilha," *O Estado de São Paulo*, 14 July 1996, http://www.estado.com.br/.

76. Silva, "Guerrilha do Araguaia: 30 anos."

77. Mobilization and pressure on the Brazilian government has also occurred outside the country's borders. In 1995 James Cavallaro, of Human Rights Watch/Americas, brought a case against the Brazilian government in the Inter-American Commission of Human Rights for failure to investigate the deaths of sixty-two guerrilla fighters in Araguaia. "Governo brasileiro será julgado sobre guerrilha," *O Estado de São Paulo*, 11 December 1995, http://

www.estado.com.br/; "Comissão procura ajuda em Marabá," *O Estado de São Paulo*, 3 July 1996, http://www.estado.com.br/.

78. Carlos Mendes, "Quintão deve falar sobre caso Araguaia," *O Estado de São Paulo*, 25 May 2001, http://www.estado.com.br/.

79. Wright Morris, lecture at Princeton University, 2 December 1971, quoted in Paul Fussell, *The Great War and Modern Memory*, 204; reprinted in John Gregory Dunne, "A Farewell to Arms," *New York Review of Books*, 13 June 2002, 4.

80. Feitlowitz, *A Lexicon of Terror*, 208–9.

81. Pauw, *Into the Heart of Darkness*, 172.

82. Ibid., 173.

83. Ibid., 172.

84. Ibid., 171.

85. Mario Kaiser, "Man in a Pink House . . . with Blood on His Hands," *Sunday Argus*, 4–5 April 1998.

86. Pauw, *Into the Heart of Darkness*, 177.

87. Paul van Vuuren, quoted in ibid., 176.

88. Ibid., 179.

89. Ibid.

90. Ibid., 179–80.

91. In contrast to this vision of Mamasela, one of the key members of the National Prosecuting Authority remarked, "I would never say that he was untrustworthy," arguing instead that Mamasela got into trouble by talking too much instead of simply, and only, providing evidence and nothing else. Interview by author, 17 May 2002, Pretoria, South Africa.

92. "Depoimento do Coronel Aviador Pedro Corrêa Cabral."

93. Kaiser, "Man in a Pink House . . . with Blood on His Hands."

94. In a performance piece about truth, Laurie Beth Clark asks individuals to tell a true story about her past in their own way. As they do, they embellish the story with elements of their own past or with invented details, making the story theirs and not hers. Laurie Beth Clark, "Yahrzeit," performance presented at the Association for Theatre in Higher Education annual conference, Chicago, Illinois, 2–5 August 2001.

95. *South Africa's Human Spirit* (CD-ROM set), vol. 4 (*Portraits of Truth*), track 3 ("This Devil's Belly").

96. Pauw, *Into the Heart of Darkness*, 178.

97. Ibid., 174.

98. *South Africa's Human Spirit*, vol. 4 (*Portraits of Truth*), track 1 ("Intriguing Characters").

99. John Yeld, "Sorry, Pebco Three Killer Mamasela Tells Widows," *Cape Argus*, 12 March 1998.

100. Pauw, *Into the Heart of Darkness*, 171.

101. Ibid., 180. Pauw further stated that Mamasela asked him for money (R100,000) for the interview. Pauw persuaded him to speak without payment by suggesting that the publicity around the book might put him in the limelight and lead to offers from foreign broadcasters. Pauw may have, inadvertently, given Mamasela more reason to embellish his story to get those deals.

102. *South Africa's Human Spirit*, vol. 4 (*Portraits of Truth*), track 4 ("Some Kind of Power").

103. Ibid.

104. Futaba, "Forced to Confess." For a discussion of the truth behind confessions, see also Brooks, *Troubling Confessions*.

105. Ken Daniels, "Mamasela Struck a Deal to Avoid Prosecution, TRC Told," *South African Press Association*, 10 March 1998.

106. Yeld, "Sorry, Pebco Three Killer Mamasela Tells Widows."

107. Joe Diamini, "Mamasela Delayed Liberation," *City Press*, 8–9 June 1996.

108. Pauw, *Into the Heart of Darkness*, 171.

109. Ibid., 180.

110. *South Africa's Human Spirit*, vol. 4 (*Portraits of Truth*), track 4 ("Some Kind of Power").

111. Zola Ntutu quoted in ibid.

112. Yeld, "Sorry, Pebco Three Killer Mamasela Tells Widows."

113. Kaiser, "Man in a Pink House . . . with Blood on His Hands."

114. *South Africa's Human Spirit*, vol. 4 (*Portraits of Truth*), track 5 ("A Black Afrikaner").

115. Scott, *Domination and the Arts of Resistance*.

116. *South Africa's Human Spirit*, vol. 4 (*Portraits of Truth*), track 5 ("A Black Afrikaner").

117. Collins, "Fixing the Past."

8. AMNESIA

Epigraph from Truth and Reconciliation Commission, Amnesty Hearing for Jeffrey T. Benzien, Cape Town, South Africa, 14 July 1997, 41–79 (transcript).

1. For artwork, see Sue Williamson's "Can't Forget, Can't Remember," in *Sue Williamson: Selected Work* (Cape Town: Double Storey Books, 2003). A fictional character modeled after Benzien is featured in Gillian Slovo's novel *Red Dust* (London: Virago Press, 2000). For a media study, see the art historian Rory Bester's "At the Edges of Apartheid Memory," paper presented at the TRC: Commissioning the Past conference, Johannesburg, South Africa, 11–14 June, 1999. For cartoons, see Wilhelm Verwoerd and Mahlubi "Chief" Mabizela's *Truths Drawn in Jest* (Cape Town: David Philip Publishers, 2000),

32, 87, 99, 136. For poetry, see Daniel P. Kunene, "Benzini?" *Communique* (spring 2002): 26. For book covers, see Else Schreiner, *Time Stretching Fear: The Detention and Solitary Confinement of 14 Anti-Apartheid Trialists, 1987–1991* (Cape Town: Robben Island Museum, 2000); and Terry Bell in collaboration with Dumisa Buhle Ntsebeza, *Unfinished Business: South Africa Apartheid and Truth* (Muizenberg, South Africa: Red Works, 2001). The South African Broadcasting Corporation's weekly television program about the TRC, *Special Report*, also featured Benzien in its opening credits.

2. Truth and Reconciliation Commission, Amnesty Hearing for Jeffrey T. Benzien, Cape Town, South Africa, 14 July 1997, 37 (transcript).

3. Both Yengeni and Ashley Forbes brought out, moreover, that when they were victims, they were unclothed, which added to the trauma and humiliation. As Forbes stated, "My pants were pulled towards my ankles and . . . thereafter the wet bag was pulled over my head and [I was] suffocated." Ibid., 47.

4. Ibid., 34.

5. Ibid., 45.

6. Ibid., 115.

7. Roger Friedman and Benny Gool, "Yengeni Reduces His Old Police Torturer to Tears," *Cape Times*, 15 July 1997.

8. Truth and Reconciliation Commission, Amnesty Hearing for Geoffrey [*sic*] Benzien, Cape Town, South Africa, 20 October 1997, 15 (transcript).

9. Ken Vernon, "I Forgive Torture Cop, Says Forbes," *Sunday Times*, 1 October 1998.

10. Truth and Reconciliation Commission, Amnesty Hearing for Jeffrey T. Benzien, Cape Town, South Africa, 14 July 1997, 34–35 (transcript).

11. Sandile Dikeni, "Didn't I Say I'm Not Gonna Write This No More . . ." *Cape Times*, 21 July 1997.

12. Gaye Davis, "Gaping Holes in Tormentor's Testimony," *Weekly Mail and Guardian*, 18 July 1997.

13. Truth and Reconciliation Commission, Amnesty Hearing for Jeffrey T. Benzien, Cape Town, South Africa, 14 July 1997, 11 (transcript). Benzien denied that he had received an order to kill the MK leader Ashley Kriel. He contended that he had killed Kriel in self-defense. But forensic and circumstantial evidence did not add up. Kriel could not have concealed a gun while opening the door to his safe house, as Benzien claimed. It also seemed highly unlikely that Kriel, who was in hiding, would have opened the door to Benzien posing as a utilities repairman. Benzien could not explain how Kriel's blood would have ended up on kitchen walls and in the bathroom, when his version of the story placed events entirely at the back of the house. Further contradicting his self-defense claim was the fact that Benzien had scrawled "one down, many to go" on a poster for Kriel's funeral hanging in the police

station. Benzien explained, "I had a reputation to live up to when interrogating terrorists, freedom fighters. I admit that it was surely in very bad taste to have it [the poster] up there, but in a certain sense it also helped with my interrogation to instill fear into the persons who I interrogated." Ibid., 31.

14. Ibid., 34.

15. Ibid.

16. Ibid., 42.

17. Apartheid police commander, interview by author, Durbanville, South Africa, 5 March 2002.

18. Sarah Maria Kotzé, Truth and Reconciliation Commission, Amnesty Hearing for Geoffrey [sic] Benzien, Cape Town, South Africa, 21 October 1997, 498 (transcript).

19. Truth and Reconciliation Commission, Amnesty Hearing for Jeffrey T. Benzien, Cape Town, South Africa, 14 July 1997, 120 (transcript).

20. Sarah Maria Kotzé testified, "Both PTSD and major depression impairs [sic] a person's or patient's memory and it became evident during therapy that Mr. Benzien has blocked out large areas of experience." Truth and Reconciliation Commission, Amnesty Hearing for Geoffrey [sic] Benzien, Cape Town, South Africa, 21 October 1997, 497–98 (transcript). The lawyer for Benzien's former victims, Michael Donen, questioned whether someone with a master's degree in psychology from the University of Stellenbosch, someone who had worked as an occupational psychologist, could effectively diagnose PTSD. He further questioned the diagnosis since PTSD requires "intense fear, helplessness or horror" and pointed out that "people who suffer from post-traumatic stress disorder are victims, they are not perpetrators who can stop the event at any time." Ibid., 500, 502.

21. Andrina Forbes-Connolly, quoted in Roger Friedman, "Picketers Blast Benzien Amnesty," Cape Times, 23 February 1999.

22. Truth and Reconciliation Commission, Amnesty Hearing for Jeffrey T. Benzien, Cape Town, South Africa, 15 July 1997, 59 (transcript).

23. R. Castell (Franschhoek), letter to the editor, "In Defense of Benzien," Cape Times, 18 July 1997.

24. David Yutar and Beauregard Tromp, "The Biko, Benzien Amnesty Poser," Cape Argus, 22 February 1999.

25. Oltramari, "Esse maldito passado," 51.

26. Ibid., 52.

27. Ibid.

28. South Africa's Human Spirit (CD-ROM set), vol. 3 (Worlds of License), disc 1, track 4 ("Bits and Pieces"). Translation by Kallie Blom.

29. Victoria Ginzberg, "Sin impunidad ni obediencia debida," Página/12, 2 October 1999.

30. "No sé si soy Astiz," *Página/12*, 20 January 1998.

31. Oltramari, "Esse maldito passado," 52.

32. Dunne, "A Farewell to Arms," 7.

33. Arnaldo Pampillon, "Un repudio a Etchecolatz," *Página/12*, 11 November 1999.

34. Interview by author, Cape Town, South Africa, 8 March 2002.

35. Interview by author, Cape Town, South Africa, 7 February 2002.

36. Interview by author, Cape Town, South Africa, 2 May 2002.

37. "Anger as Police Torturer Benzien Gets Amnesty," *Star*, 18 February 1999.

38. Jelin, *State Repression and the Labors of Memory*, 17. *Los trabajos de memoria*, 28.

9. BETRAYAL

Epigraph from "De Klerk Ordered Attack on Transkei, De Kock Trial Told," *South African Press Association*, 18 September 1996.

1. De Kock claimed he had clubbed Maponya with the spade only after he had already been shot. "It was standard practice to make sure a person was dead after they were killed." "De Kock Ordered the Murder," *Cape Times*, 16 July 1999. On hearing this defense of his actions, a *New York Times* journalist stated, "Mr. de Kock . . . has a way of making brutality sound like regulation." Suzanne Daley, "South Africa Confronts Brutalities of One Man," *New York Times*, 19 July 1999.

2. Almond Nofemela, interview by author, Pretoria, South Africa, 24 June 2002.

3. De Kock, *A Long Night's Damage*, 189.

4. Ibid., 189.

5. Craig Williamson, quoted in Pauw, *Into the Heart of Darkness*, 137.

6. Dirk Coetzee, interview by author, Johannesburg, South Africa, 8 May 2002.

7. Pauw, *Into the Heart of Darkness*, 143.

8. Jan d'Oliveira, interview by author, Pretoria, South Africa, 17 May 2002.

9. De Kock, *A Long Night's Damage*, 270.

10. Pauw, *Into the Heart of Darkness*, 142.

11. "De Kock 'Is Considering Suicide,'" *Cape Times*, 10 October 1996.

12. "De Kock Concerned He Won't Get Fair Hearing from Truth Commission," *Cape Argus*, 20 September 1996. In addition to implicating the two former apartheid presidents, de Kock implicated the former foreign minister, police ministers, police commissioners, intelligence and security-branch directors, police generals, and heads of Vlakplaas.

13. Jann Turner, "Eugene: From Apocalypse Now," *Mail and Guardian*, 28 May 1999.

14. *South Africa's Human Spirit* (CD-ROM set), vol. 3 (*Worlds of Licence*), disc 2, track 5 ("A Thousand Shades of Grey"). Translation by Johannes Oosthuizen.

15. De Kock, *A Long Night's Damage*, 277. De Kock went on to say that he did not

believe that de Klerk had promoted violence. "I think that, before he became President, he simply didn't want to face the fact that covert activity was one of the bulwarks of his party's power. Then, when he became President, he did little to stamp it out, even when its presence was shoved in his face" (ibid., 282).

16. Ibid., 36.

17. "De Kock Says He Does Not Know How Many People He Killed," *South African Press Association*, 20 September 1996.

18. De Kock, *A Long Night's Damage*, 249–50.

19. Darren Schuettler, "Eugene de Kock's Last Desperate Attempt to Be Freed from His Crimes," *Star*, 15 June 1999.

20. Peter Dickson, "A Word, a Nudge, a Drink, a Gun . . . Then Death," *Cape Argus*, 25 April 1999.

21. Fana Peete, "De Kock Tells How Vlakplas Functioned," *Star*, 25 May 1999.

22. De Kock, quoted in "De Kock Tells of Explosions," *Cape Times*, 30 July 1998.

23. On this issue, he compared himself with the former Vlakplaas commander Dirk Coetzee, who referred to his experiences at Vlakplaas as being "in the heart of the whore" (*A Long Night's Damage*, 40). For de Kock, "Coetzee was the kind of man who visits a brothel but stays in the parlour: he always had others do his dirty work for him. Furthermore, compared with me, he hadn't visited all that often. I doubt whether the whore would have recognised Coetzee in the street" (40). One of de Kock's former friends described him as "a good leader. He could lead men. Men believed in Eugene de Kock like they believed in their Bible, even more" (Riaan Stander, quoted in Pauw, *Into the Heart of Darkness*, 36).

24. Roger Friedman, "There Was No Integrity at Top," *Cape Times*, 2 October 1997.

25. Ibid.

26. Ibid.

27. David Beresford, "De Kock Spews Bile on PW," *Mail and Guardian*, 5–11 June 1998.

28. Pauw, *Into the Heart of Darkness*, 144.

29. "I Am Not Here to Buy Favours, Says de Kock," *Star*, 26 May 1999. One anonymous informer who provided legal defense for Security Branch perpetrators explained to me de Kock's fallacious reasoning. "In his mind," suggested the informant, "the medals are linked directly with the acts." But this informant explained the process of filters and codes by which lower-level officers passed information to their superiors, preventing the superiors from fully understanding the implications of the orders and the actions. He knew firsthand about how reports became sanitized before they went to the top office. "So when they say they didn't know, it was because someone slightly modified the information so that they wouldn't know." Interview by author, Pretoria, South Africa, 15 May 2002.

30. David Beresford, "Coetzee's 'Fairy Tales,'" *Mail and Guardian*, 11–17 September 1998.

31. Jonny Steinberg, "Coetzee's Application Seems on Rocky Ground," *Business Day*, 30 September 1998.

32. "Nothing New Says de Klerk," *Cape Times*, 19 September 1996.

33. Brian Stuart, "De Kock Opinions, Not Facts—NP," *Citizen*, 20 September 1996.

34. Top official at National Prosecuting Authority, interview by author, Pretoria, South Africa, 17 May 2002. The official added that de Kock could be trusted to sticking to the truth: "He said he would take his medicine and he took it like a man."

35. "Wouter Mentz at the TRC," interview by Antjie Samuels, SABC radio archives, no. T 97/392, 21 March 1997, AccNo 105215/Record BC: 19970321.

36. De Kock, *A Long Night's Damage*, 279–80.

37. Themba Molefe, "Programme Portrays de Kock as 'Hero,'" *Sowetan*, 28 October 1996.

38. Daley, "South Africa Confronts Brutalities of One Man."

39. Ibid.

40. Bird and Garda, "Reporting the Truth Commission," 340–41.

41. Stephané Bothma, "There Is Always a Time for the Truth, Court Hears," *Business Day*, 20 September 1996.

42. Pauw, *Into the Heart of Darkness*, 101.

43. "Mother of ANC Lawyer Murdered by de Kock Has Mixed Feelings," *South African Press Association*, 30 October 1996.

44. Pauw, *Into the Heart of Darkness*, 51, 56.

45. Ibid., 31.

46. Ibid. Others suggest that he joined the South African Defense Force and left only when he was lured into Koevoet to fight counterinsurgency wars.

47. Stefaans Brummer, "A Twinkle of Humour in a Most Serious Trial," *Mail and Guardian*, 21–27 July 1996.

48. De Kock, *A Long Night's Damage*, 51.

49. He added, "If we look at information I have received about the activities of the Pretoria security police [which commanded the Northern Transvaal Security Branch], we may be far back in the line. There were people who were not necessarily more effective in killing people, but maybe more cold-blooded or even sick." Pauw, *Into the Heart of Darkness*, 188.

50. "De Kock Says He Does Not Know How Many People He Killed," *South African Press Association*, 20 September 1996.

51. Maureen Isaacson, "Has de Kock Lost His Nerve?" *Cape Argus*, 11 June 2000. The day before, Berger had driven de Kock to storm out of the session. Some of the audience members interpreted de Kock's histrionics as an attempt to

mask his guilt, but others viewed him as frustrated at his inability to convince his audience of his willingness to cooperate.

52. Pauw, *Into the Heart of Darkness*.

53. De Kock, *A Long Night's Damage*, 45.

54. Ibid., 98.

55. Paul Erasmus, quoted in Pauw, *Into the Heart of Darkness*, 35.

56. Martin Ntsoelengoe, "Give Us de Kock's Blood Money!" *City Press*, 3 November 1996.

57. Pauw, *Into the Heart of Darkness*, 43.

58. Ibid., 41.

59. Ibid., 59.

60. Ibid., 54.

61. Ibid.

62. "De Kock Concerned He Won't Get Fair Hearing from Truth Commission," *Cape Argus*, 20 September 1996.

63. Pauw, *Into the Heart of Darkness*, 147.

64. Defense lawyer, interview by author, Pretoria, South Africa, 15 May 2002. An Afrikaans-speaking physician I met in the Pretoria Central Prison's parking lot echoed the pent-up emotions that described de Kock's mental state, concluding, "He'll just kill himself; I feel sorry for him."

65. De Kock's prison social worker, interview by author, Pretoria Central Prison, Pretoria, South Africa, 24 June 2002.

66. Julian Rademeyer, "De Kock Fearful of His Place in New SA," *Cape Times*, 8 June 2000.

67. Schuettler, "Eugene de Kock's Last Desperate Attempt to Be Freed from His Crimes."

68. De Kock, *A Long Night's Damage*, 54, 97.

69. " 'Prime Evil' Apologizes for Deaths," *Cape Argus*, 25 May 1999.

70. Pauw, *Into the Heart of Darkness*, 31.

71. "This Is How God Is Punishing Me . . . ," *Cape Argus*, 9 October 1996.

72. Stephané Bothma, "Truth Commission Is Told ANC Offered De Kock Job," *Business Day*, 31 July 1998.

73. De Kock stated that making these royalties available to the victims would "be a small gesture towards reconciliation. It is minimal but it is all I can do at this stage. . . . The money should be put into a trust fund and the families on both sides of the spectrum should benefit from the fund, especially the youth." Truth and Reconciliation Commission, Amnesty Hearings, Port Elizabeth, South Africa, 1 October 1997 (transcript).

74. Rademeyer, "De Kock Fearful of His Place in New SA."

75. The scholars Heribert and Kanya Adam distinguish these apartheid assassins from others who "tried to save their skins by applying for amnesty or turning

state witness without recognising the moral turpitude of their actions." It is difficult to know who they might put in that category since so many used the language of "remorse," without successfully convincing their victims of the sincerity of their words. Adam and Adam, "The Politics of Memory in Divided Societies," 43.

76. Rademeyer, "De Kock Fearful of His Place in New SA."

77. Pauw, *Into the Heart of Darkness*, 67.

78. "De Kock Tells of Ambush against Four Suspected ANC members," *South African Press Association*, 19 September 1996.

79. "De Kock Concerned He Won't Get Fair Hearing from Truth Commission," *Cape Argus*, 20 September 1996.

80. Pauw, *Into the Heart of Darkness*, 124.

81. Bothma, "Truth Commission Is Told ANC Offered De Kock Job."

82. "De Kock praises former ANC officer," *Sowetan*, 16 February 2000.

83. "If I Was Black I Would Have Supported the Freedom Struggle," *Star*, 16 February 2000.

84. Roger Friedman, "Apology 'Came from the Heart,'" *Cape Times*, 2 October 1997.

85. Dickson, "A Word, a Nudge, a Drink, a Gun . . . Then Death."

86. Widow of a Cradock Four activist, interview by author, Cape Town, South Africa, 5 February 2002.

87. Dorothy Mguduka, *Special Report on the Truth and Reconciliation Commission*, SABC-TV, 22 March 1998.

88. Isaacson, "Has De Kock Lost His Nerve?"

89. Pearl Faku, quoted in Friedman, "Apology 'Came from the Heart.'"

90. Gobodo-Madikizela, "Eugene de Kock, and Symbols of Blood and Dirt," 107.

91. *Special Report on the Truth and Reconciliation Commission*, SABC-TV, 22 March 1998.

92. Turner, "Eugene."

93. The prosecuting attorney Anton Ackerman stated, "You actually suffer from megalomania. All the operations which you participated in as a policeman were successful, and the ones you did not take part in were flops." Bothma, "There Is Always a Time for the Truth, Court Hears."

94. Prison guard, interview by author, Pretoria Central Prison, Pretoria, South Africa, 24 June 2002.

95. Gobodo-Madikizela, *A Human Being Died that Night*.

96. Nofemela was convinced that de Kock had tried to kill him before he went to jail. He had become suspicious when de Kock invited him to a party, which he had never done before. He feels certain that de Kock had planned to poison him at that party. De Kock made at least two attempts to murder Coetzee, a man he referred to as "a traitor." In the first attempt de Kock enlisted the help of Ulster Unionists in monitoring Coetzee's movements

and paid R100,000 to "take out" Coetzee. De Kock, *A Long Night's Damage*, 111. The second, more tragic attempt involved sending a mail bomb to Coetzee, who was in exile. Coetzee refused to open it, suspecting foul play, and returned it to the sender. It ended up in the hands of Bheki Mlangeni, the young civil-rights lawyer the ANC had assigned to Coetzee. Mlangeni put on the earphones, turned on the cassette player that was in the package, and was blown to pieces.

97. Brood van Heerden, quoted in Pauw, *Into the Heart of Darkness*, 141.

98. Jacques Pauw, quoted in Schuettler, "Eugene De Kock's Last Desperate Attempt to Be Freed from His Crimes."

99. Pauw, quoted in Tina Rosenberg, "Recovering from Apartheid," *New Yorker*, 18 November 1996, 95.

100. Isaacson, "Has De Kock Lost His Nerve?"; Rademeyer, "De Kock Fearful of His Place in New SA."

101. Pauw, *Into the Heart of Darkness*, 51.

102. Russel Molefe, "De Kock: Legacy of Pain," *Sowetan*, 2 September, 1996.

103. Marco Granelli, "He'll Serve Time Despite Amnesty," *Pretoria News*, 31 October 1996.

104. Roger Friedman, "Countdown to Amnesty Cut-off," *Cape Times*, 2 September 1996. By telling the truth, de Kock forced some individuals to apply for amnesty. The police commissioner Johan van der Merwe, for example, was compelled to admit to having ordered assassinations. He stated that he had ordered a raid into Lesotho in which de Kock was involved and which killed eight ANC members and three Lesotho nationals. He defended that action by stating that at the time the government policy was that "terrorists should be fought and combated wherever they are. Actions were supposed to be covert and not traceable to the government. They [the government] did not want the rest of the world to think South Africa was a police state." He added, "I personally signed a written recommendation that the members involved in the raid should be awarded the South Africa Police medal for bravery." "I Ordered Raid on ANC, Says van der Merwe," *Star*, 29 February 2000.

105. Prosecuting attorney, interview by author, Pretoria, South Africa, 17 May 2002.

106. TRC commissioner, interview by author, Cape Town, South Africa, 3 July 2002.

107. Bizos, *No One to Blame?* 236.

108. Claudio Renato, interview in *O Estado de São Paulo*, 23 December 1996, reprinted in Gaspari, *A ditadura escancarada*, 23.

109. This led to the quote, cited in chapter 5 of this volume, "Although it is painful to admit it, this is the only army in the world that, when the time comes, the generals have failed to take responsibility for the orders they gave." "Ex Agente acusa ejército no reconocer responsabilidad abusos," *Efe*, 5 April 1999.

110. Dirk Coetzee resembles de Kock in some, but not all, ways. Like de Kock, he fought in Rhodesia and subsequently became the commander of Vlakplaas. Under his command, Vlakplaas carried out high-profile murders, the most notable being that of Durban civil-rights attorney Griffiths Mxenge. The culture of impunity in Vlakplaas led Coetzee, like de Kock and others, to steal and smuggle goods for personal gain. Coetzee also, like de Kock, described himself as antiracist, fiercely loyal to his men, and sold out by his superiors. Coetzee, however, faced more difficulties within the security forces than de Kock, due to insubordination and misconduct. During the apartheid era, he was demoted to the narcotics bureau and brought up on seven charges of misconduct before he applied for a medical leave for diabetes. Coetzee rightly doubted that the security forces would come to his defense, given his background, and took the offensive with his betrayal confession.

111. Muñoz (also known as "El Encapuchado del Estadio Nacional"), in testimony to the Vicaría de Solidaridad, reprinted in Soto, *Voces de muerte*, 2:22.

112. Coetzee, quoted in Rosenberg, "Recovering from Apartheid," 88.

113. "La confesión de Schneider, 'El Barba,'" *Rocinante*, November 2002, 28–30.

114. Bizos, *No One to Blame?* 235.

115. *South Africa's Human Spirit*, vol. 3 (*Worlds of Licence*), disc 1, track 6 ("Raking through the Rubble").

116. Verbitsky, *El vuelo*, 158.

117. Ibid., 171, 172.

118. Ibid., 167.

119. Feitlowitz, *A Lexicon of Terror*, 203.

120. Verbitsky, *El vuelo*, 173.

121. Ibid., 170–71.

122. Ibid., 168.

123. Ibid., 170.

124. "Ex agente acusa ejército no reconocer responsabilidad abusos," *Efe*, 5 April 1999.

125. Verbitsky, *El vuelo*, 162.

126. Ibid., 170; also in "Grabación de Pernías y Rolón," *Ámbito Financiero*, 26 October 1994, 16.

127. Asamblea Permanente por los Derechos Humanos, "Cartas," *Página/12*, 3 February 1994.

128. Jorge Grecco, *Clarín*, 21 October 21, 1994, 3.

129. "Bittel los defiende, pero sin entusiasmo," *Clarín*, 21 October 1994, 2.

130. Ernesto Tenembaum, "A veces torturar está bien," *Página/12*, 2 January 1994, 2.

131. "La cuñada de Molina Pico y los dos torturadores," *Página/12*, 8 January 1994, 10.

132. "Marinos con mar de fondo," *Página/12*, 22 October 1994, 5.

133. "Alsogaray no apoya la tortura," *Página/12*, 29 October 1994, 4–5.

134. *Special Report on the Truth and Reconciliation Commission*, SABC-TV, 21 July 1996.

135. Eduardo Pavlovsky, "Opinión: El Sr. Galíndez," *Página/12*, 28 October 1994.

CONCLUSION

Epigraph from Dorfman, *Death and the Maiden*, 55.

1. Holmes, "Gag Rules or the Politics of Omission," 203, 204.

2. Dahl, *Polyarchy*.

3. McCoy, *A Question of Torture*, 110.

4. McCoy includes examples from the *Washington Post, Los Angeles Times, Wall Street Journal, Newsweek*, and PBS's *McLaughlin Group* as part of the "media swagger" in favor of torture. McCoy, *A Question of Torture*, 110–11. Memos discussing the use of torture in the war on terror, which were prepared for the George W. Bush administration, have been reproduced in Danner, *Torture and Truth*, 78–214. The ticking-bomb defense from self-identified liberals include Alan M. Dershowitz's *Why Terrorism Works* and Michael Levin's "The Case for Torture," which refers to the use of torture in some situations as "morally mandatory." Michael Ignatieff makes a similar, but more nuanced argument, in "Lesser Evils."

5. Whitney, Introduction, vii.

6. McCoy, *A Question of Torture*, 150, 179, 180.

7. Danner, *Torture and Truth*, 22–23.

8. Sontag, "Regarding the Torture of Others."

9. See, for example, Mourad Benchellali's testimony about his experiences in the Guantánamo Bay prison, in a book written with Antoine Audouard and excerpted as "Detainees in Despair," *New York Times*, 14 June 2006, A23.

10. Charles Babington, "Lawmakers Are Stunned," *Washington Post*, 13 May 2004, A1.

11. Sontag, "Regarding the Torture of Others."

12. McCoy, *A Question of Torture*, 186.

13. "McCain's Effort Saves Nation's Soul: Anti-torture Measure Wins Because It Keeps America on Right Side Legally," *Buffalo News*, 21 December 2005, A8.

14. Danner, *Torture and Truth*, 27.

15. Sontag, "Regarding the Torture of Others."

16. Quoted in ibid.

17. Deborah Solomon, "Questions for Trent Lott," *New York Times Magazine*, 20 June 2004, 15, quoted in McCoy, *A Question of Torture*, 153.

18. McCoy, *A Question of Torture*, 150.

19. David E. Sanger and Jim Rutenberg, "Bush and Blair Concede Errors, but Defend War," *New York Times*, 26 May 2006, A12.

20. Jane Mayer, "Outsourcing Torture: The Secret History of America's 'Extraordinary Rendition' Program," *New Yorker*, 14 February 2005, 106.

21. Eric Schmitt, "Pentagon Rethinking Manual with Interrogation Methods," *New York Times*, 14 June 2006, A19.

22. Memorandum Opinion for the Deputy Attorney General, 30 December 2004, www.usdoj.gov/.

23. Alfred McCoy reviews the career trajectory of these individuals, including those of Alberto Gonzales, president's counsel, who famously referred to the Geneva Convention's limitations on interrogations as "obsolete" and "quaint"; Jay Bybee, assistant attorney general, who prepared the memos for Gonzales, thus creating the legal cover for torture in Iraq and elsewhere; and John Yoo, the justice-department lawyer who drafted the notion of the "unitary executive," which argued for a secret emergency constitution that would give the president unlimited powers in the "war on terror." McCoy, *A Question of Torture*, 160–61.

24. "Veto? Who Needs a Veto?" *New York Times*, 5 May 2006, A22.

25. McCoy, *A Question of Torture*, 188–209.

26. Danner, *Torture and Truth*, 9.

27. Art, *The Politics of the Nazi Past in Germany and Austria*, 14.

28. Lelyveld, "Interrogating Ourselves," 39.

29. Danner, *Torture and Truth*, xiv.

30. Sontag, "Regarding the Torture of Others."

31. Downs, "Racial Incitement Law and Policy in the United States," 117–18.

32. Ibid., 128.

Ackerman, Bruce. "Why Dialogue?" *Journal of Philosophy* 86, no. 1 (January 1989): 5–22.

Acuña, Carlos H., and Catarina Smulovitz. "Ni olvido, ni perdón: Derechos humanos y tensiones cívico-militares en la transición Argentina." *Documento CEDES*, no. 69. Buenos Aires: CEDES, 1991.

Adam, Heribert, and Kanya Adam. "The Politics of Memory in Divided Societies." In *After the TRC: Reflections on Truth and Reconciliation in South Africa*, edited by Wilmot James and Linda van de Vijver, 32–47. Athens: Ohio University Press, 2000.

Adorno, T. W., Else Frenkel-Brunswik, Daniel J. Levinson, and R. Nevitt Sanford, eds. *The Authoritarian Personality*. New York: Harper and Brothers, 1950.

Almeida, Criméia Alice S. de, ed. *História da guerrilha do Araguaia*. Eremias Delizoicov Centro de Documentação. http://www.desaparecidospoliticos.org.br/.

Altemeyer, Bob. *Enemies of Freedom: Understanding Right-Wing Authoritarianism*. San Francisco: Jossey-Bass, 1988.

Arce, Luz. *El infierno*. Santiago: Planeta, 1993.

Archdiocese of São Paulo. *Torture in Brazil: A Shocking Report on the Pervasive Use of Torture by Brazilian Military Governments, 1964–1979*. Edited by Joan Dassin. Translated by Jaime Wright. New York: Vintage Books, 1986. Originally published as *Brasil: Nunca mais* (Petrópolis: Editora Vozes, 1985).

Art, David. *The Politics of the Nazi Past in Germany and Austria*. Cambridge: Cambridge University Press, 2006.

Auslander, Philip. "Liveness: Performance and the Anxiety of Simulation." In

Performance and Cultural Politics, edited by Elin Diamond, 196–213. London: Routledge, 1996.

——. *Liveness: Performance in a Mediatized Culture*. London: Routledge, 1999.

Austin, J. L. *How to Do Things with Words*. Cambridge, Mass.: Harvard University Press, 1962.

Behr, Mark. "Living in the Fault Lines." *Security Dialogue* 28, no. 1 (1997): 115–19.

Benhabib, Seyla. "Toward a Deliberative Model of Democratic Legitimacy." In *Democracy and Difference: Contesting the Boundaries of the Political*, edited by Seyla Benhabib, 67–94. Princeton, N.J.: Princeton University Press, 1996.

Bennett, Susan. *Theatre Audiences: A Theory of Production and Reception*. London: Routledge, 1997.

Beverley, John. "The Real Thing." In *The Real Thing: Testimonial Discourse and Latin America*, edited by Georg M. Gugelberger, 266–86. Durham, N.C.: Duke University Press, 1996.

Bird, Edward, and Zureida Garda. "Reporting the Truth Commission: Analysis of Media Coverage of the Truth and Reconciliation Commission of South Africa." *Gazette* 59, nos. 4–5 (1997): 331–43.

Bizos, George. *No One to Blame? In Pursuit of Justice in South Africa*. Cape Town: David Philip Publishers, 1998.

Blixen, Samuel. "Para que no haya mas Scilingos." *Brecha*, no. 549 (7 June 1996). http://www.brecha.com.uy/.

Boal, Augusto. "The Theatre as Discourse." In *The Twentieth-Century Performance Reader*, edited by Michael Huxley and Noel Witts, 85–98. New York: Routledge, 1996.

Boraine, Alex. *A Country Unmasked: Inside South Africa's Truth and Reconciliation Commission*. New York: Oxford University Press, 2000.

Branch, Taylor, and Eugene M. Propper. *Labyrinth*. New York: Viking Press, 1982.

Brooks, Peter. *Troubling Confessions: Speaking Guilt in Law and Literature*. Chicago: University of Chicago Press, 2001.

Brysk, Alison. *The Politics of Human Rights in Argentina: Protest, Change, and Democratization*. Stanford, Calif.: Stanford University Press, 1994.

Burke, Kenneth. *A Grammar of Motives*. New York: Prentice-Hall, 1952.

Cabral, Pedro Corrêa. *Xambioá: Guerrilha do Araguaia*. Rio de Janeiro: Editora Record, 1993.

Campos Filho, Romualdo Pessoa. *Guerrilha do Araguaia: a esquerda em armas*. Goiânia: Editora UFG, 1997.

Carlson, Marvin. *Performance: A Critical Introduction*. London: Routledge, 1996.

Carvalho, Alessandra, and Ludmila da Silva Catela. "31 de marzo de 1964 en Brasil: Memórias deshilachadas." In *Las conmemoraciones: Las disputas en las fechas "in-felices,"* edited by Elizabeth Jelin, 195–242. Madrid: Siglo Veintiuno, 2002.

Carvalho, Luiz Maklouf. *O colonel rompe o silêncio: Lício Augusto Ribeiro, que matou e levou tiros na caçada aos guerrilheiros do Araguaia, conta sua história*. Rio de Janeiro: Objetiva, 2004.

Castillo, Carmen, and Guy Girard. *La flaca Alejandra: Vidas y muertes de una mujer Chilena*. Bry-Sur-Marne Cedex, France: Institut Nacional de L'audiovisuel, Channel 4, 1994.

Cerruti, Gabriela. "El asesino está entre nosotros." *Trespuntos*, 14 January 1998, 6–11.

Chandler, David. *Voices from S-21: Terror and History in Pol Pot's Secret Prison*. Berkeley: University of California Press, 1999.

Ciancaglini, Sergio, and Martín Granovsky. *Nada más que la verdad: El juicio a las juntas*. Buenos Aires: Editorial Planeta Argentina, 1995.

Cohn, Carol. "Sex and Death in the Rational World of Defense Intellectuals." *Signs* 12, no. 4 (summer 1987): 687–718.

Coimbra, Cecília. "Torture in Brazil." *Torture* 6, no. 4 (1996): 89–90.

Collins, John M. "Fixing the Past: Stockpiling, Storytelling, and Palestinian Political Strategy in the Wake of the 'Peace Process.'" Paper presented at Legacies of Authoritarianism: Cultural Production, Collective Trauma, and Global Justice, University of Wisconsin, Madison, 3–5 April 1998.

Comisión Nacional Sobre la Desaparición de Personas. *Nunca más*. Buenos Aires: Editorial Universitaria de Buenos Aires, 1992.

Comissão de familiares de mortos e desaparecidos politicos, Instituto de Estudos da Violência do Estado (IEVE), Grupo Tortura Nunca Mais (RJ/PE). *Dossiê dos mortos e desaparecidos politicos a partir de 1964*. Recife, Pernambuco, Brazil: Companhia Editora de Pernambuco, 1995.

Contreiras, Hélio. *Militares: Confissões: Histórias secretas do Brasil*. Rio de Janeiro: MAUAD, 1998.

Contreras Sepúlveda, Manuel. *La verdad histórica: El ejército guerrillero*. Santiago, Chile: Ediciones Encina, 2000.

——. *La verdad histórica II: ¿Desaparecidos?* Santiago, Chile: Ediciones Encina, 2001.

Crownshaw, Richard. "Performing Memory in Holocaust Museums." *Performance Research* 5, no. 3 (winter 2000): 18–27.

Dahl, Robert A. *Polyarchy: Participation and Opposition*. New Haven, Conn.: Yale University Press, 1971.

Danner, Mark. *Torture and Truth: America, Abu Ghraib, and the War on Terror*. New York: New York Review of Books, 2004.

D'Araujo, Maria Celina, and Celso Castro, eds. *Ernesto Geisel*. Rio de Janeiro: Fundação Getulio Vargas, 1997.

D'Araujo, Maria Celina, Gláucio Ary Dillon Soares, and Celso Castro, eds. *Os anos de chumbo: A memória militar sobre a repressão*. Rio de Janeiro: Relume-Dumará, 1994.

——. *Visóes do golpe: A memória militar sobre 1964*. Rio de Janeiro: Relume-Dumará, 1994.

de Kock, Eugene. *A Long Night's Damage: Working for the Apartheid State*. Saxon-wold, South Africa: Contra Press, 1998.

"Depoimento do Coronel Aviador Pedro Corrêa Cabral a Comissão de Direitos Humanos da Câmara Federal." Movimento Tortura Nunca Mais, Pernambuco. http://www.torturanuncamais.org.br/mtnm_mil/mil_denuncias/depoimento CoronelAviador.htm.

Dershowitz, Alan M. *Why Terrorism Works: Understanding the Threat, Responding to the Challenge*. New Haven, Conn.: Yale University Press, 2002.

Dorfman, Ariel. *Death and the Maiden*. New York: Penguin Books, 1991.

Downs, Donald A. "Racial Incitement Law and Policy in the United States: Draw-ing the Line between Free Speech and Protection against Racism." In *Under the Shadow of Weimar: Democracy, Law, and Racial Incitement in Six Countries*, edited by Louis Greenspan and Cyril Levitt, 107–30. Westport, Conn.: Praeger, 1993.

Edelman, Murray. *Constructing the Political Spectacle*. Chicago: University of Chi-cago Press, 1988.

——. *The Symbolic Uses of Politics*. Urbana: University of Illinois Press, 1985.

Elster, Jon, ed. *Deliberative Democracy*. Cambridge: Cambridge University Press, 1998.

Etchecolatz, Miguel O. *La otra campana del nunca más*. Unpublished manuscript, Argentina, n.d.

Fair, Jo Ellen, and Lisa Parks. "Africa on Camera: Television News Coverage and Aerial Imaging of Rwandan Refugees." *Africa Today* 48, no. 2 (2001): 34–57.

Feitlowitz, Marguerite. *A Lexicon of Terror: Argentina and the Legacies of Torture*. New York: Oxford University Press, 1998.

Feld, Claudia. *Del estrado a la pantalla: Las imágenes del juicio a los ex comandantes en Argentina*. Madrid: Siglo Veintiuno de España Editores, 2002.

Feldman, Martha S. *Strategies for Interpreting Qualitative Data*. Qualitative Re-search Methods Series. Thousand Oaks, Calif.: Sage Publications, 1995.

Fish, Stanley. *Is There a Text in This Class? The Authority of Interpretive Communities*. Cambridge, Mass.: Harvard University Press, 1980.

Flanigan, Beverly. *Forgiving the Unforgivable*. New York: Macmillan, 1992.

Foster, Don, Paul Haupt, and Marésa de Beer. *The Theatre of Violence: Narratives of Protagonists in the South African Conflict*. Cape Town: HSRC Press, 2005.

Fuoss, Kirk. "Lynching Performances, Theatres of Violence." *Text and Perfor-mance Quarterly* 19, no. 1 (January 1999): 1–37.

Futaba, Igarashi. "Forced to Confess." Translated by Gavan McCormack. In *De-mocracy in Contemporary Japan*, edited by Gavan McCormack and Yoshio Sugi-moto, 195–214. Armonk, N.Y.: M. E. Sharpe, 1986.

Gaspari, Elio. *A ditadura escancarada*. São Paulo: Companhia das Letras, 2002.

Gobodo-Madikizela, Pumla. "Eugene de Kock, and Symbols of Blood and Dirt." In *Truths Drawn in Jest: Commentary on the Truth and Reconciliation Commission through Cartoons*, edited by Wilhelm Verwoerd and Mahlubi "Chief" Mabizela, 103–16. Cape Town: David Philip Publishers, 2000.

——. *A Human Being Died that Night: A South African Story of Forgiveness*. New York: Houghton Mifflin, 2003.

Goffman, Erving. *Encounters: Two Studies in the Sociology of Interaction*. Indianapolis: Bobbs-Merrill, 1961.

——. "Performances." In *Ritual, Play, and Performance: Readings in the Social Sciences/Theatre*, edited by Richard Schechner and Mady Schuman, 89–96. New York: Seabury Press, 1976.

——. *The Presentation of Self in Everyday Life*. New York: Anchor Books, 1959.

Goleman, Daniel. *Vital Lies, Simple Truths: The Psychology of Self-Deception*. New York: Simon and Schuster, 1985.

Goñi, Uki. *Judas: La verdadera historia de Alfredo Astiz, el infiltrado*. Buenos Aires: Sudamericana, 1996.

González, Eduardo. "Brazil: Between the Politics of Memory and Transitional Justice." Draft document, International Center on Transitional Justice, July 2005.

Graziano, Frank. *Divine Violence: Spectacle, Psychosexuality, and Radical Christianity in the Argentine "Dirty War."* Boulder, Colo.: Westview Press, 1992.

Guzmán, Nancy. *Romo: Confesiones de un torturador*. Santiago: Editorial Planeta, 2000.

Hitchens, Christopher. *The Trial of Henry Kissinger*. New York: Verso, 2001.

Holmes, Stephen. "Gag Rules or the Politics of Omission." In *Passions and Constraint: On the Theory of Liberal Democracy*, edited by Stephen Holmes, 202–35. Chicago: University of Chicago Press, 1995.

Huggins, Martha K., Mika Haritos-Fatouros, and Philip G. Zimbardo. *Violence Workers: Police Torturers and Murderers Reconstruct Brazilian Atrocities*. Berkeley: University of California Press, 2002.

Ignatieff, Michael. "Articles of Faith." *Index on Censorship* 5 (September 1996): 110–22.

——. "Lesser Evils." *New York Times Magazine*, 2 May 2004.

Institute for Justice and Reconciliation. "Brian Mitchell: Staying Power." Unpublished manuscript, Cape Town, South Africa, n.d.

Jarry, Alfred. "Of the Futility of the 'Theatrical' in Theater." In *The Twentieth-Century Performance Reader*, edited by Michael Huxley and Noel Witts, 209–15. New York: Routledge, 1996.

Jeffrey, Paul. "Guatemala: Bishops Record Violent History." *Latinamerica Press* 27, no. 17 (11 May 1995): 8.

Jelin, Elizabeth. *Los trabajos de la memoria*. Madrid: Siglo XXI de España Editores/Siglo XXI de Argentina Editores, 2002.

——. *State Repression and the Labors of Memory*. Translated from *Los trabajos de la*

memoria by Judy Rein and Marcial Godoy-Anatiria. Minneapolis: University of Minnesota Press, 2003.

Krog, Antjie. *Country of My Skull: Guilt, Sorrow and the Limits of Forgiveness in the New South Africa.* New York: Three Rivers Press, 2000.

Laub, Dori. "Bearing Witness or the Vicissitudes of Listening." In *Testimony: Crises of Witnessing in Literature, Psychoanalysis and History,* edited by Shoshana Felman and Dori Laub, 57–74. New York: Routledge, 1992.

Lelyveld, Joseph. "Interrogating Ourselves." *New York Times Magazine,* 12 June 2005, 36–43, 60, 66–69.

Levin, Michael. "The Case for Torture." *Newsweek,* 7 June 1982, 13.

Levinson, Sanford, ed. *Torture: A Collection.* Oxford: Oxford University Press, 2004.

Lifton, Robert Jay. *The Nazi Doctors: Medical Killing and the Psychology of Genocide.* New York: Basic Books, 1986.

Lincoln, Bruce. *Authority: Construction and Corrosion.* Chicago: University of Chicago Press, 1994.

Malamud Goti, Jaime. "Trials from Within and from Without." Paper presented at the Social Science Research Council Program on Global Security and Cooperation, International Law, and International Relations, Workshop on International Criminal Accountability, Washington, 6–7 November 2003.

Mansbridge, Jane. "Using Power/Fighting Power: The Polity." In *Democracy and Difference: Contesting the Boundaries of the Political,* edited by Seyla Benhabib, 46–66. Princeton, N.J.: Princeton University Press, 1996.

Martins Filho, João Roberto. "A memória militar sobre a tortura." In *Mortos e desaparecidos políticos: Reparação ou impunidade?* edited by Janaína Teles, 91–97. São Paulo: Humanitas, 2000.

May, Richard. "Memo for Workshop on International Criminal Accountability." Paper presented at the Social Science Research Council Program on Global Security and Cooperation, International Law, and International Relations, Workshop on International Criminal Accountability, Washington, 6–7 November 2003.

McCoy, Alfred W. *A Question of Torture: CIA Interrogation, from the Cold War to the War on Terror.* New York: Metropolitan Books, 2006.

Méndez, Juan E. "Accountability for Past Abuses." *Human Rights Quarterly* 19, no. 2 (May 1997): 255–82.

Messinger, Sheldon L., Harold Sampson, and Robert D. Towne. "Life as Theater: Some Notes on the Dramaturgical Approach to Social Reality." *Sociometry* 25, no. 1 (March 1962): 98–110.

Mezarobba, Glenda. *Um acerto de contas com o futuro: A anistia e suas conseqüencias: um estudo do caso brasileiro.* São Paulo: FAPESP, 2006.

Milgram, Stanley. *Obedience to Authority: An Experimental View.* New York: Harper and Row, 1974.

Morais, Taís, and Eumano Silva. *Operação Araguaia: Os arquivos secretos da guerrilha.* São Paulo: Geração Editorial, 2005.

Morris, Madeline. "International Humanitarian Law: State Collusion and the Conundrum of Jurisdiction." Paper presented at the Social Science Research Council Program on Global Security and Cooperation, International Law, and International Relations, Workshop on International Criminal Accountability, Washington, 6–7 November 2003.

Ndebele, Njabulo. "Memory, Metaphor, and the Triumph of Narrative." In *Negotiating the Past: The Making of Memory in South Africa*, edited by Sarah Nuttall and Carli Coetzee, 19–28. Cape Town: Oxford University Press, 1998.

"A ocultação dos mortos." In *História da guerilha do Araguaia*, edited by Criméia Alice S. de Almeida. Eremias Delizoicov Centro de Documentação. http://www.desaparecidospoliticos.org.br/.

O'Donnell, Guillermo, and Philippe C. Schmitter. *Transitions from Authoritarian Rule: Tentative Conclusions about Uncertain Democracies.* Baltimore: Johns Hopkins University Press, 1986.

Oltramari, Alexandre. "Torturei uns trinta." *Veja*, 9 December 1998, 44–46.

Orentlicher, Diane F. "Settling Accounts: The Duty to Prosecute Human Rights Violations of a Prior Regime." *Yale Law Journal* 100, no. 8 (June 1991): 2537–615.

Osiel, Mark J. *Mass Atrocity, Ordinary Evil, and Hannah Arendt: Criminal Consciousness in Argentina's Dirty War.* New Haven, Conn.: Yale University Press, 2001.

Palmer, Richard. "Toward a Postmodern Hermeneutics of Performance." In *Performance in Postmodern Culture*, edited by Michel Benamou and Charles Caramello, 19–32. Madison, Wisc.: Coda Press, 1997.

Partnoy, Alicia. *The Little School: Tales of Disappearance and Survival in Argentina.* Pittsburgh: Cleis Press, 1986.

Patraka, Vivian M. "Spectacles of Suffering: Performing Presence, Absence, and Historical Memory at U.S. Holocaust Museums." In *Performance and Cultural Politics*, edited by Elin Diamond, 89–107. London: Routledge, 1996.

——. *Spectacles of Suffering: Theatre, Fascism and the Holocaust.* Bloomington: Indiana University Press, 1996.

Pauw, Jacques. *Into the Heart of Darkness: Confessions of Apartheid's Assassins.* Johannesburg: Jonathan Ball Publishers, 1997.

Pavlovsky, Eduardo. "Opinión: El Sr. Galídez." *Página/12*, 28 October 1994.

Phelan, Peggy. *Unmarked: The Politics of Performance.* London: Routledge, 1993.

Roach, Joseph. "Kinship, Intelligence, and Memory as Improvisation: Culture and Performance in New Orleans." In *Performance and Cultural Politics*, edited by Elin Diamond, 217–36. London: Routledge, 1996.

Rosenberg, Tina. *Children of Cain: Violence and the Violent in Latin America.* New York: William Morrow, 1991.

——. "Recovering from Apartheid." *New Yorker*, 18 November 1996, 86–87.

Scartezini, Antonio Carlos. *Segredos de Médici.* São Paulo: Marco Zero, 1985.

Scilingo, Adolfo Francisco. *Por siempre nunca más.* Buenos Aires: Editorial Del Plata S.A., n.d.

Scott, James C. *Domination and the Arts of Resistance: Hidden Transcripts*. New Haven, Conn.: Yale University Press, 1990.

Scott, Marvin B., and Stanford M. Lyman. "Accounts." *American Sociological Review* 33, no. 1 (February 1968): 46–62.

"O silêncio e a fala dos militares." In *História da guerrilha do Araguaia*, edited by Criméia Alice S. de Almeida. Eremias Delizoicov Centro de Documentação. http:// www.desaparecidospoliticos.org.br/.

Sontag, Susan. "Regarding the Torture of Others." *New York Times Magazine*, 23 May 2004, 24–29, 42.

Soto, Hernán, ed. *Voces de muerte*. 2 vols. Santiago: LOM Ediciones, 1998.

South Africa's Human Spirit: An Oral Memoir of the Truth and Reconciliation Commission. 5 vols. CD-ROM. Johannesburg: SABC News Production, 2000. http://www.sabctruth.co.za/.

Stiglmayer, Alexandra. "The Rapes in Bosnia-Herzegovina." In *Mass Rape*, edited by Alexandra Stiglmayer, 82–169, 147–55. Lincoln: University of Nebraska Press, 1994.

Sullivan, John L., James Piereson, and George E. Marcus. "An Alternative Conceptualization of Political Tolerance: Illusory Increases 1950s–1970s." *American Political Science Review* 73, no. 3 (September 1979): 781–94.

Taylor, Diana. "Performing Gender: Las Madres de la Plaza de Mayo." In *Negotiating Performance: Gender, Sexuality, and Theatricality in Latin/o America*, edited by Diana Taylor and Juan Villegas, 275–305. Durham, N.C.: Duke University Press, 1994.

Taylor, Jane. *Ubu and the Truth Commission*. Cape Town: University of Cape Town Press, 1998.

Timerman, Jacobo. *Prisoner without a Name, Cell without a Number*. Translated by Toby Talbot. New York: Vintage Books, 1982.

Turner, Jann. "Eugene: From Apocalypse Now to Scotland the Brave." *Mail and Guardian*, 28 May 1999. http://www.jannturner.co.za.

Turner, Victor. *From Ritual to Theatre: The Human Seriousness of Play*. New York: Performing Arts Journal Publications, 1982.

Ustra, Carlos Alberto Brilhante. *Rompendo o silêncio*. Brasília: Editerra Editorial, 1987.

Valenzuela, Luisa. *Other Weapons*. Translated by Deborah Bonner. Hanover, N.H.: Ediciones del Norte, 1985.

van Zyl, Paul. "Transitional Justice in Iraq: Observations on Process and Policy." Paper presented at the Social Science Research Council Program on Global Security and Cooperation, International Law, and International Relations, Workshop on International Criminal Accountability, Washington, 6–7 November 2003.

Verbitsky, Horacio. *The Flight: Confessions of an Argentine Dirty Warrior*. Translated by Esther Allen. New York: New Press, 1996.

———. *El vuelo*. Buenos Aires: Planeta, 1995.

Vergez, Héctor. *Yo fui Vargas: El antiterrorismo por dentro.* Buenos Aires: self-published, 1995.

Whitney, Craig R. Introduction to *The Abu Ghraib Investigations: The Official Reports of the Independent Panel and the Pentagon on the Shocking Prisoner Abuse in Iraq*, edited by Steven Strasser, vii–xxiii. New York: Public Affairs, 2004.

Wolin, Sheldon S. "Fugitive Democracy." In *Democracy and Difference: Contesting the Boundaries of the Political*, edited by Seyla Benhabib, 31–45. Princeton, N.J.: Princeton University Press, 1996.

Young, Iris Marion. "Communication and the Other: Beyond Deliberative Democracy." In *Democracy and Difference: Contesting the Boundaries of the Political*, edited by Seyla Benhabib, 120–35. Princeton, N.J.: Princeton University Press, 1996.

Young, James E. *The Texture of Memory: Holocaust Memorials and Meaning.* New Haven, Conn.: Yale University Press, 1993.

Zalaquett, José. "Balancing Ethical Imperatives and Political Constraints: The Dilemma of New Democracies Confronting Past Human Rights Violations." *Hastings Law Journal* 43, no. 6 (August 1992): 1425–38.

NEWSPAPERS, MAGAZINES, AND JOURNALS

Agence France-Presse (French Newswire Services)
Buenos Aires Herald (Argentina)
Business Day (South Africa)
Cape Argus (South Africa)
Cape Times (South Africa)
Caras (Chile)
CHIP [Chile Information Project]
Clarín (Argentina)
La Cuarta (Chile)
Diario Popular (Argentina)
Efe (Spanish Newswire Services)
O Estado de São Paulo (Brazil)
Folha de São Paulo (Brazil)
Global News Wire Service
Jornal do Brasil (Brazil)
Mail and Guardian (South Africa)
El Mercurio (Chile)
La Nación (Argentina)
La Nación (Chile)
Página/12 (Argentina)
El País (Spain)
Perfil (Argentina)

La Prensa (Argentina)
Punto Final (Chile)
Servicio Universal de Noticias–InfoLatina
South African Press Association (South Africa)
Sowetan (South Africa)
Star (South Africa)
Sunday Independent (South Africa)
La Tercera (Chile)
Trespuntos (Argentina)
Las Últimas Noticias (Chile)
Veja (Brazil)
Weekly Mail and Guardian (South Africa)

Almeida, Criméia, 213

Almeida, Joana, 211

Alsogaray, Álvaro, 275

Alvear, Soledad, 314n.61

AMIA bombing (Argentine Jewish cultural center), 160, 161–62, 322n.95

amnesia, 10–11; audiences as filling in the gaps, 246–48, 249; effectiveness of, 239–40, 248–50; media's role in, 245–46, 249; mental illness associated with, 244; motives for, 20; preexisting conditions contributing to, 243–44; PTSD's role in, 236, 242, 333n.20; trials' role in, 244–46; trivial details remembered and, 242–44; victims' political agenda and, 247, 248, 249; willful, 240–41. See also Benzien, Jeffrey, confession of

amnesty: in Argentina, 4–5, 6–7, 11, 288; for Michael Bellingan, denied, 221–22; for Benzien, 236–39; in Brazil, 4, 9, 11, 29, 176, 288, 324n.25; in Chile, 4, 8, 120, 288; the disappeared and, 145; prosecution and, 288; in South Africa, 3, 4, 10, 11, 67, 190, 239, 288, 310n.91; by truth commissions, 3–5, 10, 11, 67, 190, 239, 310n.91; for Williamson, 102, 103–4, 190, 311nn.115–16

Amnesty Commission (Brazil), 176

Amnesty Committee (South Africa), 31

ANC (African National Congress): apartheid regime defeated by, 4; apartheid victims and survivors represented by, 11; askaris working for, 60; de Kock on, 264–65; in exile, 254; Fransch's death and, 64; headquarters bombed by Williamson (1982), 93; Lesotho massacre of members of, 186–87, 339n.104; London headquarters bombed, 253, 258. See also Mamasela, Joe

Anos rebeldes (TV-Globo), 181

apartheid regime (South Africa): acquittals following, 33; black-on-black violence under, 253; Cape Town Church Street bombing under, 61–62; collaborators with, 56, 60, 302n.54; delegitimation and defeat of, 4; Goldstone Commission on, 254, 255; Harms Commission on, 218, 254; plausible-deniability defense used by, 163–64; police vs. military silence following, 186–87, 194, 325n.45; remorseful confessions following, 56–59; war-based justifications for, 61–62. See also Benzien, Jeffrey, confession of; Botha, P. W.; Mamasela, Joe; PEBCO 3; TRC; Vlakplaas; Williamson, Craig

APDH (Permanent Assembly for Human Rights; Argentina), 134, 169, 308n.44

April Fool's Day (Brazil), 182

Araguaia massacre (Brazil): awards given to perpetrators of, 324n.28; Cabral's role in, 199, 201, 207–10, 220 (see also *Xambioá: Guerrilha no Araguaia*); CIE's role in, 203, 204, 207–8; disposal of bodies (Operation Clean-up), 199, 204–5, 206, 207, 210–11, 214; evidence for and documentation on, 202, 209, 212–13, 214, 326n.5, 326n.12, 327n.19; Human Rights Commission on, 209, 210; Inter-American Commission of Human Rights case against Brazil, 330n.77; justice following, 213, 214; memorializing and remembering, 213–14; military's reign of terror, 200, 326nn.6–7; military vs. villagers' accounts of, 199–200, 210–11; number and whereabouts of disappeared following, 197, 212–13,

ibility of, 269; effectiveness of, 11, 272–74; loyalty and subordination of perpetrators and, 271, 273; motives for, 269–71, 340n.109; plea bargaining and, 22, 278; reprisals following and protection for confessors, 277, 278; rewards for confessors, 275–76; venues for, 270–71. *See also* de Kock, Eugene, confession of

Bianchi de Carcano, Emilio, 50

Biko, Steve, 167, 238–39

Bin Laden, Osama, 97

Bittel, Deolindo, 275

Bizos, George, 268, 272, 310n.91

black-on-black violence, 253

Boal, Augusto, 27

Bonadío, Claudio, 88–89

Bonafini, Hebe de, 91–92, 305n.3

Bonasso, Miguel, 83, 306n.13

Bonino, Mario, 80

"born again" narratives, 18, 302n.57. *See also* religious rebirth

Bosnian War (1992–1995), 62–63, 132–33

Botha, Carl, 62

Botha, Dawn, 266–67

Botha, P. W., 98–99, 100–101, 291

Botha, Pik, 164, 258

Brasil: Nunca mais (*Torture in Brazil*), 9, 125, 133, 175–76, 328n.47. *See also* never again

Bravo, Alfredo, 87, 161, 162, 166, 169

Brazil: amnesty in, 4, 9, 11, 29, 176, 288, 324n.25; civil cases against torturers in, 180–81, 324n.25; coup anniversary celebrations in, 176–78, 181–82; democracy in, 179; human-rights violations investigated in, 9, 11, 290; low level of repression in, 9, 11, 175; military silence in, 173, 175–82; mobilization in, 179–80, 290; repressive era in (1969–74), 173, 175–

76, 178, 181, 323n.3; restorative justice in, 181; torture used in, 125–26, 315n.86. *See also* Araguaia massacre; *Brasil: Nunca mais;* Cabral, Pedro Corrêa, confession of

Brazilian Air Force (FAB), 326n.7. *See also* Araguaia massacre

Brazilian Bar Association (OAB), 209, 210

Brazilian Expeditionary Force (FEB), 200

Breaking the Silence (*Rompendo o silêncio;* C. A. B. Ustra), 180–81, 323n.8

Brecht, Bertolt, 296n.50

Bromberg, Ellen, 222

Brown, William, 185

Brull, Mónica, 131–32

Brunner, José Joaquín, 120

Bueno da Cruz, Adalberto, 209

Bush, George W., 282, 283–84, 285, 287, 289–90, 291, 341n.4

Bussi, Antonio Domingo, 84–85, 164

Bussi, Hortensia, 152, 318–19n.38

Bybee, Jay, 342n.23

Cabral, Pedro Corrêa, confession of: amnesia of Cabral, 205; on the Araguaia massacre, 199, 201, 207–10, 220 (see also *Xambioá: Guerrilha no Araguaia*); on CIE executions, 204; military reaction to, 209–10, 328n.54; on Operation Clean-up, 204; overview of, 9–10; religious conversion's role in, 205–6, 218; remorse in, 220; on the victims, 205

Camilión, Oscar, 300n.35

Cape Argus, 263, 265

Cape Times, 265

Cape Town Church Street bombing (South Africa), 61–62

Caravan of Death (Chile), 145

Cardoso, Alberto, 173

Commando Cueva (Cave Commando), 82, 307n.27

Commission of Disappeared Political Activists (Brazil), 214

Communist Party (Brazil). *See* PC do B

Communist Party (Chile), 102, 156–57, 311n.110, 320n.50

CONADEP (National Commission on the Disappeared; Argentina), 6, 41, 43, 162, 215

confessional performance: audience interpretations of, 4, 26–35, 296n.53, 298n.69; audience's role in, 15, 36, 294n.8; as Catholic byproduct, 5; chains of confession, 25; contentious coexistence and, 4, 12, 18–19, 34–40; democratic politics affected by, 5; as documenting violence, 31; as doing, 13, 15, 293n.2 (ch. 1); effectiveness of, 18, 22; healing approach to, 30–32, 296–97nn.59–60; images and psyches of perpetrators and, 16–18, 294n.15; instrumental, 27, 296n.51; live, 23; "mediatized," 5, 23, 295n.43; memory as selective and reconstructed in, 19–20; metaphor of performance, 15; motives for, 5–6; perpetrators as actors, 15–19; perpetrators changed by, 36–37; perpetrators' failure to question "missions" and, 20–21; vs. political talk, 13, 15; public attention on perpetrators vs. victims and, 15–16; punishment and, 32; rarity of, 5–6; retributive approach to, 32–33, 297n.67; salvational approach to, 33–34; scripts for, 19–22; staging and timing of, 6, 11–12, 15, 22–26, 289, 295n.39; as transgressive, 34–35; traumatic approach to, 28–29; types of (*see* amnesia; betrayal confessions; denial; heroic confessions;

remorse; sadistic confessions; silence); use of "perpetrator," 16, 294n.14

conflictual dialogue, 3

Congress of South African Trade Unions, 263

contentious coexistence, 279–92; Abu Ghraib photographs and, 282–84; confessional performance and, 4, 12, 18–19, 34–40; democracy as fostered by, 3–4, 12, 28–30, 34–40, 279, 284, 285; examples of (*see specific confessions*); vs. gag orders, 281, 291; vs. healing truth, 279, 281, 284, 290; political groups' reactions to unsettling accounts and, 286–87; political transformations via, 288–91; realism and effectiveness of, 291–92; reinterpretation of unsettling accounts and, 284–85; success factors for, 289–90

Contreras Sepúlveda, Manuel, confession of, 141–58; Arce's testimony and, 145, 157; background and military career of Contreras, 143; books by and websites of Contreras, 146, 151; on Hortensia Bussi, 318–19n.38; CIA's relationship with Contreras and, 144–45, 151, 318n.34; denials in, 141, 143, 146–49, 151, 157–59, 318n.34, 318n.36; the disappeared and, investigation and prosecution for, 145–46, 147–49, 157, 317n.24; extradition requests following, 143; house arrest for Contreras following imprisonment, 319n.47; human-rights community's reaction to, 145, 151–53, 157; "just war" defense in, 149, 151–52, 159; lack of support from military colleagues and, 144–45; on Marxists, 147–48, 149–51, 317n.27, 318n.31; media coverage of Con-

Malan, Rian, 98

Mall, Hassen E., 70

Mamasela, Joe: on ANC, 224; appearance of, 217, 221; confession and lies by, 215–18, 219–20, 224–25, 330n.91; media attention on, 16; religious conversion of, 218; remorse of, 220; sale of his story, 218, 220–21, 331n.101; staging by, 222–25; success of testimony of, 223–24

Mandela, Nelson, 4, 167. *See also* ANC

Mansbridge, Jane, 37–38

Maponya, Japie, 251, 253, 334n.1

Maponya, Odirile, 260, 267

Marcos, Ferdinand, 96

Marcus, George E., 16

Mariani, Clara Analí, 244

Marín, Gladys, 153

Marrón, Carlos, 87

Martínez, Aurelio ("Za Za"), 87, 88

Martínez, Claudio, 122

Martínez de Buck, Perla, 309n.66

Martins Peri, Enzo, 177

Marxists (Chile), 147–48, 149–51, 317n.27, 318n.31

Massera, Emilio, 49, 54, 86, 87, 99–100, 307n.27, 308n.57

Massimino, Elisa, 287

Massu, Jacques, 304–5n.93

Matthei, Fernando, 21, 295n.34

May, Richard, 297n.68

Mbeki, Thabo, 190

Mbelo, Thapelo, 56–57, 58–59, 60, 72

McCain, John, 284

McCoy, Alfred, 282, 286, 341n.4, 342n.23

MEDH (Ecumenical Human Rights Movement; Argentina), 308n.44

media: amnesia, role in, 245–46, 249; Astiz's confession covered by, 75–78, 81, 307n.25; authoritarian regimes' control of, 21; Benzien in, 229, 331–

32n.1; Coetzee in, 16; Contreras in, 146; de Kock in, 16, 255, 259, 260, 265; on denial, 165–66; failure to cover confessions, 190–91; Mamasela in, 16; opposition presses, 270–71; performance in, 5, 23–24, 295n.43; on perpetrators vs. victims, 15–16; Romo in, 191, 289; sadistic confessions manipulated by, 127, 130–33; Scilingo in, 48–49, 61, 91–92, 307n.25; on torture, 341n.4

Médici, Emílio Garrastazú, 100, 178, 200, 202–3. *See also* Araguaia massacre

Mediodía con Mauro, 131–32, 135, 138–39, 316n.96

Melchor Basterra, Víctor, 53

memory: entrepreneurs and militants of, 37; as healing, 29–32; lies, 215; motives of, 104; saturation by and backlash against, 37, 298n.76; selective and reconstructed, 19–20

Mena, Odlanier, 144

Mendes, Chico, 182

Mendía, Luis María, 54, 302n.52

Menem, Carlos: Astiz and, 81, 83, 305n.3; Scilingo and, 50–51, 92, 183–84

Menéndez, Luciano Benjamin, 299–300n.26

Mentz, Wouter, 258–59, 267

Merino, Marcia, 59–60, 110, 302n.59

Meroño, Mercedes, 91

Meschiatti, Teresa, 166

Meyer, Leon, 266

Meyer, Roelf, 258

Mignone, Emilio, 52, 85, 275

Milgram, Stanley, 16

Military Club (Brazil), 177

Military Confessions, 178, 179

Milosevic, Slobodan, 99

Milton, John, 16

41–43, 55, 61; divisiveness of, 225; finances of Scilingo following, 301n.49; on following orders, 41, 44, 302n.52; imprisonment of Scilingo following, 50, 54–55, 61, 73, 300n.31, 302n.52; internal conflict and religious rebirth of Scilingo and, 43–44, 59; kidnapping of and threats to Scilingo following, 51–52, 54, 61, 277, 300n.36, 301n.50; language and euphemisms in, 46–47, 61; legal complaints by Scilingo following, 54–55, 302n.52; media attention to, 48–49, 61, 91–92, 307n.25; motives for, 43–45, 47–48; on Nazi concentration camps, 43; overview of, 7; on the past, 41; perpetrators identified during, 53–54, 301n.46; remorse of, 46, 47, 55, 59, 66, 73; responses to, 48; retraction of, 61, 190; silence broken by, 41, 43, 298–99n.2; silencing of Scilingo attempted, 49, 51–52, 183–84; as transforming Scilingo, 46–47, 59; Verbitsky's role in, 45–47, 48, 62, 70, 270–71, 299n.4, 301n.46; victims not identified during, 53

Scorpion (alias of Ricardo Scifo Modica), 300n.29

Scott, James, 104

September 11 terrorist attacks (U.S., 2001), 282

Serbs. *See* Bosnian War

SERPAJ (Peace and Justice Service; Argentina), 308n.44

Setorio, Osvaldo, 244

Shakespeare, William, 13, 16

Sharia laws, 281

Sibonge, Fostus, 67–68

Sidebe, Glory, 264

SIFA (Air Force Intelligence Service; Chile), 144, 188, 271

silence: ambiguity and, 185; of apartheid police vs. military, 186–87, 194, 325n.45; on Araguaia massacre, 200–202; of the Brazilian military, 173, 175–82; of the Chilean military, 184–85, 194; democracy and, 179; effectiveness of, 194; guilt implied by, 180, 185–86; as healthy, 183–85; human-rights community on, 180; human-rights community's strategies to force confessions, 191–94; interpretations of, 185–86; media's failure to cover confessions, 190–91; on military and specialized issues, 184; motives for, 20, 24, 187–90, 194; overview of, 10; partial, 183, 194; on personal acts, 184; prosecution avoided via, 190; public act of breaking of, 194–95; public recrimination avoided via, 190; remorse and, 65, 68; for self-protection against reprisals, 187–90, 194, 325n.47, 325n.49; in Trial of the Generals, 190–91, 194; victims' silencing of perpetrators, 28–29. *See also* Cabral, Pedro Corrêa, confession of; censorship

Silva, Luiz Inácio da ("Lula"), 11, 177–78

Simón, Julio ("El Turco Julián"), 127, 130–32, 134, 135, 137, 316n.96

Sinclair, Santiago, 155

Singing Myself a Lullaby (D. Rosenberg and E. Bromberg), 222

Slovo, Gillian, 331–32n.1

Slovo, Joe, 93, 95

The Smell of Apples (Behr), 69, 304n.89

SNI (National Intelligence Service; Argentina), 77

Socialist Party (Chile), 110, 189

socialization, 16, 20, 294n.15

Solarz de Osatinsky, Sara, 166

Soler, Mercedes, 111, 118, 122

Leigh A. Payne is a professor of political science at the University of Wisconsin, Madison. She is the author of *Uncivil Movements: The Armed Right Wing and Democracy in Latin America* (2000) and *Brazilian Industrialists and Democratic Change* (1994). She is the editor of (with Ernest Bartell) *Business and Democracy in Latin America* (1995) and (with Ksenija Bilbija, Jo Ellen Fair, and Cynthia Milton) *The Art of Truth-telling about Authoritarian Rule* (2005).

Library of Congress Cataloging-in-Publication Data

Payne, Leigh A.
Unsettling accounts : neither truth nor reconciliation
in confessions of state violence / Leigh A. Payne.
p. cm. — (The cultures and practice of violence series)
"A John Hope Franklin Center Book."
Includes bibliographical references and index.
ISBN-13: 978-0-8223-4061-4 (cloth : alk. paper)
ISBN-13: 978-0-8223-4082-9 (pbk. : alk. paper)
1. Political violence—Case studies. 2. Confession (Law)—Case studies.
3. Democratization—Case studies. I. Title.
JC328.6.P39 2007
303.6'9—dc22   2007026682